PRESS

ROTH,M
CONTRACT/TEM
/07372-64D
CITIZEN, CON

NEXT OF KIN

ORGAN DONOR: Y
BLOOD TYPE

DMZ
BODY OF A JOURNALIST

BODY OF A JOURNALIST
BRIAN WOOD WRITER
RICCARDO BURCHIELLI ARTIST

ZEE, NYC
BRIAN WOOD WRITER
KRISTIAN DONALDSON ARTIST

NEW YORK TIMES
BRIAN WOOD STORY & ART

JEROMY COX
COLORIST

JARED K. FLETCHER
LETTERER

ORIGINAL SERIES COVERS BY
BRIAN WOOD

INTRODUCTION BY
D. RANDALL BLYTHE

DMZ CREATED BY
BRIAN WOOD AND
RICCARDO BURCHIELLI

Karen Berger Senior VP-Executive Editor
Will Dennis Editor-original series
Casey Seijas Assistant Editor-original series
Bob Harras Editor-collected edition
Robbin Brosterman Senior Art Director
Paul Levitz President & Publisher
Georg Brewer VP-Design & DC Direct Creative
Richard Bruning Senior VP-Creative Director
Patrick Caldon Executive VP-Finance & Operations
Chris Caramalis VP-Finance
John Cunningham VP-Marketing
Terri Cunningham VP-Managing Editor
Stephanie Fierman Senior VP-Sales & Marketing
Alison Gill VP-Manufacturing
Hank Kanalz VP-General Manager, WildStorm
Jim Lee Editorial Director-WildStorm
Paula Lowitt Senior VP-Business & Legal Affairs
MaryEllen McLaughlin VP-Advertising & Custom Publishing
John Nee VP-Business Development
Gregory Noveck Senior VP-Creative Affairs
Cheryl Rubin Senior VP-Brand Management
Jeff Trojan VP-Business Development, DC Direct
Bob Wayne VP-Sales

Cover illustration by Brian Wood. Logo designed by Brian Wood.
Publication design and additional photography by Amie Brockway-Metcalf.

DMZ: BODY OF A JOURNALIST. Published by DC Comics. Cover, introduction and compilation
copyright © 2007 DC Comics. All Rights Reserved. Originally published in single magazine form as DMZ 6-12. Copyright © 2006
Brian Wood and Riccardo Burchielli. All Rights Reserved. Vertigo and all characters, their distinctive likenesses and related elements
featured in this publication are trademarks of DC Comics. The stories, characters and incidents featured in this publication are entirely
fictional. DC Comics does not read or accept unsolicited submissions of ideas, stories or artwork.
DC Comics, 1700 Broadway, New York, NY 10019. A Warner Bros. Entertainment Company.
Printed in Canada. First Printing.
ISBN: 1-4012-1247-6
ISBN 13: 978-1-4012-1247-6

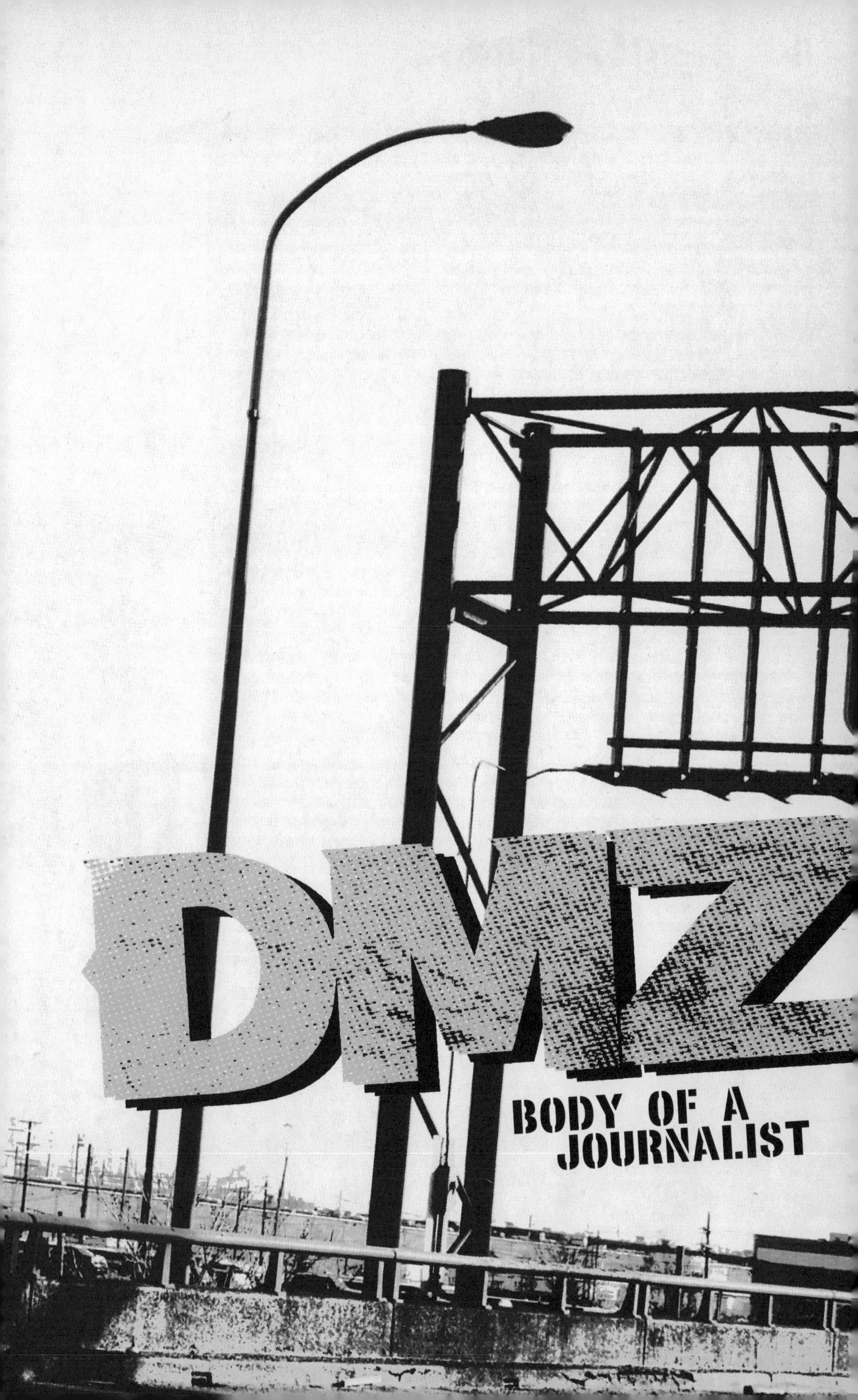
DMZ
BODY OF A JOURNALIST

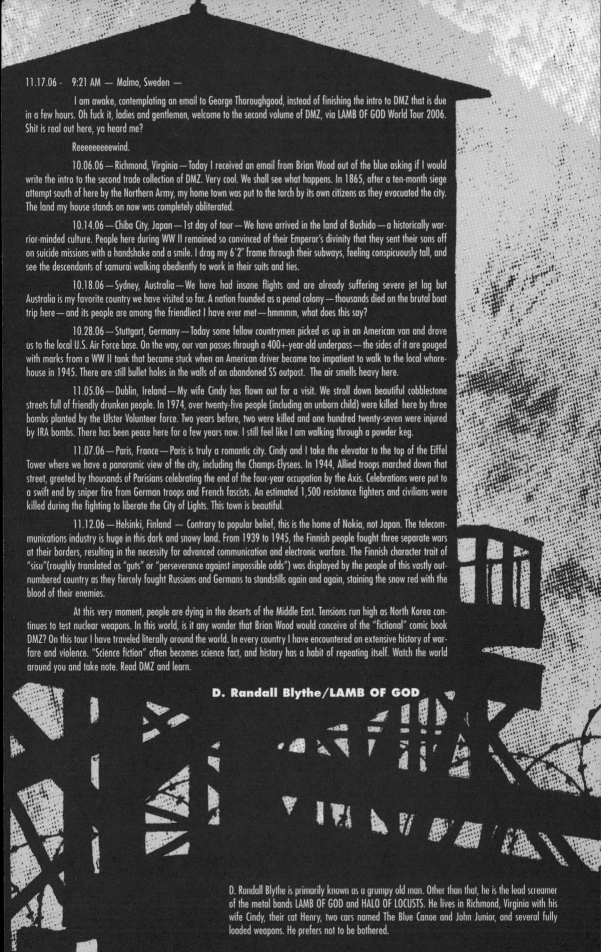

11.17.06 - 9:21 AM — Malmo, Sweden —

I am awake, contemplating an email to George Thoroughgood, instead of finishing the intro to DMZ that is due in a few hours. Oh fuck it, ladies and gentlemen, welcome to the second volume of DMZ, via LAMB OF GOD World Tour 2006. Shit is real out here, ya heard me?

Reeeeeeeeewind.

10.06.06 — Richmond, Virginia — Today I received an email from Brian Wood out of the blue asking if I would write the intro to the second trade collection of DMZ. Very cool. We shall see what happens. In 1865, after a ten-month siege attempt south of here by the Northern Army, my home town was put to the torch by its own citizens as they evacuated the city. The land my house stands on now was completely obliterated.

10.14.06 — Chiba City, Japan — 1st day of tour — We have arrived in the land of Bushido — a historically warrior-minded culture. People here during WW II remained so convinced of their Emperor's divinity that they sent their sons off on suicide missions with a handshake and a smile. I drag my 6'2" frame through their subways, feeling conspicuously tall, and see the descendants of samurai walking obediently to work in their suits and ties.

10.18.06 — Sydney, Australia — We have had insane flights and are already suffering severe jet lag but Australia is my favorite country we have visited so far. A nation founded as a penal colony — thousands died on the brutal boat trip here — and its people are among the friendliest I have ever met — hmmmm, what does this say?

10.28.06 — Stuttgart, Germany — Today some fellow countrymen picked us up in an American van and drove us to the local U.S. Air Force base. On the way, our van passes through a 400+-year-old underpass — the sides of it are gouged with marks from a WW II tank that became stuck when an American driver became too impatient to walk to the local whorehouse in 1945. There are still bullet holes in the walls of an abandoned SS outpost. The air smells heavy here.

11.05.06 — Dublin, Ireland — My wife Cindy has flown out for a visit. We stroll down beautiful cobblestone streets full of friendly drunken people. In 1974, over twenty-five people (including an unborn child) were killed here by three bombs planted by the Ulster Volunteer force. Two years before, two were killed and one hundred twenty-seven were injured by IRA bombs. There has been peace here for a few years now. I still feel like I am walking through a powder keg.

11.07.06 — Paris, France — Paris is truly a romantic city. Cindy and I take the elevator to the top of the Eiffel Tower where we have a panoramic view of the city, including the Champs-Elysees. In 1944, Allied troops marched down that street, greeted by thousands of Parisians celebrating the end of the four-year occupation by the Axis. Celebrations were put to a swift end by sniper fire from German troops and French fascists. An estimated 1,500 resistance fighters and civilians were killed during the fighting to liberate the City of Lights. This town is beautiful.

11.12.06 — Helsinki, Finland — Contrary to popular belief, this is the home of Nokia, not Japan. The telecommunications industry is huge in this dark and snowy land. From 1939 to 1945, the Finnish people fought three separate wars at their borders, resulting in the necessity for advanced communication and electronic warfare. The Finnish character trait of "sisu"(roughly translated as "guts" or "perseverance against impossible odds") was displayed by the people of this vastly outnumbered country as they fiercely fought Russians and Germans to standstills again and again, staining the snow red with the blood of their enemies.

At this very moment, people are dying in the deserts of the Middle East. Tensions run high as North Korea continues to test nuclear weapons. In this world, is it any wonder that Brian Wood would conceive of the "fictional" comic book DMZ? On this tour I have traveled literally around the world. In every country I have encountered an extensive history of warfare and violence. "Science fiction" often becomes science fact, and history has a habit of repeating itself. Watch the world around you and take note. Read DMZ and learn.

D. Randall Blythe/LAMB OF GOD

D. Randall Blythe is primarily known as a grumpy old man. Other than that, he is the lead screamer of the metal bands LAMB OF GOD and HALO OF LOCUSTS. He lives in Richmond, Virginia with his wife Cindy, their cat Henry, two cars named The Blue Canoe and John Junior, and several fully loaded weapons. He prefers not to be bothered.

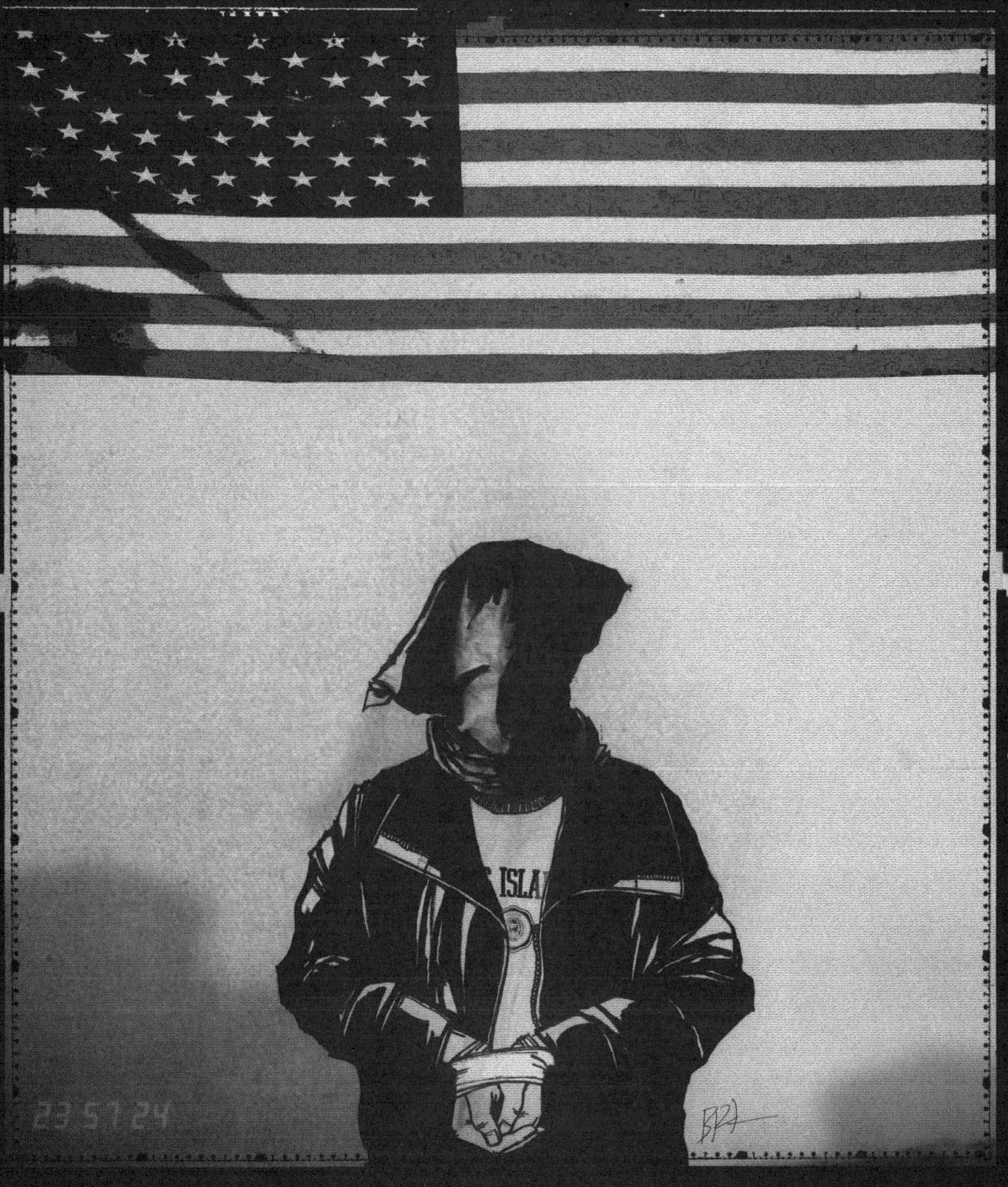
23 5 7 24

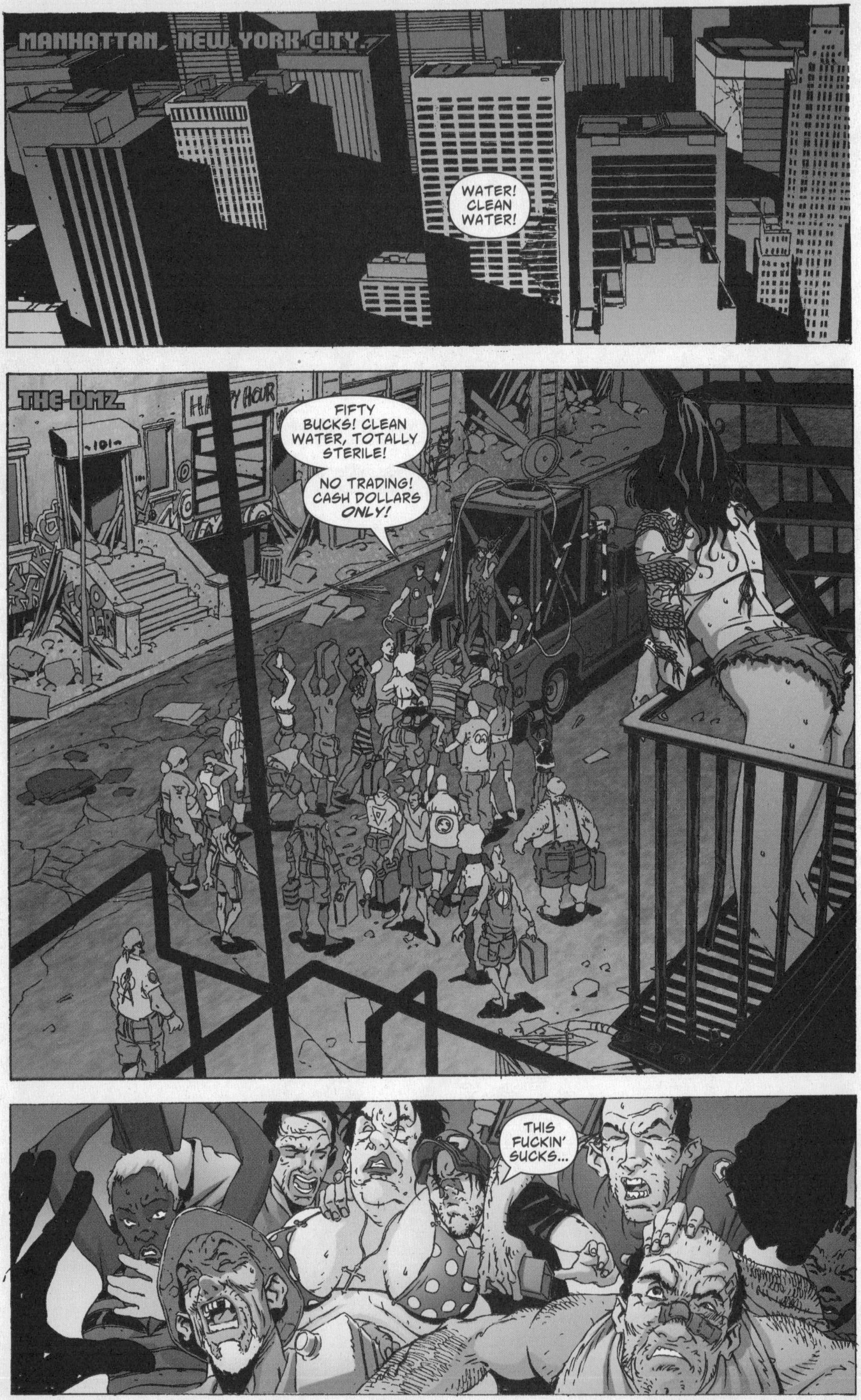
MANHATTAN, NEW YORK CITY.
WATER! CLEAN WATER!
THE DMZ.
FIFTY BUCKS! CLEAN WATER, TOTALLY STERILE!
NO TRADING! CASH DOLLARS ONLY!
THIS FUCKIN' SUCKS...

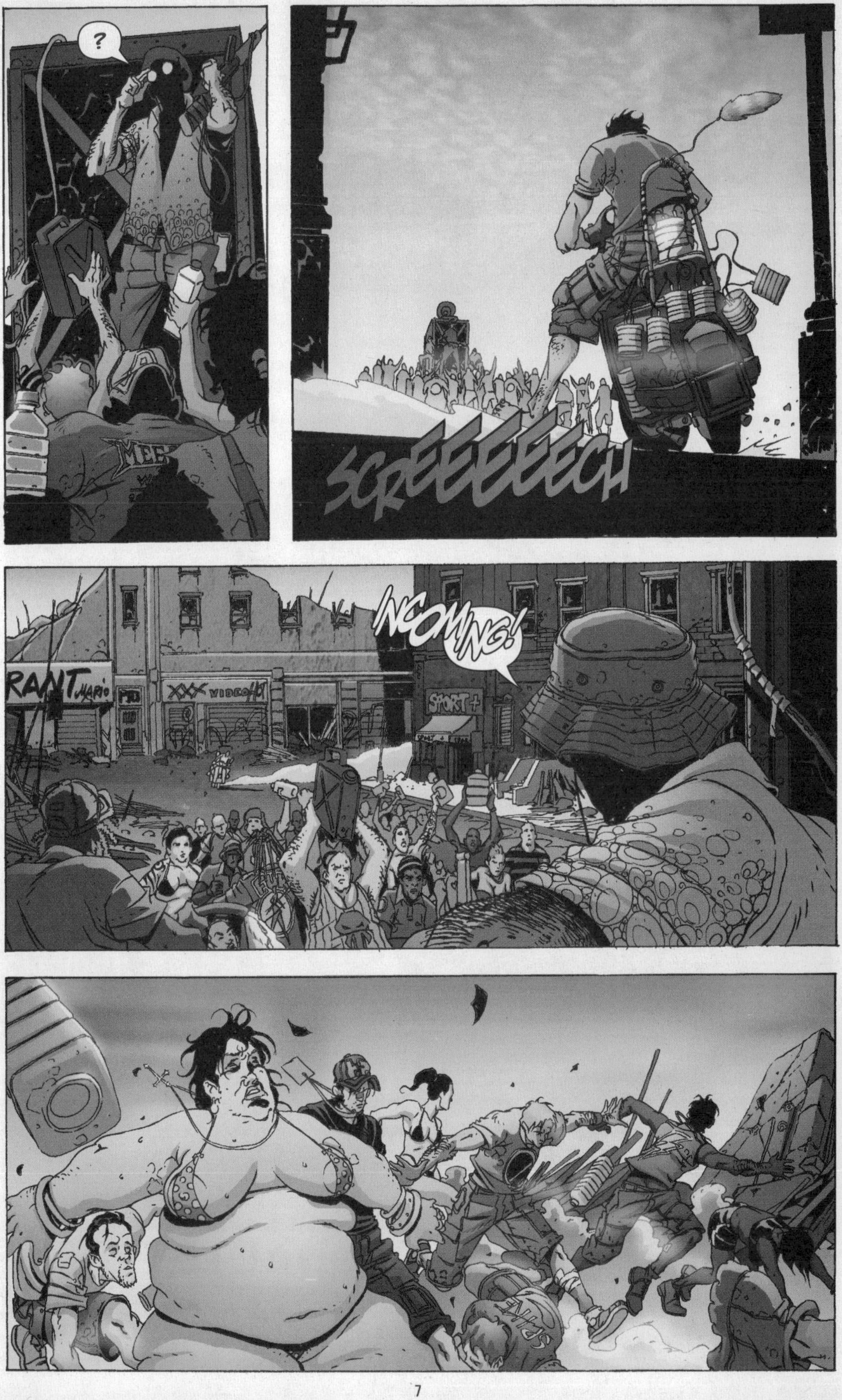
?
SCREEEEECH
RANT mario
XXX VIDEO
SPORT +
INCOMING!

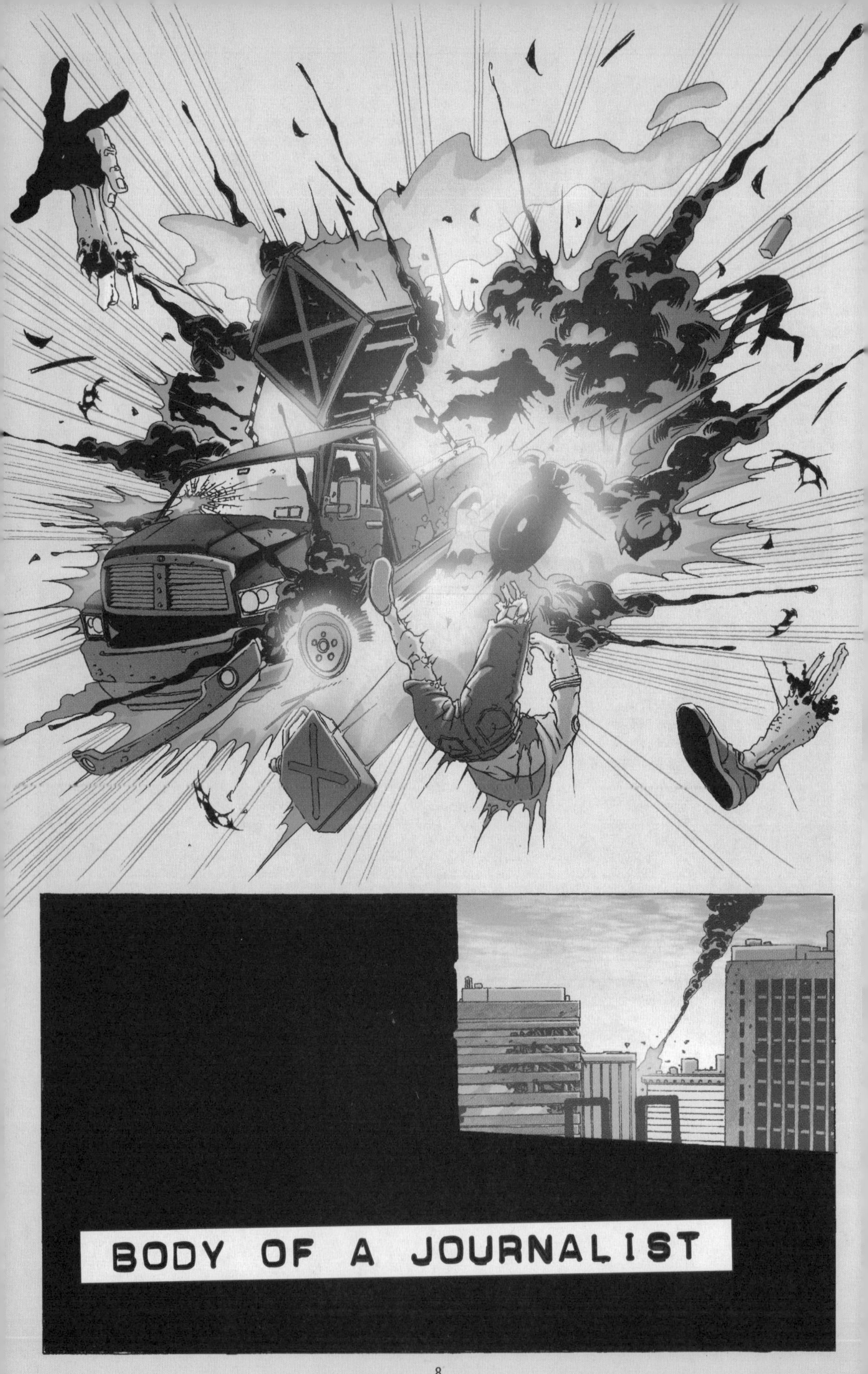
BODY OF A JOURNALIST

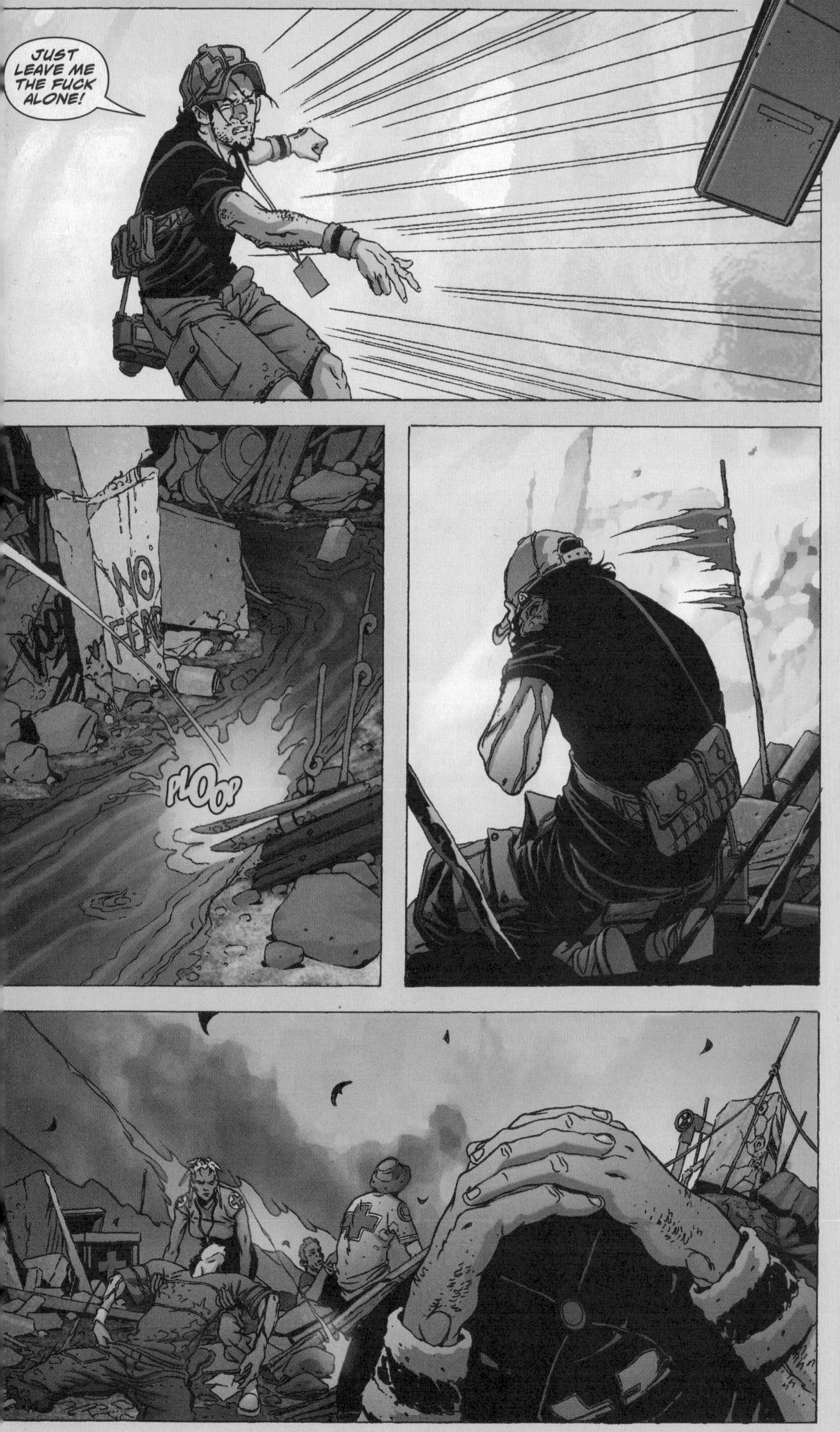
JUST LEAVE ME THE FUCK ALONE!
NO FEAR
PLOOP

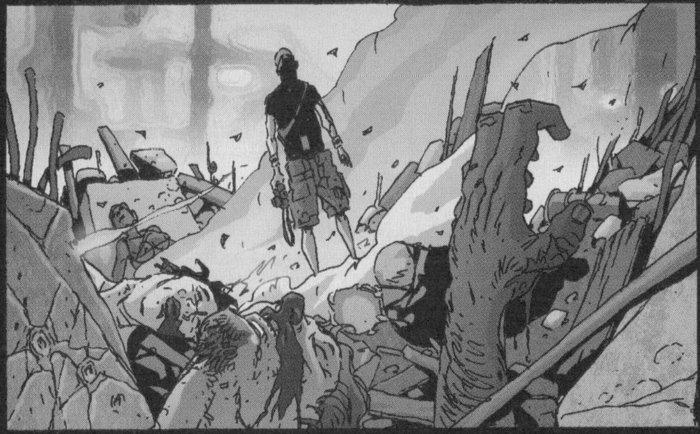

In one of the deadliest days in recent weeks, a suicide-bombing deep in what was once Manhattan's Little Italy claimed the lives of seventeen civilians and three local insurgents, as well as the bomber himself.

Liberty News' Matthew Roth will be providing exclusive images from the scene.

The suspected target was a water delivery truck that was providing drinking water for the area residents. The city's been particularly hard hit by the recent heat wave, with clean, safe water in short supply.

This delivery was not believed to be sanctioned by the tribal bosses who have claimed governance over the area, and the bombing is thought to be retribution.

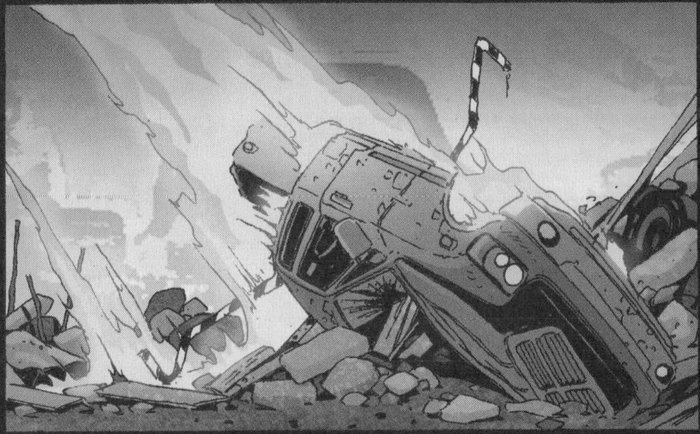

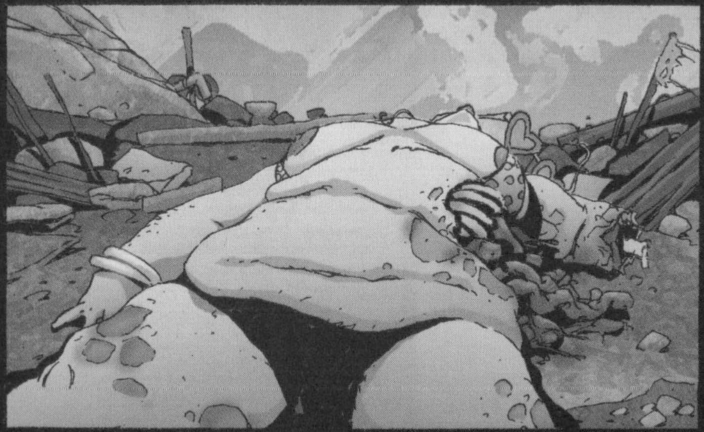

American Military, claiming extraordinary circumstances in the face of increased insurgent violence, have resumed aerial reconnaissance of the city.

This comes despite their having agreed to a mutual no-fly situation with the self-labeled "Free States" earlier this year.

Military spokesmen declined comment.

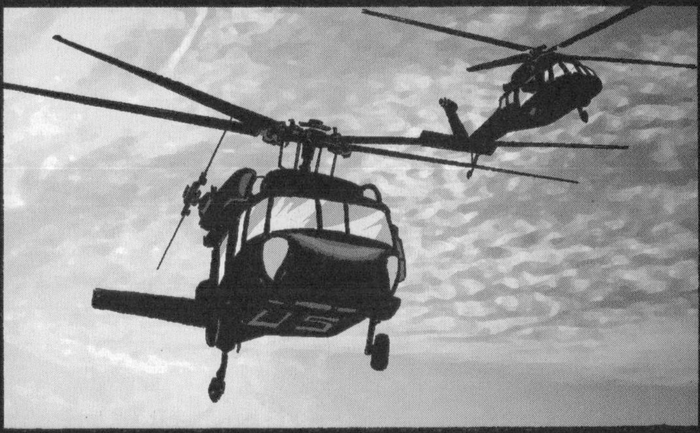

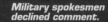

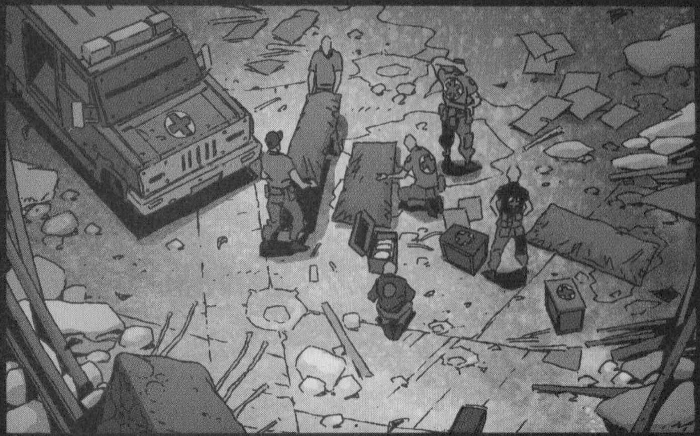

In related news, sniper fire claimed the lives of six American servicemen in Staten Island this morning.

Flatbush Avenue in U.S.-Controlled Brooklyn erupted in violence overnight with a series of drive-by shootings on military housing that eyewitnesses on the scene described as "coordinated."

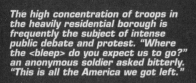

The high concentration of troops in the heavily residential borough is frequently the subject of intense public debate and protest. "Where the <bleep> do you expect us to go?" an anonymous soldier asked bitterly. "This is all the America we got left."

Seven people were wounded, two fatally.

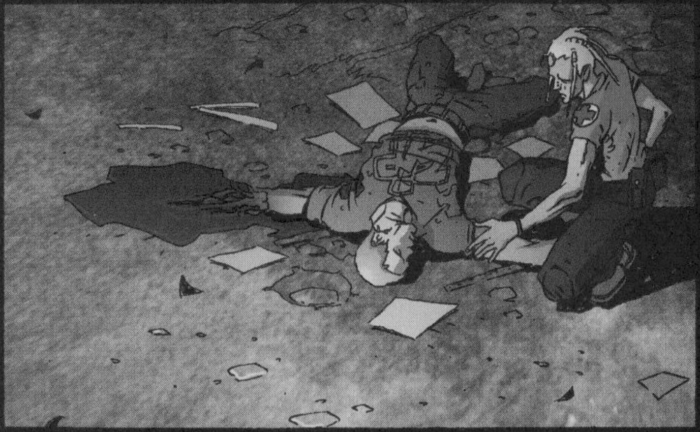

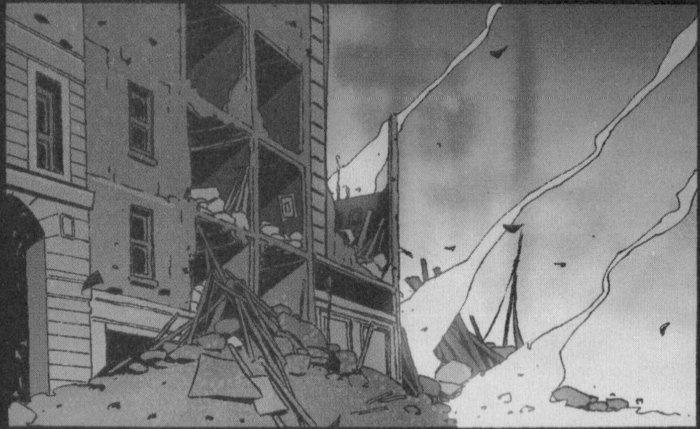

The Pentagon released its official findings concerning a suspected "dirty explosion" recorded in the vicinity of the Statue of Liberty two days ago. Radiation levels came back high, and a general advisory was issued, warning all to avoid the landmark for the next 120-180 days.

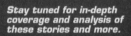

Stay tuned for in-depth coverage and analysis of these stories and more.

This has been a Liberty News summary.

News for America, and Americans.

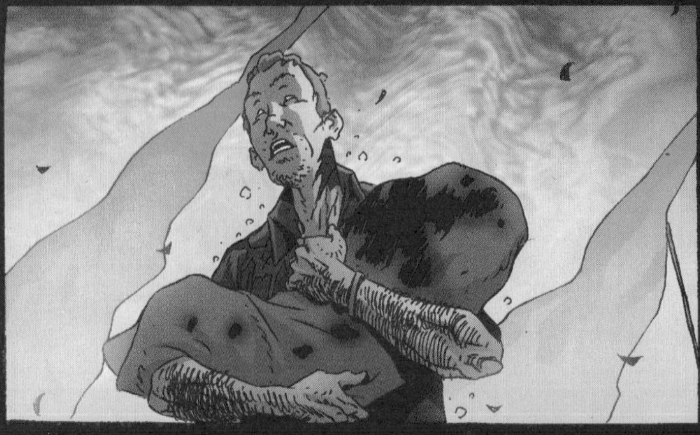

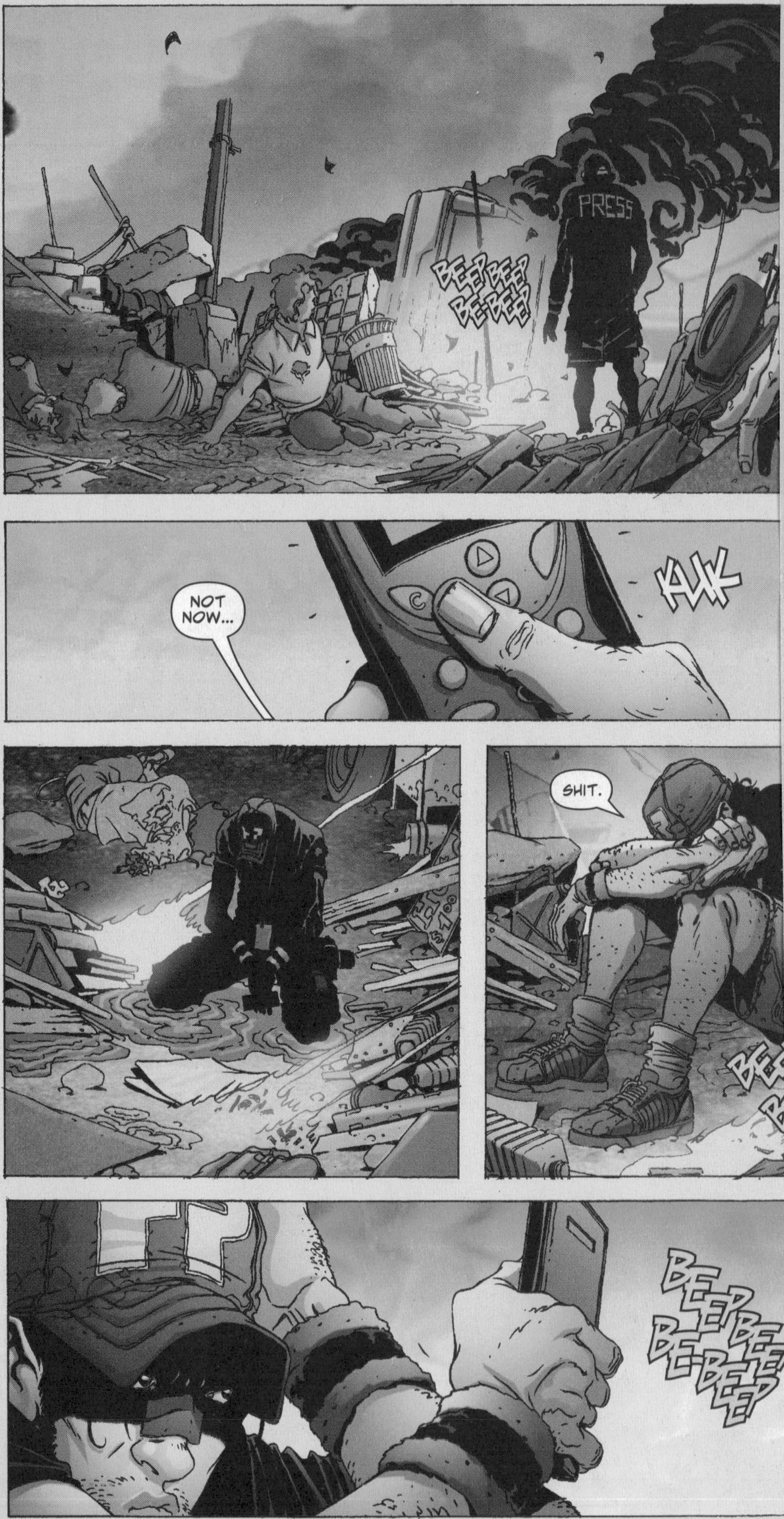
PRESS
BEEPBEEP BE-BEEP
NOT NOW...
KLIK
SHIT.
BEEPBEEP BE-BEEP

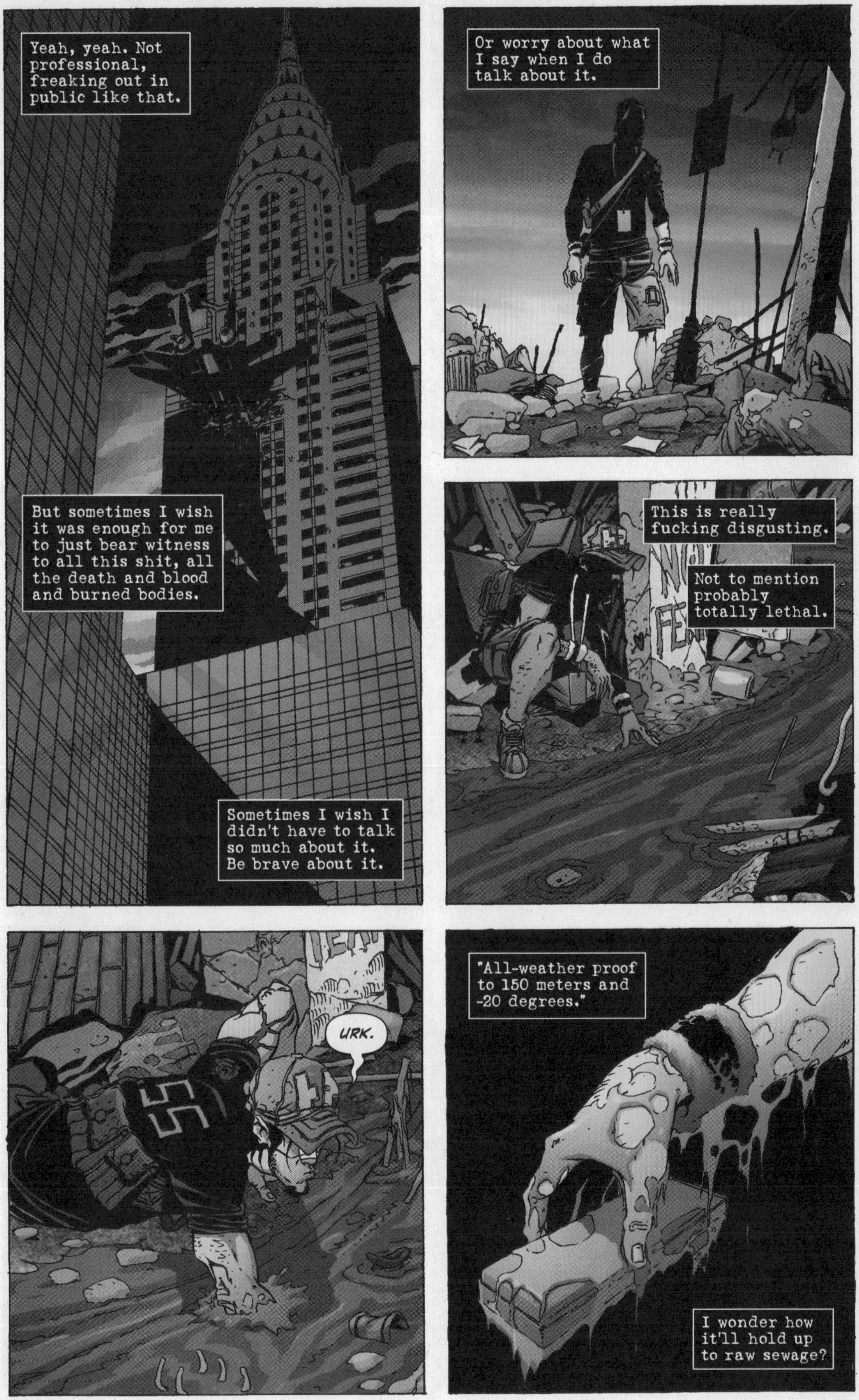
Yeah, yeah. Not professional, freaking out in public like that.
But sometimes I wish it was enough for me to just bear witness to all this shit, all the death and blood and burned bodies.
Sometimes I wish I didn't have to talk so much about it. Be brave about it.
Or worry about what I say when I do talk about it.
This is really fucking disgusting.
Not to mention probably totally lethal.
URK.
"All-weather proof to 150 meters and -20 degrees."
I wonder how it'll hold up to raw sewage?

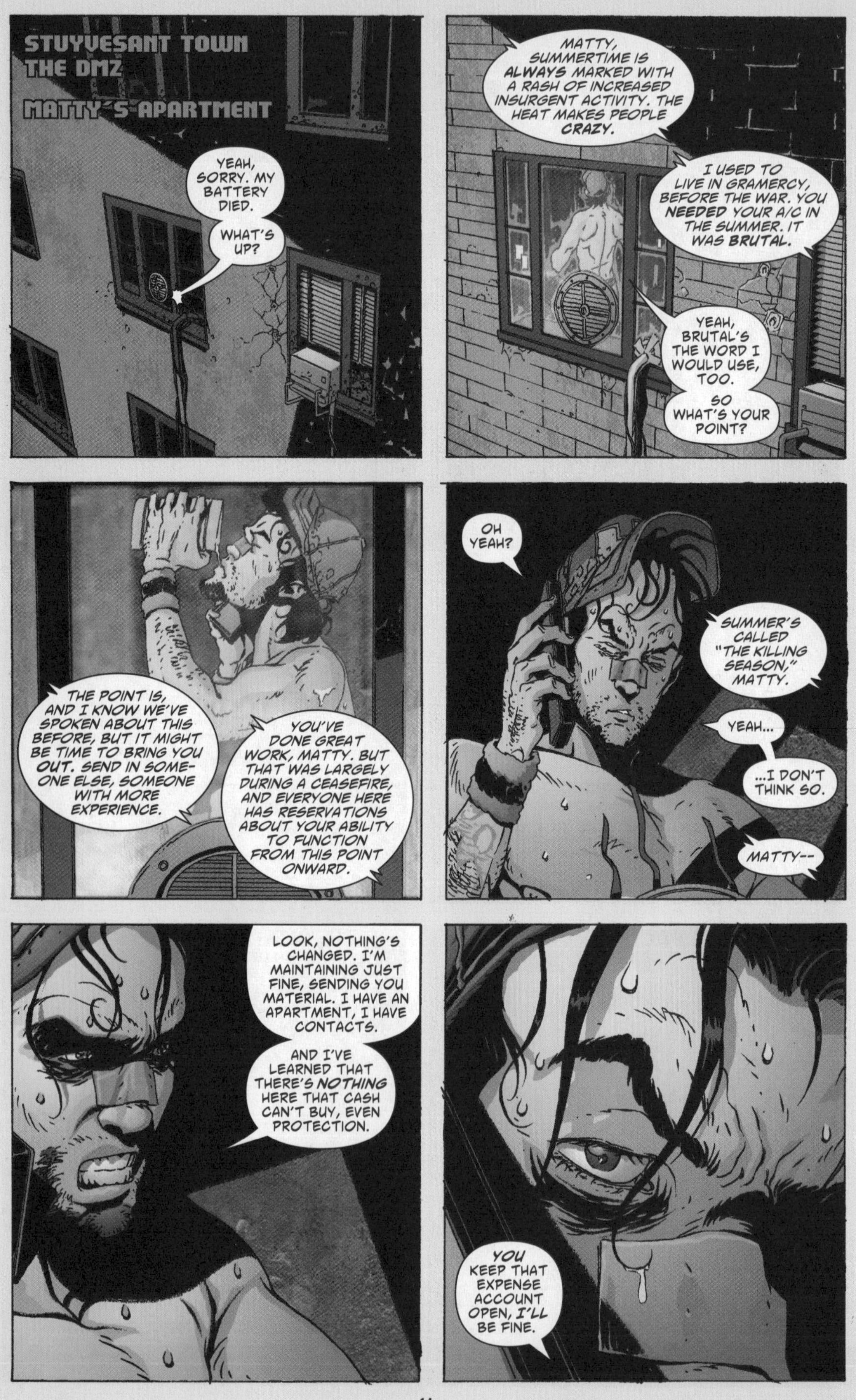
STUYVESANT TOWN
THE DMZ
MATTY'S APARTMENT
YEAH, SORRY. MY BATTERY DIED.
WHAT'S UP?
MATTY, SUMMERTIME IS ALWAYS MARKED WITH A RASH OF INCREASED INSURGENT ACTIVITY. THE HEAT MAKES PEOPLE CRAZY.
I USED TO LIVE IN GRAMERCY, BEFORE THE WAR. YOU NEEDED YOUR A/C IN THE SUMMER. IT WAS BRUTAL.
YEAH, BRUTAL'S THE WORD I WOULD USE, TOO.
SO WHAT'S YOUR POINT?
THE POINT IS, AND I KNOW WE'VE SPOKEN ABOUT THIS BEFORE, BUT IT MIGHT BE TIME TO BRING YOU OUT. SEND IN SOMEONE ELSE, SOMEONE WITH MORE EXPERIENCE.
YOU'VE DONE GREAT WORK, MATTY. BUT THAT WAS LARGELY DURING A CEASEFIRE, AND EVERYONE HERE HAS RESERVATIONS ABOUT YOUR ABILITY TO FUNCTION FROM THIS POINT ONWARD.
OH YEAH?
SUMMER'S CALLED "THE KILLING SEASON," MATTY.
YEAH...
...I DON'T THINK SO.
MATTY--
LOOK, NOTHING'S CHANGED. I'M MAINTAINING JUST FINE, SENDING YOU MATERIAL. I HAVE AN APARTMENT, I HAVE CONTACTS.
AND I'VE LEARNED THAT THERE'S NOTHING HERE THAT CASH CAN'T BUY, EVEN PROTECTION.
YOU KEEP THAT EXPENSE ACCOUNT OPEN, I'LL BE FINE.

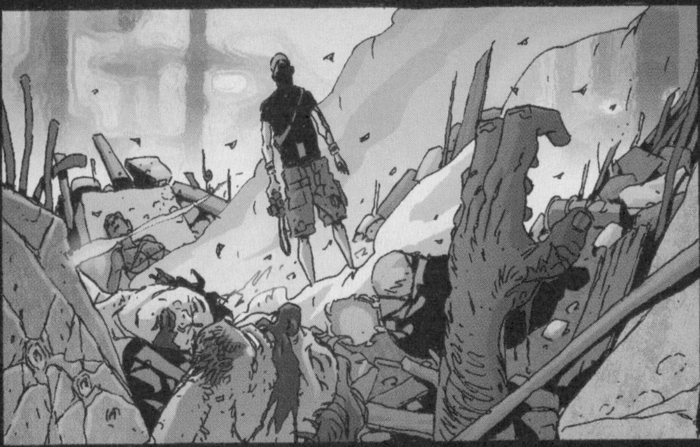

In one of the deadliest days in recent weeks, a suicide-bombing deep in what was once Manhattan's Little Italy claimed the lives of seventeen civilians and three local insurgents, as well as the bomber himself.

Liberty News' Matthew Roth will be providing exclusive images from the scene.

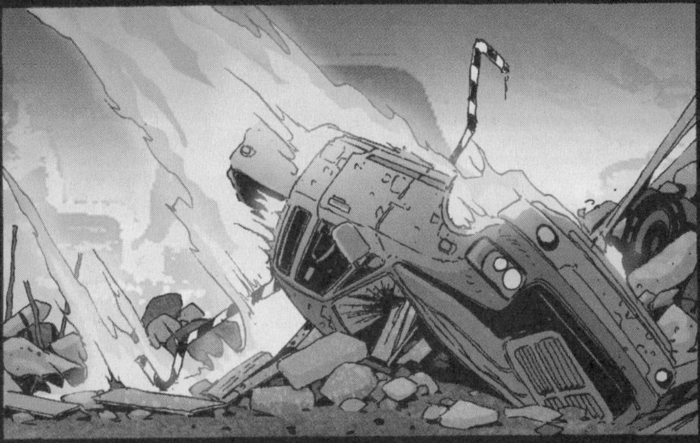

The suspected target was a water delivery truck that was providing drinking water for the area residents. The city's been particularly hard hit by the recent heat wave, with clean, safe water in short supply.

This delivery was not believed to be sanctioned by the tribal bosses who have claimed governance over the area, and the bombing is thought to be retribution.

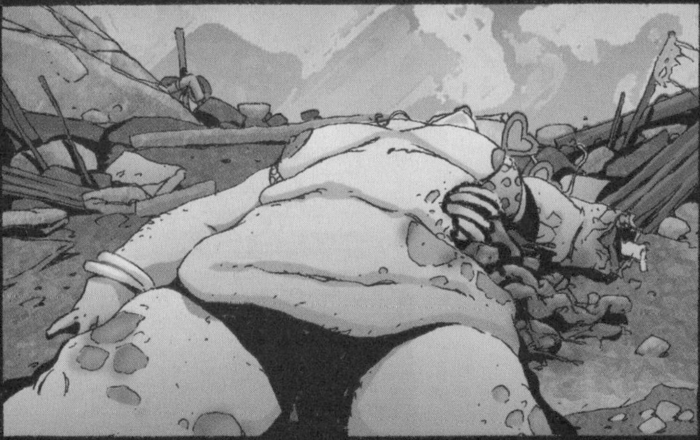

American Military, claiming extraordinary circumstances in the face of increased insurgent violence, have resumed aerial reconnaissance of the city.

This comes despite their having agreed to a mutual no-fly situation with the self-labeled "Free States" earlier this year.

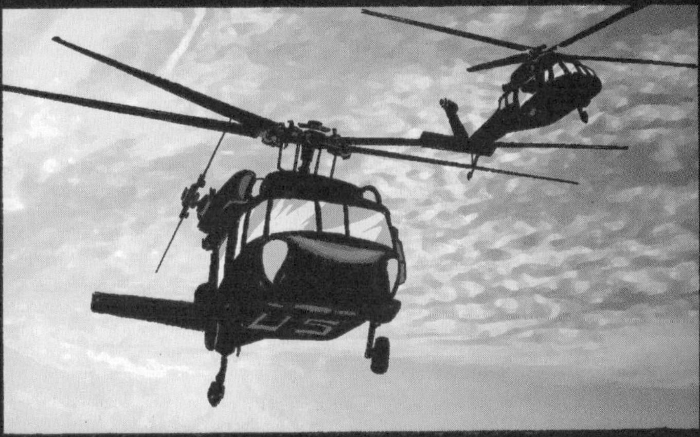

Military spokesmen declined comment.

In related news, sniper fire claimed the lives of six American servicemen in Staten Island this morning.

Flatbush Avenue in U.S.-Controlled Brooklyn erupted in violence overnight with a series of drive-by shootings on military housing that eyewitnesses on the scene described as "coordinated."

The high concentration of troops in the heavily residential borough is frequently the subject of intense public debate and protest. "Where the <bleep> do you expect us to go?" an anonymous soldier asked bitterly. "This is all the America we got left."

Seven people were wounded, two fatally.

The Pentagon released its official findings concerning a suspected "dirty explosion" recorded in the vicinity of the Statue of Liberty two days ago. Radiation levels came back high, and a general advisory was issued, warning all to avoid the landmark for the next 120-180 days.

Stay tuned for in-depth coverage and analysis of these stories and more.

This has been a Liberty News summary.

News for America, and Americans.

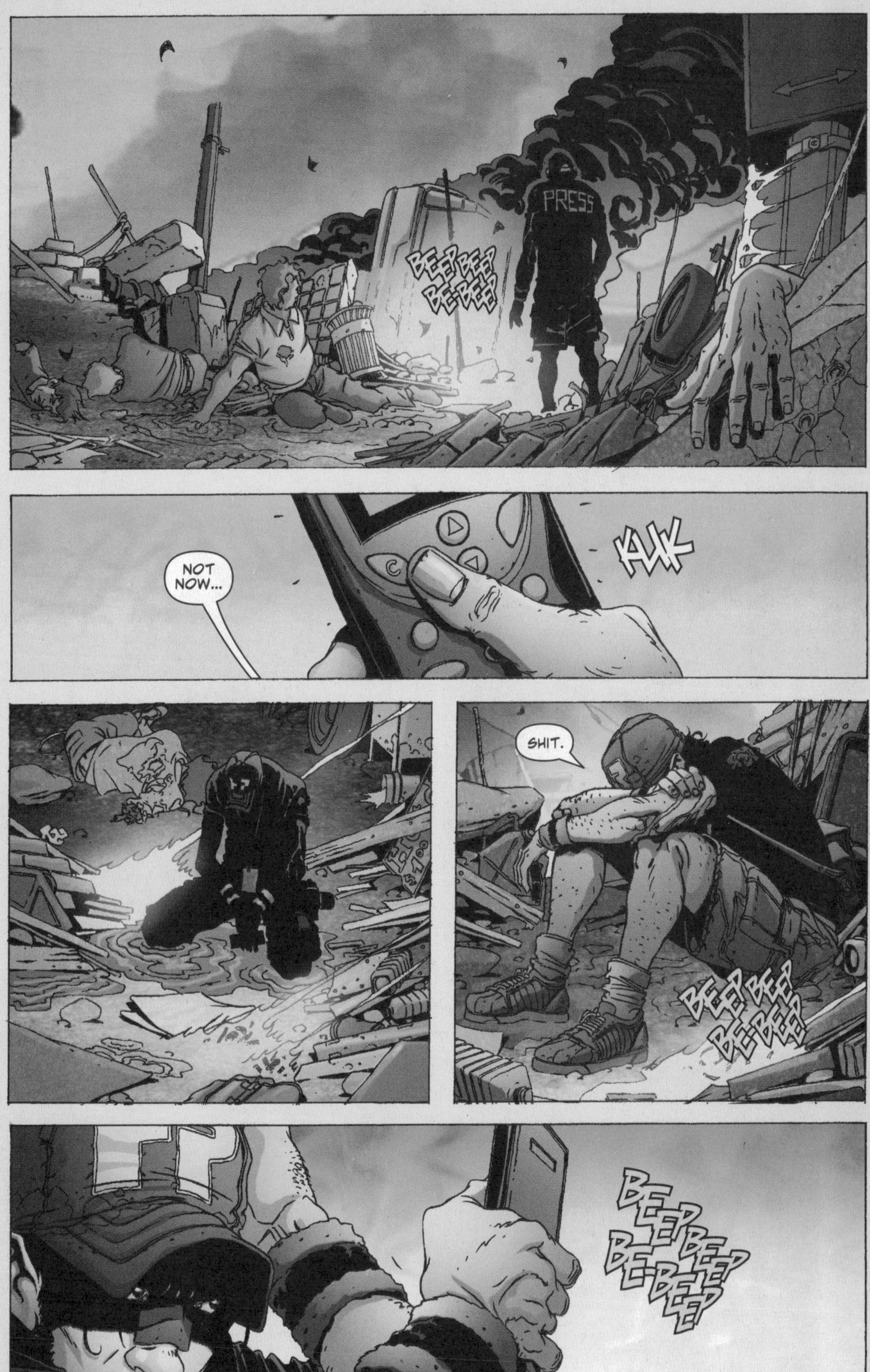
PRESS
BEEP BEEP BE-BEEP
NOT NOW...
KLIK
SHIT.
BEEP BEEP BE-BEEP
BEEP BEEP BE-BEEP

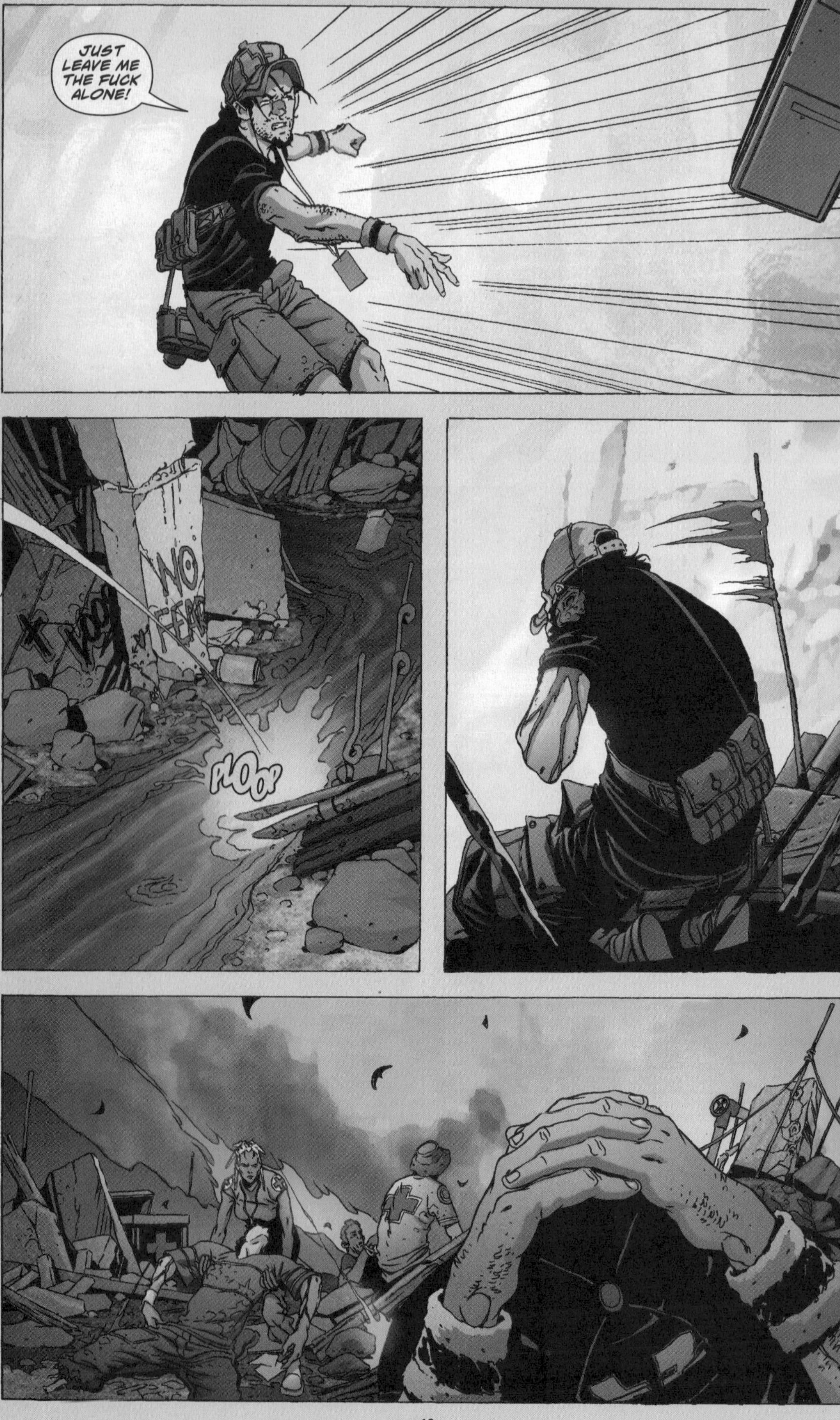
JUST LEAVE ME THE FUCK ALONE!
NO FEAR
PLOOP

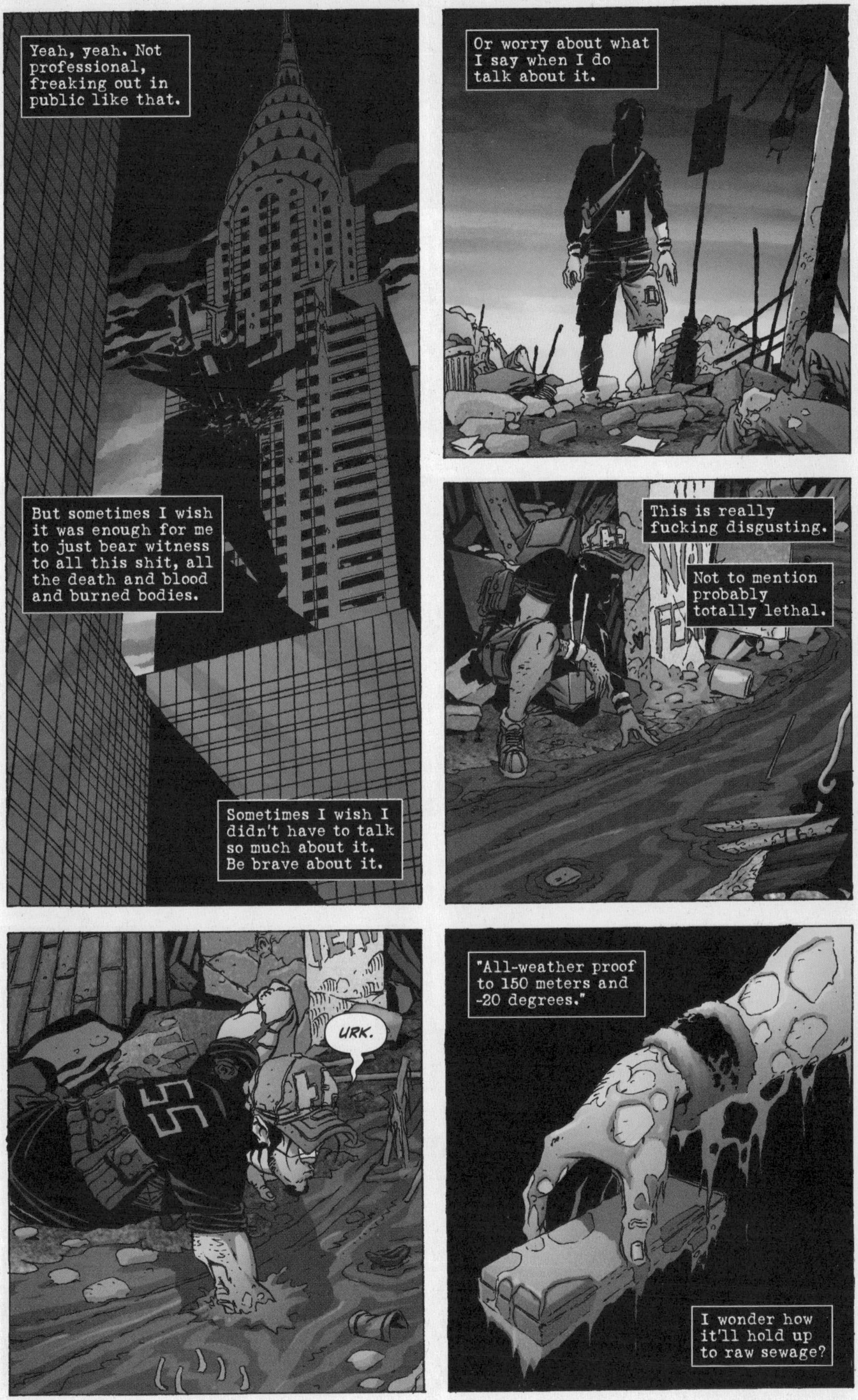
Yeah, yeah. Not professional, freaking out in public like that.
But sometimes I wish it was enough for me to just bear witness to all this shit, all the death and blood and burned bodies.
Sometimes I wish I didn't have to talk so much about it. Be brave about it.
Or worry about what I say when I do talk about it.
This is really fucking disgusting.
Not to mention probably totally lethal.
URK.
"All-weather proof to 150 meters and -20 degrees."
I wonder how it'll hold up to raw sewage?

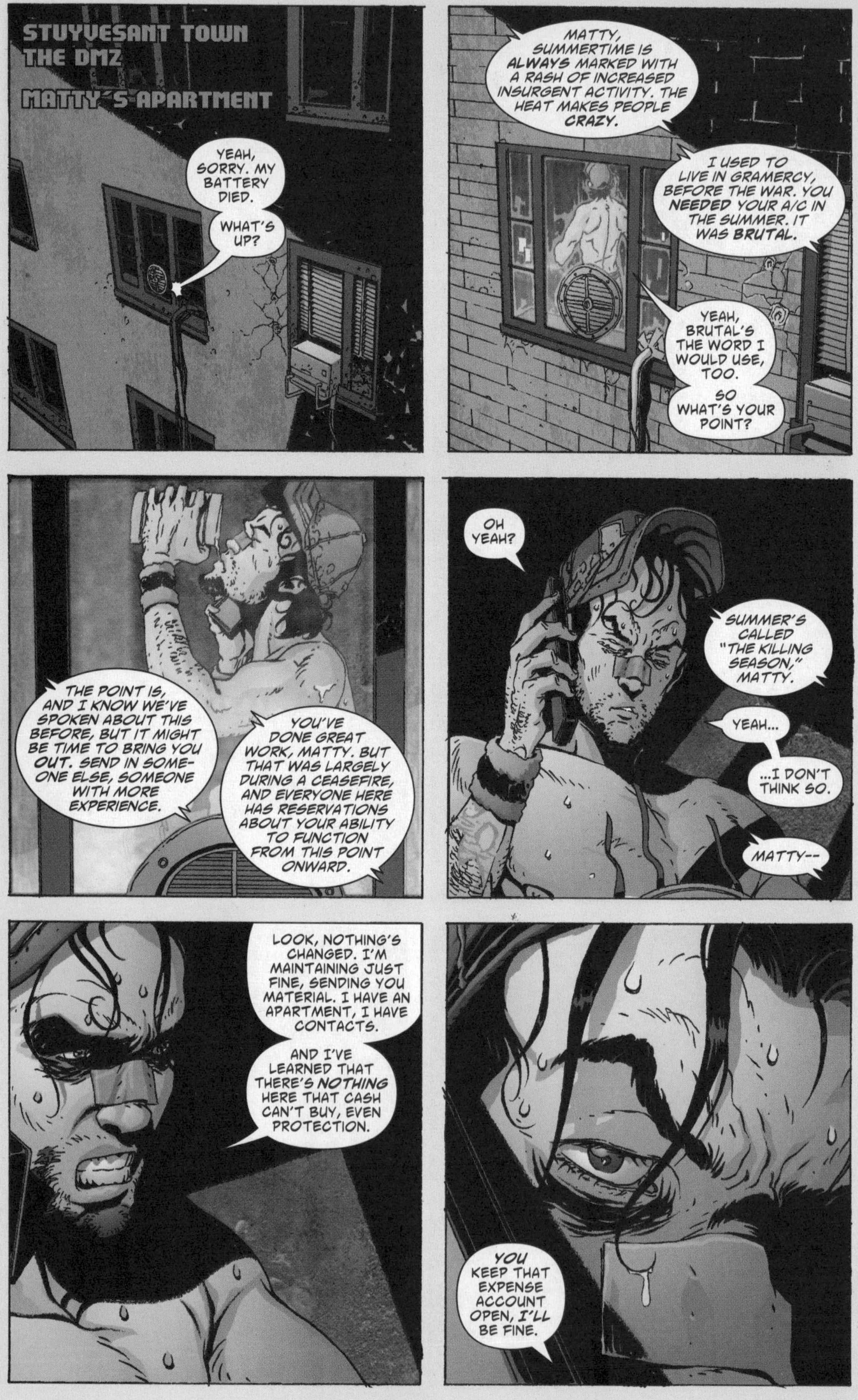

STUYVESANT TOWN
THE DMZ
MATTY'S APARTMENT
YEAH, SORRY. MY BATTERY DIED.
WHAT'S UP?
MATTY, SUMMERTIME IS ALWAYS MARKED WITH A RASH OF INCREASED INSURGENT ACTIVITY. THE HEAT MAKES PEOPLE CRAZY.
I USED TO LIVE IN GRAMERCY, BEFORE THE WAR. YOU NEEDED YOUR A/C IN THE SUMMER. IT WAS BRUTAL.
YEAH, BRUTAL'S THE WORD I WOULD USE, TOO.
SO WHAT'S YOUR POINT?
THE POINT IS, AND I KNOW WE'VE SPOKEN ABOUT THIS BEFORE, BUT IT MIGHT BE TIME TO BRING YOU OUT. SEND IN SOMEONE ELSE, SOMEONE WITH MORE EXPERIENCE.
YOU'VE DONE GREAT WORK, MATTY. BUT THAT WAS LARGELY DURING A CEASEFIRE, AND EVERYONE HERE HAS RESERVATIONS ABOUT YOUR ABILITY TO FUNCTION FROM THIS POINT ONWARD.
OH YEAH?
SUMMER'S CALLED "THE KILLING SEASON," MATTY.
YEAH...
...I DON'T THINK SO.
MATTY--
LOOK, NOTHING'S CHANGED. I'M MAINTAINING JUST FINE, SENDING YOU MATERIAL. I HAVE AN APARTMENT, I HAVE CONTACTS.
AND I'VE LEARNED THAT THERE'S NOTHING HERE THAT CASH CAN'T BUY, EVEN PROTECTION.
YOU KEEP THAT EXPENSE ACCOUNT OPEN, I'LL BE FINE.

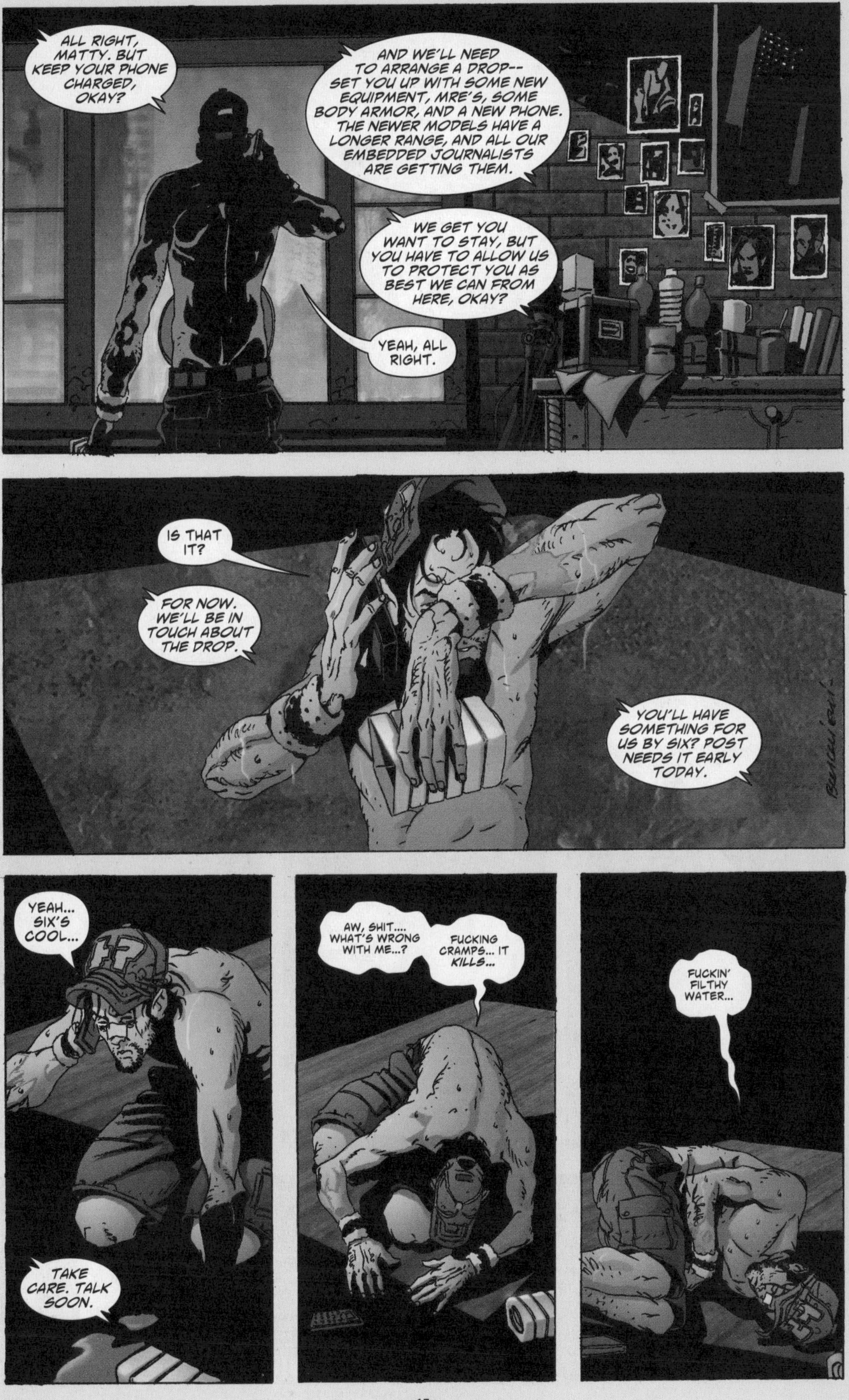
ALL RIGHT, MATTY. BUT KEEP YOUR PHONE CHARGED, OKAY?
AND WE'LL NEED TO ARRANGE A DROP-- SET YOU UP WITH SOME NEW EQUIPMENT, MRE'S, SOME BODY ARMOR, AND A NEW PHONE. THE NEWER MODELS HAVE A LONGER RANGE, AND ALL OUR EMBEDDED JOURNALISTS ARE GETTING THEM.
WE GET YOU WANT TO STAY, BUT YOU HAVE TO ALLOW US TO PROTECT YOU AS BEST WE CAN FROM HERE, OKAY?
YEAH, ALL RIGHT.
IS THAT IT?
FOR NOW. WE'LL BE IN TOUCH ABOUT THE DROP.
YOU'LL HAVE SOMETHING FOR US BY SIX? POST NEEDS IT EARLY TODAY.
YEAH... SIX'S COOL...
TAKE CARE. TALK SOON.
AW, SHIT.... WHAT'S WRONG WITH ME...?
FUCKING CRAMPS... IT KILLS...
FUCKIN' FILTHY WATER...

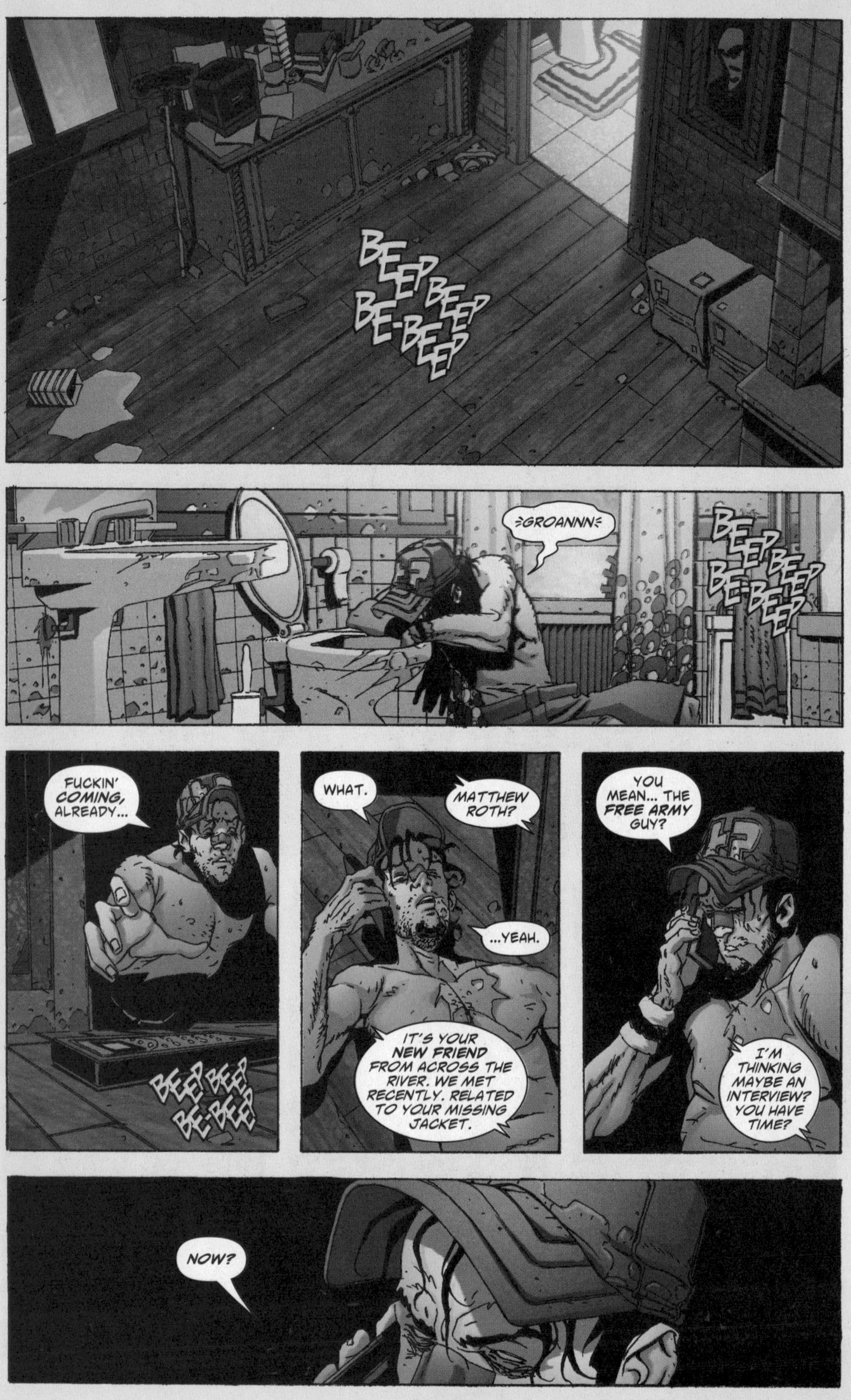
BEEP BEEP BE-BEEP
GROANNN
BEEP BEEP BE-BEEP
FUCKIN' COMING, ALREADY...
BEEP BEEP BE-BEEP
WHAT.
MATTHEW ROTH?
...YEAH.
IT'S YOUR NEW FRIEND FROM ACROSS THE RIVER. WE MET RECENTLY. RELATED TO YOUR MISSING JACKET.
YOU MEAN... THE FREE ARMY GUY?
I'M THINKING MAYBE AN INTERVIEW? YOU HAVE TIME?
NOW?

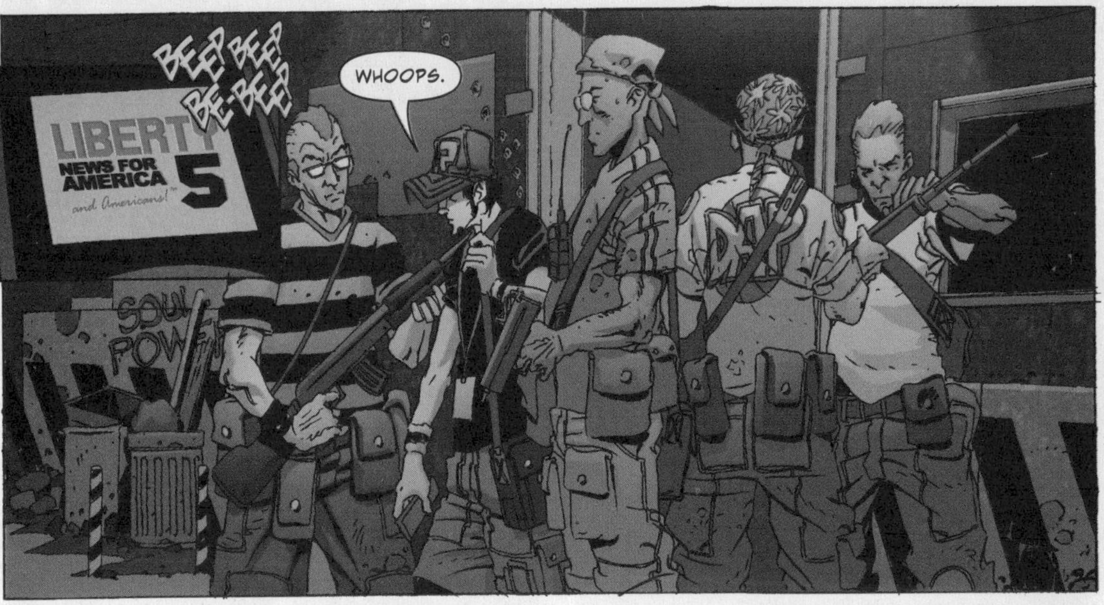
BEEP BEEP BE-BEEP
LIBERTY
NEWS FOR AMERICA
5
and Americans!™
WHOOPS.

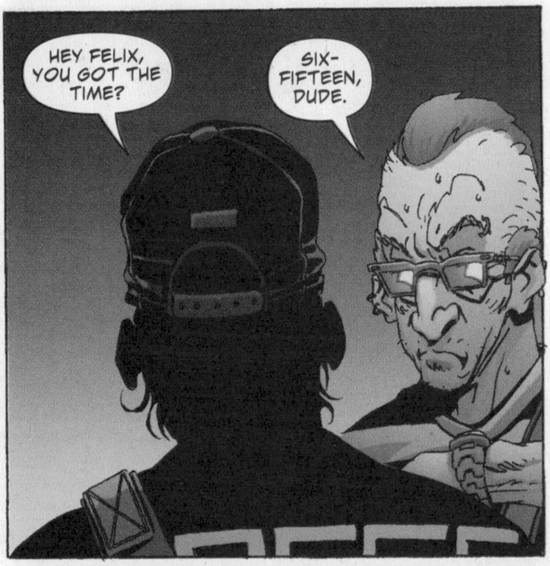
HEY FELIX, YOU GOT THE TIME?
SIX-FIFTEEN, DUDE.

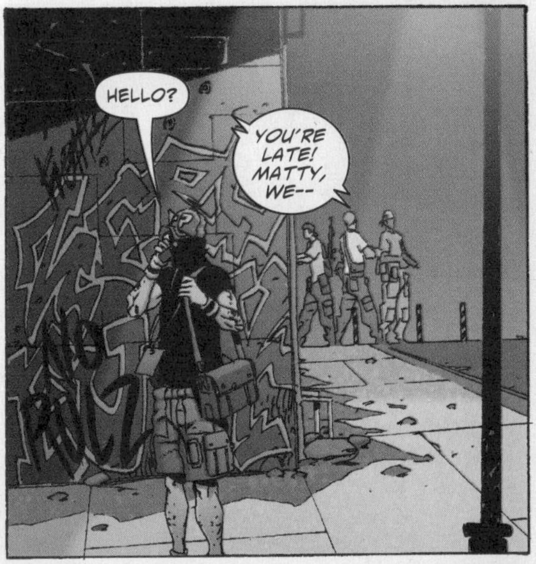
HELLO?
YOU'RE LATE! MATTY, WE--

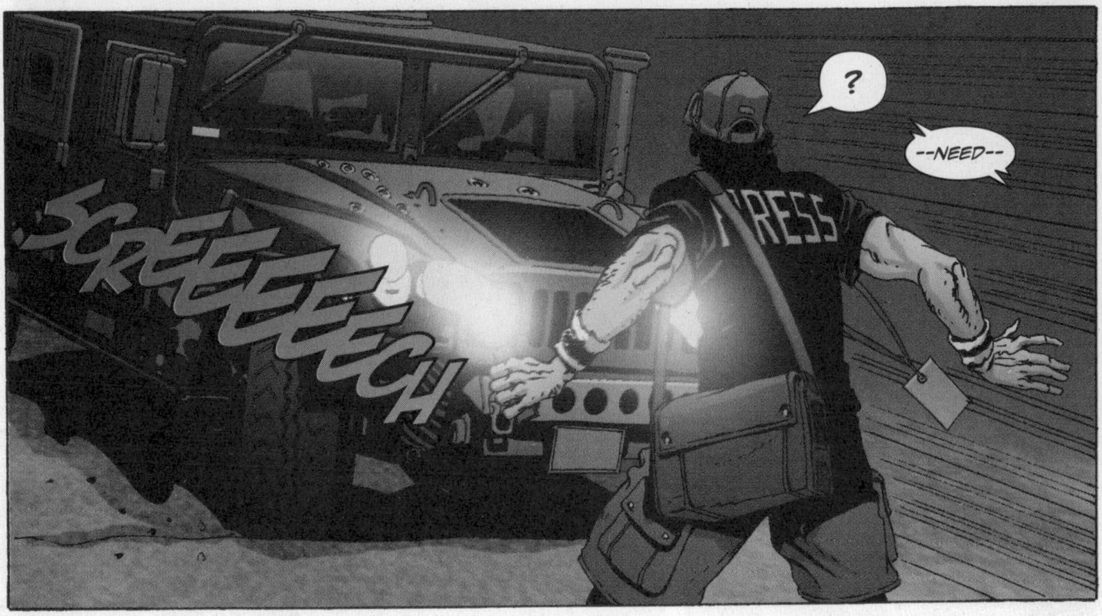
SCREEEEEEECH
?
--NEED--

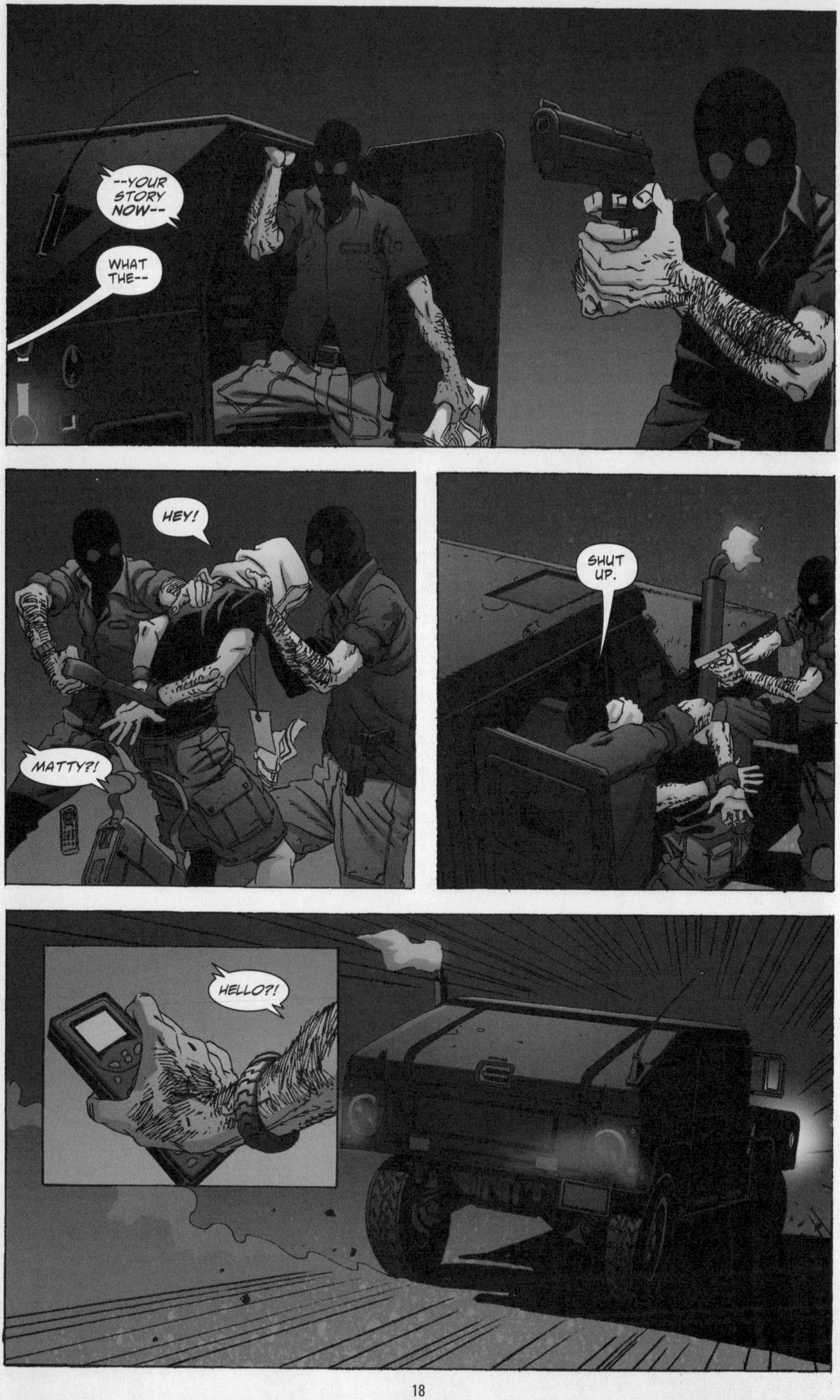
--YOUR STORY NOW--
WHAT THE--
HEY!
MATTY?!
SHUT UP.
HELLO?!

HEY! WHO THE FUCK *ARE* YOU PEOPLE? DO YOU KNOW WHO I--

GAH!

CRACK

SHUT UP!

PLIK

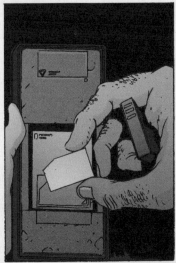

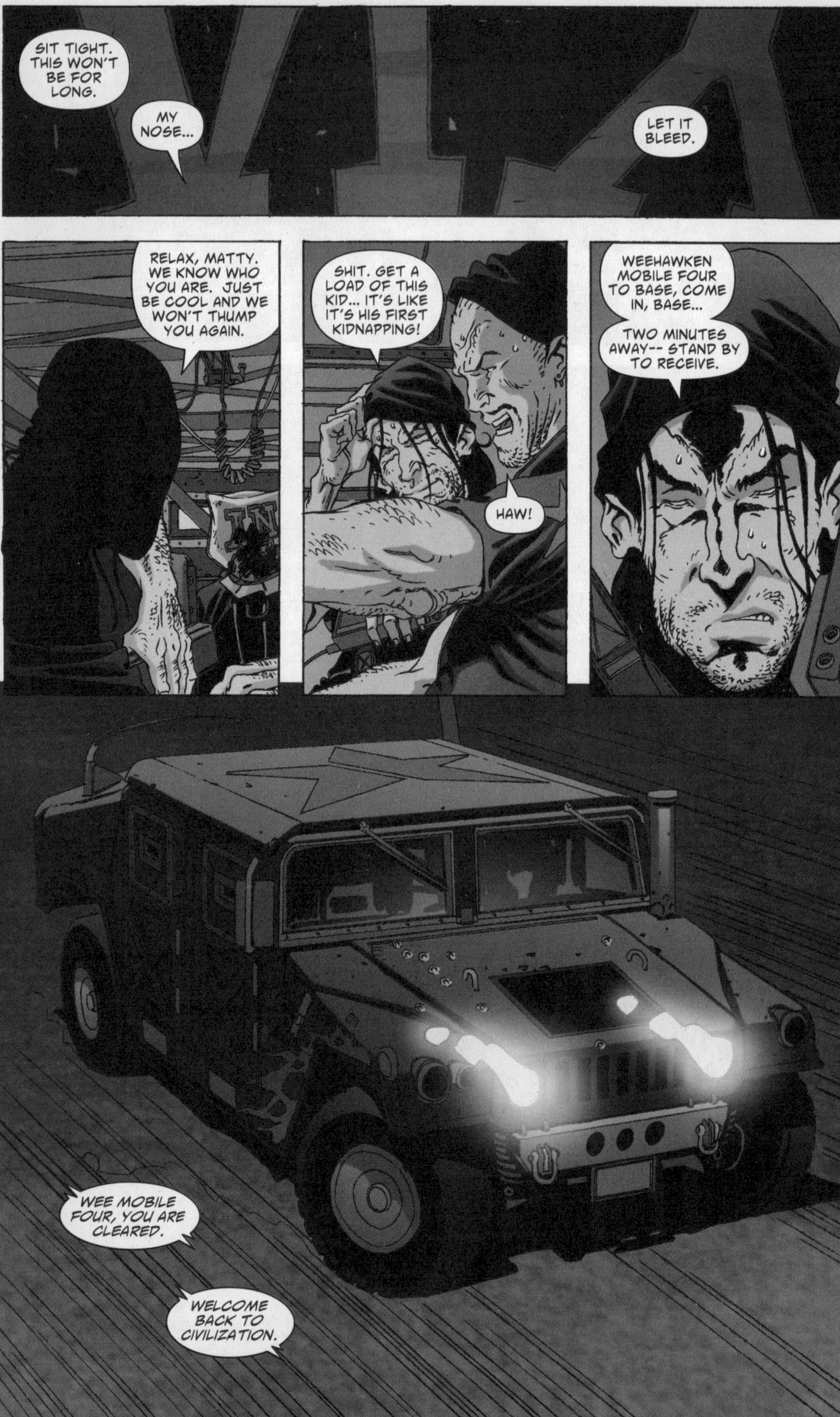
SIT TIGHT. THIS WON'T BE FOR LONG.
MY NOSE...
LET IT BLEED.
RELAX, MATTY. WE KNOW WHO YOU ARE. JUST BE COOL AND WE WON'T THUMP YOU AGAIN.
SHIT. GET A LOAD OF THIS KID... IT'S LIKE IT'S HIS FIRST KIDNAPPING!
HAW!
WEEHAWKEN MOBILE FOUR TO BASE, COME IN, BASE...
TWO MINUTES AWAY-- STAND BY TO RECEIVE.
WEE MOBILE FOUR, YOU ARE CLEARED.
WELCOME BACK TO CIVILIZATION.

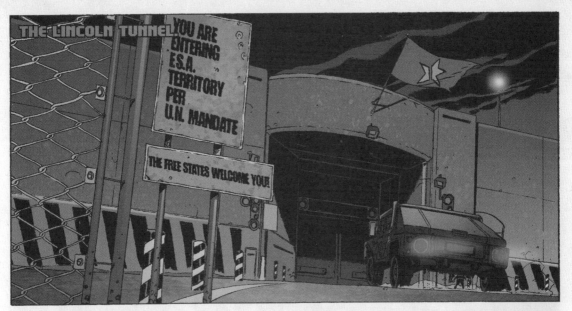

YOU ARE
ENTERING
E.S.A.
TERRITORY
PER
U.N. MANDATE

THE FREE STATES WELCOME YOU!

OK, WE'RE CLOSE.

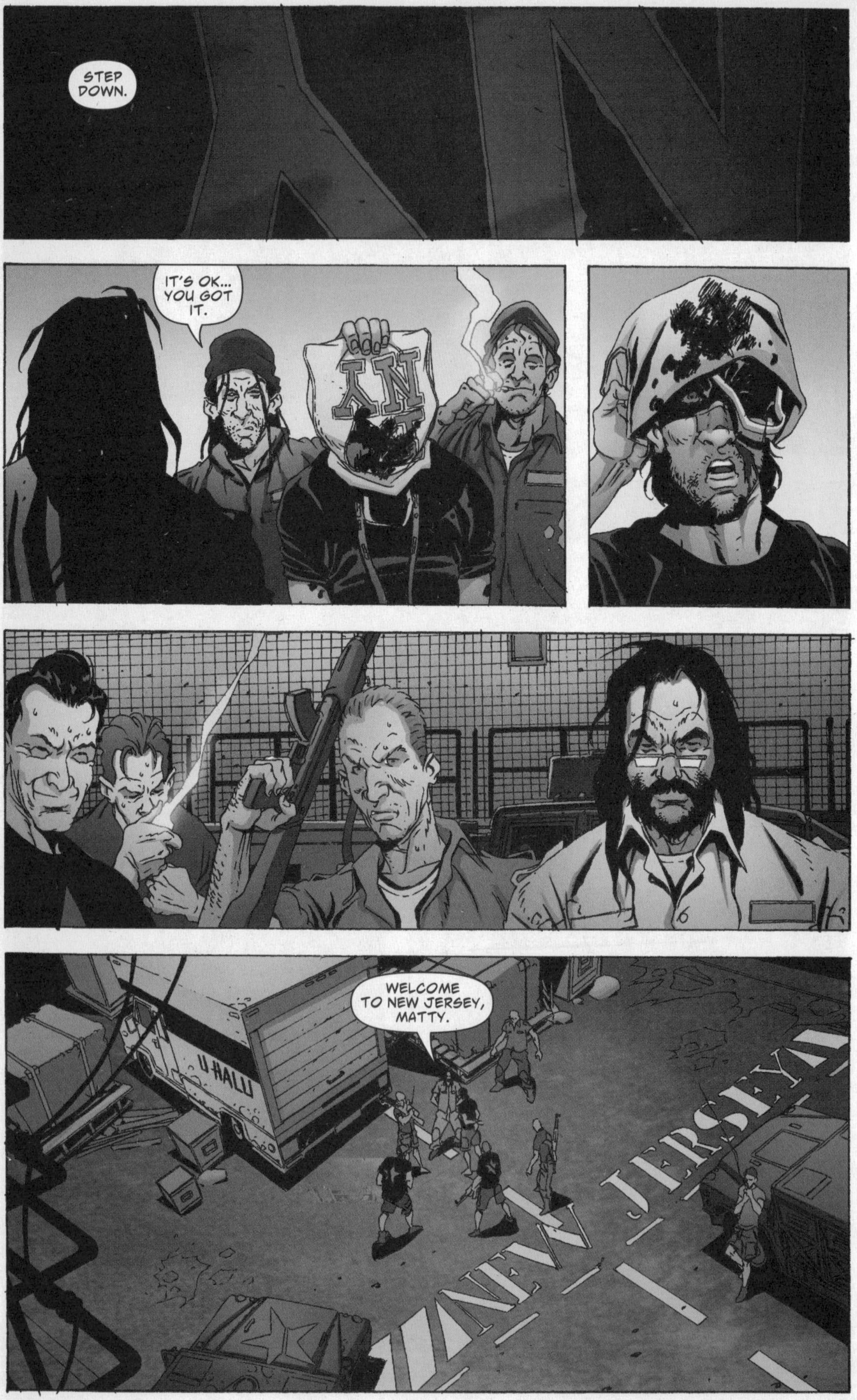
STEP DOWN.
IT'S OK... YOU GOT IT.
WELCOME TO NEW JERSEY, MATTY.
NEW JERSEY

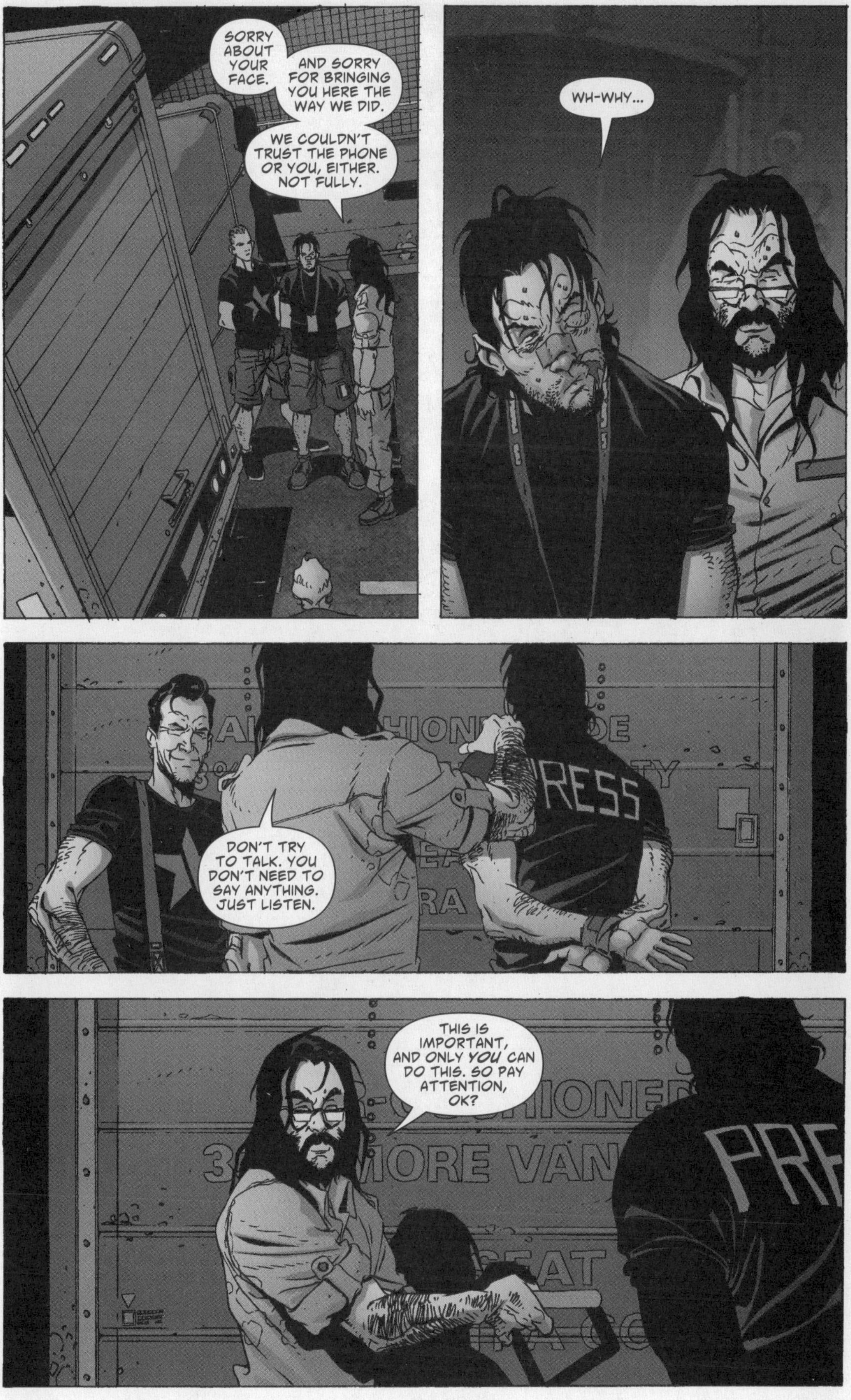
SORRY ABOUT YOUR FACE.
AND SORRY FOR BRINGING YOU HERE THE WAY WE DID.
WE COULDN'T TRUST THE PHONE OR YOU, EITHER. NOT FULLY.
WH-WHY...
DON'T TRY TO TALK. YOU DON'T NEED TO SAY ANYTHING. JUST LISTEN.
THIS IS IMPORTANT, AND ONLY *YOU* CAN DO THIS. SO PAY ATTENTION, OK?

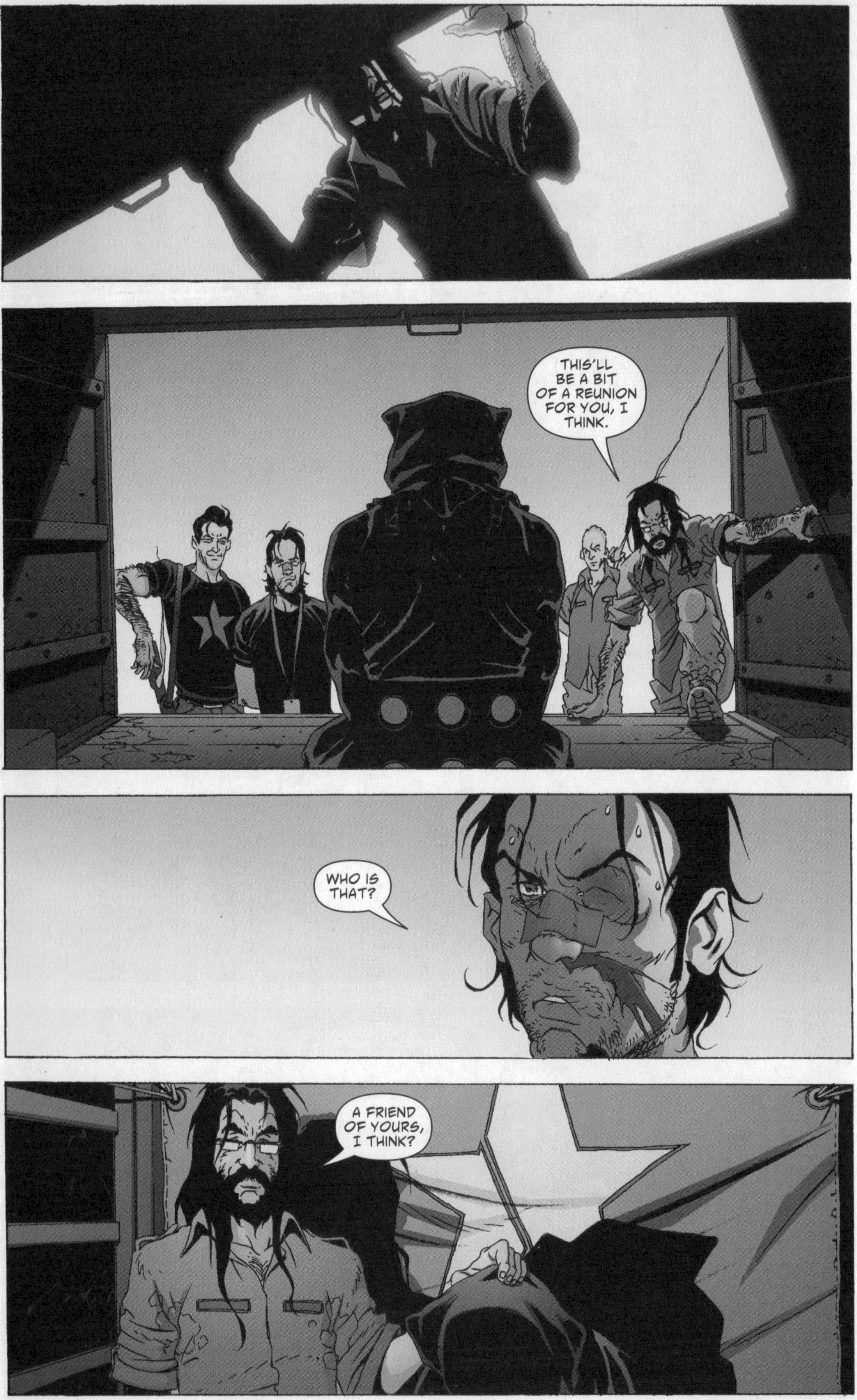
THIS'LL BE A BIT OF A REUNION FOR YOU, I THINK.
WHO IS THAT?
A FRIEND OF YOURS, I THINK?

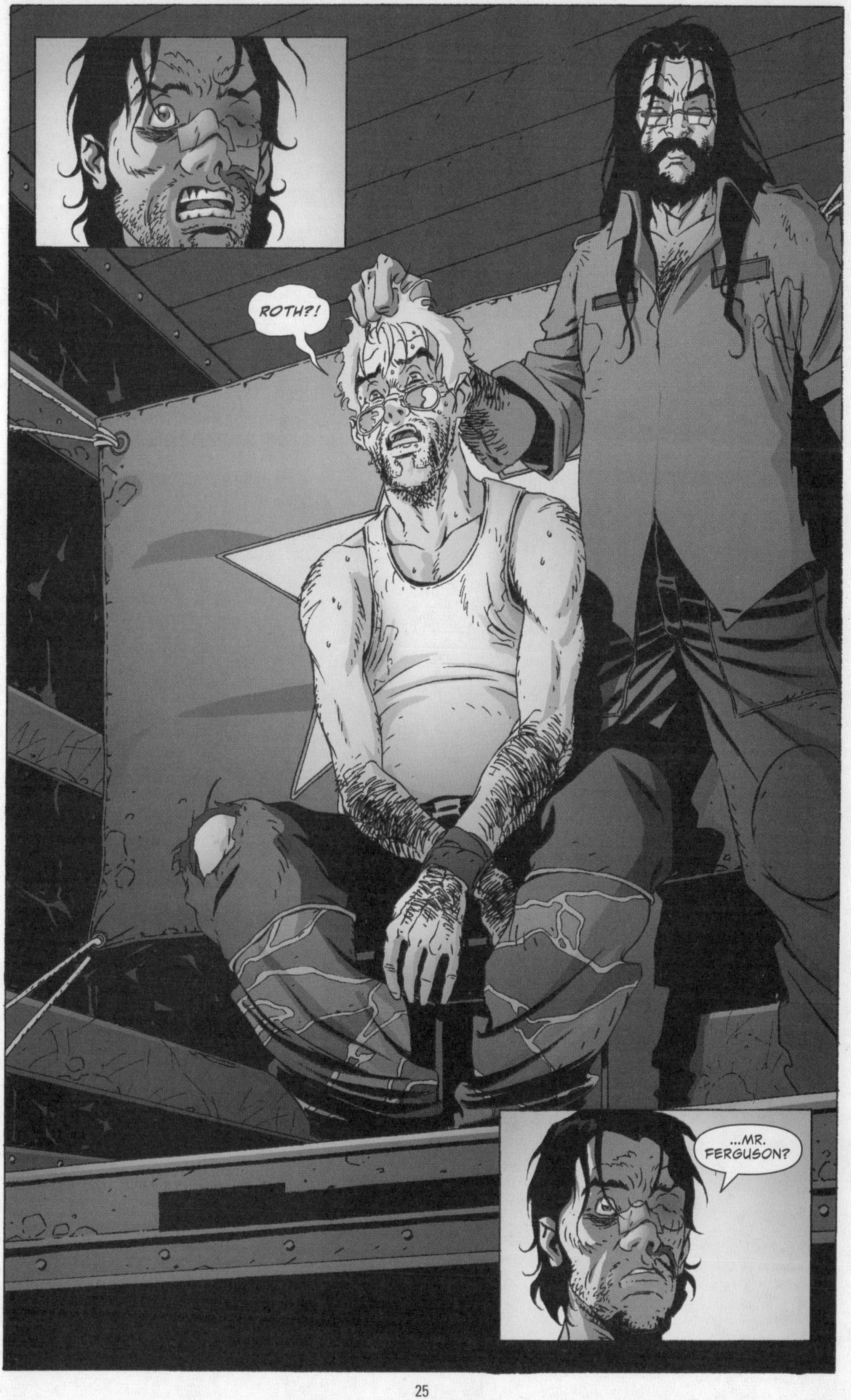
ROTH?!
...MR. FERGUSON?

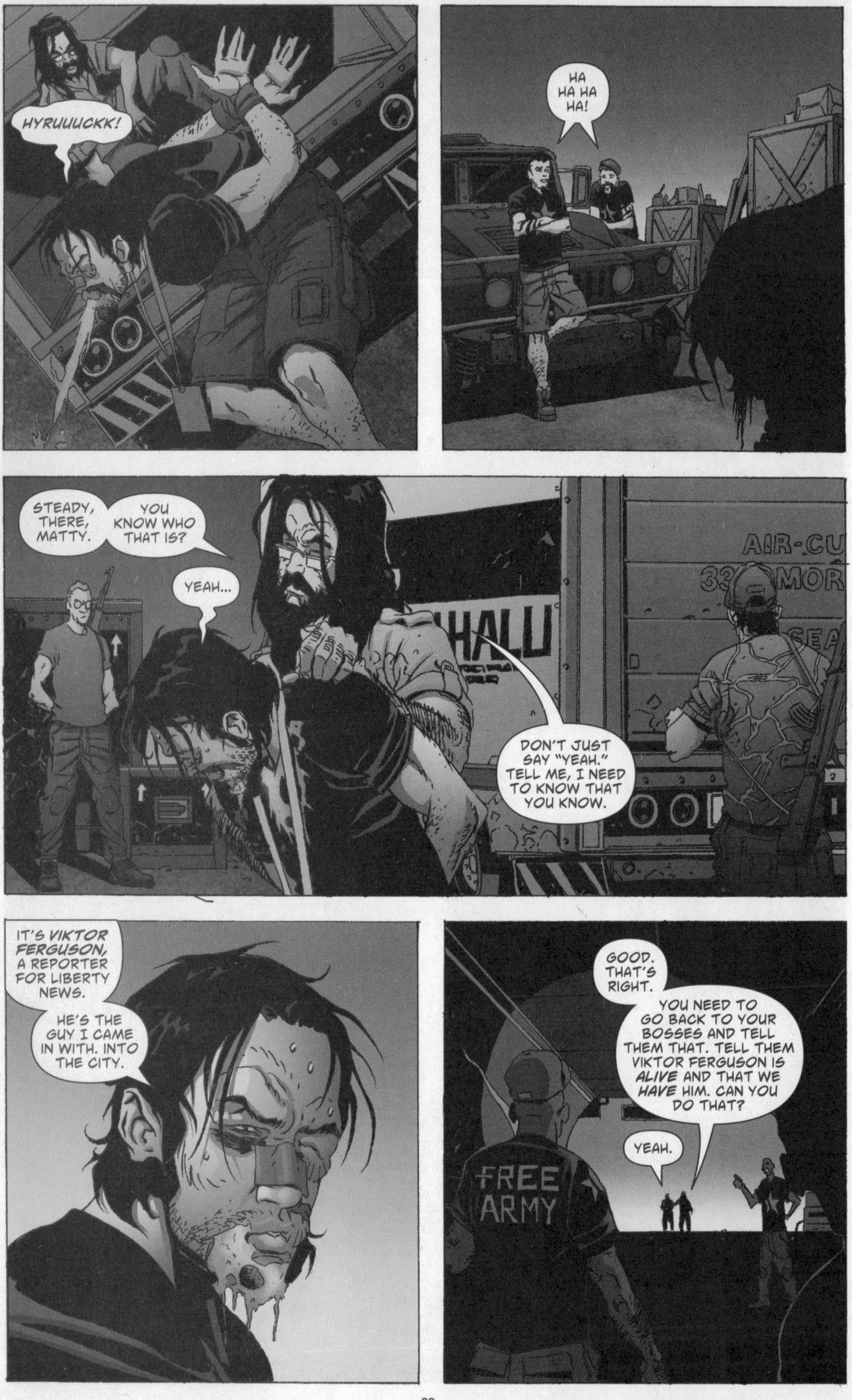
HYRUUUCKK!
HA HA HA HA!
STEADY, THERE, MATTY.
YOU KNOW WHO THAT IS?
YEAH...
DON'T JUST SAY "YEAH." TELL ME, I NEED TO KNOW THAT YOU KNOW.
IT'S *VIKTOR FERGUSON,* A REPORTER FOR LIBERTY NEWS.
HE'S THE GUY I CAME IN WITH. INTO THE CITY.
GOOD. THAT'S RIGHT.
YOU NEED TO GO BACK TO YOUR BOSSES AND TELL THEM THAT. TELL THEM VIKTOR FERGUSON IS *ALIVE* AND THAT WE *HAVE* HIM. CAN YOU DO THAT?
YEAH.
FREE ARMY

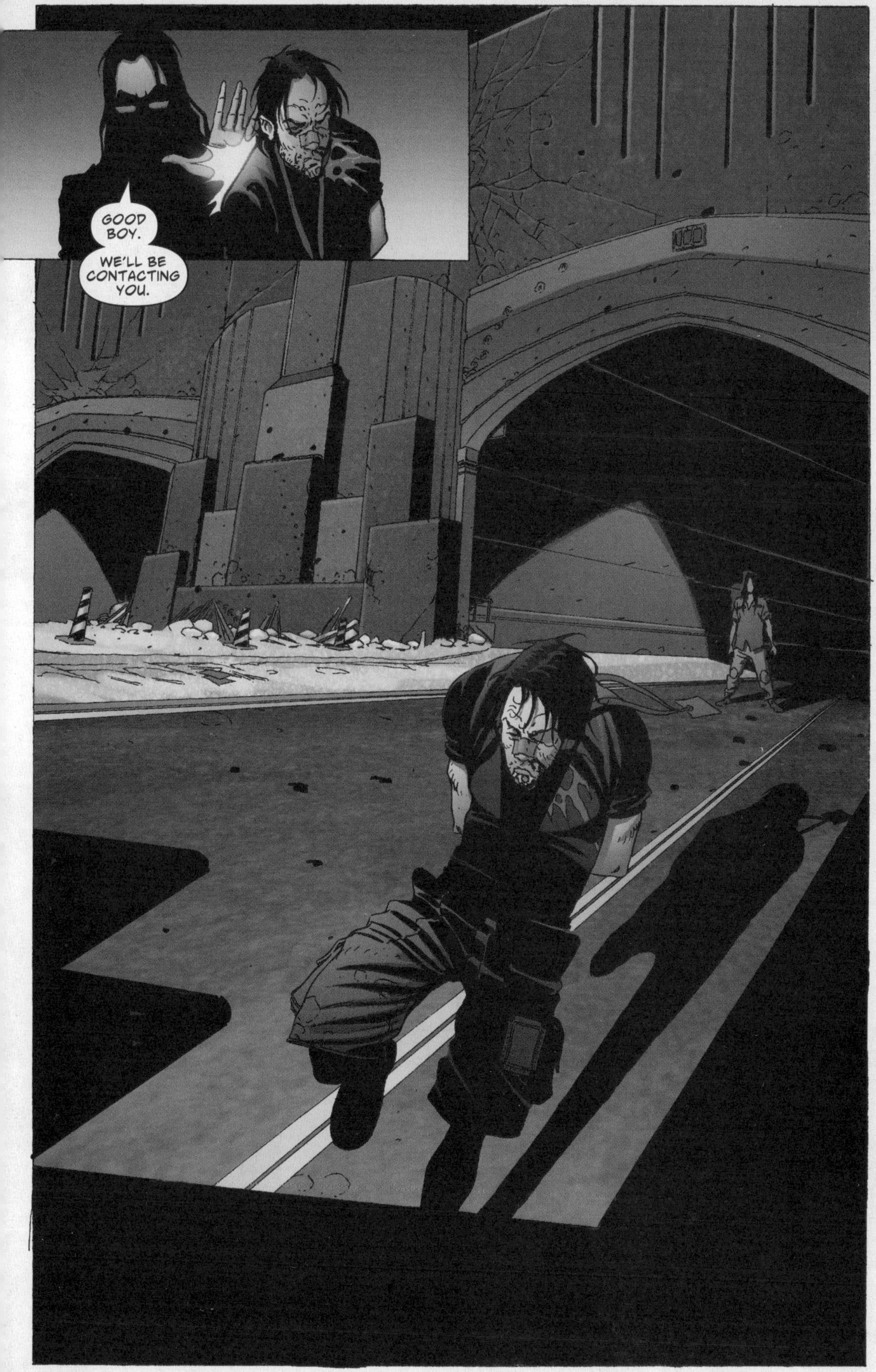
GOOD BOY.
WE'LL BE CONTACTING YOU.

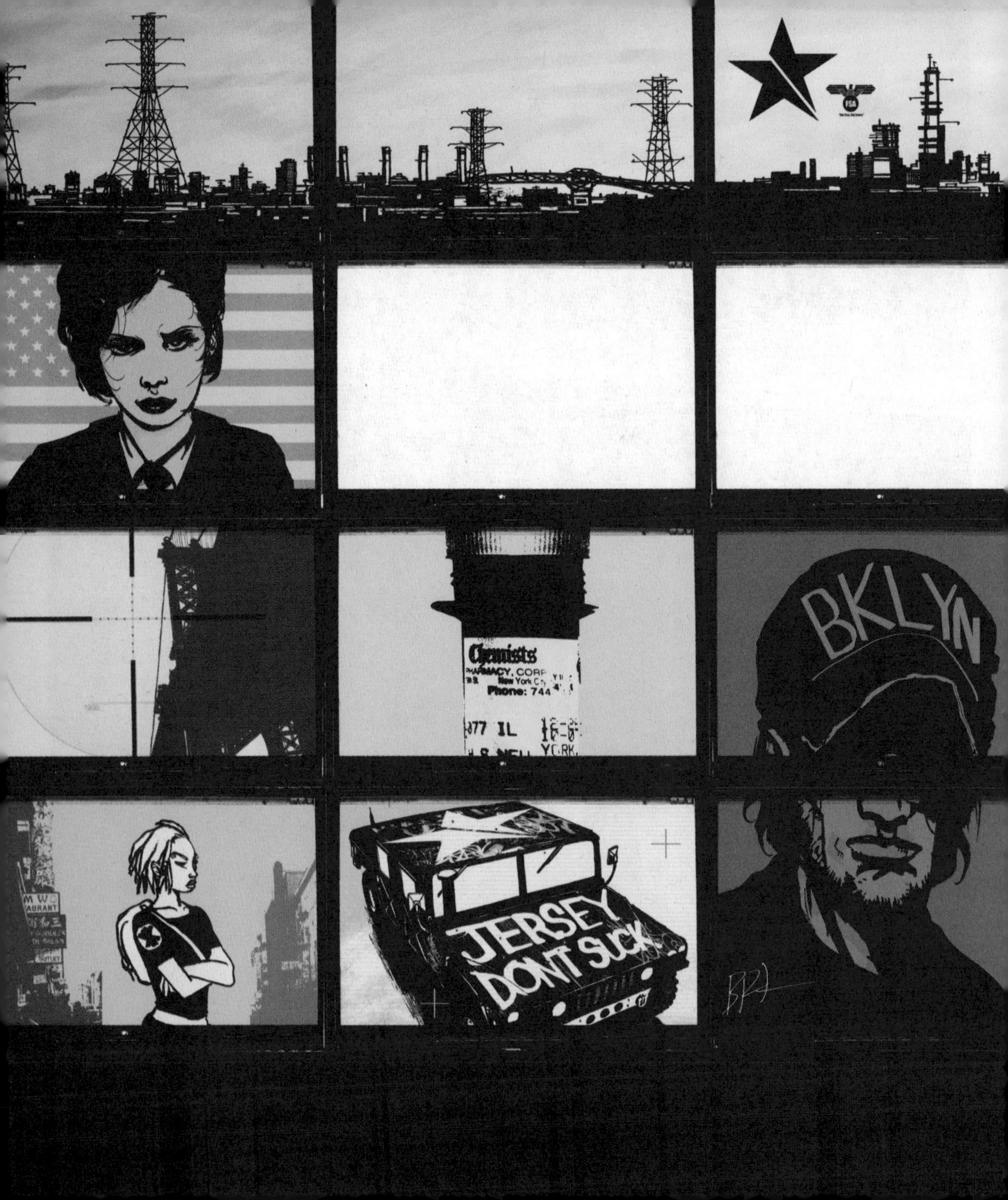

Chemists
PHARMACY, CORP
New York City
Phone: 744
BKLYN
JERSEY
DONT SUCK

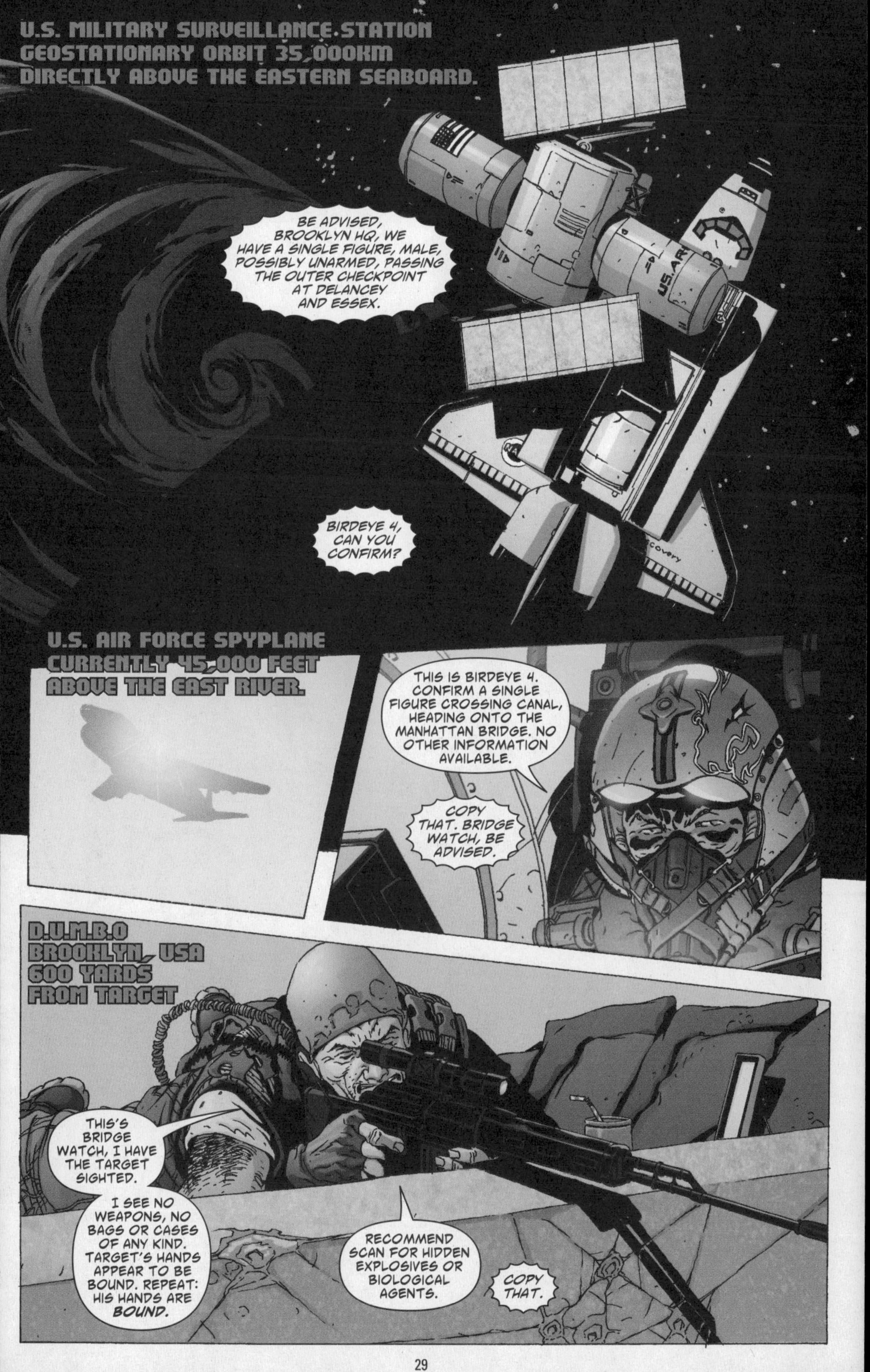

U.S. MILITARY SURVEILLANCE STATION
GEOSTATIONARY ORBIT 35,000KM
DIRECTLY ABOVE THE EASTERN SEABOARD.
BE ADVISED, BROOKLYN HQ, WE HAVE A SINGLE FIGURE, MALE, POSSIBLY UNARMED, PASSING THE OUTER CHECKPOINT AT DELANCEY AND ESSEX.
BIRDEYE 4, CAN YOU CONFIRM?
U.S. AIR FORCE SPYPLANE
CURRENTLY 45,000 FEET
ABOVE THE EAST RIVER.
THIS IS BIRDEYE 4. CONFIRM A SINGLE FIGURE CROSSING CANAL, HEADING ONTO THE MANHATTAN BRIDGE. NO OTHER INFORMATION AVAILABLE.
COPY THAT. BRIDGE WATCH, BE ADVISED.
D.U.M.B.O
BROOKLYN, USA
600 YARDS
FROM TARGET
THIS'S BRIDGE WATCH, I HAVE THE TARGET SIGHTED.
I SEE NO WEAPONS, NO BAGS OR CASES OF ANY KIND. TARGET'S HANDS APPEAR TO BE BOUND. REPEAT: HIS HANDS ARE BOUND.
RECOMMEND SCAN FOR HIDDEN EXPLOSIVES OR BIOLOGICAL AGENTS.
COPY THAT.

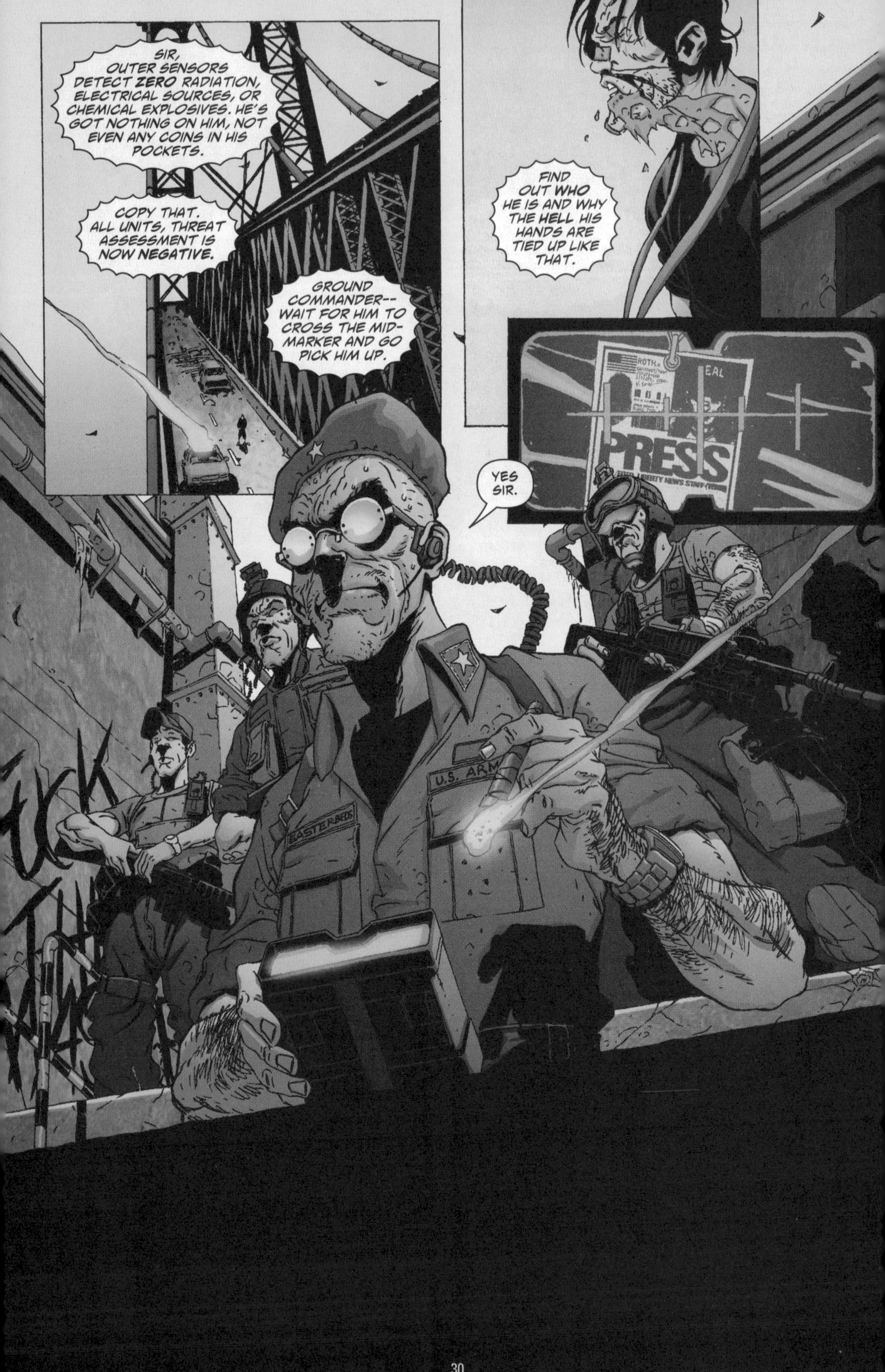
SIR, OUTER SENSORS DETECT ZERO RADIATION, ELECTRICAL SOURCES, OR CHEMICAL EXPLOSIVES. HE'S GOT NOTHING ON HIM, NOT EVEN ANY COINS IN HIS POCKETS.
COPY THAT. ALL UNITS, THREAT ASSESSMENT IS NOW NEGATIVE.
GROUND COMMANDER-- WAIT FOR HIM TO CROSS THE MID-MARKER AND GO PICK HIM UP.
FIND OUT WHO HE IS AND WHY THE HELL HIS HANDS ARE TIED UP LIKE THAT.
PRESS
YES SIR.

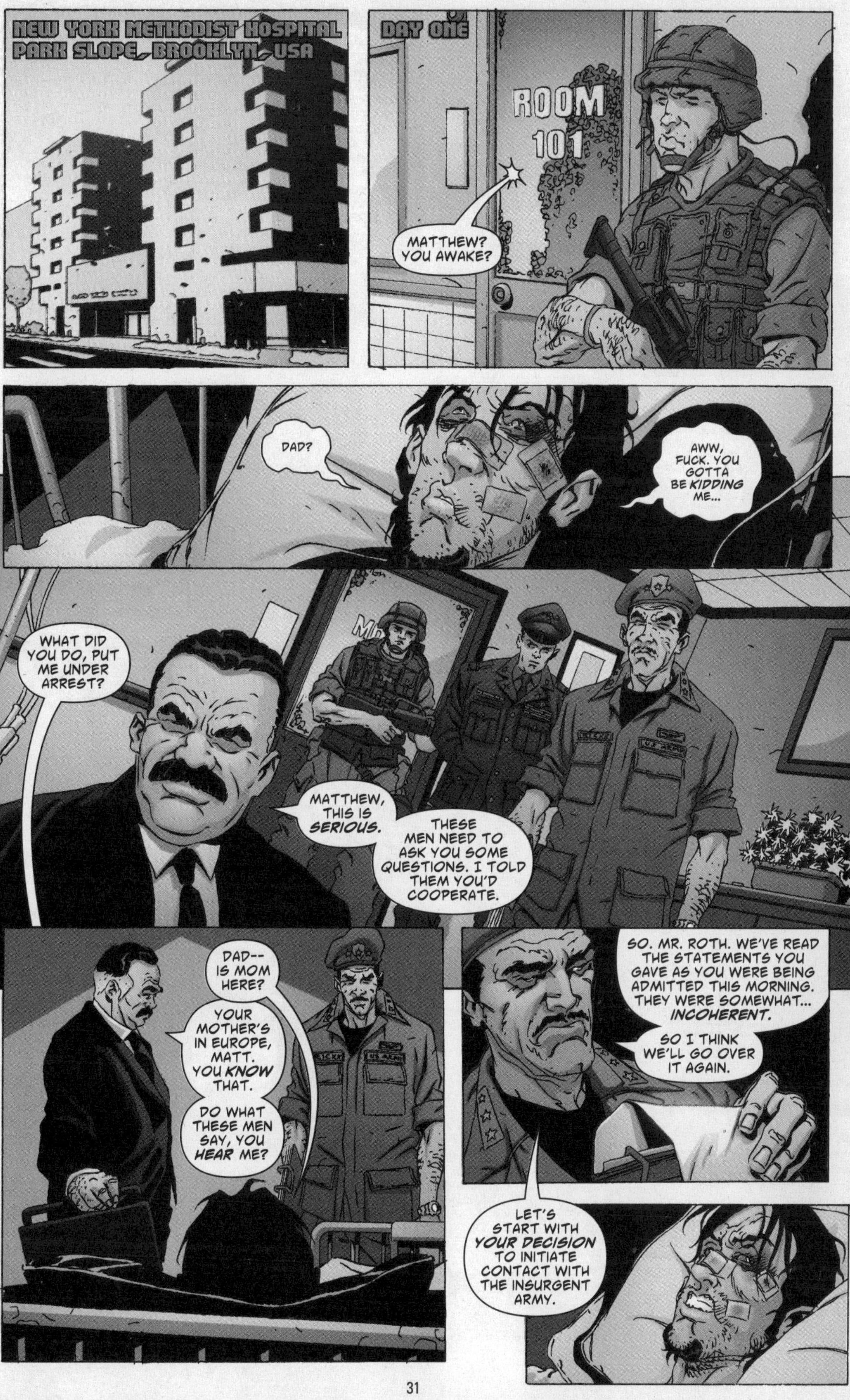
NEW YORK METHODIST HOSPITAL
PARK SLOPE, BROOKLYN, USA
DAY ONE
ROOM 101
MATTHEW? YOU AWAKE?
DAD?
AWW, FUCK. YOU GOTTA BE *KIDDING* ME...
WHAT DID YOU DO, PUT ME UNDER ARREST?
MATTHEW, THIS IS *SERIOUS.*
THESE MEN NEED TO ASK YOU SOME QUESTIONS. I TOLD THEM YOU'D COOPERATE.
DAD-- IS MOM HERE?
YOUR MOTHER'S IN EUROPE, MATT. YOU *KNOW* THAT.
DO WHAT THESE MEN SAY, YOU *HEAR* ME?
SO. MR. ROTH. WE'VE READ THE STATEMENTS YOU GAVE AS YOU WERE BEING ADMITTED THIS MORNING. THEY WERE SOMEWHAT... *INCOHERENT.*
SO I THINK WE'LL GO OVER IT AGAIN.
LET'S START WITH *YOUR DECISION* TO INITIATE CONTACT WITH THE INSURGENT ARMY.

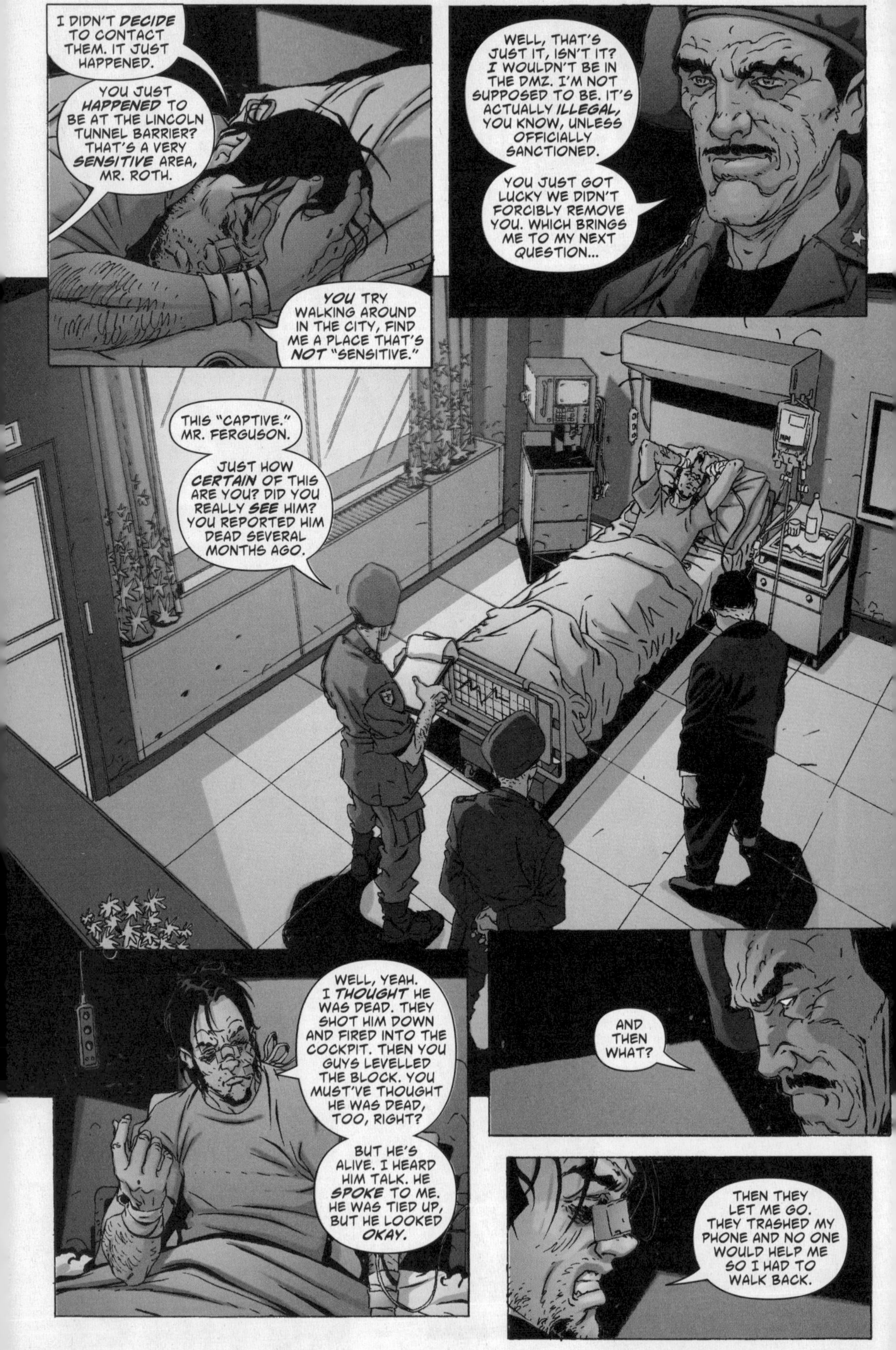
I DIDN'T DECIDE TO CONTACT THEM. IT JUST HAPPENED.
YOU JUST HAPPENED TO BE AT THE LINCOLN TUNNEL BARRIER? THAT'S A VERY SENSITIVE AREA, MR. ROTH.
YOU TRY WALKING AROUND IN THE CITY, FIND ME A PLACE THAT'S NOT "SENSITIVE."
WELL, THAT'S JUST IT, ISN'T IT? I WOULDN'T BE IN THE DMZ. I'M NOT SUPPOSED TO BE. IT'S ACTUALLY ILLEGAL, YOU KNOW, UNLESS OFFICIALLY SANCTIONED.
YOU JUST GOT LUCKY WE DIDN'T FORCIBLY REMOVE YOU. WHICH BRINGS ME TO MY NEXT QUESTION...
THIS "CAPTIVE." MR. FERGUSON.
JUST HOW CERTAIN OF THIS ARE YOU? DID YOU REALLY SEE HIM? YOU REPORTED HIM DEAD SEVERAL MONTHS AGO.
WELL, YEAH. I THOUGHT HE WAS DEAD. THEY SHOT HIM DOWN AND FIRED INTO THE COCKPIT. THEN YOU GUYS LEVELLED THE BLOCK. YOU MUST'VE THOUGHT HE WAS DEAD, TOO, RIGHT?
BUT HE'S ALIVE. I HEARD HIM TALK. HE SPOKE TO ME. HE WAS TIED UP, BUT HE LOOKED OKAY.
AND THEN WHAT?
THEN THEY LET ME GO. THEY TRASHED MY PHONE AND NO ONE WOULD HELP ME SO I HAD TO WALK BACK.

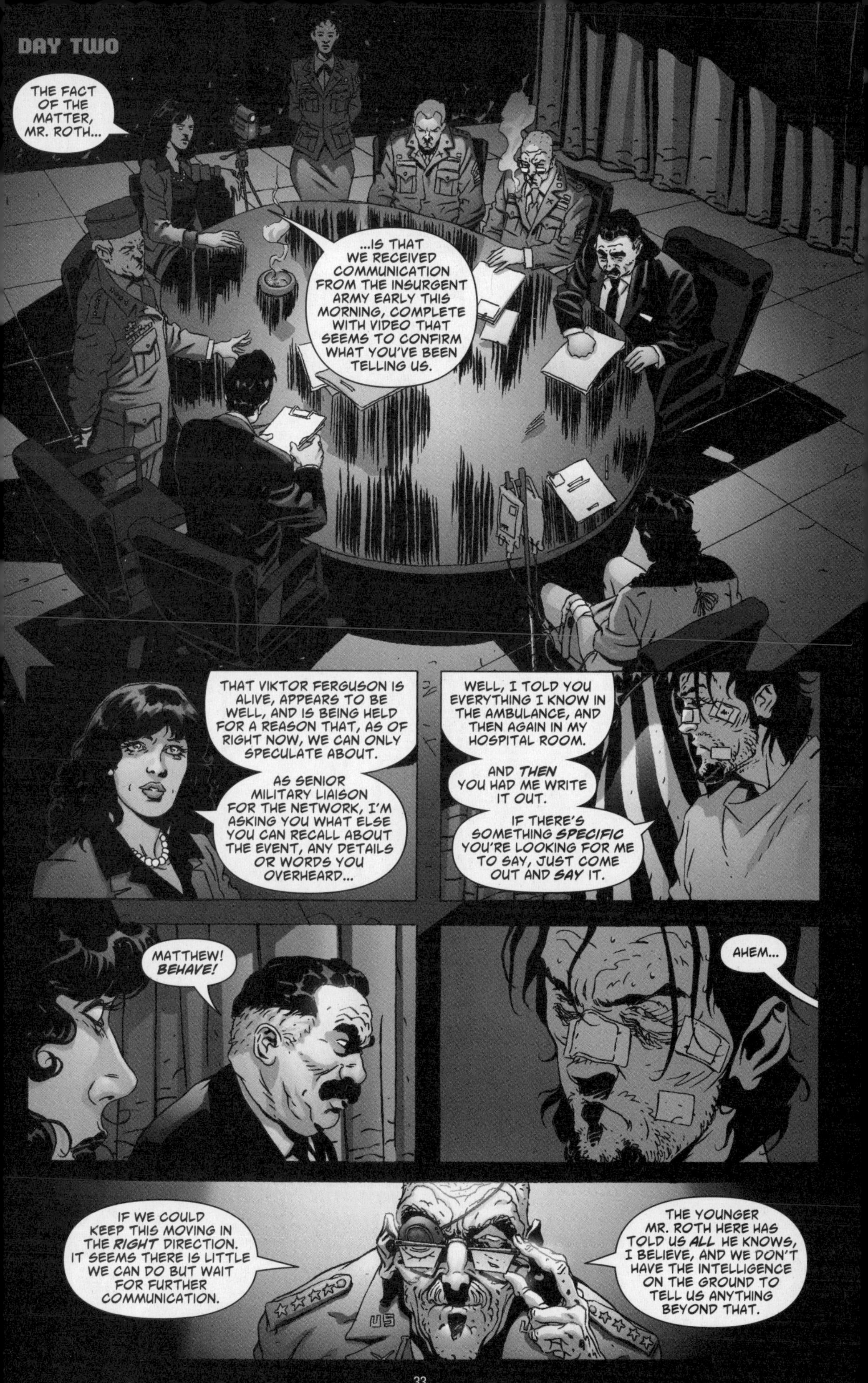
DAY TWO
THE FACT OF THE MATTER, MR. ROTH...
...IS THAT WE RECEIVED COMMUNICATION FROM THE INSURGENT ARMY EARLY THIS MORNING, COMPLETE WITH VIDEO THAT SEEMS TO CONFIRM WHAT YOU'VE BEEN TELLING US.
THAT VIKTOR FERGUSON IS ALIVE, APPEARS TO BE WELL, AND IS BEING HELD FOR A REASON THAT, AS OF RIGHT NOW, WE CAN ONLY SPECULATE ABOUT.
AS SENIOR MILITARY LIAISON FOR THE NETWORK, I'M ASKING YOU WHAT ELSE YOU CAN RECALL ABOUT THE EVENT, ANY DETAILS OR WORDS YOU OVERHEARD...
WELL, I TOLD YOU EVERYTHING I KNOW IN THE AMBULANCE, AND THEN AGAIN IN MY HOSPITAL ROOM.
AND *THEN* YOU HAD ME WRITE IT OUT.
IF THERE'S SOMETHING *SPECIFIC* YOU'RE LOOKING FOR ME TO SAY, JUST COME OUT AND *SAY* IT.
MATTHEW! *BEHAVE!*
AHEM...
THE YOUNGER MR. ROTH HERE HAS TOLD US *ALL* HE KNOWS, I BELIEVE, AND WE DON'T HAVE THE INTELLIGENCE ON THE GROUND TO TELL US ANYTHING BEYOND THAT.
IF WE COULD KEEP THIS MOVING IN THE *RIGHT* DIRECTION. IT SEEMS THERE IS LITTLE WE CAN DO BUT WAIT FOR FURTHER COMMUNICATION.

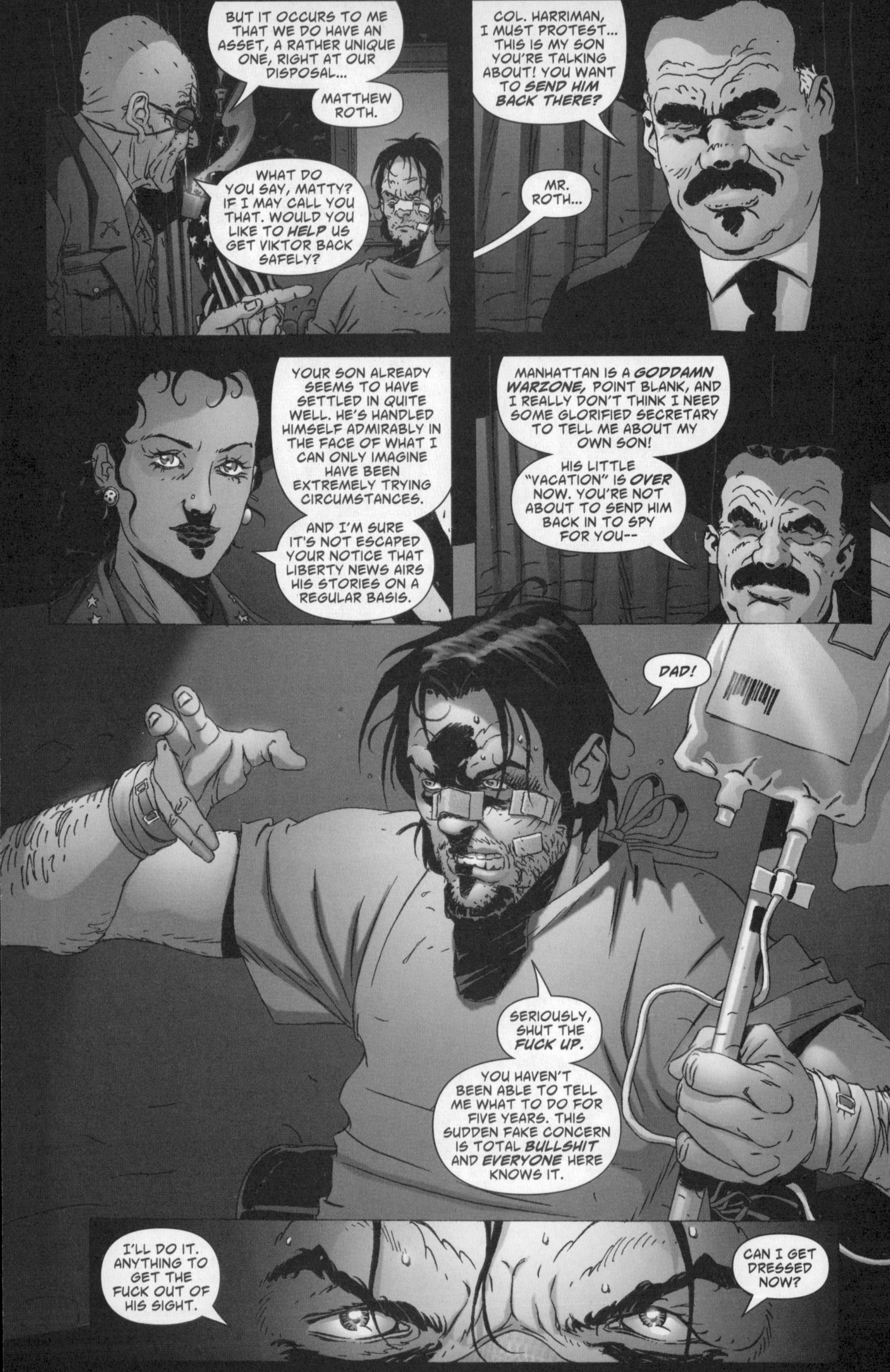
BUT IT OCCURS TO ME THAT WE DO HAVE AN ASSET, A RATHER UNIQUE ONE, RIGHT AT OUR DISPOSAL...
MATTHEW ROTH.
WHAT DO YOU SAY, MATTY? IF I MAY CALL YOU THAT. WOULD YOU LIKE TO HELP US GET VIKTOR BACK SAFELY?
COL. HARRIMAN, I MUST PROTEST... THIS IS MY SON YOU'RE TALKING ABOUT! YOU WANT TO SEND HIM BACK THERE?
MR. ROTH...
YOUR SON ALREADY SEEMS TO HAVE SETTLED IN QUITE WELL. HE'S HANDLED HIMSELF ADMIRABLY IN THE FACE OF WHAT I CAN ONLY IMAGINE HAVE BEEN EXTREMELY TRYING CIRCUMSTANCES.
AND I'M SURE IT'S NOT ESCAPED YOUR NOTICE THAT LIBERTY NEWS AIRS HIS STORIES ON A REGULAR BASIS.
MANHATTAN IS A GODDAMN WARZONE, POINT BLANK, AND I REALLY DON'T THINK I NEED SOME GLORIFIED SECRETARY TO TELL ME ABOUT MY OWN SON!
HIS LITTLE "VACATION" IS OVER NOW. YOU'RE NOT ABOUT TO SEND HIM BACK IN TO SPY FOR YOU--
DAD!
SERIOUSLY, SHUT THE FUCK UP.
YOU HAVEN'T BEEN ABLE TO TELL ME WHAT TO DO FOR FIVE YEARS. THIS SUDDEN FAKE CONCERN IS TOTAL BULLSHIT AND EVERYONE HERE KNOWS IT.
I'LL DO IT. ANYTHING TO GET THE FUCK OUT OF HIS SIGHT.
CAN I GET DRESSED NOW?

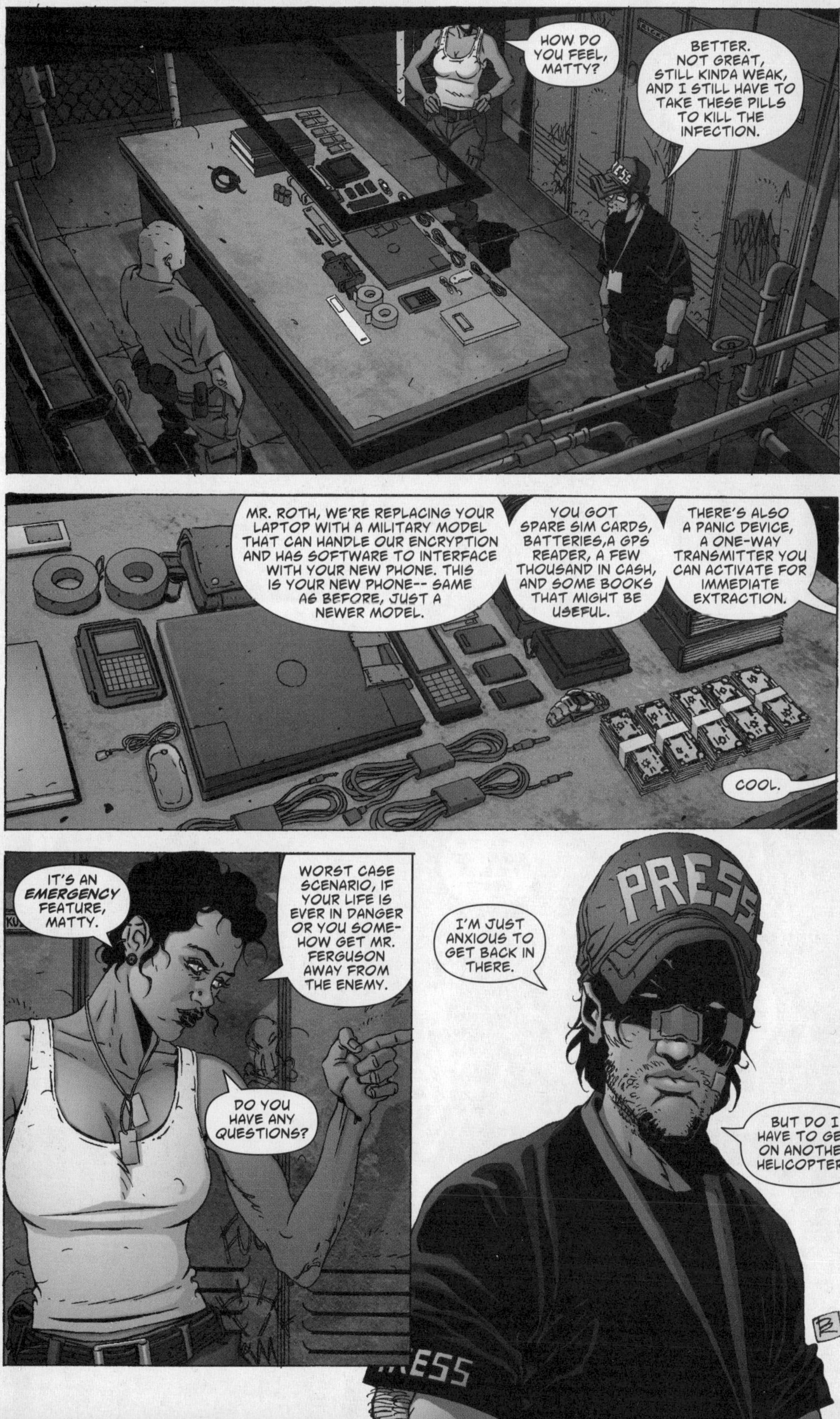
HOW DO YOU FEEL, MATTY?
BETTER. NOT GREAT, STILL KINDA WEAK, AND I STILL HAVE TO TAKE THESE PILLS TO KILL THE INFECTION.
MR. ROTH, WE'RE REPLACING YOUR LAPTOP WITH A MILITARY MODEL THAT CAN HANDLE OUR ENCRYPTION AND HAS SOFTWARE TO INTERFACE WITH YOUR NEW PHONE. THIS IS YOUR NEW PHONE-- SAME AS BEFORE, JUST A NEWER MODEL.
YOU GOT SPARE SIM CARDS, BATTERIES,A GPS READER, A FEW THOUSAND IN CASH, AND SOME BOOKS THAT MIGHT BE USEFUL.
THERE'S ALSO A PANIC DEVICE, A ONE-WAY TRANSMITTER YOU CAN ACTIVATE FOR IMMEDIATE EXTRACTION.
COOL.
IT'S AN *EMERGENCY* FEATURE, MATTY.
WORST CASE SCENARIO, IF YOUR LIFE IS EVER IN DANGER OR YOU SOME-HOW GET MR. FERGUSON AWAY FROM THE ENEMY.
DO YOU HAVE ANY QUESTIONS?
I'M JUST ANXIOUS TO GET BACK IN THERE.
BUT DO I HAVE TO GET ON ANOTHER HELICOPTER?

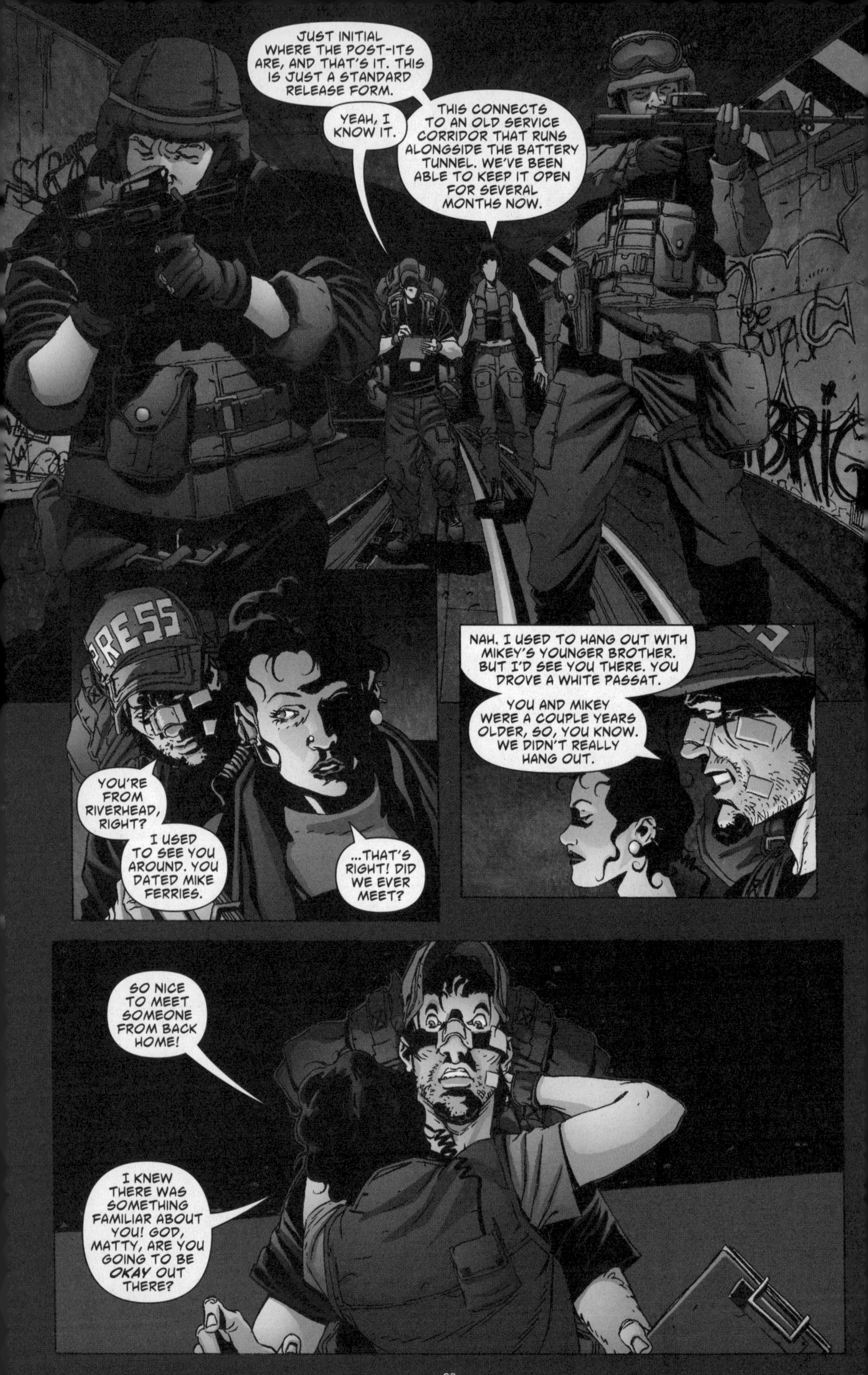
JUST INITIAL WHERE THE POST-ITS ARE, AND THAT'S IT. THIS IS JUST A STANDARD RELEASE FORM.
YEAH, I KNOW IT.
THIS CONNECTS TO AN OLD SERVICE CORRIDOR THAT RUNS ALONGSIDE THE BATTERY TUNNEL. WE'VE BEEN ABLE TO KEEP IT OPEN FOR SEVERAL MONTHS NOW.
PRESS
YOU'RE FROM RIVERHEAD, RIGHT?
I USED TO SEE YOU AROUND. YOU DATED MIKE FERRIES.
...THAT'S RIGHT! DID WE EVER MEET?
NAH. I USED TO HANG OUT WITH MIKEY'S YOUNGER BROTHER. BUT I'D SEE YOU THERE. YOU DROVE A WHITE PASSAT.
YOU AND MIKEY WERE A COUPLE YEARS OLDER, SO, YOU KNOW. WE DIDN'T REALLY HANG OUT.
SO NICE TO MEET SOMEONE FROM BACK HOME!
I KNEW THERE WAS SOMETHING FAMILIAR ABOUT YOU! GOD, MATTY, ARE YOU GOING TO BE *OKAY* OUT THERE?

YEAH, IT'LL BE OK. I KNOW MY WAY AROUND. IT'S NOT AS BAD AS THEY SAY--

PEOPLE TALK ABOUT YOU ALL THE TIME. YOUR STORIES ARE ALL OVER THE NEWS... YOU'RE A REAL *CELEBRITY.*

HEY, GIVE ME YOUR PHONE.

I'M GIVING YOU MY CELL NUMBER... JUST IN CASE YOU NEED SOME INFORMATION, OR NEED TO *TALK.*

YOU KNOW... IF YOU DON'T WANNA GO THROUGH THE NETWORK.

THAT'S COOL.

SO WHATEVER HAPPENED TO MIKE FERRIES?

HE WAS *KILLED.* THE JERSEY CITY OFFENSIVE, LAST YEAR.

...OH.

GET VIKTOR FERGUSON BACK, OKAY, MATTY?

AND DON'T *YOU* DIE, EITHER. I COULDN'T BEAR IT. HARDLY ANY-ONE'S LEFT FROM BACK HOME.

INSTRUCTIONS WILL COME AT NINETEEN-HUNDRED HOURS, TONIGHT. MAKE SURE YOUR PHONE'S ON.

SERGEANT, SEE THAT HE MAKES IT SAFELY ACROSS.

YES, MA'AM.

I Feel AS the SUN it fades to Gr

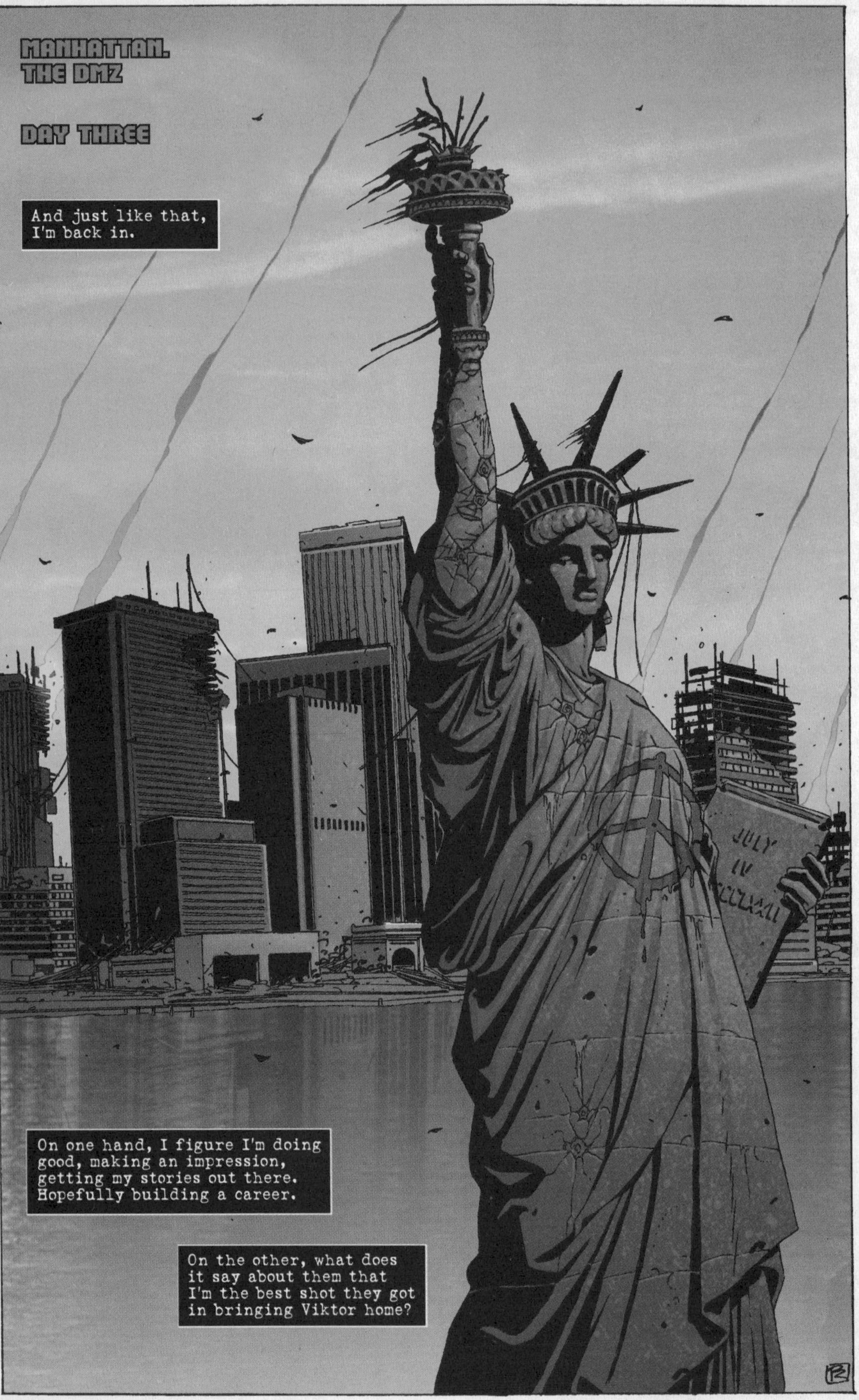
MANHATTAN.
THE DMZ
DAY THREE
And just like that, I'm back in.
On one hand, I figure I'm doing good, making an impression, getting my stories out there. Hopefully building a career.
On the other, what does it say about them that I'm the best shot they got in bringing Viktor home?
JULY IV MDCCLXXVI

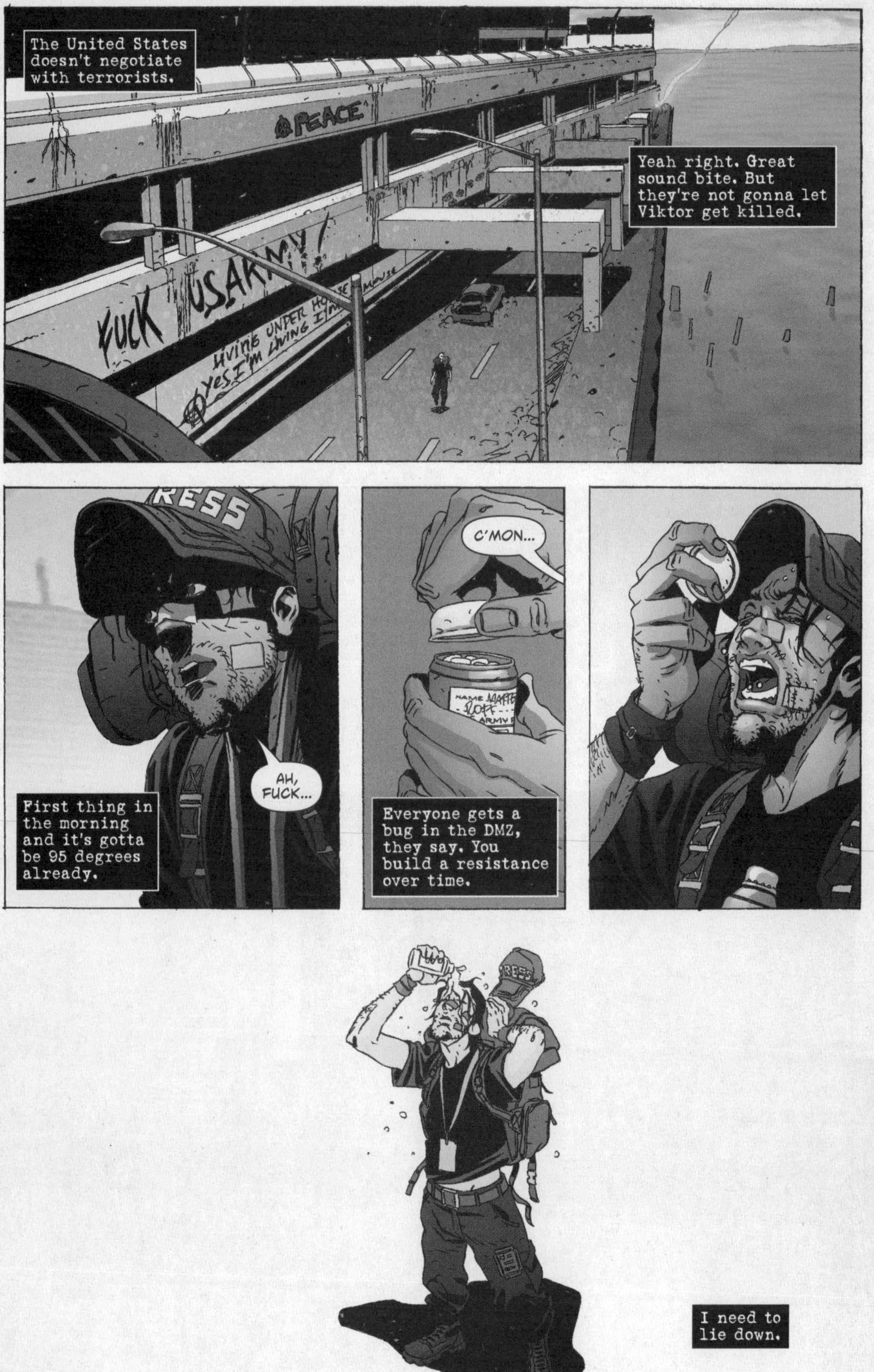
The United States doesn't negotiate with terrorists.
PEACE
Yeah right. Great sound bite. But they're not gonna let Viktor get killed.
AH, FUCK...
First thing in the morning and it's gotta be 95 degrees already.
C'MON...
Everyone gets a bug in the DMZ, they say. You build a resistance over time.
I need to lie down.

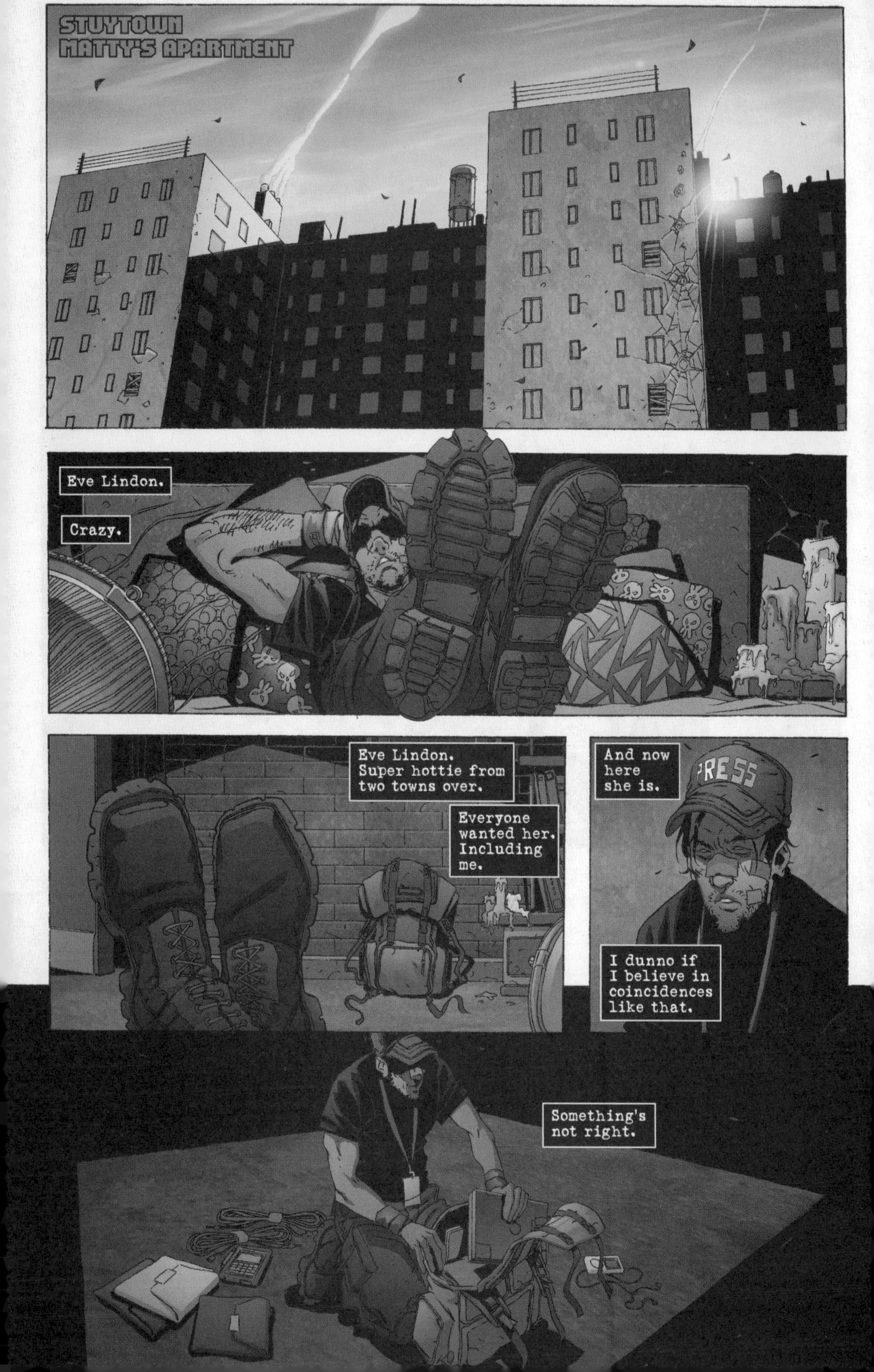
STUYTOWN
MATTY'S APARTMENT
Eve Lindon.
Crazy.
Eve Lindon. Super hottie from two towns over.
Everyone wanted her. Including me.
And now here she is.
PRESS
I dunno if I believe in coincidences like that.
Something's not right.

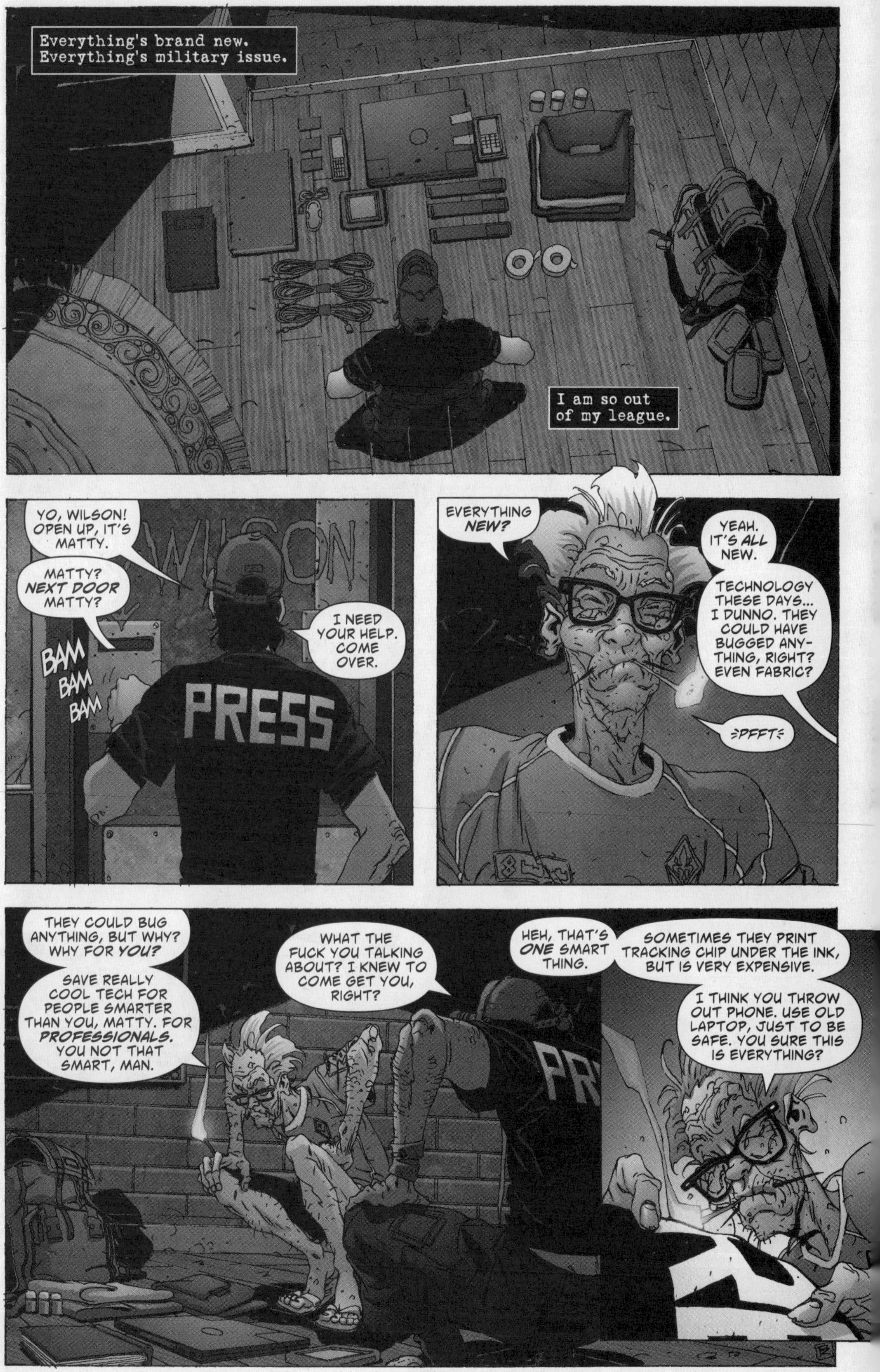
Everything's brand new. Everything's military issue.
I am so out of my league.
YO, WILSON! OPEN UP, IT'S MATTY.
MATTY? NEXT DOOR MATTY?
BAM BAM BAM
I NEED YOUR HELP. COME OVER.
WILSON
PRESS
EVERYTHING NEW?
YEAH. IT'S ALL NEW.
TECHNOLOGY THESE DAYS... I DUNNO. THEY COULD HAVE BUGGED ANYTHING, RIGHT? EVEN FABRIC?
PFFT
THEY COULD BUG ANYTHING, BUT WHY? WHY FOR YOU?
SAVE REALLY COOL TECH FOR PEOPLE SMARTER THAN YOU, MATTY. FOR PROFESSIONALS. YOU NOT THAT SMART, MAN.
WHAT THE FUCK YOU TALKING ABOUT? I KNEW TO COME GET YOU, RIGHT?
HEH, THAT'S ONE SMART THING.
SOMETIMES THEY PRINT TRACKING CHIP UNDER THE INK, BUT IS VERY EXPENSIVE.
I THINK YOU THROW OUT PHONE. USE OLD LAPTOP, JUST TO BE SAFE. YOU SURE THIS IS EVERYTHING?

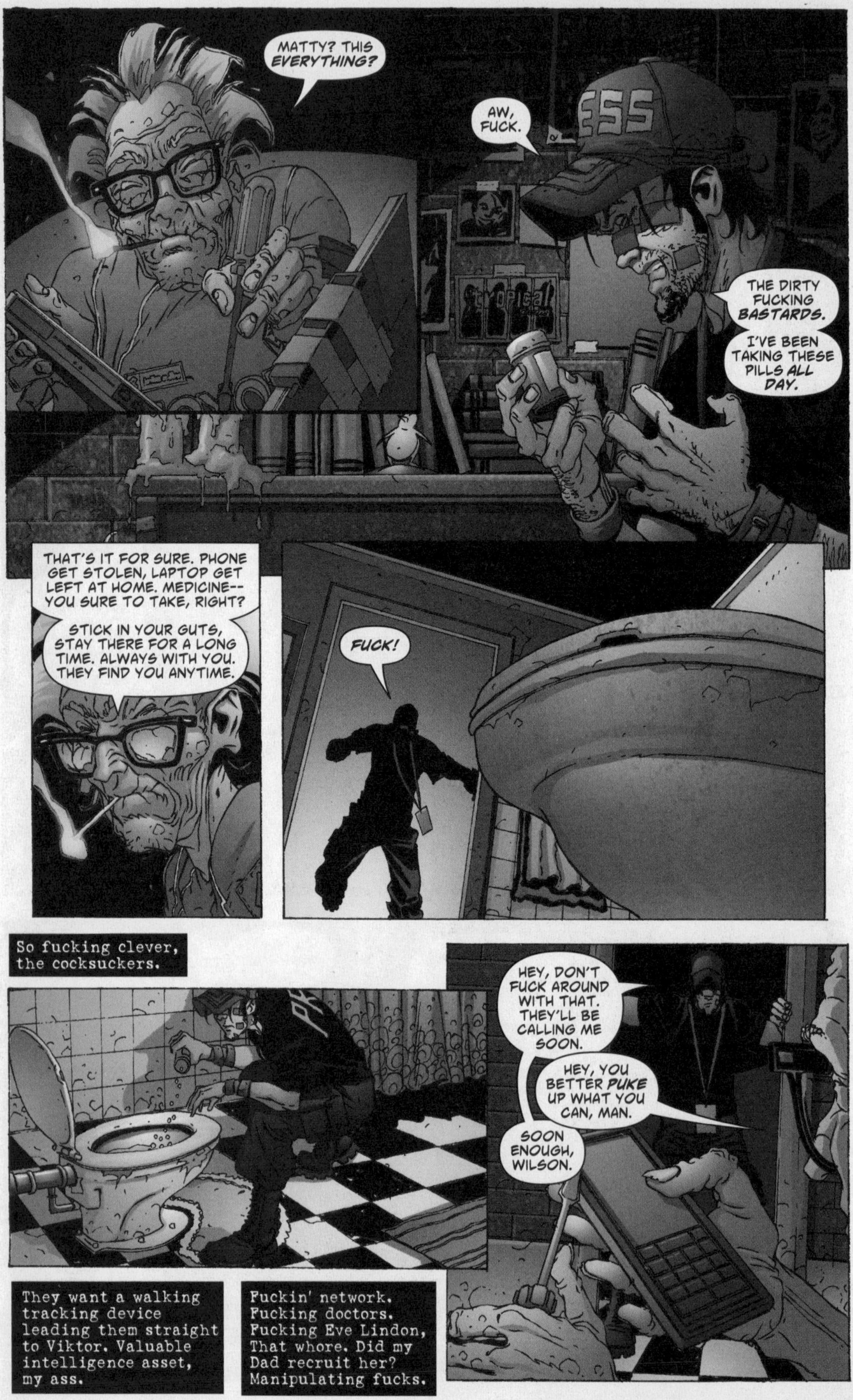
MATTY? THIS EVERYTHING?
AW, FUCK.
THE DIRTY FUCKING BASTARDS.
I'VE BEEN TAKING THESE PILLS ALL DAY.
THAT'S IT FOR SURE. PHONE GET STOLEN, LAPTOP GET LEFT AT HOME. MEDICINE--YOU SURE TO TAKE, RIGHT?
STICK IN YOUR GUTS, STAY THERE FOR A LONG TIME. ALWAYS WITH YOU. THEY FIND YOU ANYTIME.
FUCK!
So fucking clever, the cocksuckers.
HEY, DON'T FUCK AROUND WITH THAT. THEY'LL BE CALLING ME SOON.
HEY, YOU BETTER PUKE UP WHAT YOU CAN, MAN.
SOON ENOUGH, WILSON.
They want a walking tracking device leading them straight to Viktor. Valuable intelligence asset, my ass.
Fuckin' network. Fucking doctors. Fucking Eve Lindon, That whore. Did my Dad recruit her? Manipulating fucks.

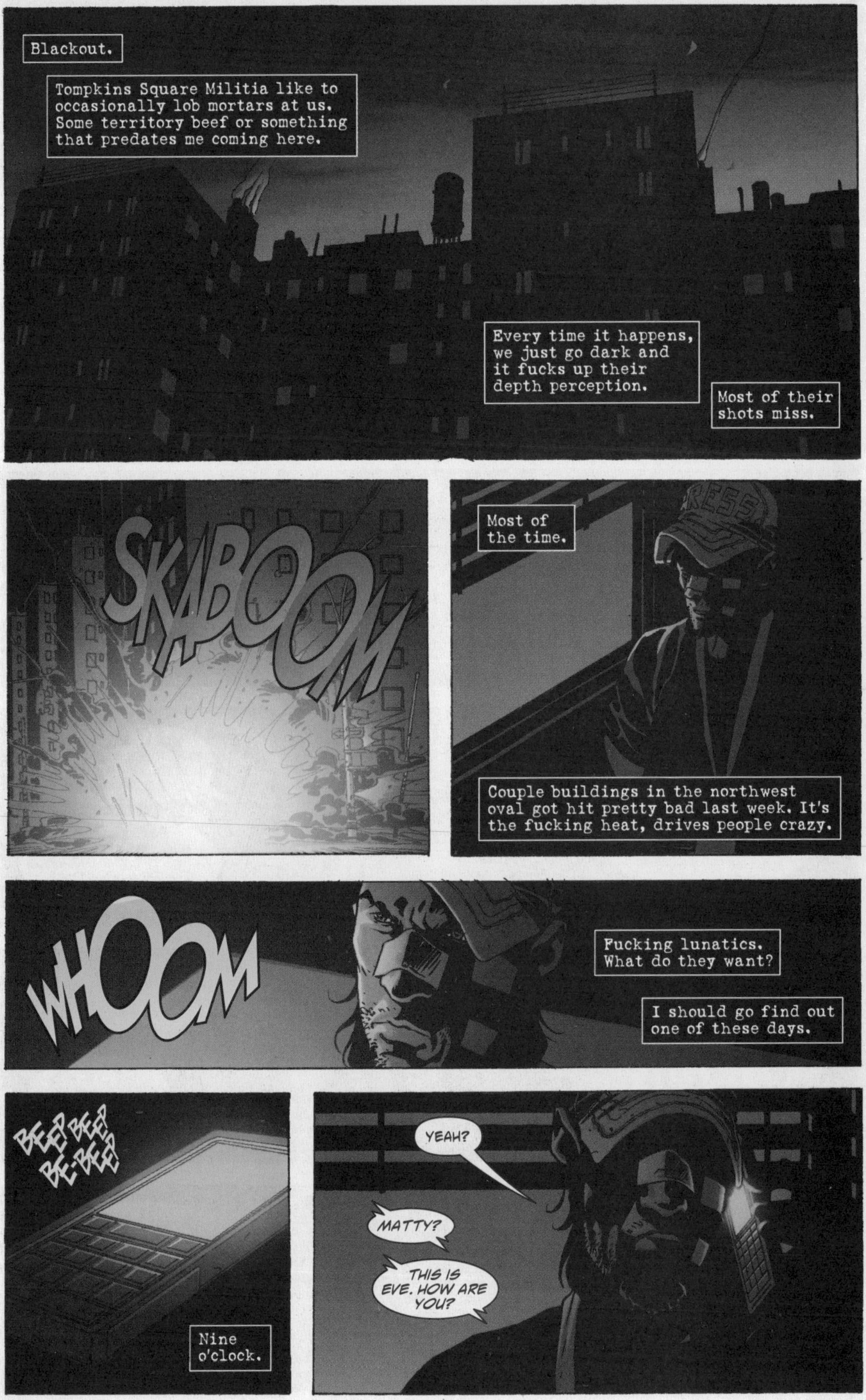

Blackout.
Tompkins Square Militia like to occasionally lob mortars at us. Some territory beef or something that predates me coming here.
Every time it happens, we just go dark and it fucks up their depth perception.
Most of their shots miss.
SKABOOM
Most of the time.
Couple buildings in the northwest oval got hit pretty bad last week. It's the fucking heat, drives people crazy.
WHOOM
Fucking lunatics. What do they want?
I should go find out one of these days.
BEEP BEEP BE-BEEP
Nine o'clock.
YEAH?
MATTY?
THIS IS EVE. HOW ARE YOU?

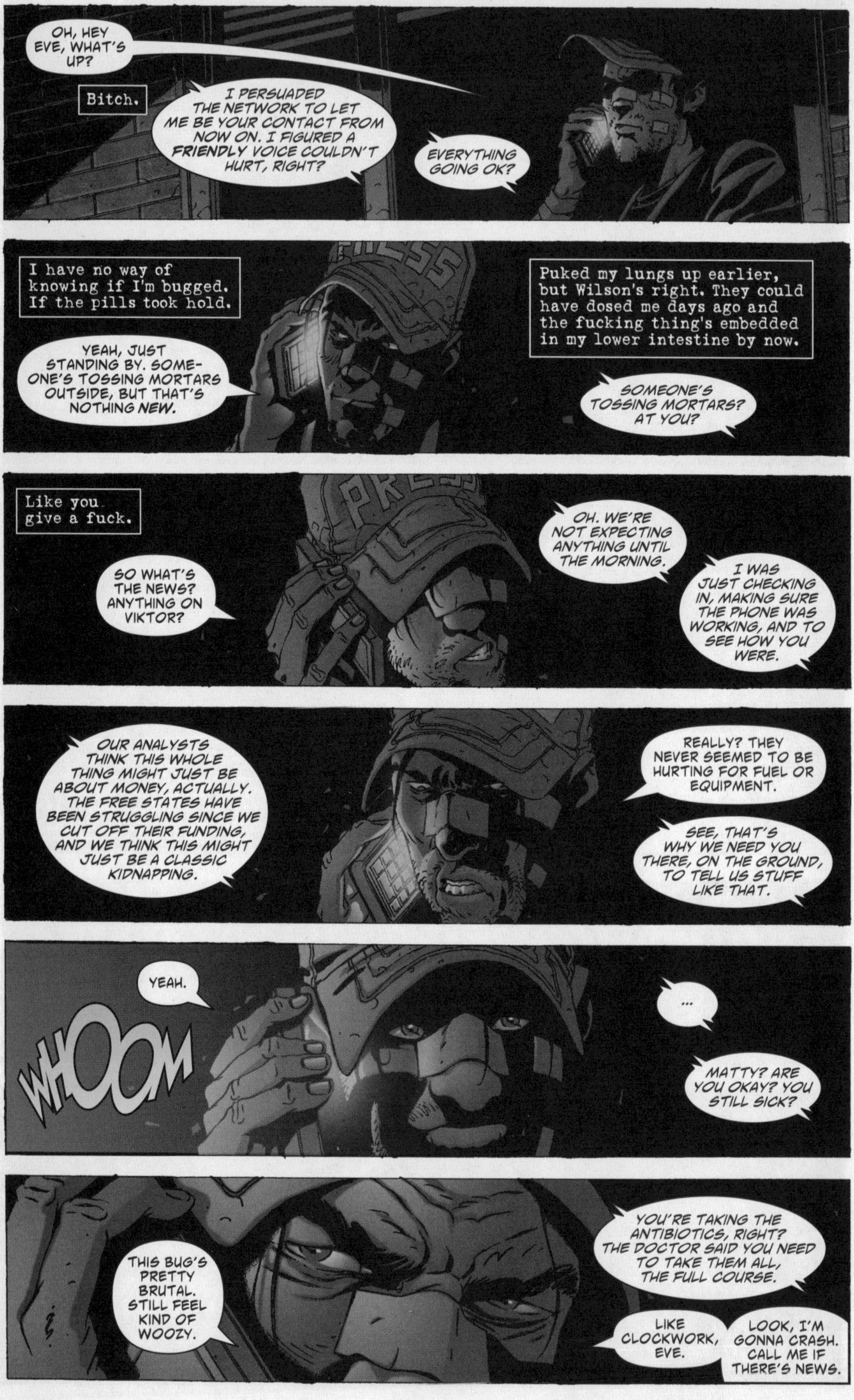
OH, HEY EVE, WHAT'S UP?
Bitch.
I PERSUADED THE NETWORK TO LET ME BE YOUR CONTACT FROM NOW ON. I FIGURED A FRIENDLY VOICE COULDN'T HURT, RIGHT?
EVERYTHING GOING OK?
I have no way of knowing if I'm bugged. If the pills took hold.
Puked my lungs up earlier, but Wilson's right. They could have dosed me days ago and the fucking thing's embedded in my lower intestine by now.
YEAH, JUST STANDING BY. SOMEONE'S TOSSING MORTARS OUTSIDE, BUT THAT'S NOTHING NEW.
SOMEONE'S TOSSING MORTARS? AT YOU?
Like you give a fuck.
SO WHAT'S THE NEWS? ANYTHING ON VIKTOR?
OH. WE'RE NOT EXPECTING ANYTHING UNTIL THE MORNING.
I WAS JUST CHECKING IN, MAKING SURE THE PHONE WAS WORKING, AND TO SEE HOW YOU WERE.
OUR ANALYSTS THINK THIS WHOLE THING MIGHT JUST BE ABOUT MONEY, ACTUALLY. THE FREE STATES HAVE BEEN STRUGGLING SINCE WE CUT OFF THEIR FUNDING, AND WE THINK THIS MIGHT JUST BE A CLASSIC KIDNAPPING.
REALLY? THEY NEVER SEEMED TO BE HURTING FOR FUEL OR EQUIPMENT.
SEE, THAT'S WHY WE NEED YOU THERE, ON THE GROUND, TO TELL US STUFF LIKE THAT.
YEAH.
WHOOM
...
MATTY? ARE YOU OKAY? YOU STILL SICK?
THIS BUG'S PRETTY BRUTAL. STILL FEEL KIND OF WOOZY.
YOU'RE TAKING THE ANTIBIOTICS, RIGHT? THE DOCTOR SAID YOU NEED TO TAKE THEM ALL, THE FULL COURSE.
LIKE CLOCKWORK, EVE.
LOOK, I'M GONNA CRASH. CALL ME IF THERE'S NEWS.

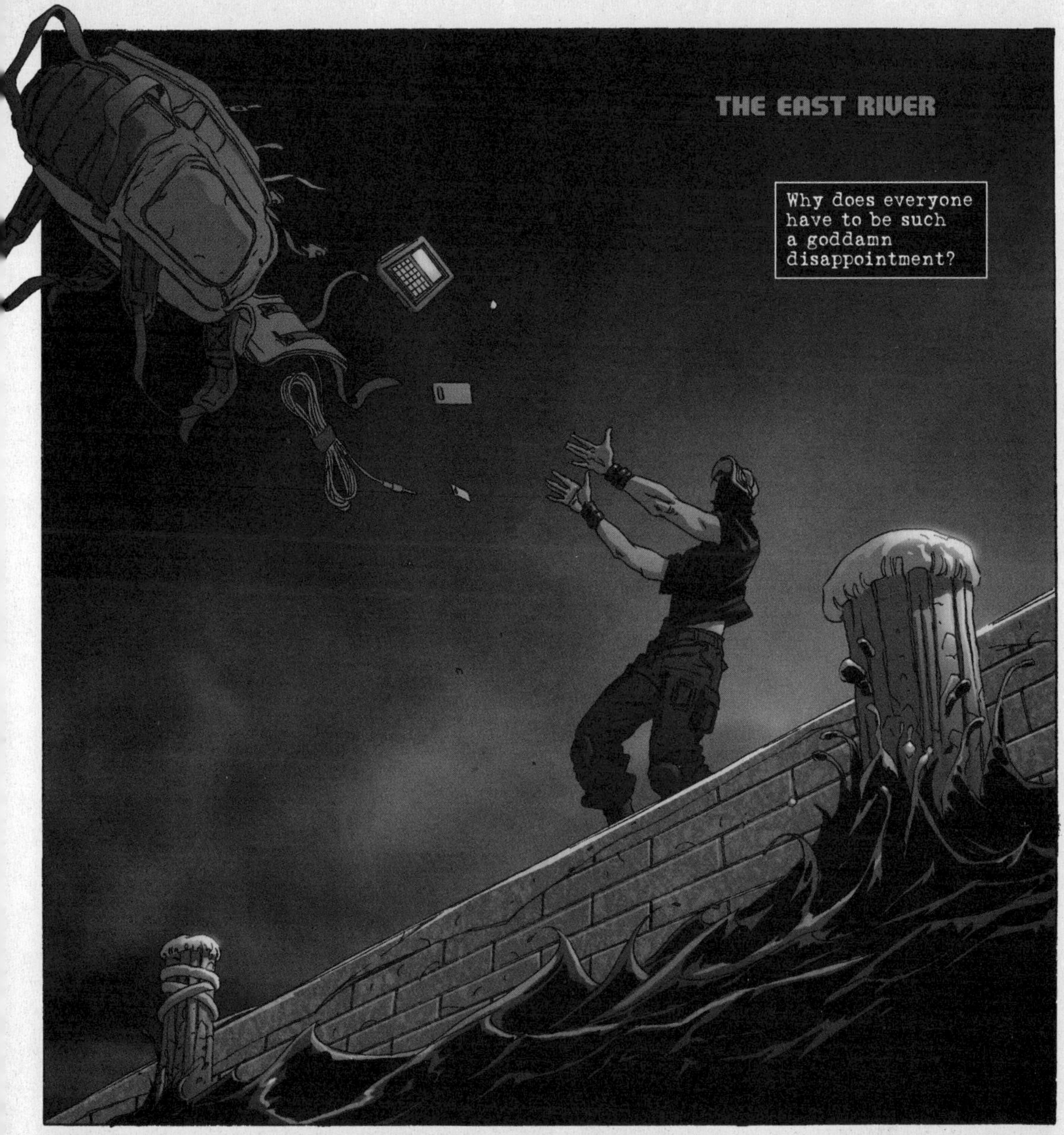
THE EAST RIVER
Why does everyone have to be such a goddamn disappointment?

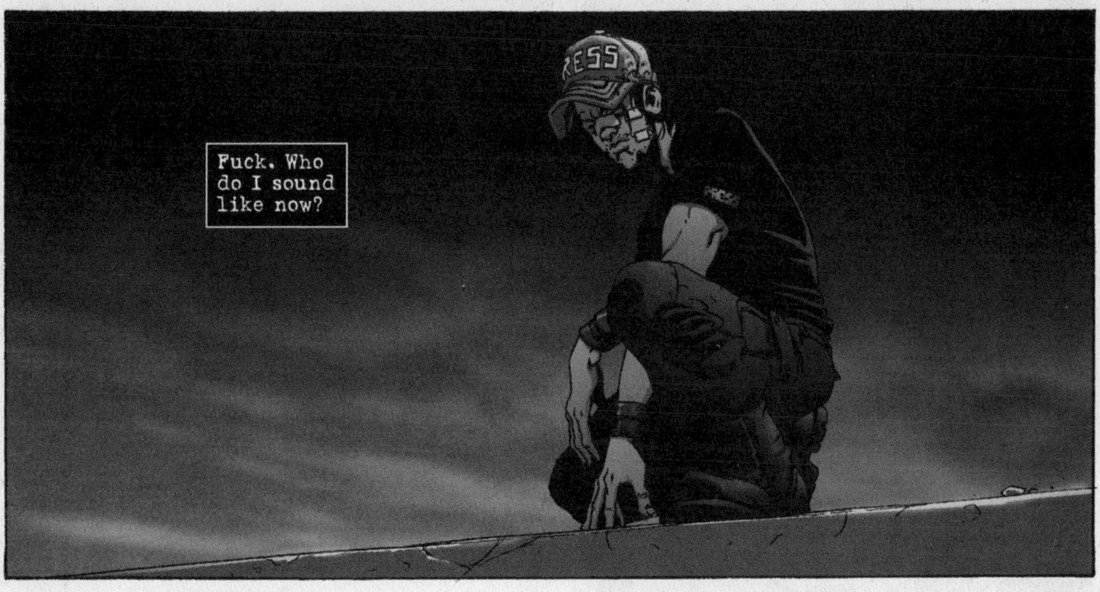
Fuck. Who do I sound like now?
PRESS

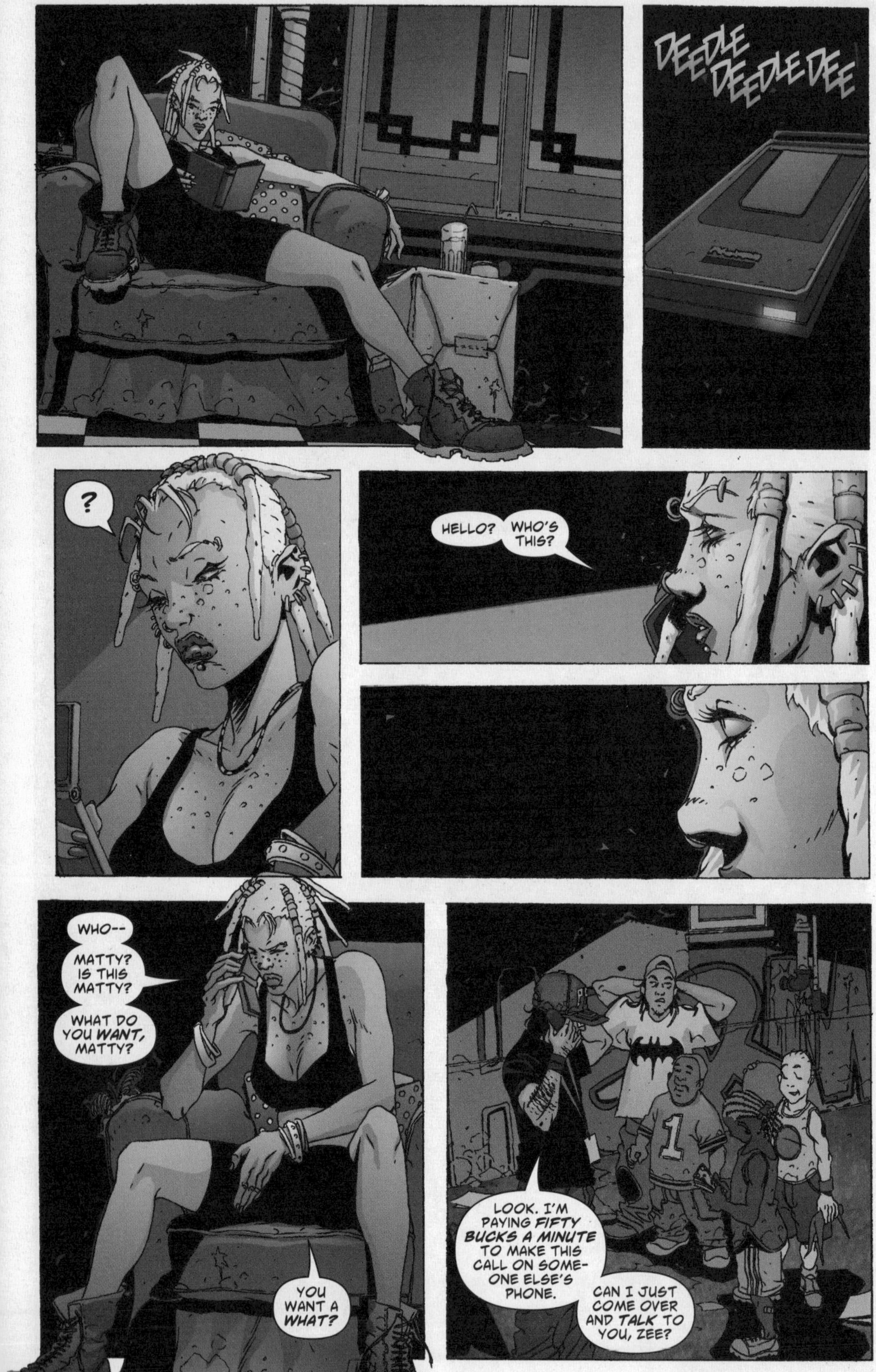
DEEDLE DEEDLE DEE
?
HELLO?
WHO'S THIS?
WHO--
MATTY? IS THIS MATTY?
WHAT DO YOU WANT, MATTY?
LOOK. I'M PAYING FIFTY BUCKS A MINUTE TO MAKE THIS CALL ON SOME-ONE ELSE'S PHONE.
CAN I JUST COME OVER AND TALK TO YOU, ZEE?
YOU WANT A WHAT?

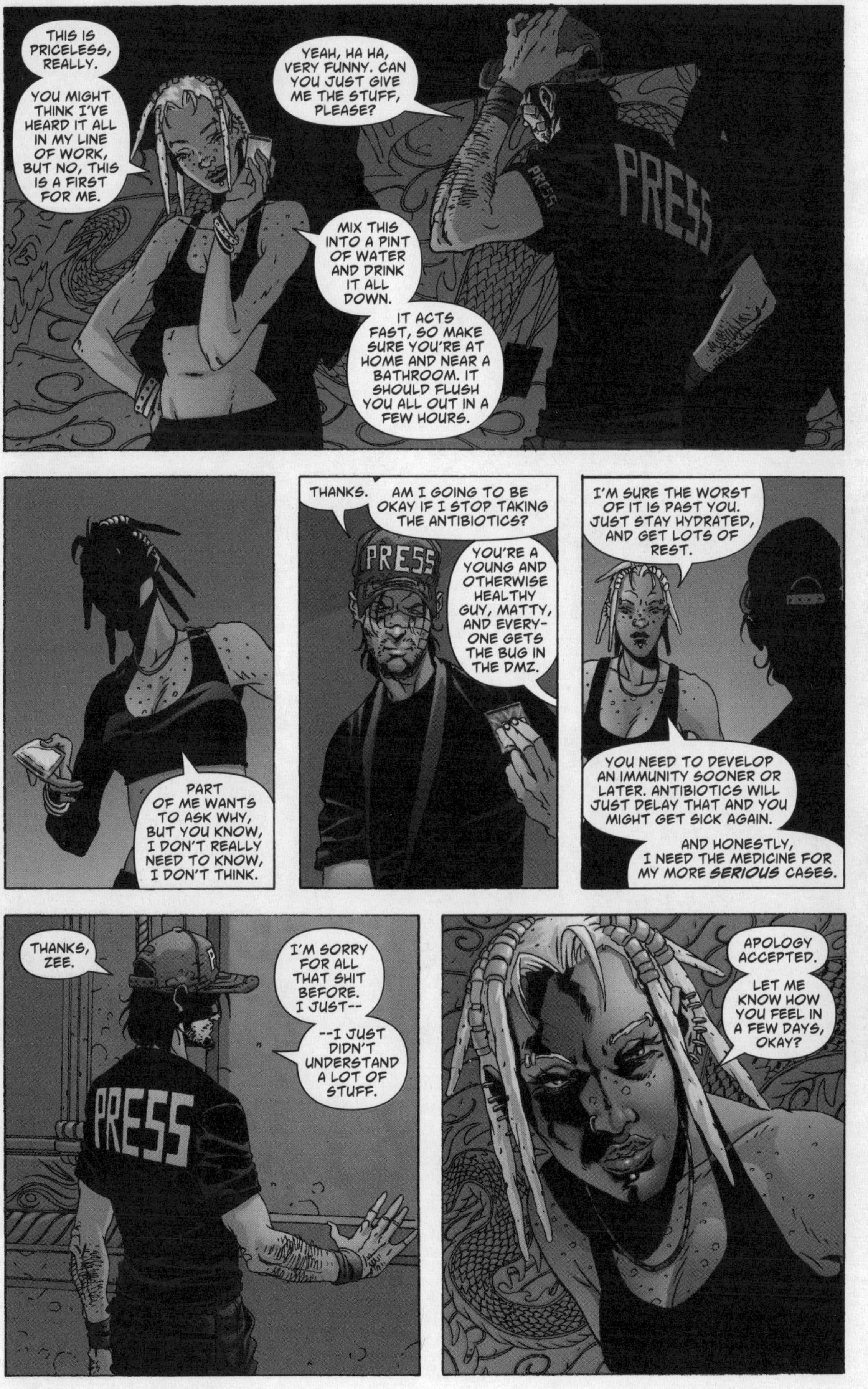

THIS IS PRICELESS, REALLY.
YOU MIGHT THINK I'VE HEARD IT ALL IN MY LINE OF WORK, BUT NO, THIS IS A FIRST FOR ME.
YEAH, HA HA, VERY FUNNY. CAN YOU JUST GIVE ME THE STUFF, PLEASE?
MIX THIS INTO A PINT OF WATER AND DRINK IT ALL DOWN.
IT ACTS FAST, SO MAKE SURE YOU'RE AT HOME AND NEAR A BATHROOM. IT SHOULD FLUSH YOU ALL OUT IN A FEW HOURS.
PRESS
PART OF ME WANTS TO ASK WHY, BUT YOU KNOW, I DON'T REALLY NEED TO KNOW, I DON'T THINK.
THANKS.
AM I GOING TO BE OKAY IF I STOP TAKING THE ANTIBIOTICS?
PRESS
YOU'RE A YOUNG AND OTHERWISE HEALTHY GUY, MATTY, AND EVERY-ONE GETS THE BUG IN THE DMZ.
I'M SURE THE WORST OF IT IS PAST YOU. JUST STAY HYDRATED, AND GET LOTS OF REST.
YOU NEED TO DEVELOP AN IMMUNITY SOONER OR LATER. ANTIBIOTICS WILL JUST DELAY THAT AND YOU MIGHT GET SICK AGAIN.
AND HONESTLY, I NEED THE MEDICINE FOR MY MORE *SERIOUS* CASES.
THANKS, ZEE.
I'M SORRY FOR ALL THAT SHIT BEFORE. I JUST--
--I JUST DIDN'T UNDERSTAND A LOT OF STUFF.
PRESS
APOLOGY ACCEPTED.
LET ME KNOW HOW YOU FEEL IN A FEW DAYS, OKAY?

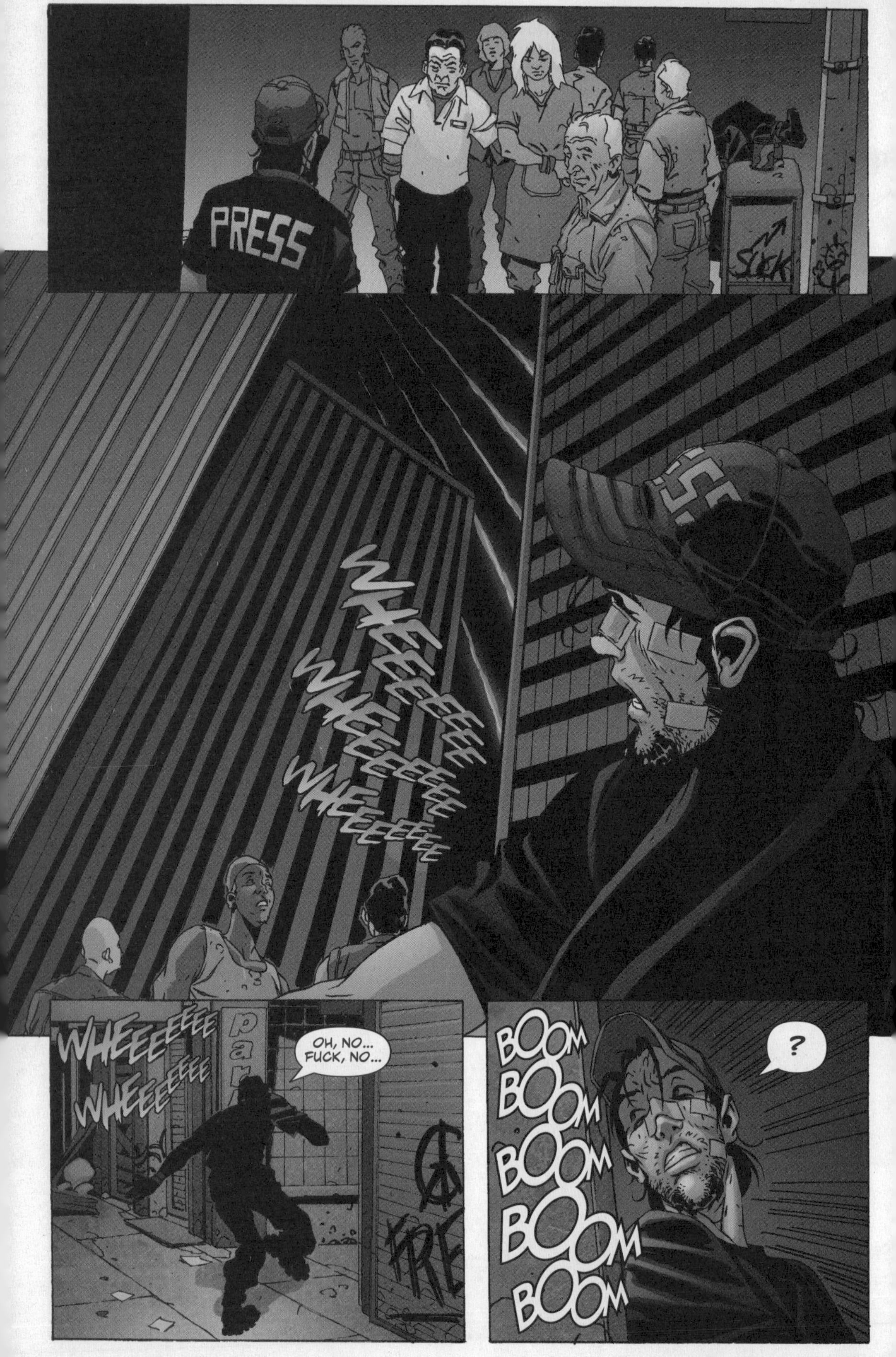
PRESS
WHEEEEEEEE
WHEEEEEEEE
WHEEEEEEEE
WHEEEEEEEE
WHEEEEEEEE
OH, NO... FUCK, NO...
BOOM
BOOM
BOOM
BOOM
BOOM
BOOM
?

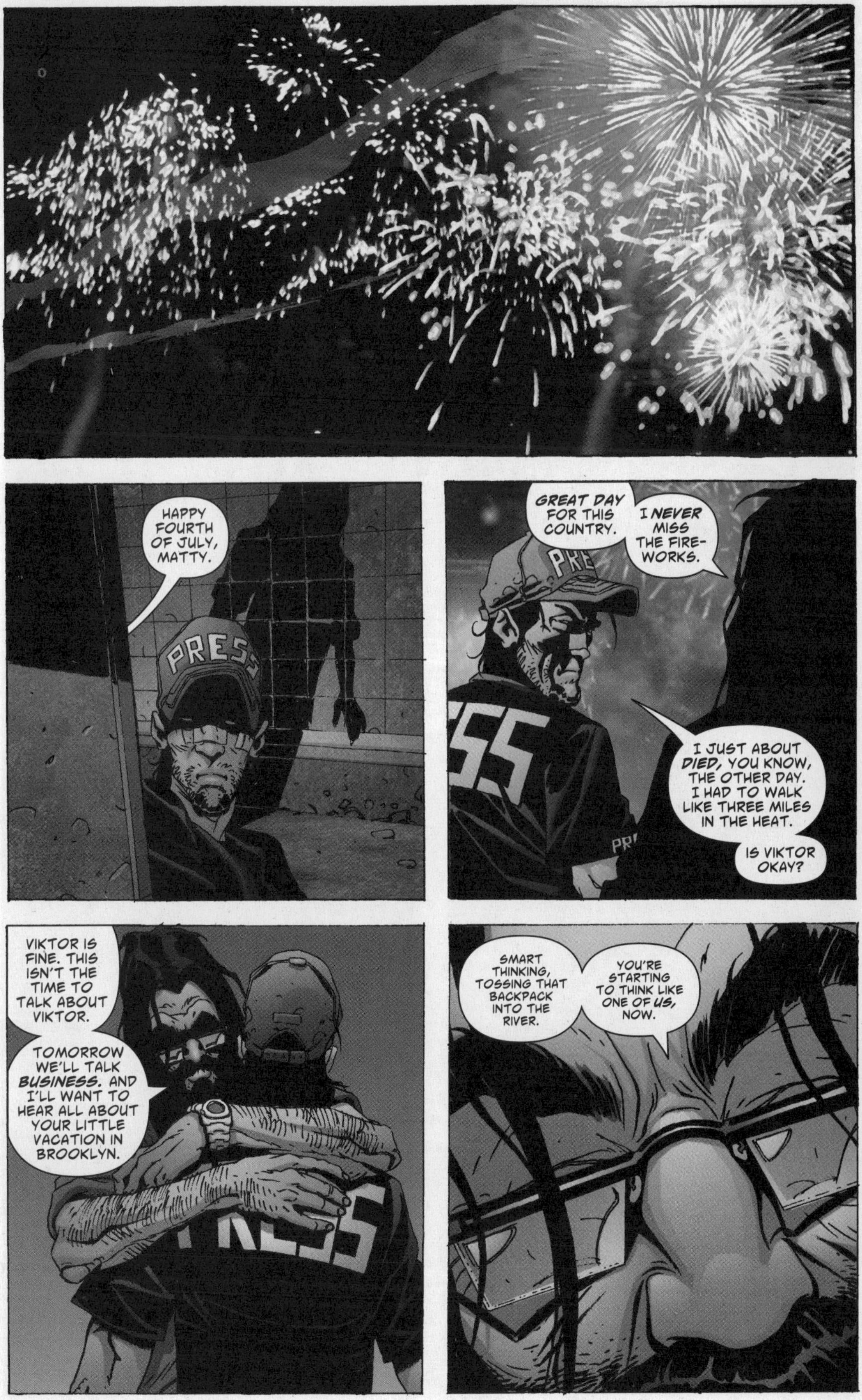
HAPPY FOURTH OF JULY, MATTY.
GREAT DAY FOR THIS COUNTRY.
I NEVER MISS THE FIRE-WORKS.
I JUST ABOUT DIED, YOU KNOW, THE OTHER DAY. I HAD TO WALK LIKE THREE MILES IN THE HEAT.
IS VIKTOR OKAY?
VIKTOR IS FINE. THIS ISN'T THE TIME TO TALK ABOUT VIKTOR.
TOMORROW WE'LL TALK BUSINESS. AND I'LL WANT TO HEAR ALL ABOUT YOUR LITTLE VACATION IN BROOKLYN.
SMART THINKING, TOSSING THAT BACKPACK INTO THE RIVER.
YOU'RE STARTING TO THINK LIKE ONE OF US, NOW.

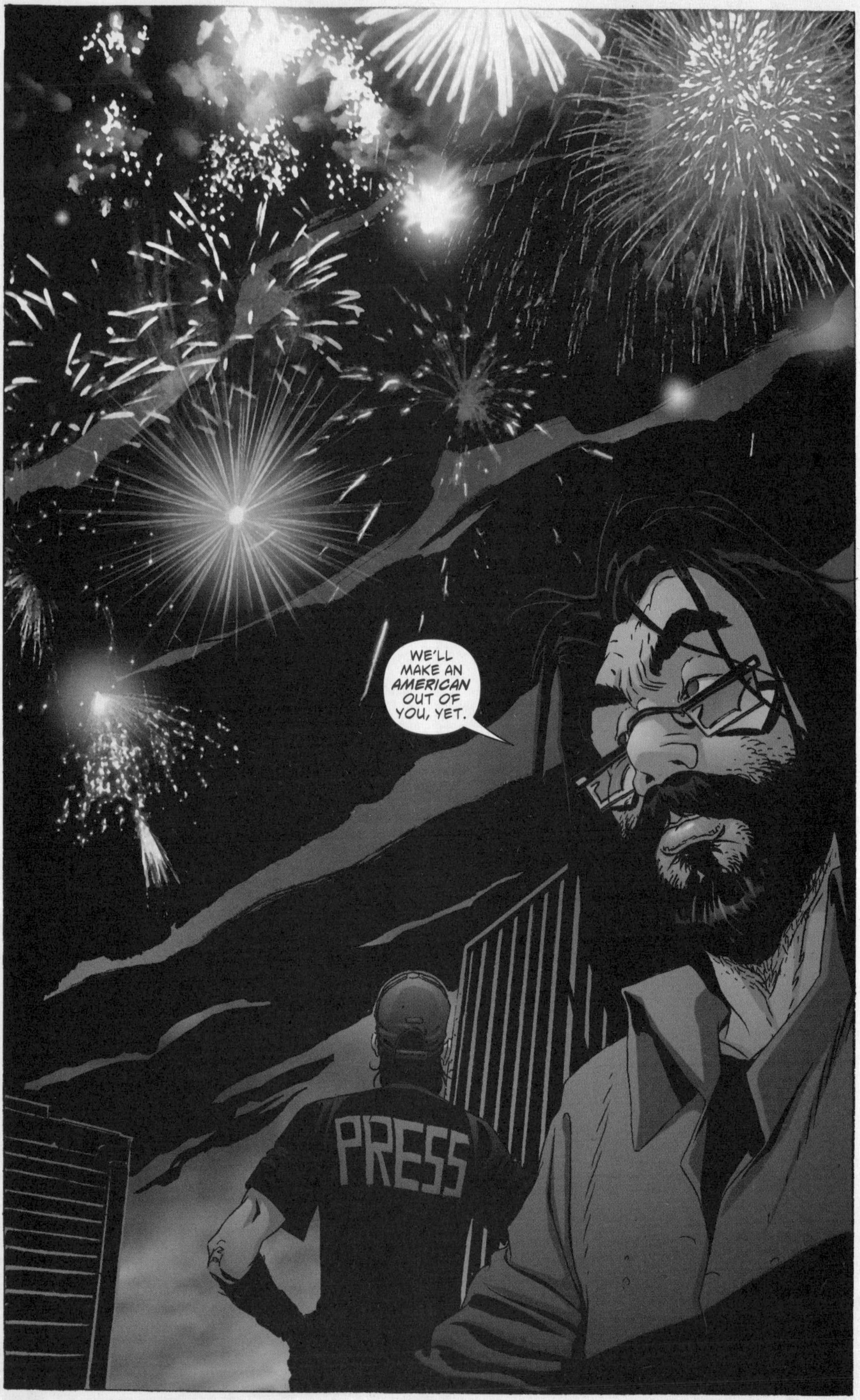
WE'LL MAKE AN *AMERICAN* OUT OF YOU, YET.
PRESS

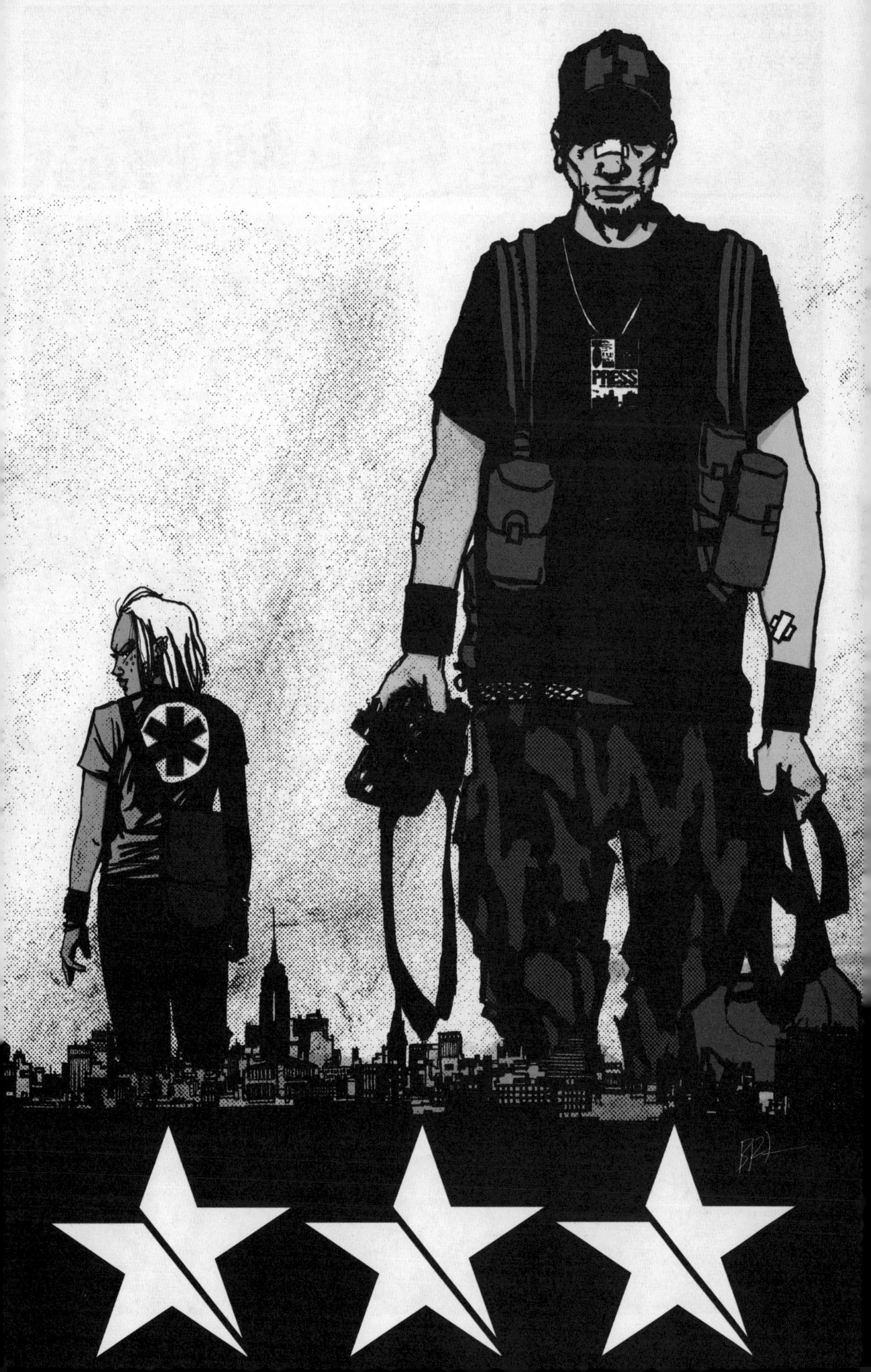
PRESS

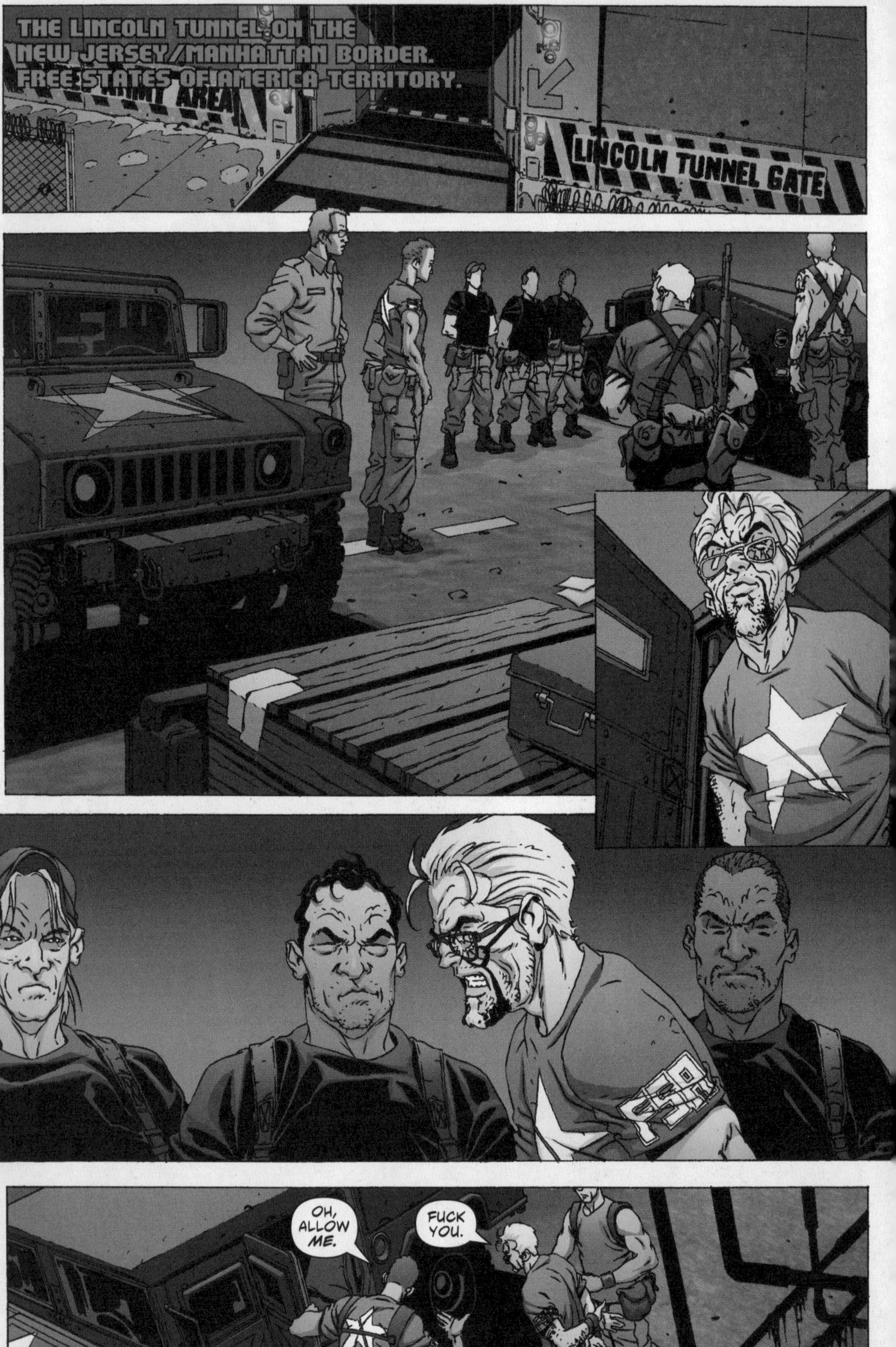
THE LINCOLN TUNNEL ON THE NEW JERSEY/MANHATTAN BORDER. FREE STATES OF AMERICA TERRITORY.
LINCOLN TUNNEL GATE
OH, ALLOW ME.
FUCK YOU.

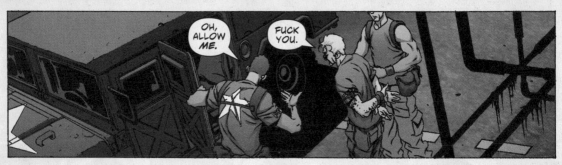

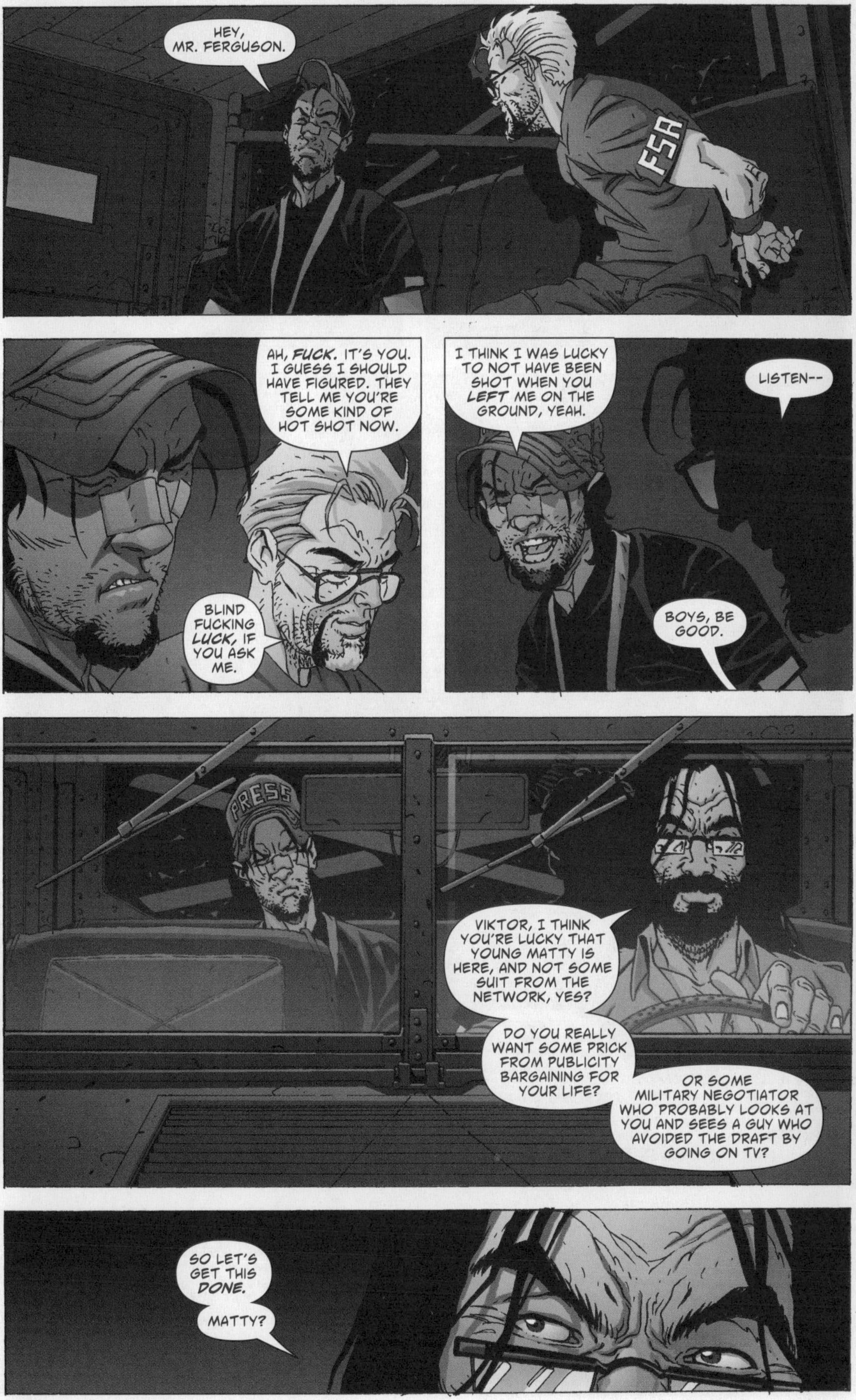
HEY, MR. FERGUSON.
AH, FUCK. IT'S YOU. I GUESS I SHOULD HAVE FIGURED. THEY TELL ME YOU'RE SOME KIND OF HOT SHOT NOW.
BLIND FUCKING LUCK, IF YOU ASK ME.
I THINK I WAS LUCKY TO NOT HAVE BEEN SHOT WHEN YOU LEFT ME ON THE GROUND, YEAH.
LISTEN--
BOYS, BE GOOD.
PRESS
VIKTOR, I THINK YOU'RE LUCKY THAT YOUNG MATTY IS HERE, AND NOT SOME SUIT FROM THE NETWORK, YES?
DO YOU REALLY WANT SOME PRICK FROM PUBLICITY BARGAINING FOR YOUR LIFE?
OR SOME MILITARY NEGOTIATOR WHO PROBABLY LOOKS AT YOU AND SEES A GUY WHO AVOIDED THE DRAFT BY GOING ON TV?
SO LET'S GET THIS DONE.
MATTY?

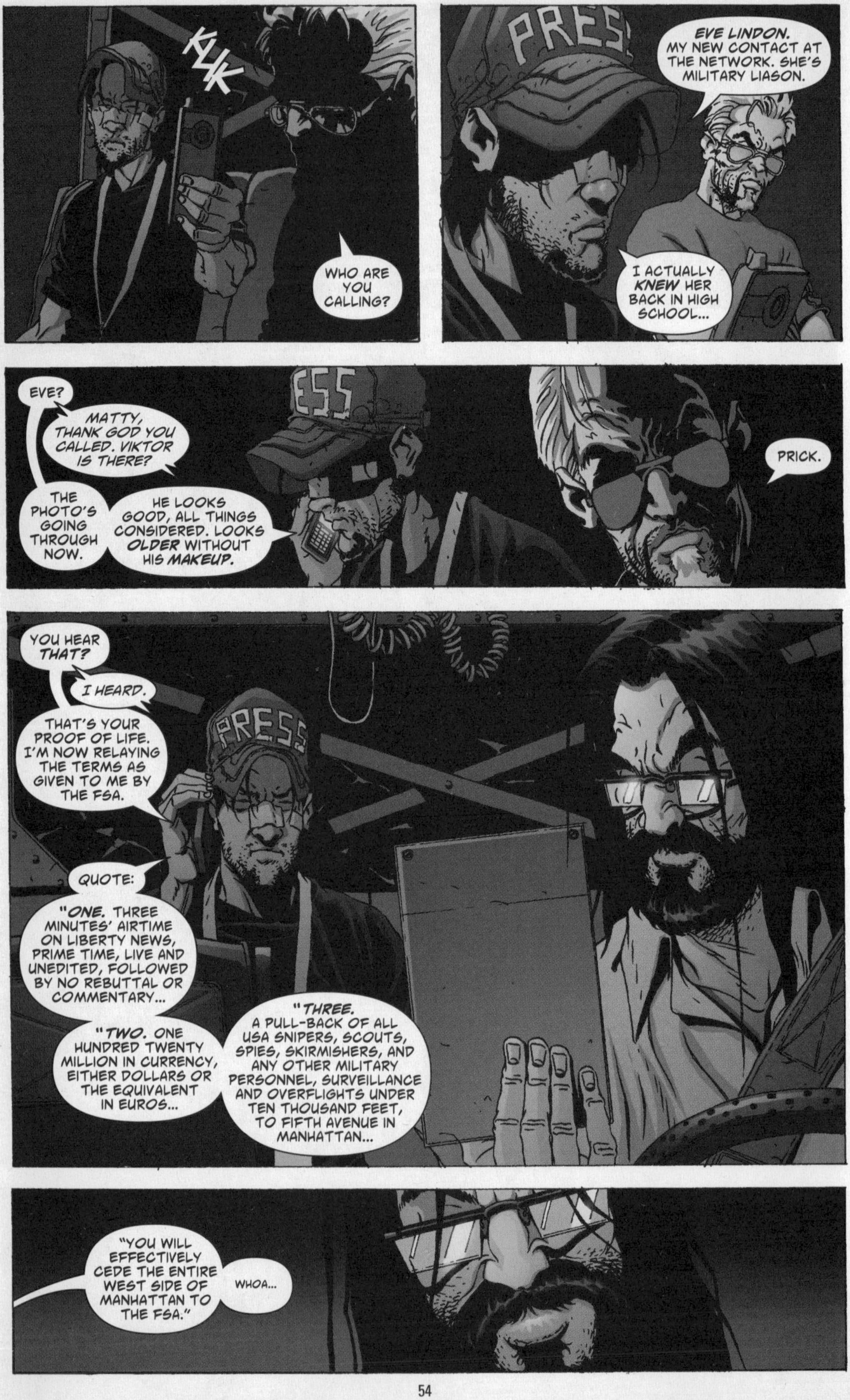
KLIK
WHO ARE YOU CALLING?
EVE LINDON. MY NEW CONTACT AT THE NETWORK. SHE'S MILITARY LIASON.
I ACTUALLY KNEW HER BACK IN HIGH SCHOOL...
EVE?
MATTY, THANK GOD YOU CALLED. VIKTOR IS THERE?
THE PHOTO'S GOING THROUGH NOW.
HE LOOKS GOOD, ALL THINGS CONSIDERED. LOOKS OLDER WITHOUT HIS MAKEUP.
PRICK.
YOU HEAR THAT?
I HEARD.
THAT'S YOUR PROOF OF LIFE. I'M NOW RELAYING THE TERMS AS GIVEN TO ME BY THE FSA.
QUOTE:
"ONE. THREE MINUTES' AIRTIME ON LIBERTY NEWS, PRIME TIME, LIVE AND UNEDITED, FOLLOWED BY NO REBUTTAL OR COMMENTARY...
"TWO. ONE HUNDRED TWENTY MILLION IN CURRENCY, EITHER DOLLARS OR THE EQUIVALENT IN EUROS...
"THREE. A PULL-BACK OF ALL USA SNIPERS, SCOUTS, SPIES, SKIRMISHERS, AND ANY OTHER MILITARY PERSONNEL, SURVEILLANCE AND OVERFLIGHTS UNDER TEN THOUSAND FEET, TO FIFTH AVENUE IN MANHATTAN...
"YOU WILL EFFECTIVELY CEDE THE ENTIRE WEST SIDE OF MANHATTAN TO THE FSA."
WHOA...

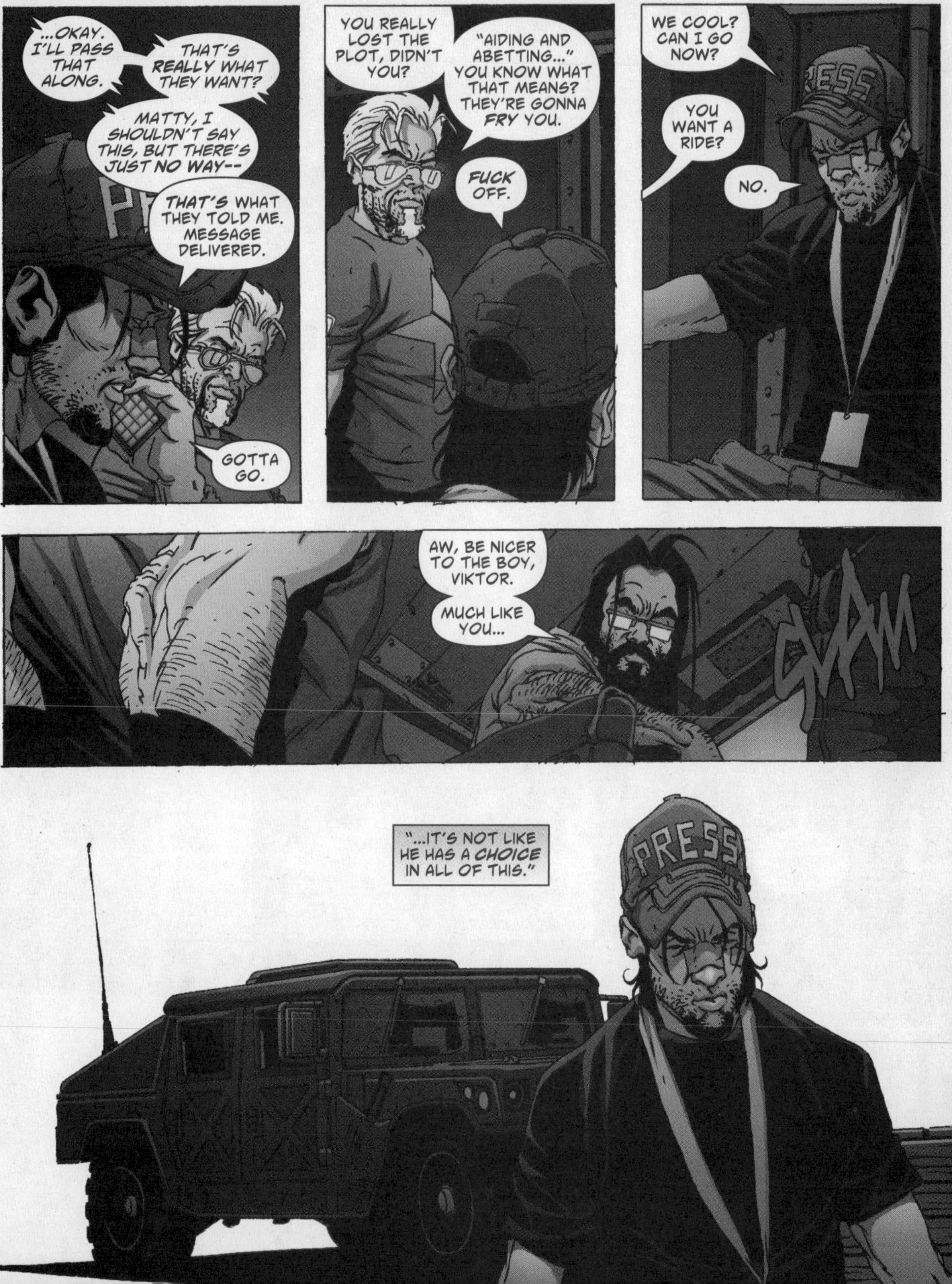
...OKAY. I'LL PASS THAT ALONG.
THAT'S REALLY WHAT THEY WANT?
MATTY, I SHOULDN'T SAY THIS, BUT THERE'S JUST NO WAY--
THAT'S WHAT THEY TOLD ME. MESSAGE DELIVERED.
GOTTA GO.
YOU REALLY LOST THE PLOT, DIDN'T YOU?
"AIDING AND ABETTING..." YOU KNOW WHAT THAT MEANS? THEY'RE GONNA FRY YOU.
FUCK OFF.
WE COOL? CAN I GO NOW?
YOU WANT A RIDE?
NO.
AW, BE NICER TO THE BOY, VIKTOR.
MUCH LIKE YOU...
"...IT'S NOT LIKE HE HAS A CHOICE IN ALL OF THIS."

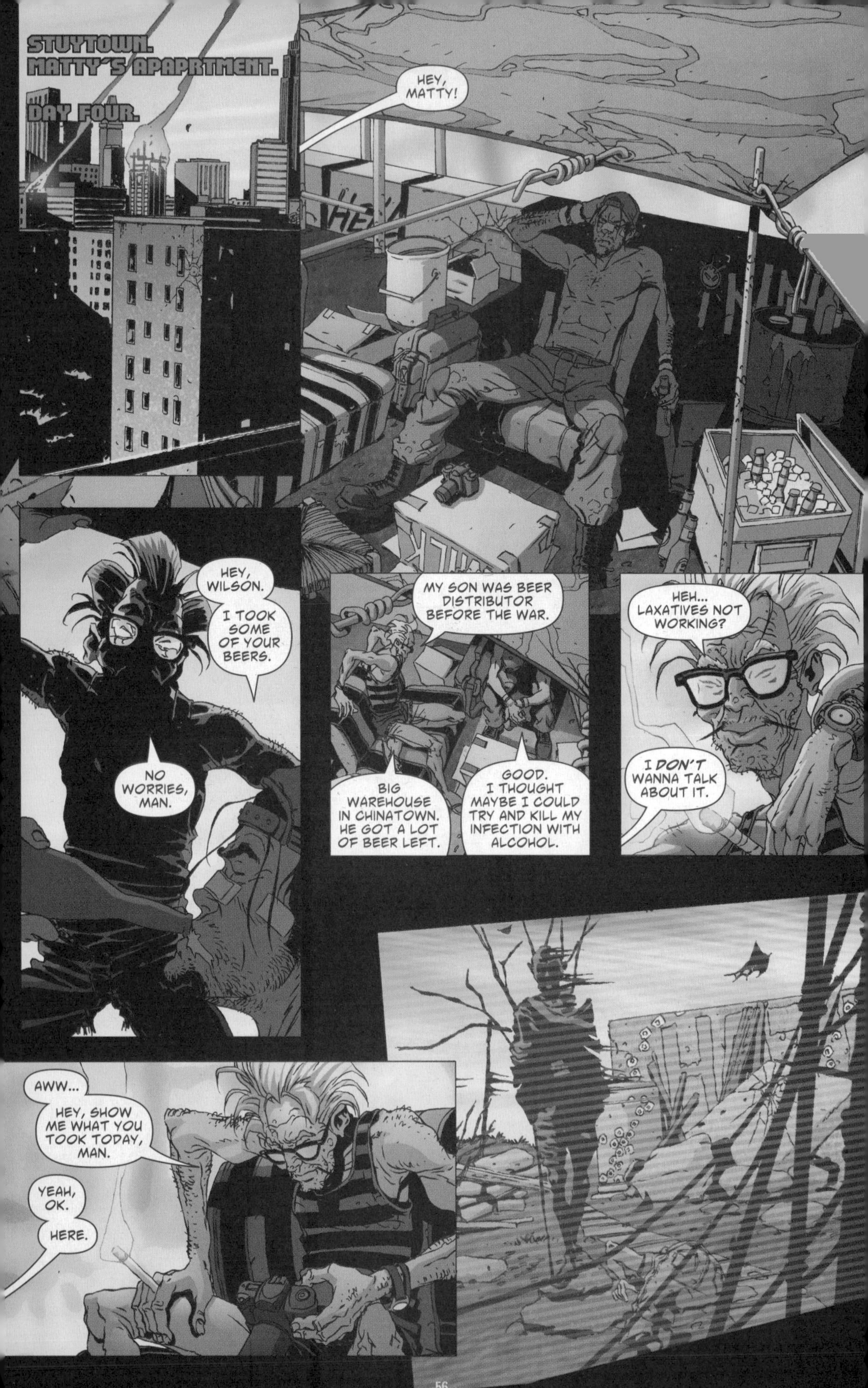
STUYTOWN.
MATTY'S APAPRTMENT.
DAY FOUR.
HEY, MATTY!
HEY, WILSON.
I TOOK SOME OF YOUR BEERS.
NO WORRIES, MAN.
MY SON WAS BEER DISTRIBUTOR BEFORE THE WAR.
BIG WAREHOUSE IN CHINATOWN. HE GOT A LOT OF BEER LEFT.
GOOD. I THOUGHT MAYBE I COULD TRY AND KILL MY INFECTION WITH ALCOHOL.
HEH... LAXATIVES NOT WORKING?
I DON'T WANNA TALK ABOUT IT.
AWW...
HEY, SHOW ME WHAT YOU TOOK TODAY, MAN.
YEAH, OK.
HERE.

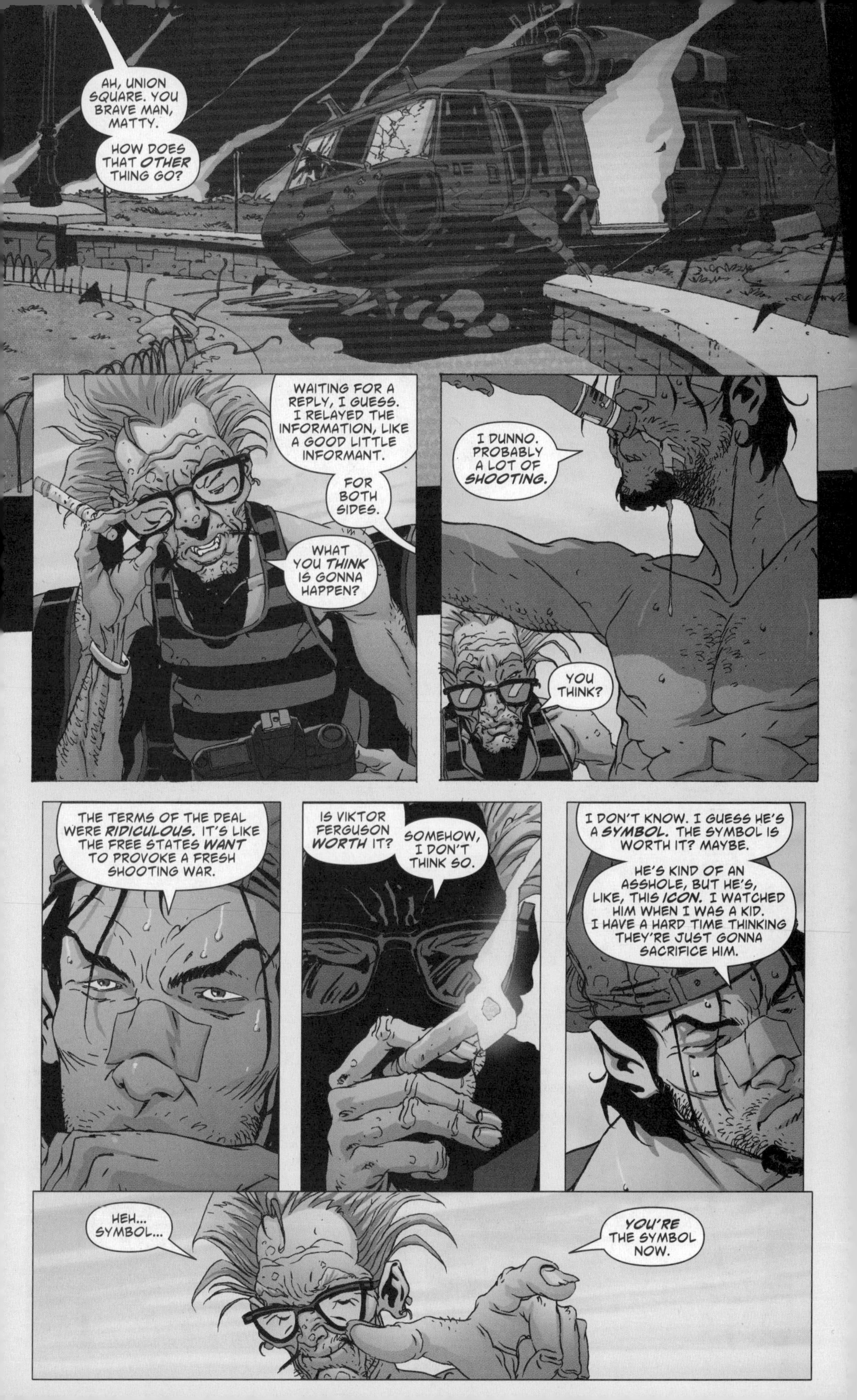
AH, UNION SQUARE. YOU BRAVE MAN, MATTY.
HOW DOES THAT OTHER THING GO?
WAITING FOR A REPLY, I GUESS. I RELAYED THE INFORMATION, LIKE A GOOD LITTLE INFORMANT.
FOR BOTH SIDES.
WHAT YOU THINK IS GONNA HAPPEN?
I DUNNO. PROBABLY A LOT OF SHOOTING.
YOU THINK?
THE TERMS OF THE DEAL WERE RIDICULOUS. IT'S LIKE THE FREE STATES WANT TO PROVOKE A FRESH SHOOTING WAR.
IS VIKTOR FERGUSON WORTH IT?
SOMEHOW, I DON'T THINK SO.
I DON'T KNOW. I GUESS HE'S A SYMBOL. THE SYMBOL IS WORTH IT? MAYBE.
HE'S KIND OF AN ASSHOLE, BUT HE'S, LIKE, THIS ICON. I WATCHED HIM WHEN I WAS A KID. I HAVE A HARD TIME THINKING THEY'RE JUST GONNA SACRIFICE HIM.
HEH... SYMBOL...
YOU'RE THE SYMBOL NOW.

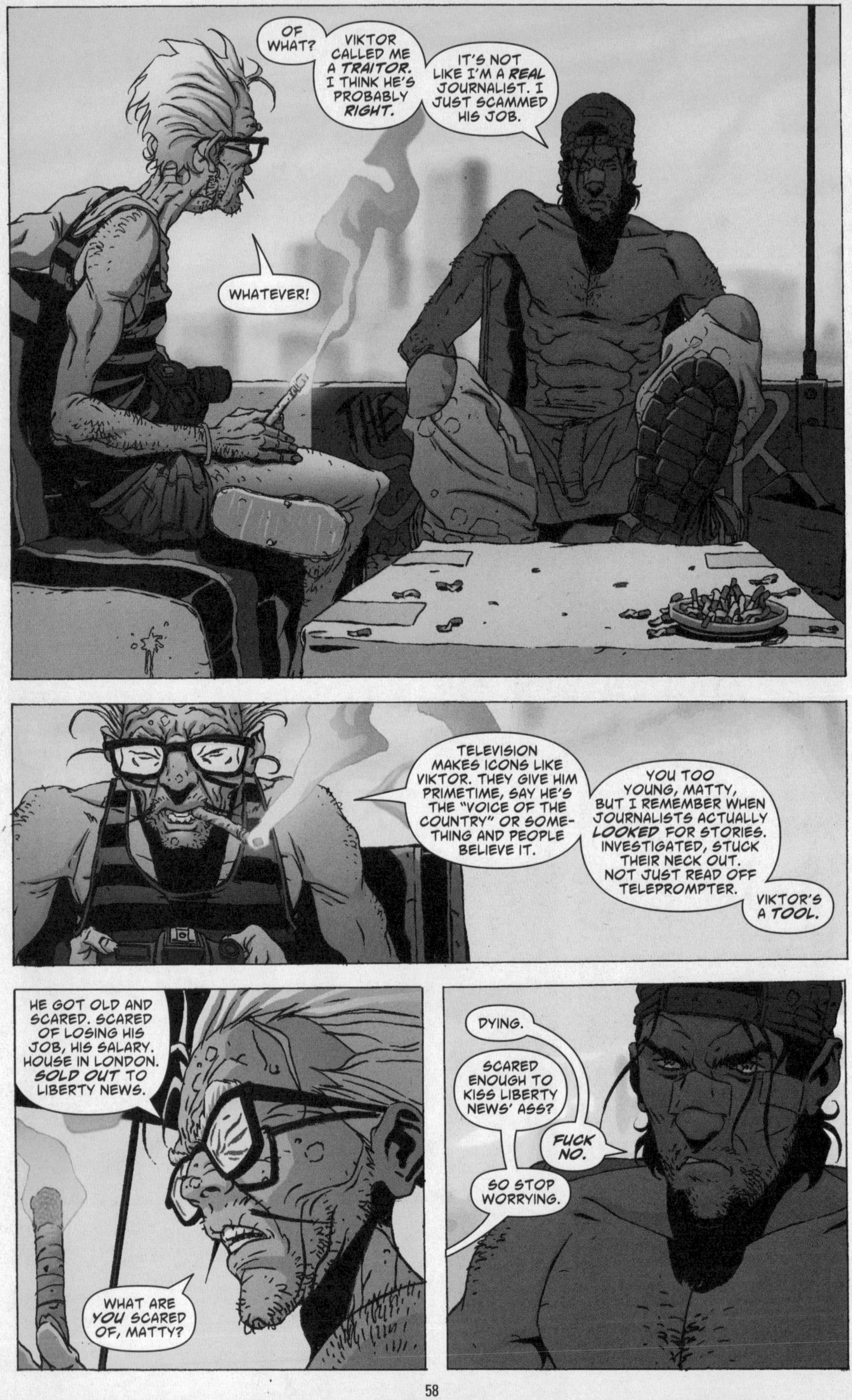
OF WHAT?
VIKTOR CALLED ME A TRAITOR. I THINK HE'S PROBABLY RIGHT.
IT'S NOT LIKE I'M A REAL JOURNALIST. I JUST SCAMMED HIS JOB.
WHATEVER!
TELEVISION MAKES ICONS LIKE VIKTOR. THEY GIVE HIM PRIMETIME, SAY HE'S THE "VOICE OF THE COUNTRY" OR SOMETHING AND PEOPLE BELIEVE IT.
YOU TOO YOUNG, MATTY, BUT I REMEMBER WHEN JOURNALISTS ACTUALLY LOOKED FOR STORIES. INVESTIGATED, STUCK THEIR NECK OUT. NOT JUST READ OFF TELEPROMPTER.
VIKTOR'S A TOOL.
HE GOT OLD AND SCARED. SCARED OF LOSING HIS JOB, HIS SALARY. HOUSE IN LONDON. SOLD OUT TO LIBERTY NEWS.
WHAT ARE YOU SCARED OF, MATTY?
DYING.
SCARED ENOUGH TO KISS LIBERTY NEWS' ASS?
FUCK NO.
SO STOP WORRYING.

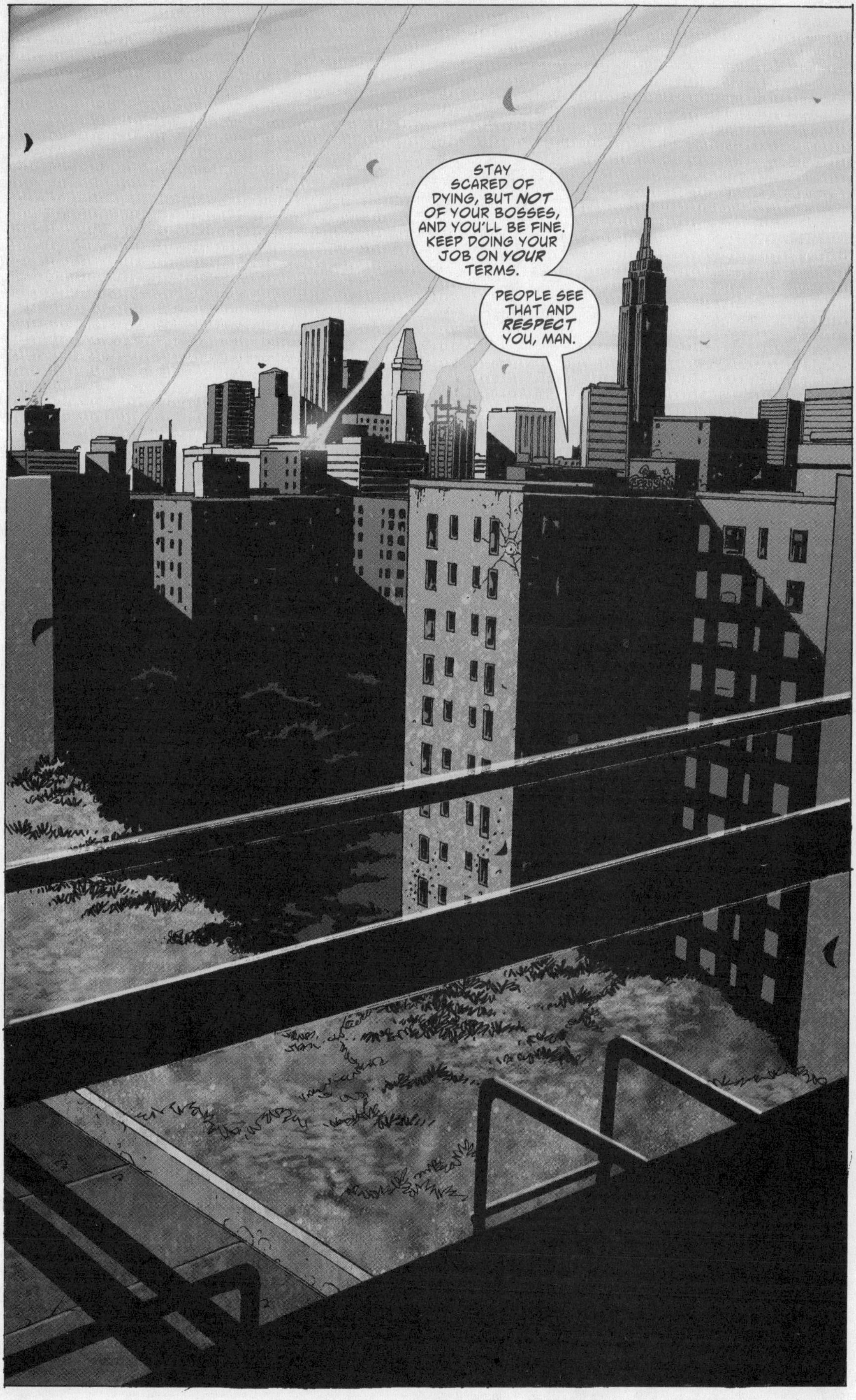
STAY SCARED OF DYING, BUT NOT OF YOUR BOSSES, AND YOU'LL BE FINE. KEEP DOING YOUR JOB ON YOUR TERMS.
PEOPLE SEE THAT AND RESPECT YOU, MAN.

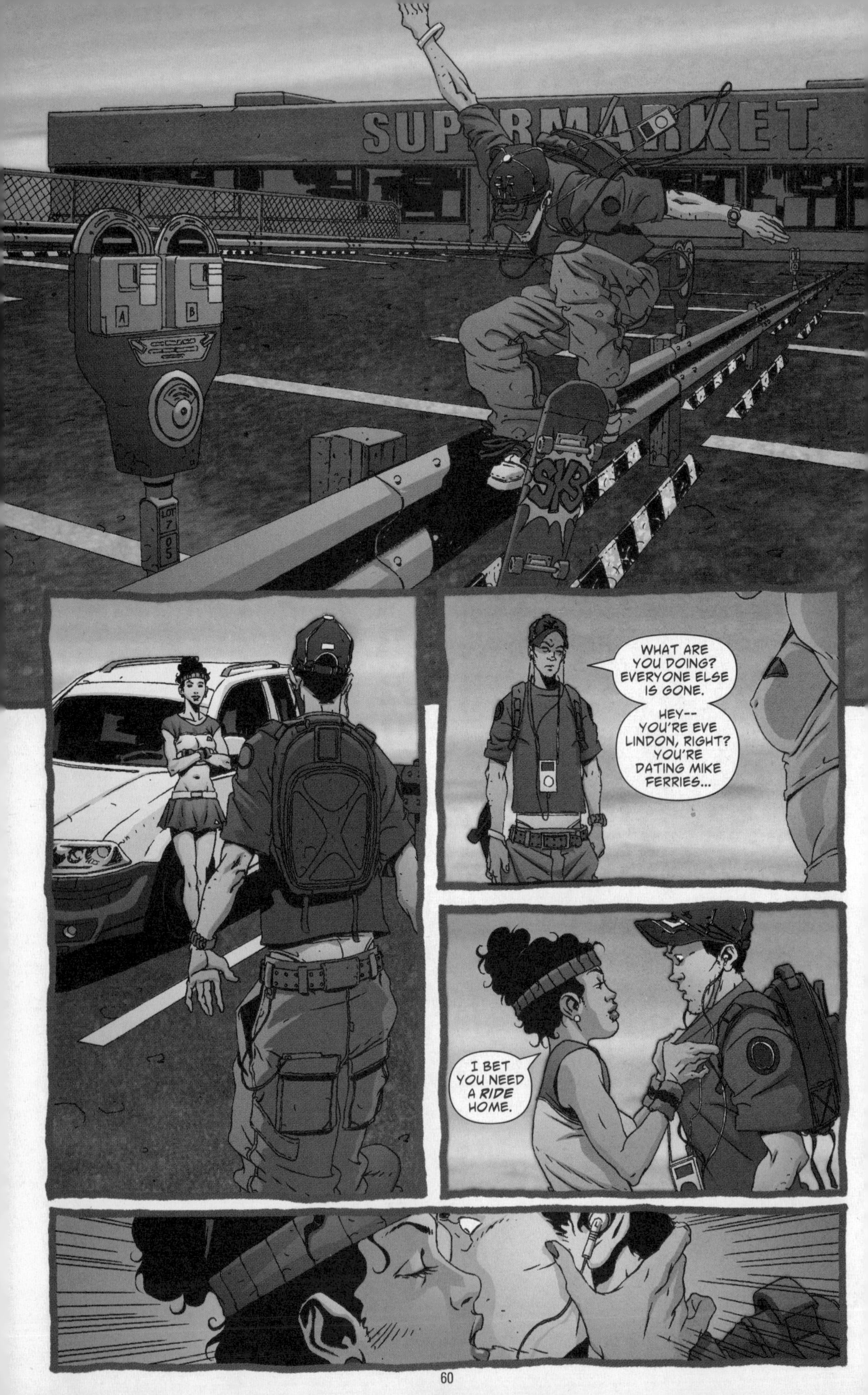
SUPERMARKET
A
B
LOT 7 05
SK8
WHAT ARE YOU DOING? EVERYONE ELSE IS GONE.
HEY-- YOU'RE EVE LINDON, RIGHT? YOU'RE DATING MIKE FERRIES...
I BET YOU NEED A *RIDE* HOME.

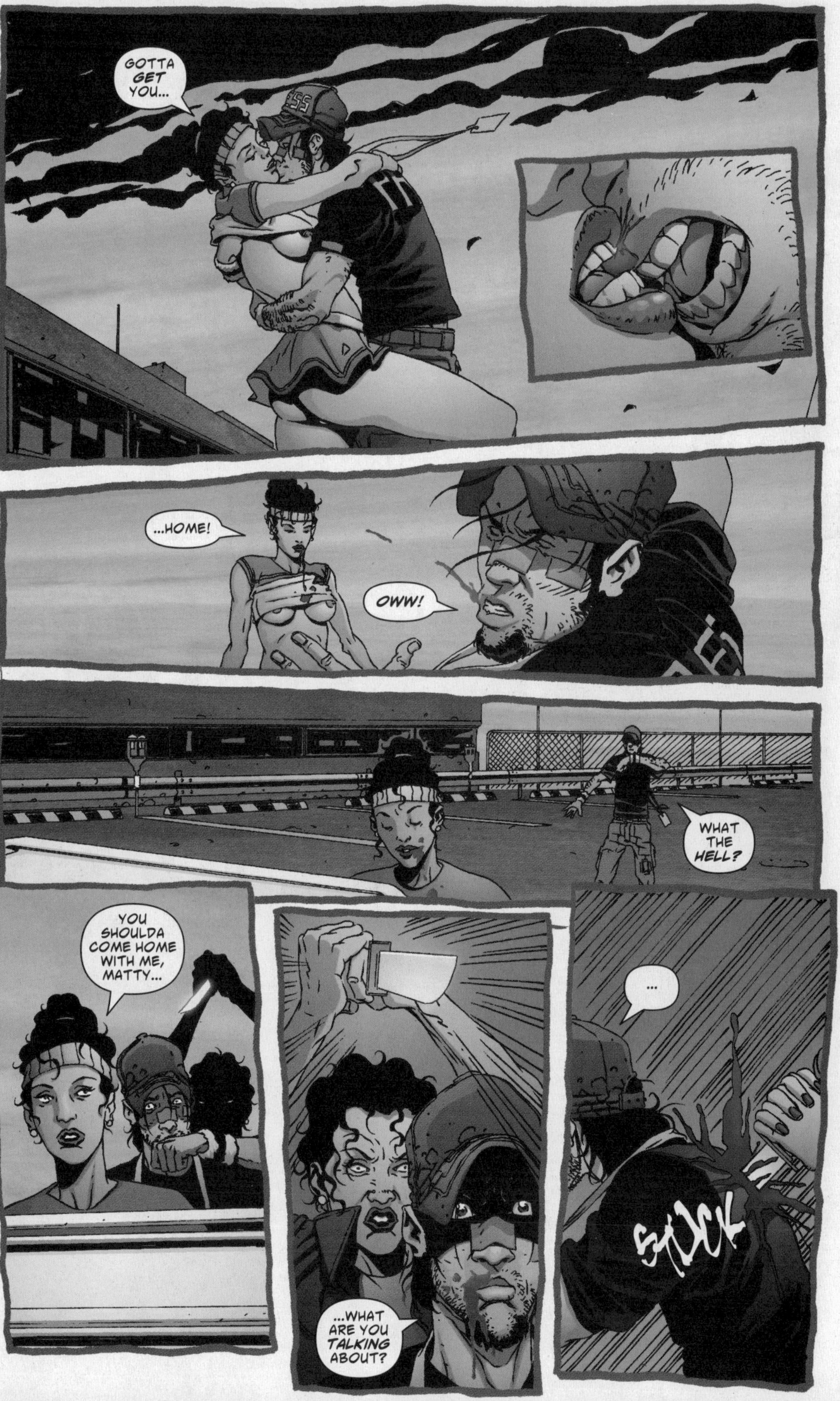

GOTTA GET YOU...
...HOME!
OWW!
WHAT THE HELL?
YOU SHOULDA COME HOME WITH ME, MATTY...
...WHAT ARE YOU TALKING ABOUT?
...

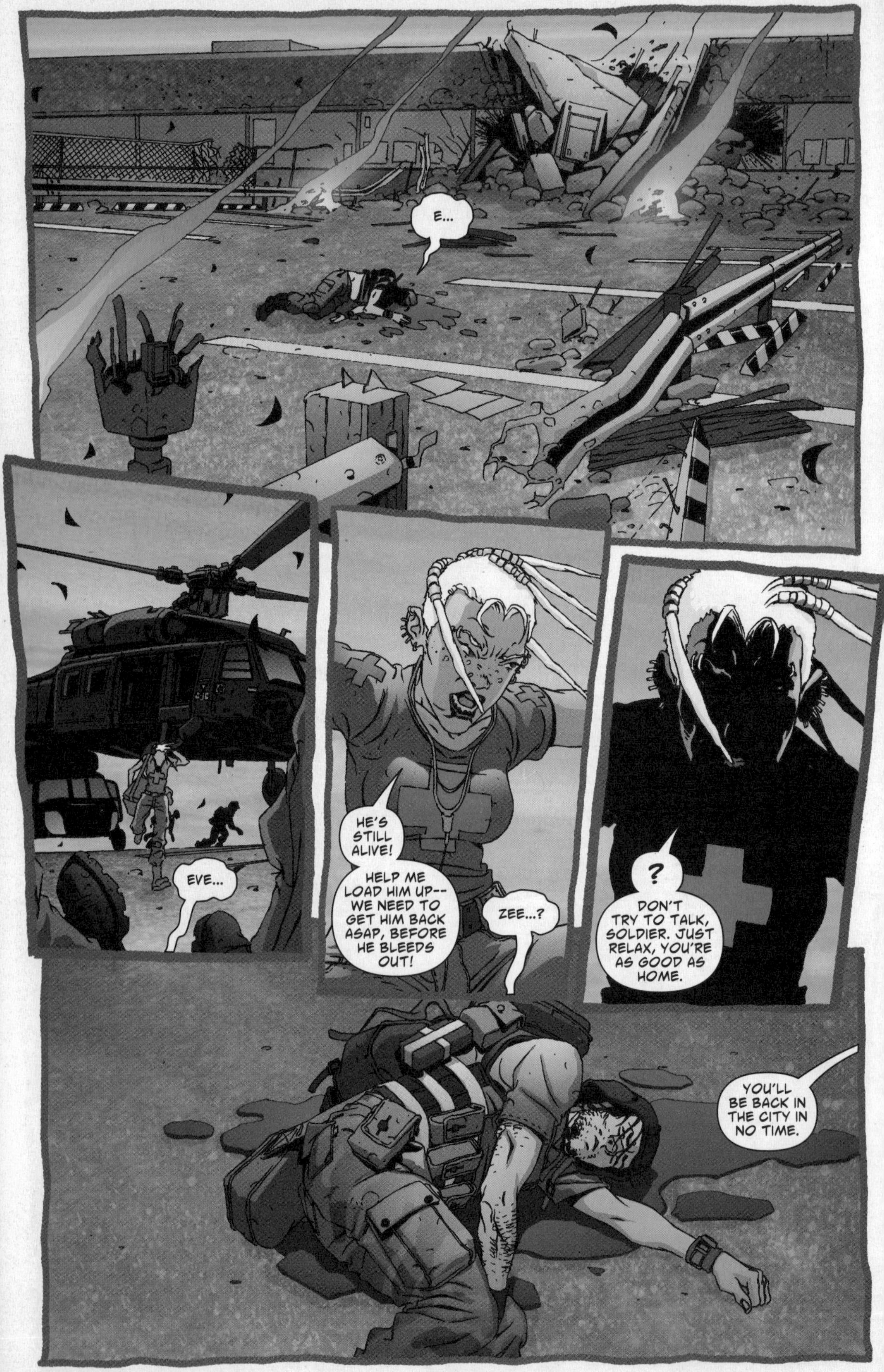
E...
EVE...
HE'S STILL ALIVE!
HELP ME LOAD HIM UP-- WE NEED TO GET HIM BACK ASAP, BEFORE HE BLEEDS OUT!
ZEE...?
?
DON'T TRY TO TALK, SOLDIER. JUST RELAX, YOU'RE AS GOOD AS HOME.
YOU'LL BE BACK IN THE CITY IN NO TIME.

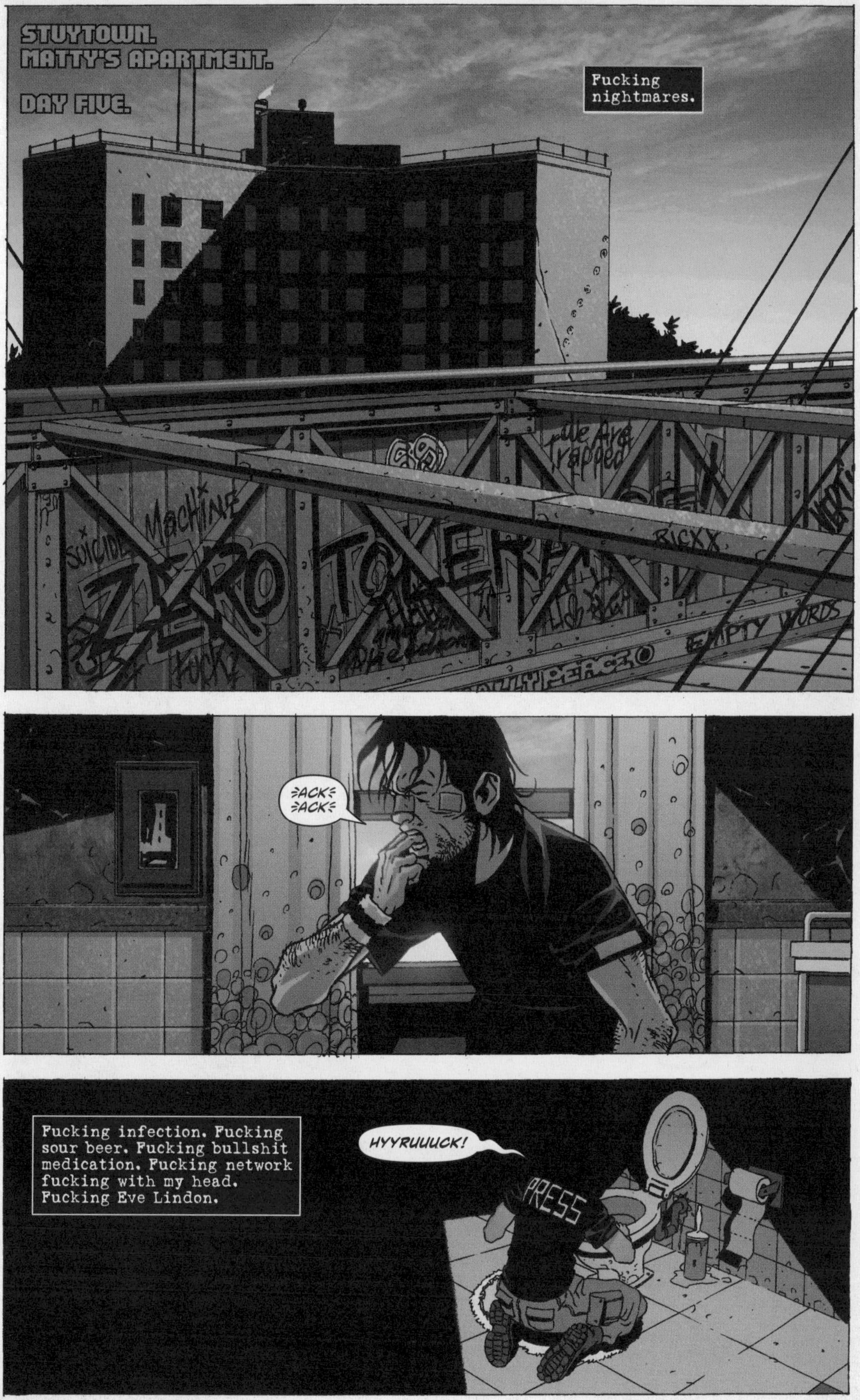
STUYTOWN.
MATTY'S APARTMENT.
DAY FIVE.
Fucking nightmares.
We Are Trapped
SUICIDE
MACHINE
ZERO
EMPTY WORDS
ACK
ACK
Fucking infection. Fucking sour beer. Fucking bullshit medication. Fucking network fucking with my head. Fucking Eve Lindon.
HYYRUUUCK!
PRESS

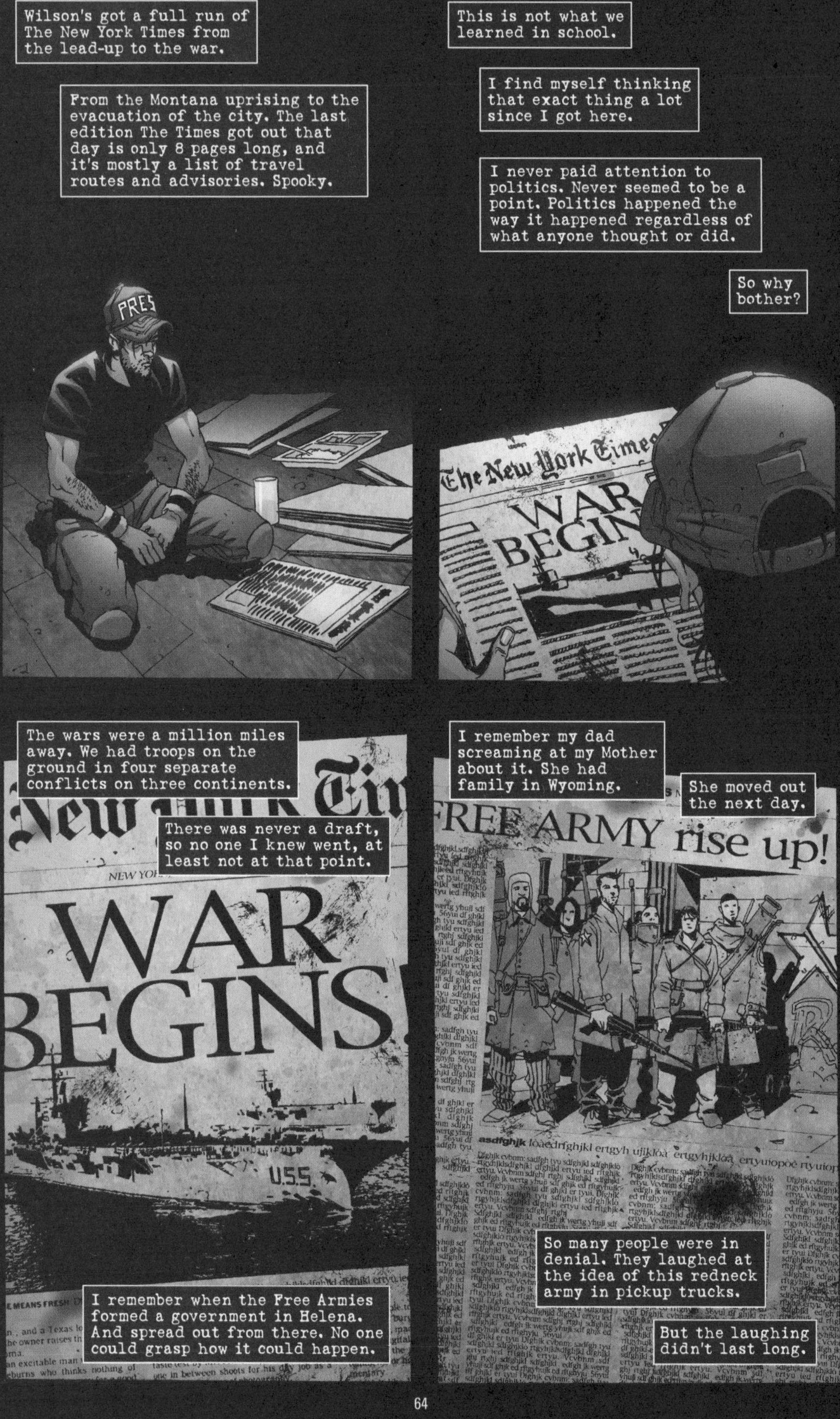
Wilson's got a full run of The New York Times from the lead-up to the war.
From the Montana uprising to the evacuation of the city. The last edition The Times got out that day is only 8 pages long, and it's mostly a list of travel routes and advisories. Spooky.
This is not what we learned in school.
I find myself thinking that exact thing a lot since I got here.
I never paid attention to politics. Never seemed to be a point. Politics happened the way it happened regardless of what anyone thought or did.
So why bother?
PRES
The New York Times
WAR BEGINS
The wars were a million miles away. We had troops on the ground in four separate conflicts on three continents.
There was never a draft, so no one I knew went, at least not at that point.
WAR BEGINS
U.S.S.
I remember when the Free Armies formed a government in Helena. And spread out from there. No one could grasp how it could happen.
I remember my dad screaming at my Mother about it. She had family in Wyoming.
She moved out the next day.
FREE ARMY rise up!
So many people were in denial. They laughed at the idea of this redneck army in pickup trucks.
But the laughing didn't last long.

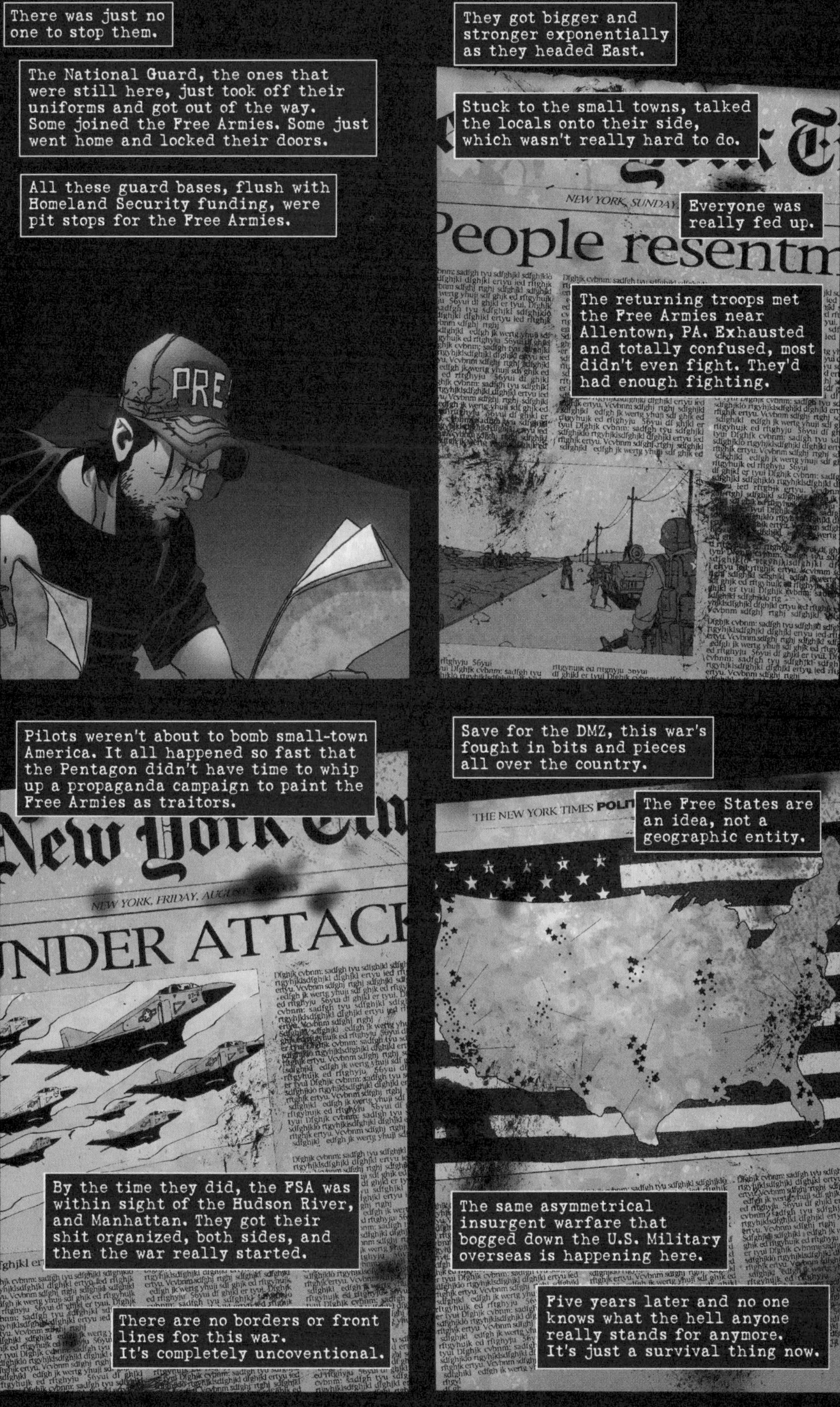
There was just no one to stop them.
The National Guard, the ones that were still here, just took off their uniforms and got out of the way. Some joined the Free Armies. Some just went home and locked their doors.
All these guard bases, flush with Homeland Security funding, were pit stops for the Free Armies.
PRE
They got bigger and stronger exponentially as they headed East.
Stuck to the small towns, talked the locals onto their side, which wasn't really hard to do.
NEW YORK, SUNDAY
Everyone was really fed up.
People resentm
The returning troops met the Free Armies near Allentown, PA. Exhausted and totally confused, most didn't even fight. They'd had enough fighting.
Pilots weren't about to bomb small-town America. It all happened so fast that the Pentagon didn't have time to whip up a propaganda campaign to paint the Free Armies as traitors.
NEW YORK, FRIDAY, AUGUST
NDER ATTAC
By the time they did, the FSA was within sight of the Hudson River, and Manhattan. They got their shit organized, both sides, and then the war really started.
There are no borders or front lines for this war. It's completely unconventional.
Save for the DMZ, this war's fought in bits and pieces all over the country.
THE NEW YORK TIMES POLI
The Free States are an idea, not a geographic entity.
The same asymmetrical insurgent warfare that bogged down the U.S. Military overseas is happening here.
Five years later and no one knows what the hell anyone really stands for anymore. It's just a survival thing now.

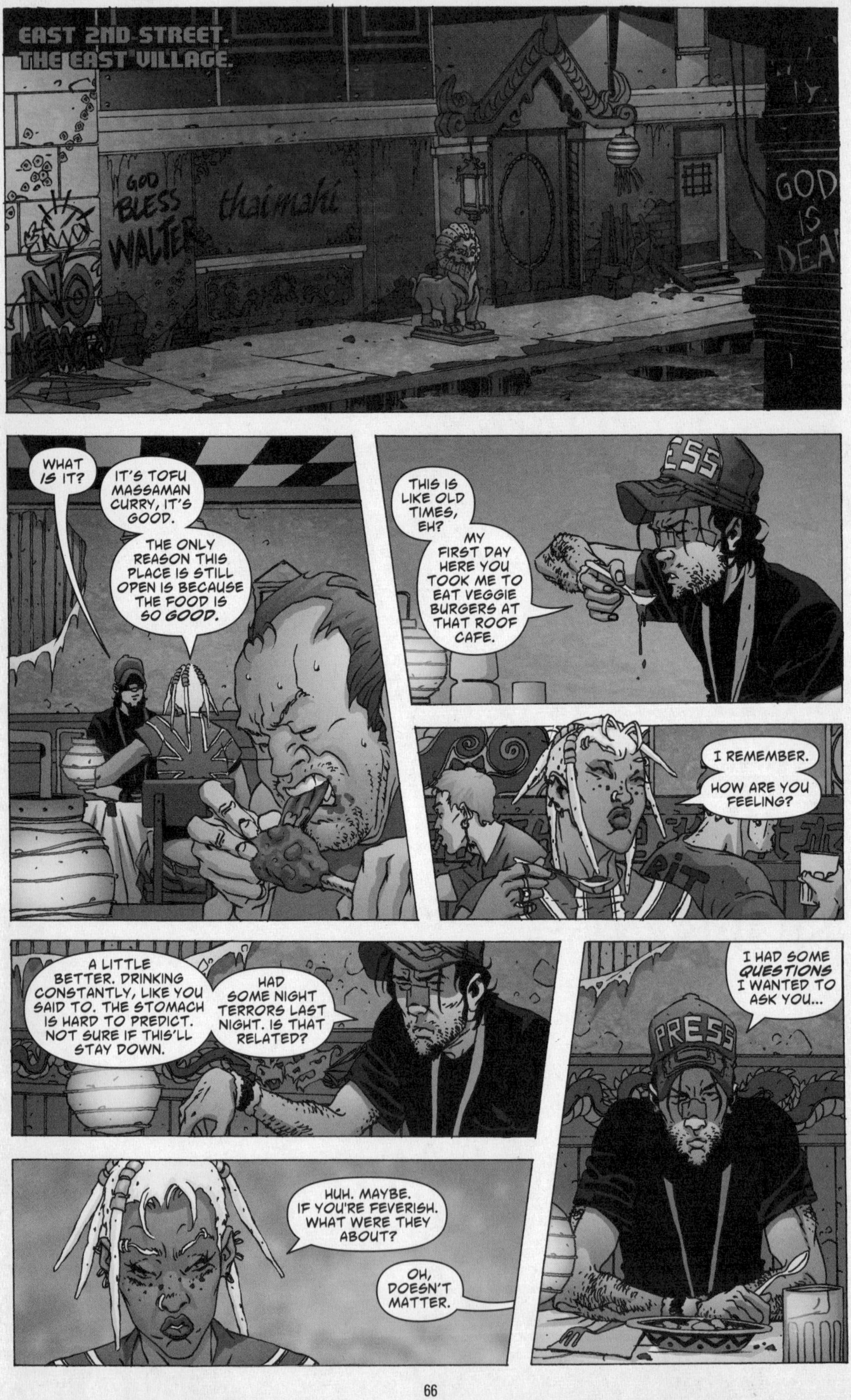
EAST 2ND STREET. THE EAST VILLAGE.
GOD BLESS WALTER
thaimaki
NO MEMORY
GOD IS DEAD
WHAT IS IT?
IT'S TOFU MASSAMAN CURRY, IT'S GOOD.
THE ONLY REASON THIS PLACE IS STILL OPEN IS BECAUSE THE FOOD IS SO GOOD.
THIS IS LIKE OLD TIMES, EH?
MY FIRST DAY HERE YOU TOOK ME TO EAT VEGGIE BURGERS AT THAT ROOF CAFE.
I REMEMBER.
HOW ARE YOU FEELING?
A LITTLE BETTER. DRINKING CONSTANTLY, LIKE YOU SAID TO. THE STOMACH IS HARD TO PREDICT. NOT SURE IF THIS'LL STAY DOWN.
HAD SOME NIGHT TERRORS LAST NIGHT. IS THAT RELATED?
I HAD SOME QUESTIONS I WANTED TO ASK YOU...
PRESS
HUH. MAYBE. IF YOU'RE FEVERISH. WHAT WERE THEY ABOUT?
OH, DOESN'T MATTER.

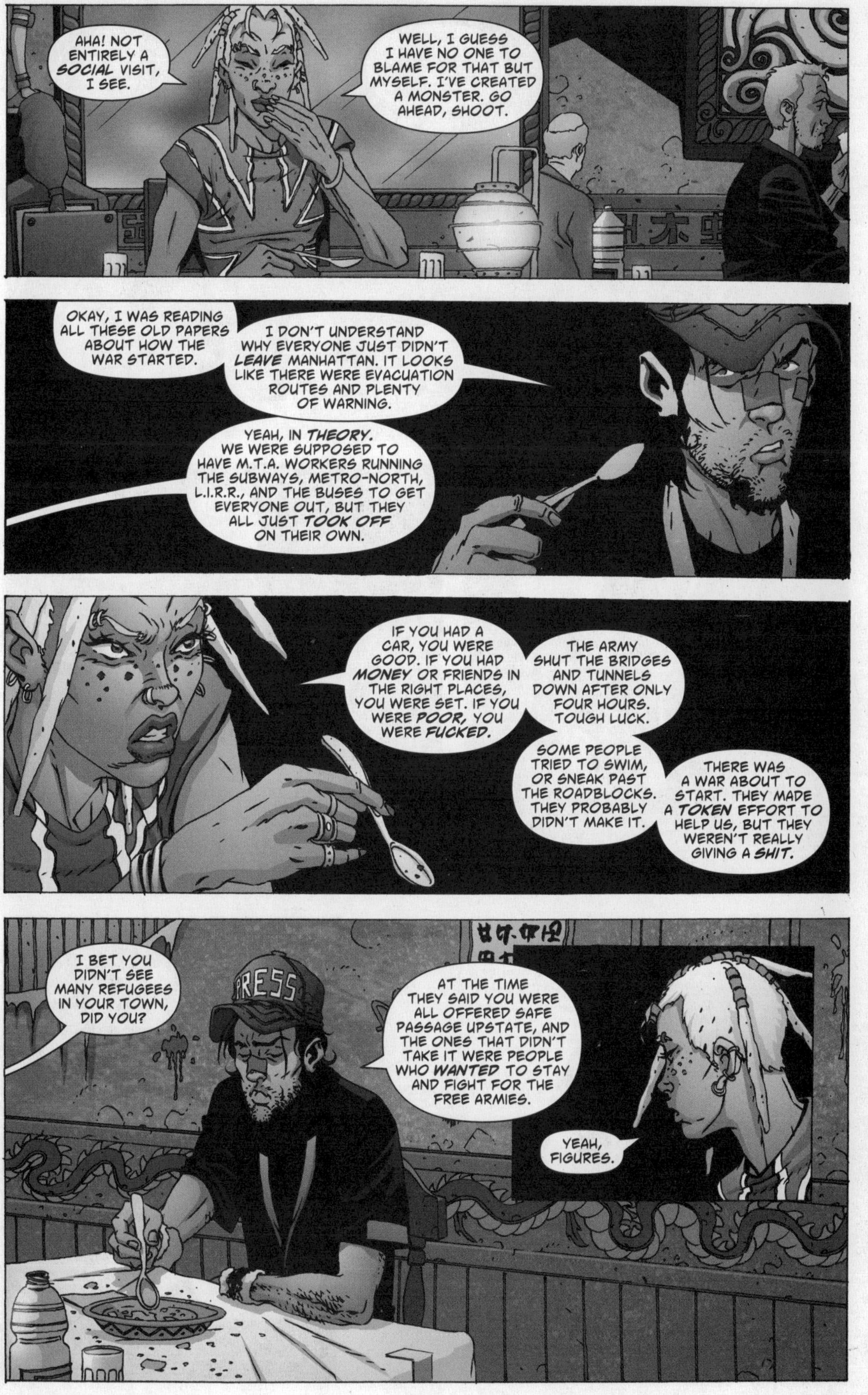
AHA! NOT ENTIRELY A *SOCIAL* VISIT, I SEE.
WELL, I GUESS I HAVE NO ONE TO BLAME FOR THAT BUT MYSELF. I'VE CREATED A MONSTER. GO AHEAD, SHOOT.
OKAY, I WAS READING ALL THESE OLD PAPERS ABOUT HOW THE WAR STARTED.
I DON'T UNDERSTAND WHY EVERYONE JUST DIDN'T *LEAVE* MANHATTAN. IT LOOKS LIKE THERE WERE EVACUATION ROUTES AND PLENTY OF WARNING.
YEAH, IN *THEORY.* WE WERE SUPPOSED TO HAVE M.T.A. WORKERS RUNNING THE SUBWAYS, METRO-NORTH, L.I.R.R., AND THE BUSES TO GET EVERYONE OUT, BUT THEY ALL JUST *TOOK OFF* ON THEIR OWN.
IF YOU HAD A CAR, YOU WERE GOOD. IF YOU HAD *MONEY* OR FRIENDS IN THE RIGHT PLACES, YOU WERE SET. IF YOU WERE *POOR,* YOU WERE *FUCKED.*
THE ARMY SHUT THE BRIDGES AND TUNNELS DOWN AFTER ONLY FOUR HOURS. TOUGH LUCK.
SOME PEOPLE TRIED TO SWIM, OR SNEAK PAST THE ROADBLOCKS. THEY PROBABLY DIDN'T MAKE IT.
THERE WAS A WAR ABOUT TO START. THEY MADE A *TOKEN* EFFORT TO HELP US, BUT THEY WEREN'T REALLY GIVING A *SHIT.*
I BET YOU DIDN'T SEE MANY REFUGEES IN YOUR TOWN, DID YOU?
PRESS
AT THE TIME THEY SAID YOU WERE ALL OFFERED SAFE PASSAGE UPSTATE, AND THE ONES THAT DIDN'T TAKE IT WERE PEOPLE WHO *WANTED* TO STAY AND FIGHT FOR THE FREE ARMIES.
YEAH, FIGURES.

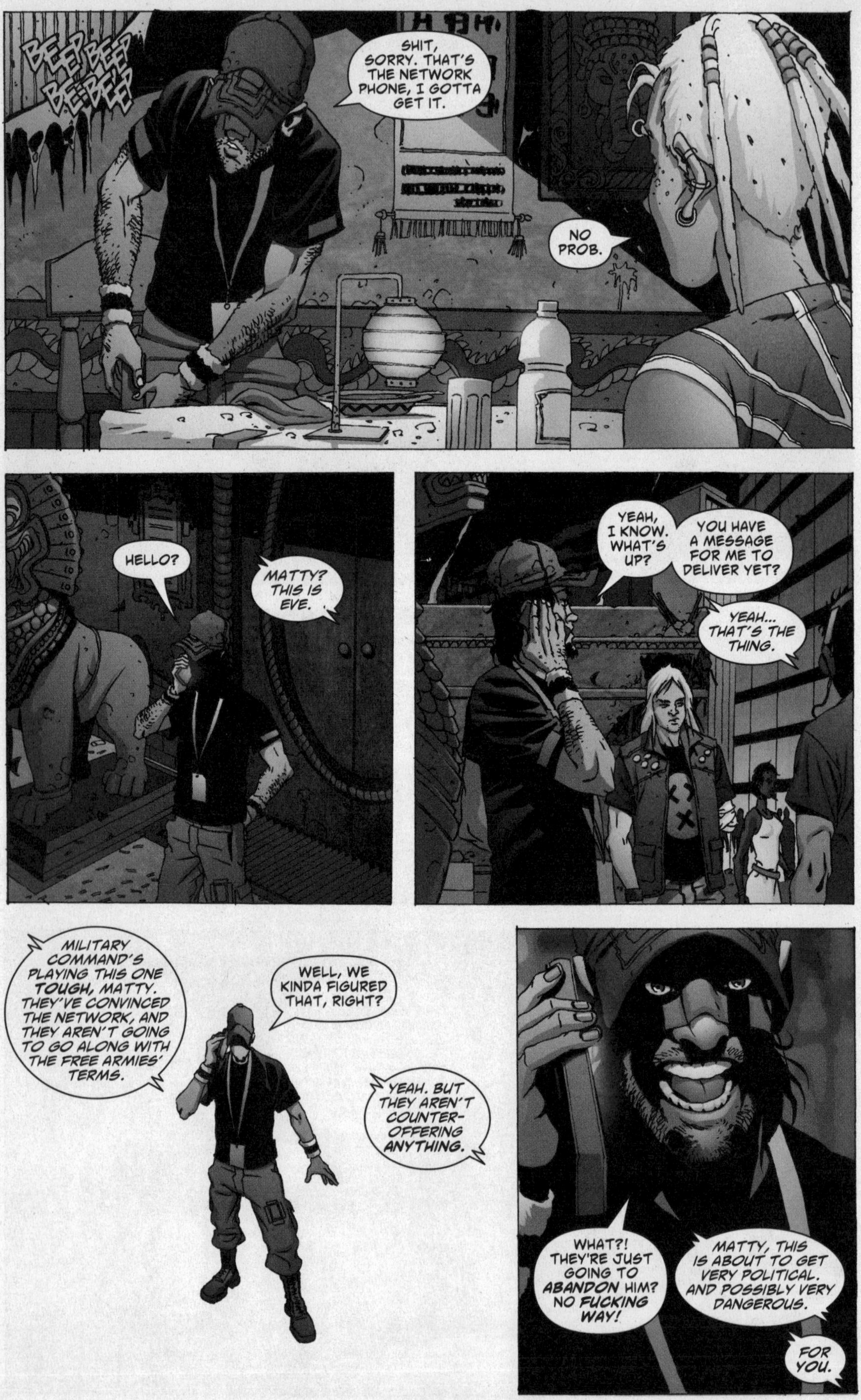
BEEP BEEP BEEP BE-BEEP
SHIT, SORRY. THAT'S THE NETWORK PHONE, I GOTTA GET IT.
NO PROB.
HELLO?
MATTY? THIS IS EVE.
YEAH, I KNOW. WHAT'S UP?
YOU HAVE A MESSAGE FOR ME TO DELIVER YET?
YEAH... THAT'S THE THING.
MILITARY COMMAND'S PLAYING THIS ONE TOUGH, MATTY. THEY'VE CONVINCED THE NETWORK, AND THEY AREN'T GOING TO GO ALONG WITH THE FREE ARMIES' TERMS.
WELL, WE KINDA FIGURED THAT, RIGHT?
YEAH. BUT THEY AREN'T COUNTER-OFFERING ANYTHING.
WHAT?! THEY'RE JUST GOING TO ABANDON HIM? NO FUCKING WAY!
MATTY, THIS IS ABOUT TO GET VERY POLITICAL. AND POSSIBLY VERY DANGEROUS.
FOR YOU.

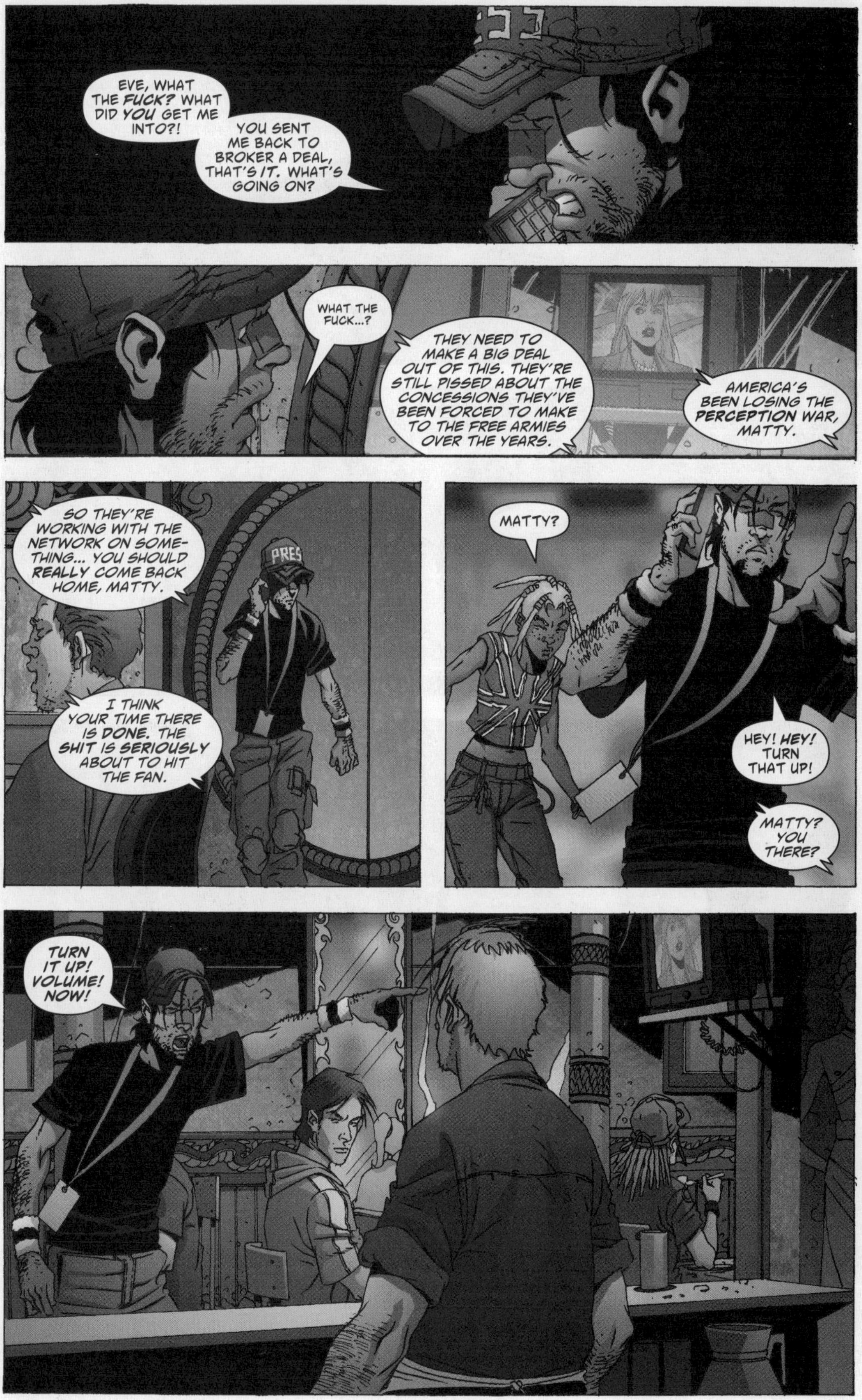
EVE, WHAT THE FUCK? WHAT DID YOU GET ME INTO?!
YOU SENT ME BACK TO BROKER A DEAL, THAT'S IT. WHAT'S GOING ON?
WHAT THE FUCK...?
THEY NEED TO MAKE A BIG DEAL OUT OF THIS. THEY'RE STILL PISSED ABOUT THE CONCESSIONS THEY'VE BEEN FORCED TO MAKE TO THE FREE ARMIES OVER THE YEARS.
AMERICA'S BEEN LOSING THE PERCEPTION WAR, MATTY.
SO THEY'RE WORKING WITH THE NETWORK ON SOME-THING... YOU SHOULD REALLY COME BACK HOME, MATTY.
PRES
I THINK YOUR TIME THERE IS DONE. THE SHIT IS SERIOUSLY ABOUT TO HIT THE FAN.
MATTY?
HEY! HEY! TURN THAT UP!
MATTY? YOU THERE?
TURN IT UP! VOLUME! NOW!

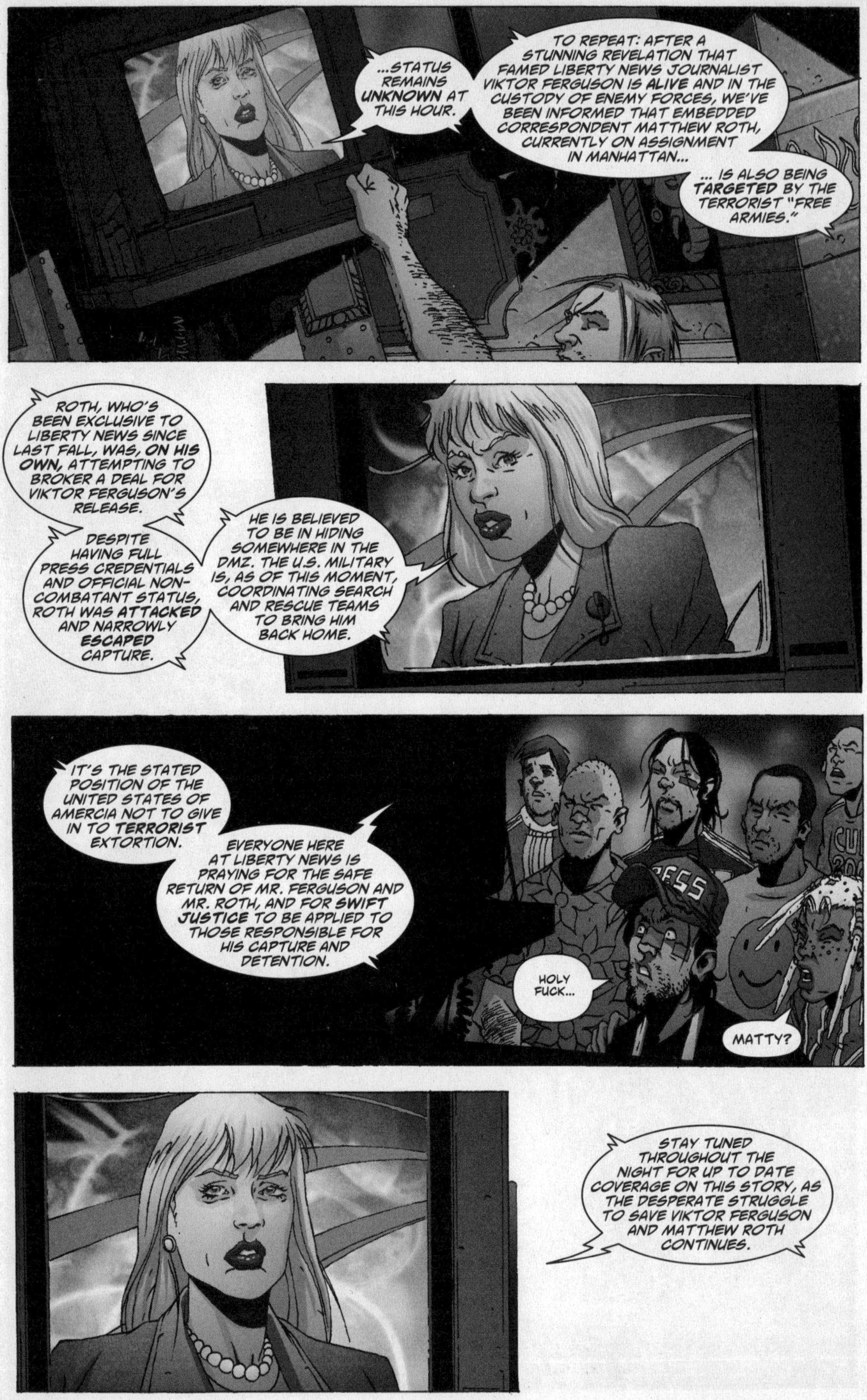
...STATUS REMAINS UNKNOWN AT THIS HOUR.
TO REPEAT: AFTER A STUNNING REVELATION THAT FAMED LIBERTY NEWS JOURNALIST VIKTOR FERGUSON IS ALIVE AND IN THE CUSTODY OF ENEMY FORCES, WE'VE BEEN INFORMED THAT EMBEDDED CORRESPONDENT MATTHEW ROTH, CURRENTLY ON ASSIGNMENT IN MANHATTAN...
... IS ALSO BEING TARGETED BY THE TERRORIST "FREE ARMIES."
ROTH, WHO'S BEEN EXCLUSIVE TO LIBERTY NEWS SINCE LAST FALL, WAS, ON HIS OWN, ATTEMPTING TO BROKER A DEAL FOR VIKTOR FERGUSON'S RELEASE.
DESPITE HAVING FULL PRESS CREDENTIALS AND OFFICIAL NON-COMBATANT STATUS, ROTH WAS ATTACKED AND NARROWLY ESCAPED CAPTURE.
HE IS BELIEVED TO BE IN HIDING SOMEWHERE IN THE DMZ. THE U.S. MILITARY IS, AS OF THIS MOMENT, COORDINATING SEARCH AND RESCUE TEAMS TO BRING HIM BACK HOME.
IT'S THE STATED POSITION OF THE UNITED STATES OF AMERCIA NOT TO GIVE IN TO TERRORIST EXTORTION.
EVERYONE HERE AT LIBERTY NEWS IS PRAYING FOR THE SAFE RETURN OF MR. FERGUSON AND MR. ROTH, AND FOR SWIFT JUSTICE TO BE APPLIED TO THOSE RESPONSIBLE FOR HIS CAPTURE AND DETENTION.
HOLY FUCK...
MATTY?
STAY TUNED THROUGHOUT THE NIGHT FOR UP TO DATE COVERAGE ON THIS STORY, AS THE DESPERATE STRUGGLE TO SAVE VIKTOR FERGUSON AND MATTHEW ROTH CONTINUES.

MATTY? MATTY?

WHAT THE *FUCK* DID YOU JUST DO TO ME?

THAT WAS COMPLETE AND UTTER *BULL-SHIT*, AND YOU *KNOW* IT!

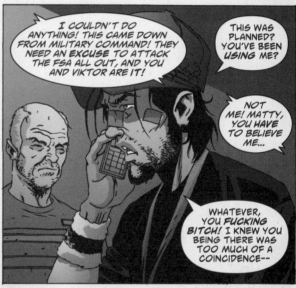

I COULDN'T DO ANYTHING! THIS CAME DOWN FROM MILITARY COMMAND! THEY NEED AN EXCUSE TO ATTACK THE FSA ALL OUT, AND YOU AND VIKTOR ARE IT!

THIS WAS PLANNED? YOU'VE BEEN USING ME?

NOT ME! MATTY, YOU HAVE TO BELIEVE ME...

WHATEVER, YOU *FUCKING BITCH!* I KNEW YOU BEING THERE WAS TOO MUCH OF A COINCIDENCE--

WAIT... WHAT "RESCUE TEAMS"? THEY SAID "RESCUE TEAMS"--

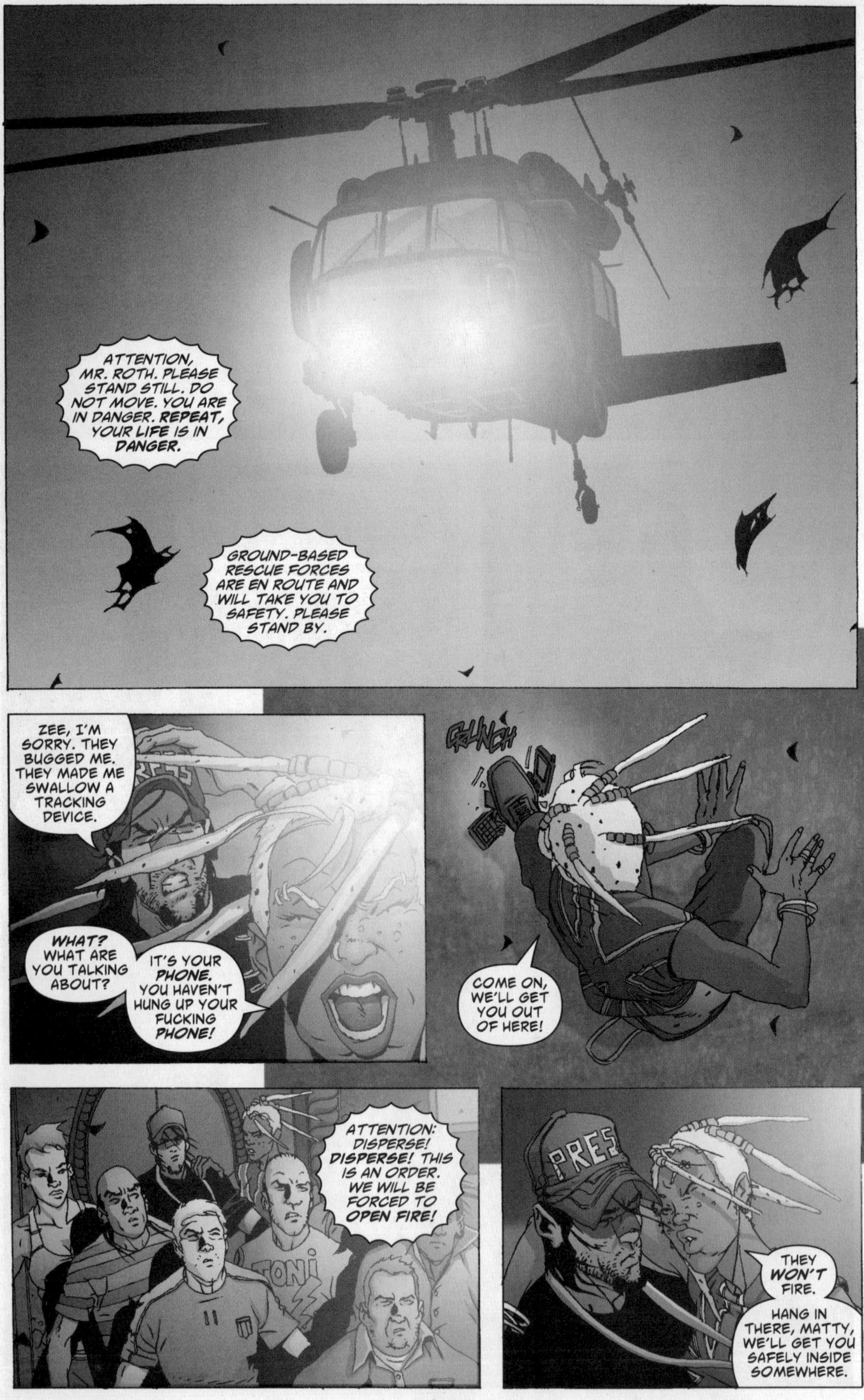
ATTENTION, MR. ROTH. PLEASE STAND STILL. DO NOT MOVE. YOU ARE IN DANGER. REPEAT, YOUR LIFE IS IN DANGER.
GROUND-BASED RESCUE FORCES ARE EN ROUTE AND WILL TAKE YOU TO SAFETY. PLEASE STAND BY.
ZEE, I'M SORRY. THEY BUGGED ME. THEY MADE ME SWALLOW A TRACKING DEVICE.
WHAT? WHAT ARE YOU TALKING ABOUT?
IT'S YOUR PHONE. YOU HAVEN'T HUNG UP YOUR FUCKING PHONE!
CRUNCH
COME ON, WE'LL GET YOU OUT OF HERE!
ATTENTION: DISPERSE! DISPERSE! THIS IS AN ORDER. WE WILL BE FORCED TO OPEN FIRE!
THEY WON'T FIRE.
HANG IN THERE, MATTY, WE'LL GET YOU SAFELY INSIDE SOMEWHERE.

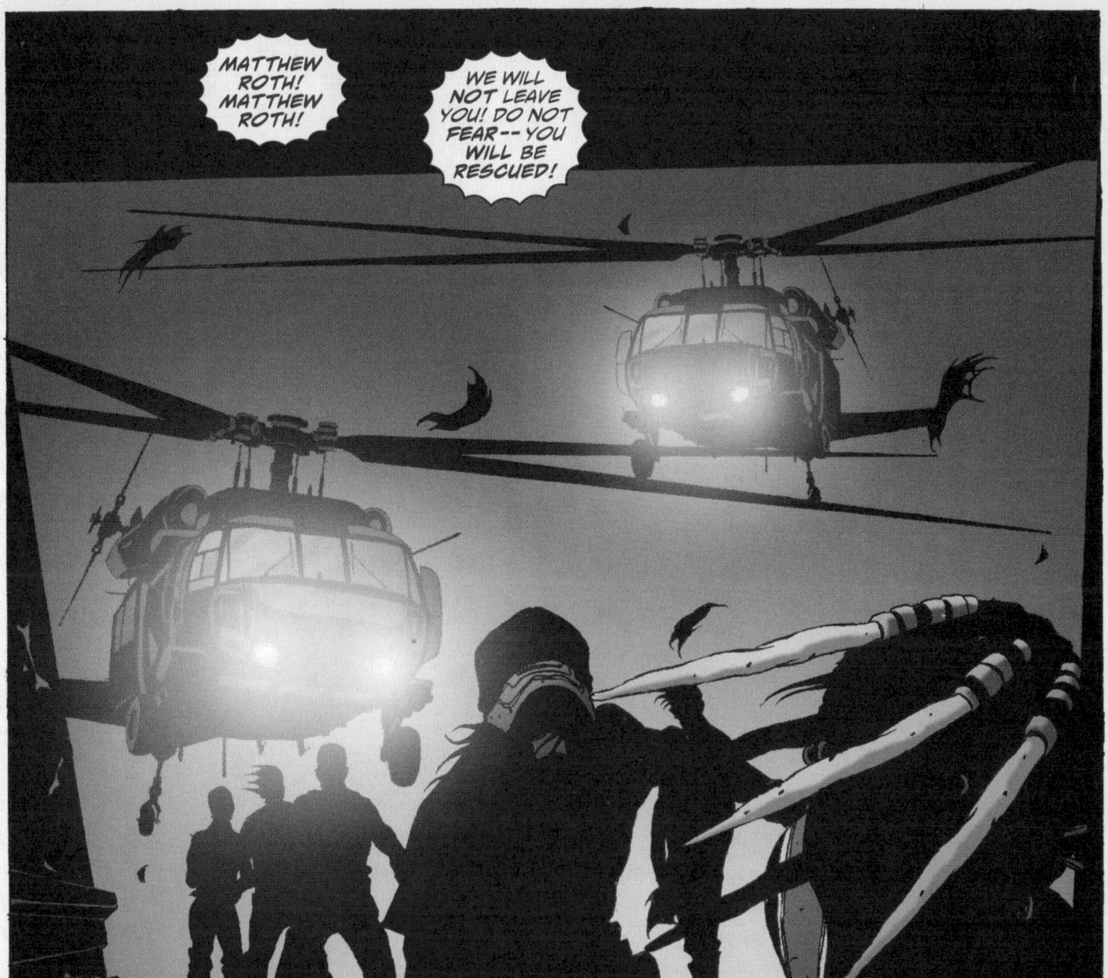
MATTHEW ROTH! MATTHEW ROTH!
WE WILL NOT LEAVE YOU! DO NOT FEAR-- YOU WILL BE RESCUED!

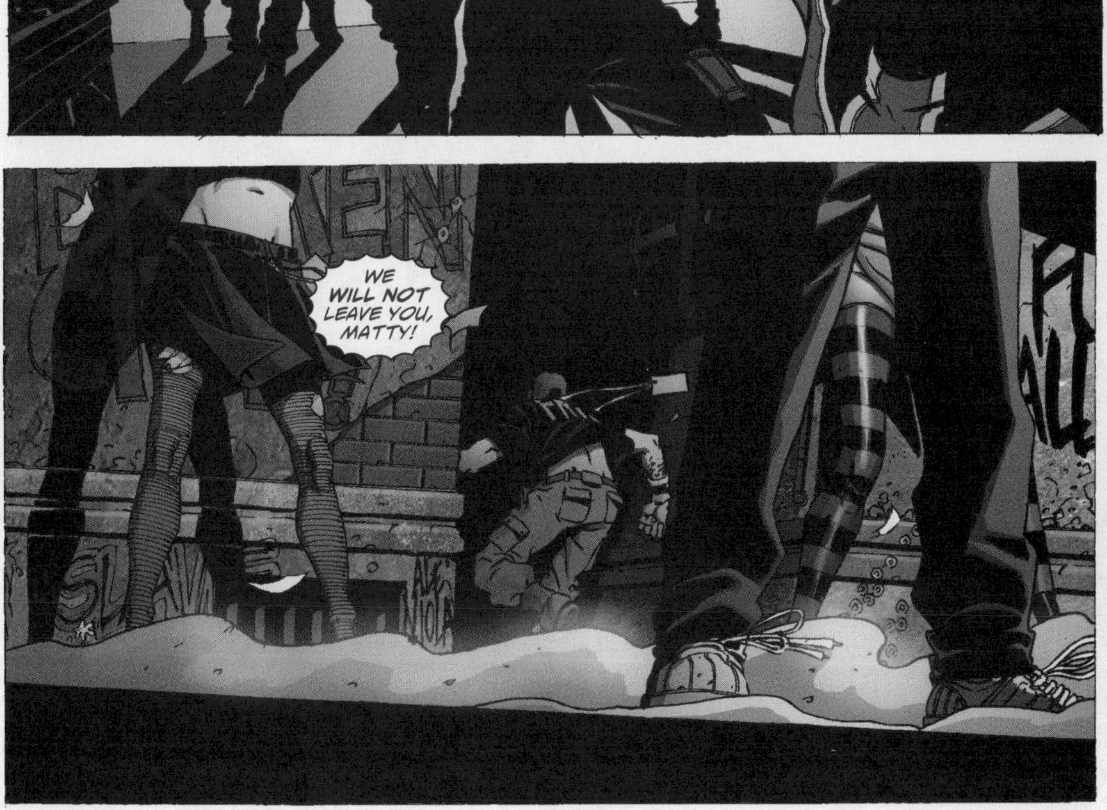
WE WILL NOT LEAVE YOU, MATTY!

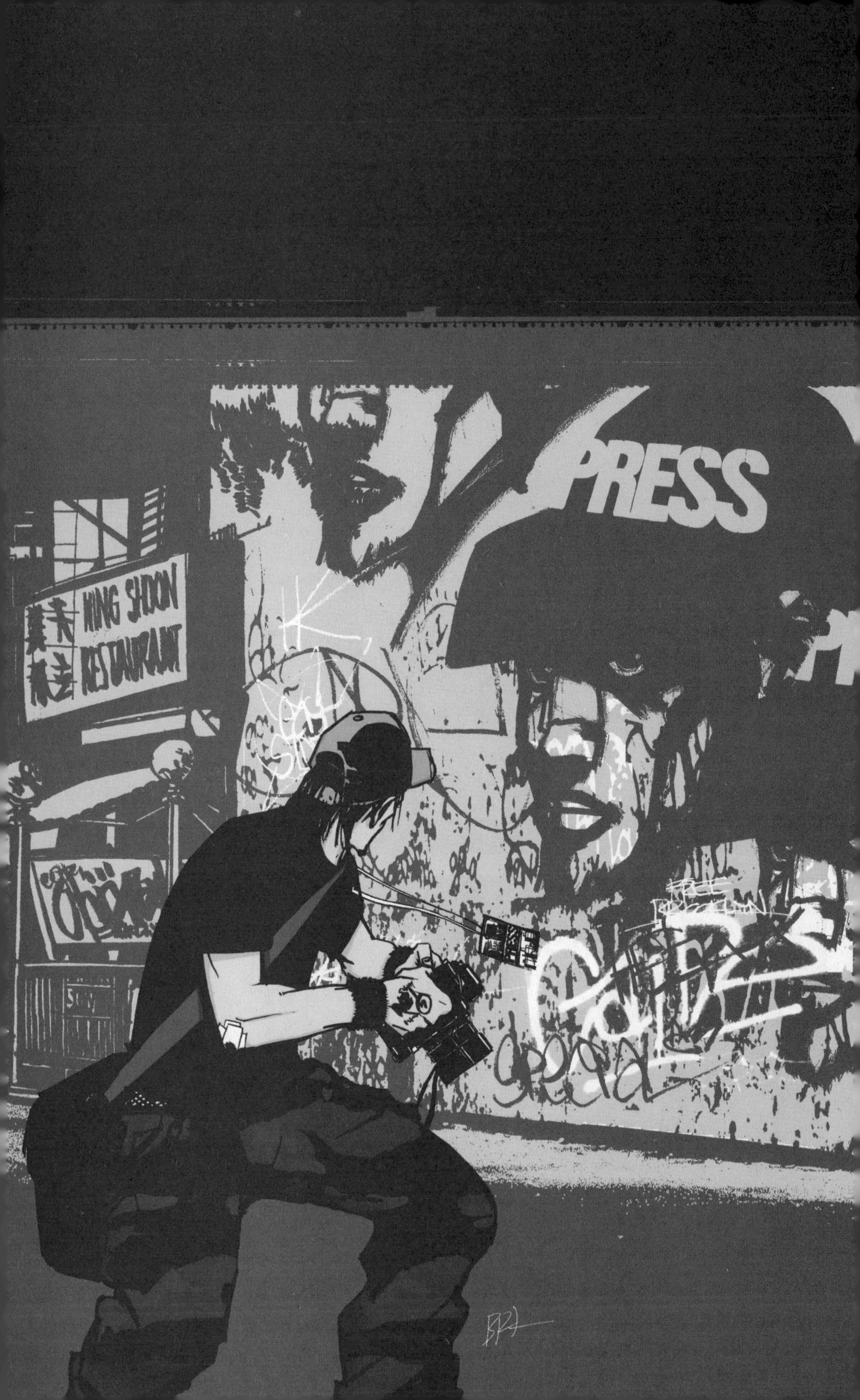
PRESS
WING SHOON
RESTAURANT

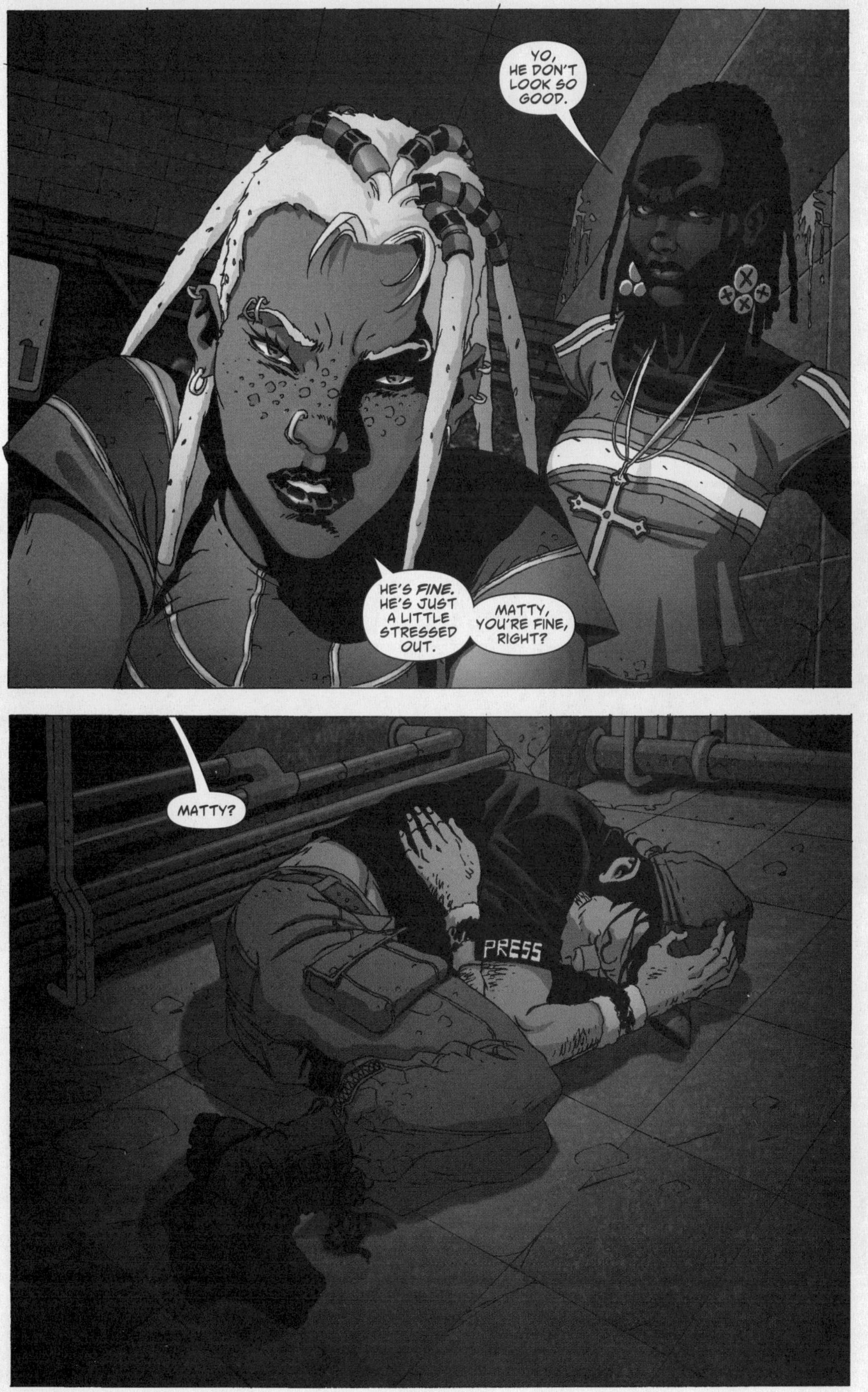
YO, HE DON'T LOOK SO GOOD.
HE'S *FINE*. HE'S JUST A LITTLE STRESSED OUT.
MATTY, YOU'RE FINE, RIGHT?
MATTY?
PRESS

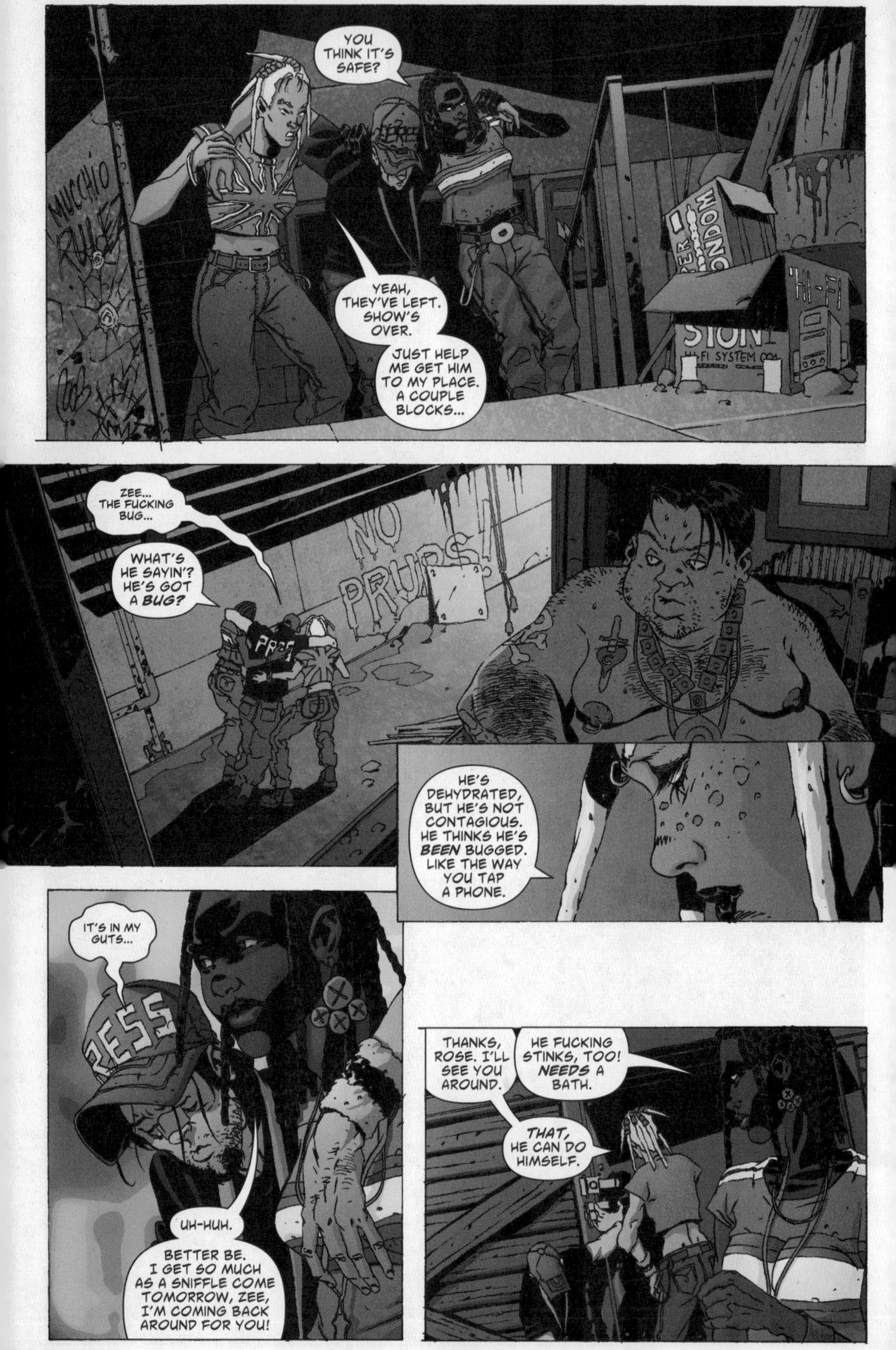
YOU THINK IT'S SAFE?
YEAH, THEY'VE LEFT. SHOW'S OVER.
JUST HELP ME GET HIM TO MY PLACE. A COUPLE BLOCKS...
MUCCHIO RULEZ
HI-FI
ZEE... THE FUCKING BUG...
WHAT'S HE SAYIN'? HE'S GOT A *BUG?*
NO PRUPS
HE'S DEHYDRATED, BUT HE'S NOT CONTAGIOUS. HE THINKS HE'S *BEEN* BUGGED. LIKE THE WAY YOU TAP A PHONE.
IT'S IN MY GUTS...
UH-HUH.
BETTER BE. I GET SO MUCH AS A SNIFFLE COME TOMORROW, ZEE, I'M COMING BACK AROUND FOR YOU!
THANKS, ROSE. I'LL SEE YOU AROUND.
HE FUCKING STINKS, TOO! *NEEDS* A BATH.
THAT, HE CAN DO HIMSELF.

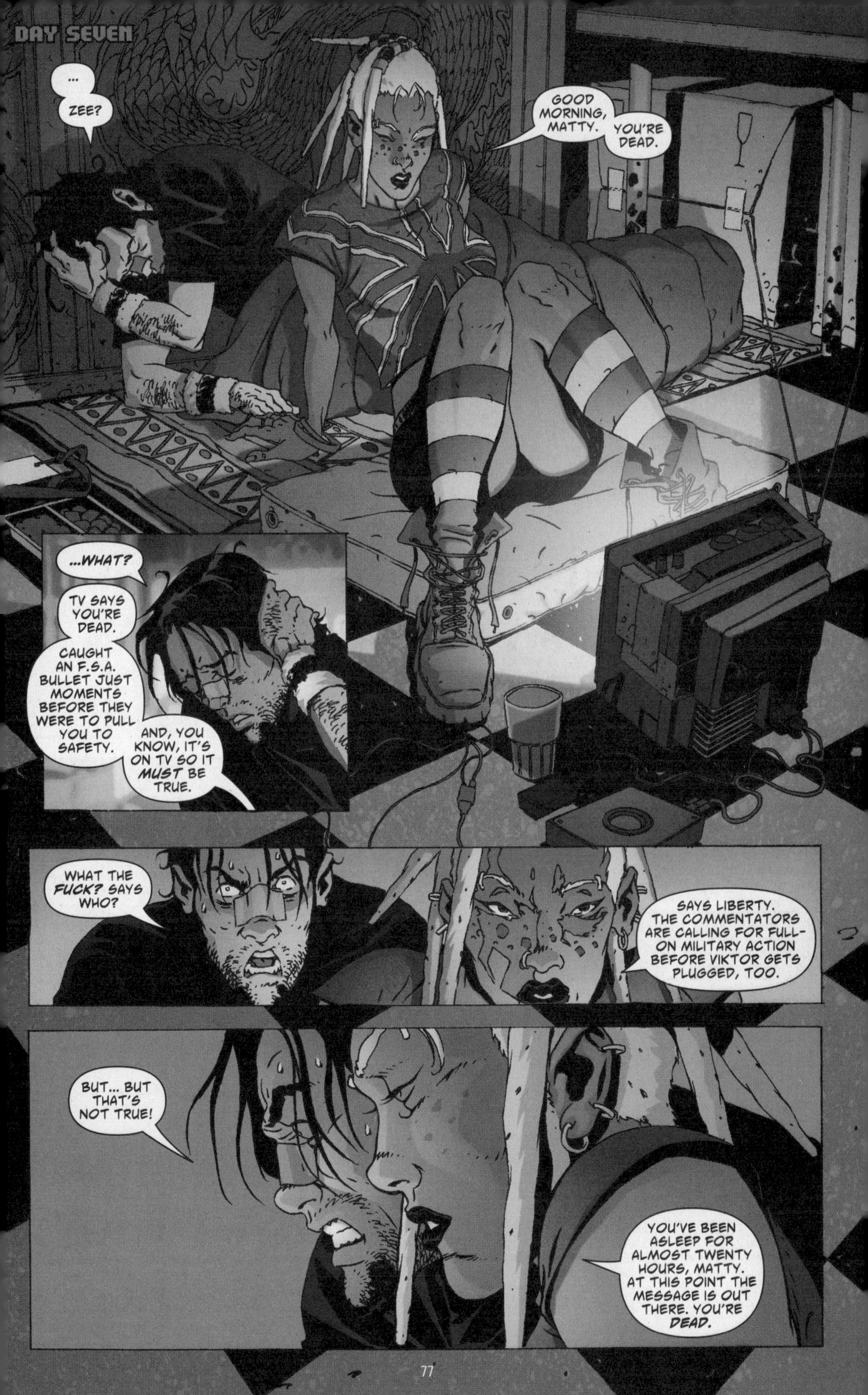
...
ZEE?
GOOD MORNING, MATTY.
YOU'RE DEAD.
...WHAT?
TV SAYS YOU'RE DEAD.
CAUGHT AN F.S.A. BULLET JUST MOMENTS BEFORE THEY WERE TO PULL YOU TO SAFETY.
AND, YOU KNOW, IT'S ON TV SO IT MUST BE TRUE.
WHAT THE FUCK? SAYS WHO?
SAYS LIBERTY. THE COMMENTATORS ARE CALLING FOR FULL-ON MILITARY ACTION BEFORE VIKTOR GETS PLUGGED, TOO.
BUT... BUT THAT'S NOT TRUE!
YOU'VE BEEN ASLEEP FOR ALMOST TWENTY HOURS, MATTY. AT THIS POINT THE MESSAGE IS OUT THERE. YOU'RE DEAD.

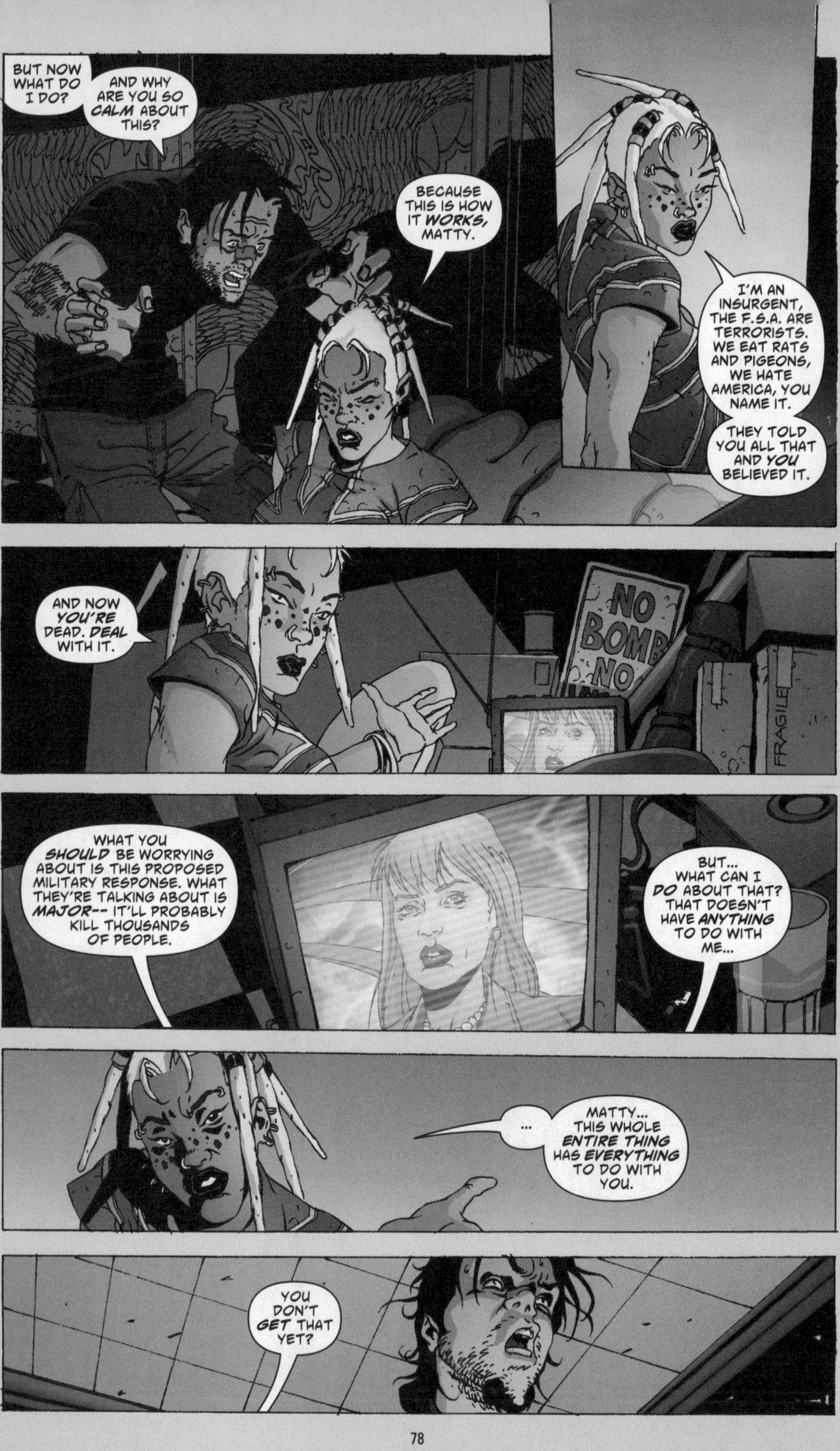
BUT NOW WHAT DO I DO?
AND WHY ARE YOU SO CALM ABOUT THIS?
BECAUSE THIS IS HOW IT WORKS, MATTY.
I'M AN INSURGENT, THE F.S.A. ARE TERRORISTS. WE EAT RATS AND PIGEONS, WE HATE AMERICA, YOU NAME IT.
THEY TOLD YOU ALL THAT AND YOU BELIEVED IT.
AND NOW YOU'RE DEAD. DEAL WITH IT.
NO BOMB NO
FRAGILE
WHAT YOU SHOULD BE WORRYING ABOUT IS THIS PROPOSED MILITARY RESPONSE. WHAT THEY'RE TALKING ABOUT IS MAJOR-- IT'LL PROBABLY KILL THOUSANDS OF PEOPLE.
BUT... WHAT CAN I DO ABOUT THAT? THAT DOESN'T HAVE ANYTHING TO DO WITH ME...
...
MATTY... THIS WHOLE ENTIRE THING HAS EVERYTHING TO DO WITH YOU.
YOU DON'T GET THAT YET?

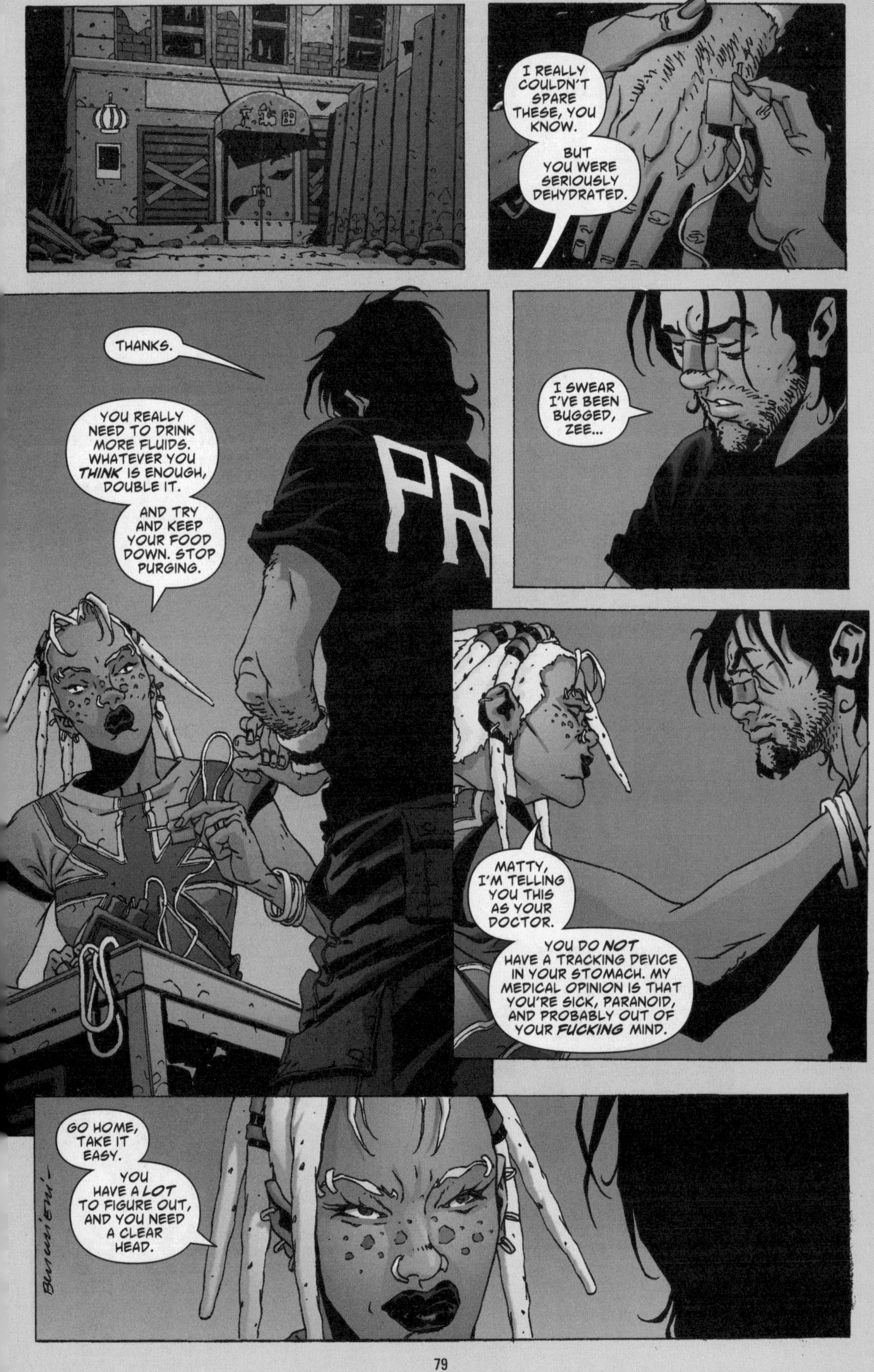
I REALLY COULDN'T SPARE THESE, YOU KNOW.
BUT YOU WERE SERIOUSLY DEHYDRATED.
THANKS.
YOU REALLY NEED TO DRINK MORE FLUIDS. WHATEVER YOU *THINK* IS ENOUGH, DOUBLE IT.
AND TRY AND KEEP YOUR FOOD DOWN. STOP PURGING.
I SWEAR I'VE BEEN BUGGED, ZEE...
MATTY, I'M TELLING YOU THIS AS YOUR DOCTOR.
YOU DO **NOT** HAVE A TRACKING DEVICE IN YOUR STOMACH. MY MEDICAL OPINION IS THAT YOU'RE SICK, PARANOID, AND PROBABLY OUT OF YOUR ***FUCKING*** MIND.
GO HOME, TAKE IT EASY.
YOU HAVE A ***LOT*** TO FIGURE OUT, AND YOU NEED A CLEAR HEAD.

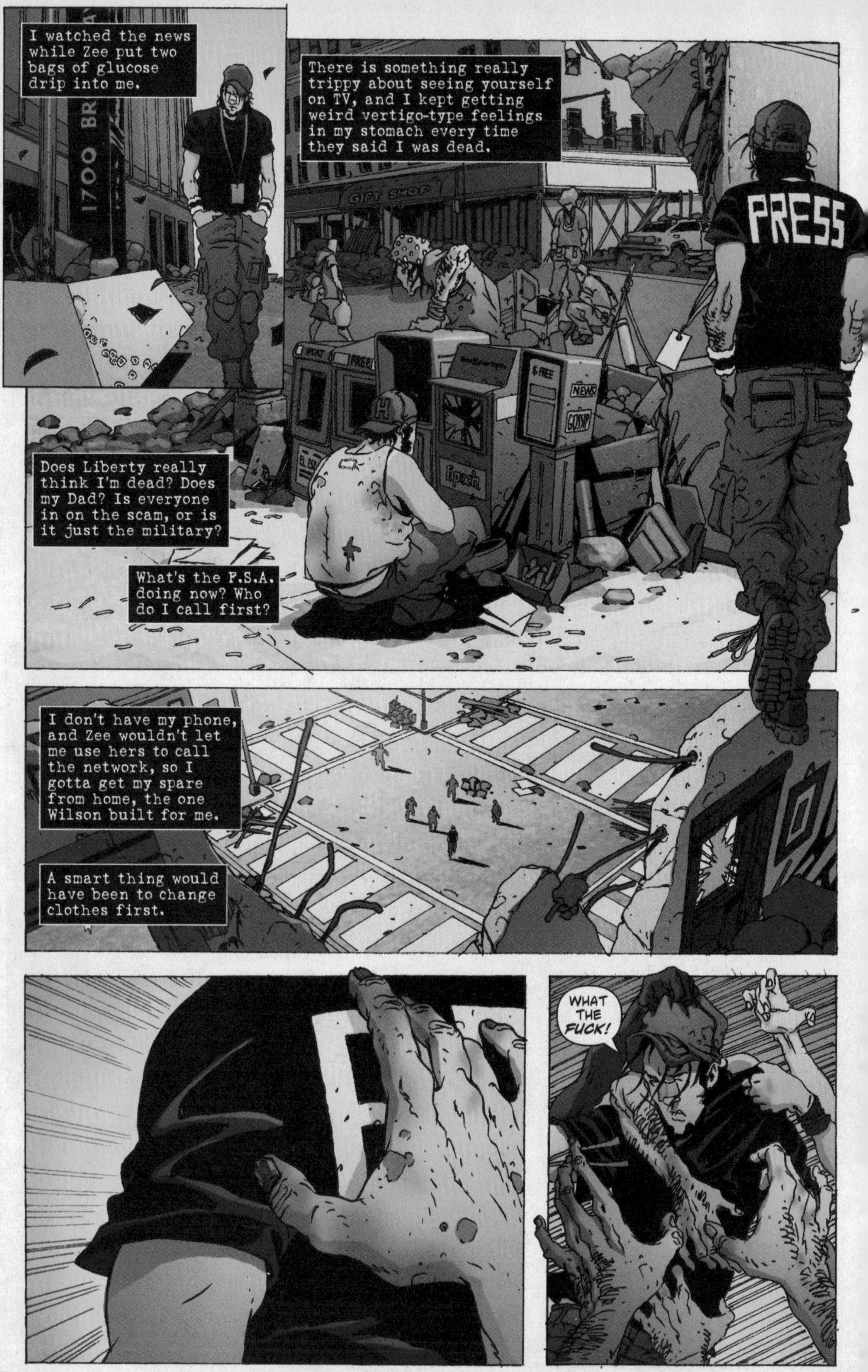
I watched the news while Zee put two bags of glucose drip into me.
1700 BR
There is something really trippy about seeing yourself on TV, and I kept getting weird vertigo-type feelings in my stomach every time they said I was dead.
GIFT SHOP
PRESS
Does Liberty really think I'm dead? Does my Dad? Is everyone in on the scam, or is it just the military?
What's the F.S.A. doing now? Who do I call first?
I don't have my phone, and Zee wouldn't let me use hers to call the network, so I gotta get my spare from home, the one Wilson built for me.
A smart thing would have been to change clothes first.
WHAT THE FUCK!

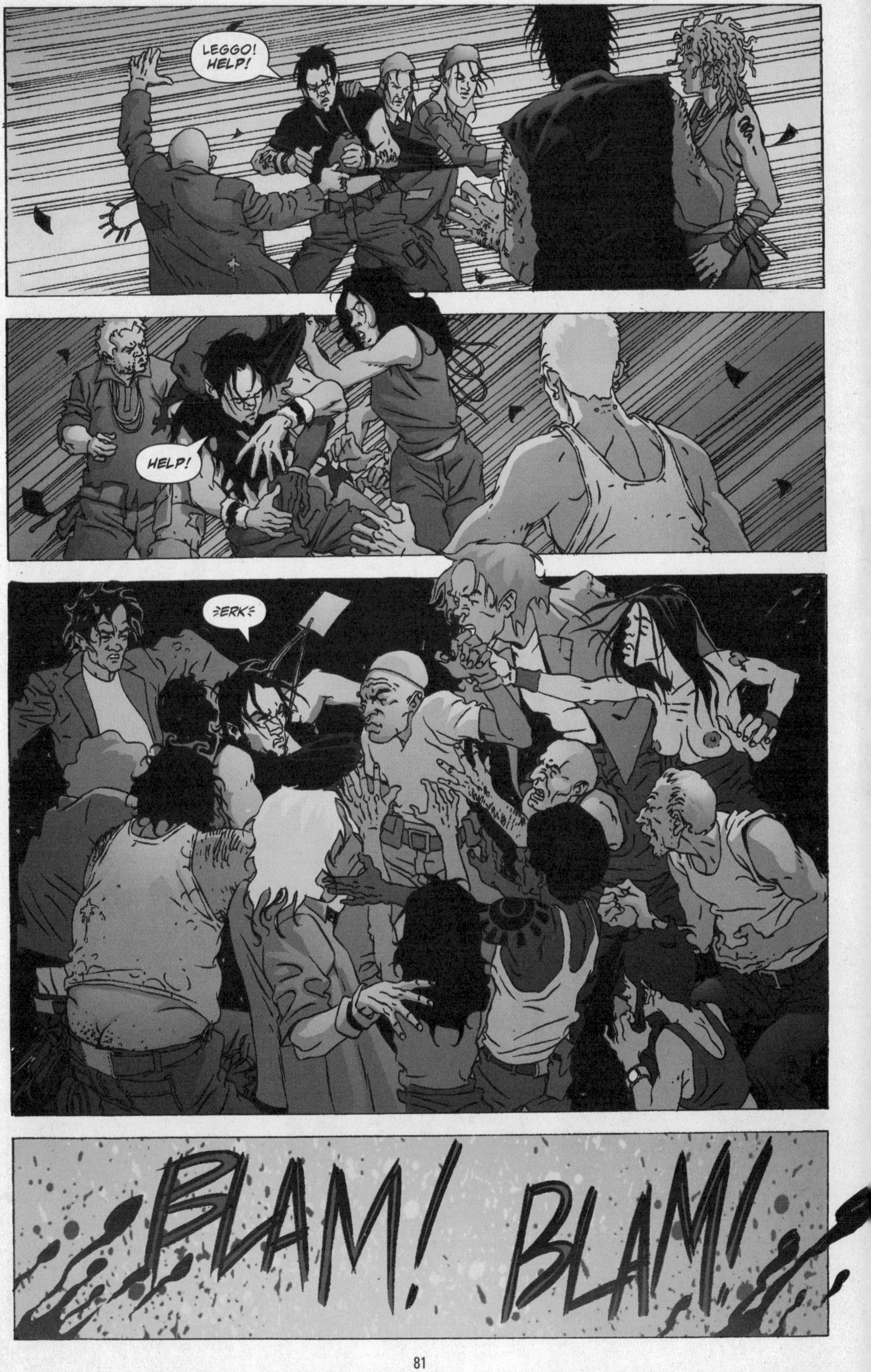
LEGGO! HELP!
HELP!
ERK
BLAM! BLAM!

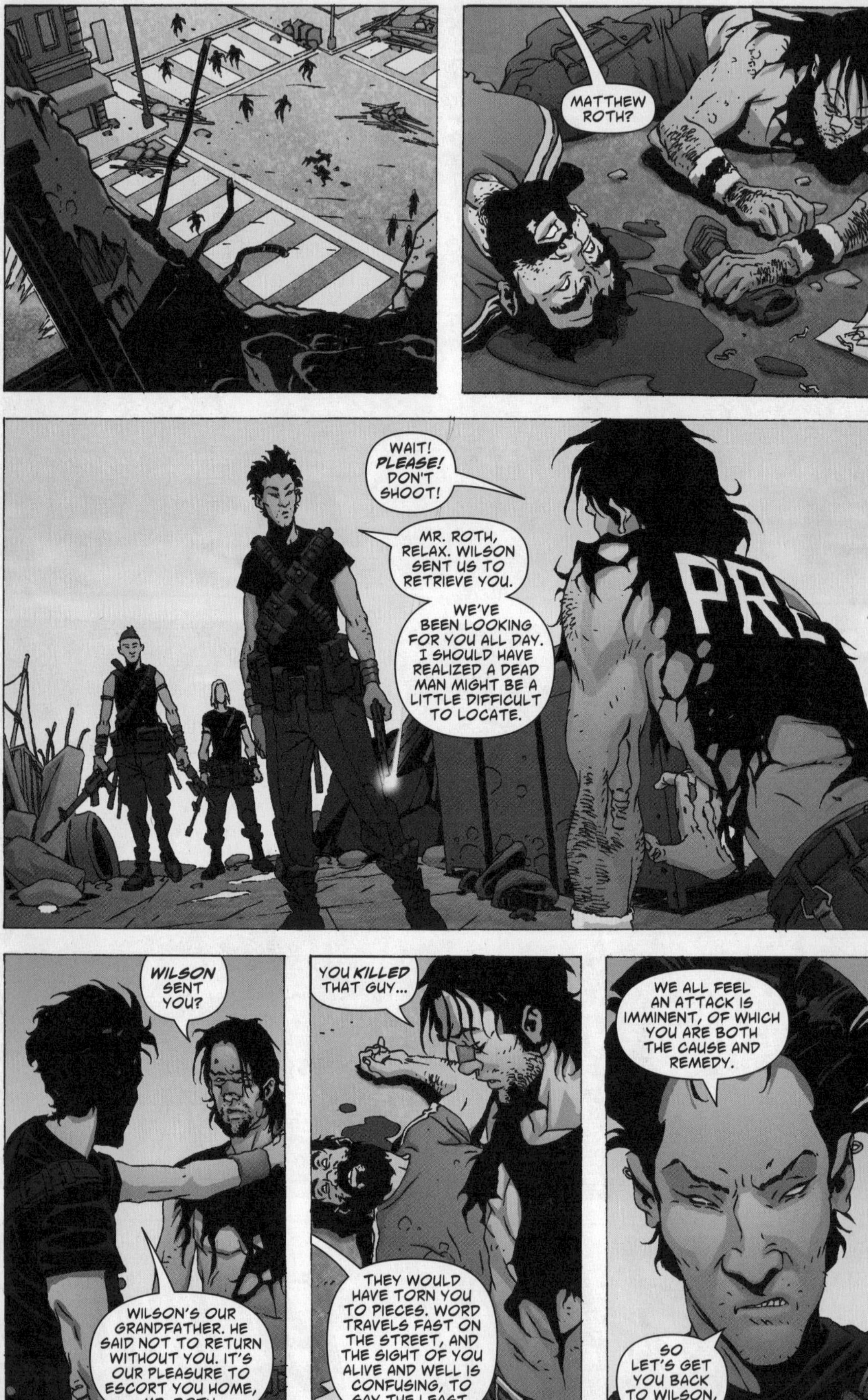

MATTHEW ROTH?
WAIT! PLEASE! DON'T SHOOT!
MR. ROTH, RELAX. WILSON SENT US TO RETRIEVE YOU.
WE'VE BEEN LOOKING FOR YOU ALL DAY. I SHOULD HAVE REALIZED A DEAD MAN MIGHT BE A LITTLE DIFFICULT TO LOCATE.
PRE
WILSON SENT YOU?
WILSON'S OUR GRANDFATHER. HE SAID NOT TO RETURN WITHOUT YOU. IT'S OUR PLEASURE TO ESCORT YOU HOME, MR. ROTH.
YOU KILLED THAT GUY...
THEY WOULD HAVE TORN YOU TO PIECES. WORD TRAVELS FAST ON THE STREET, AND THE SIGHT OF YOU ALIVE AND WELL IS CONFUSING, TO SAY THE LEAST.
WE ALL FEEL AN ATTACK IS IMMINENT, OF WHICH YOU ARE BOTH THE CAUSE AND REMEDY.
SO LET'S GET YOU BACK TO WILSON, OKAY?

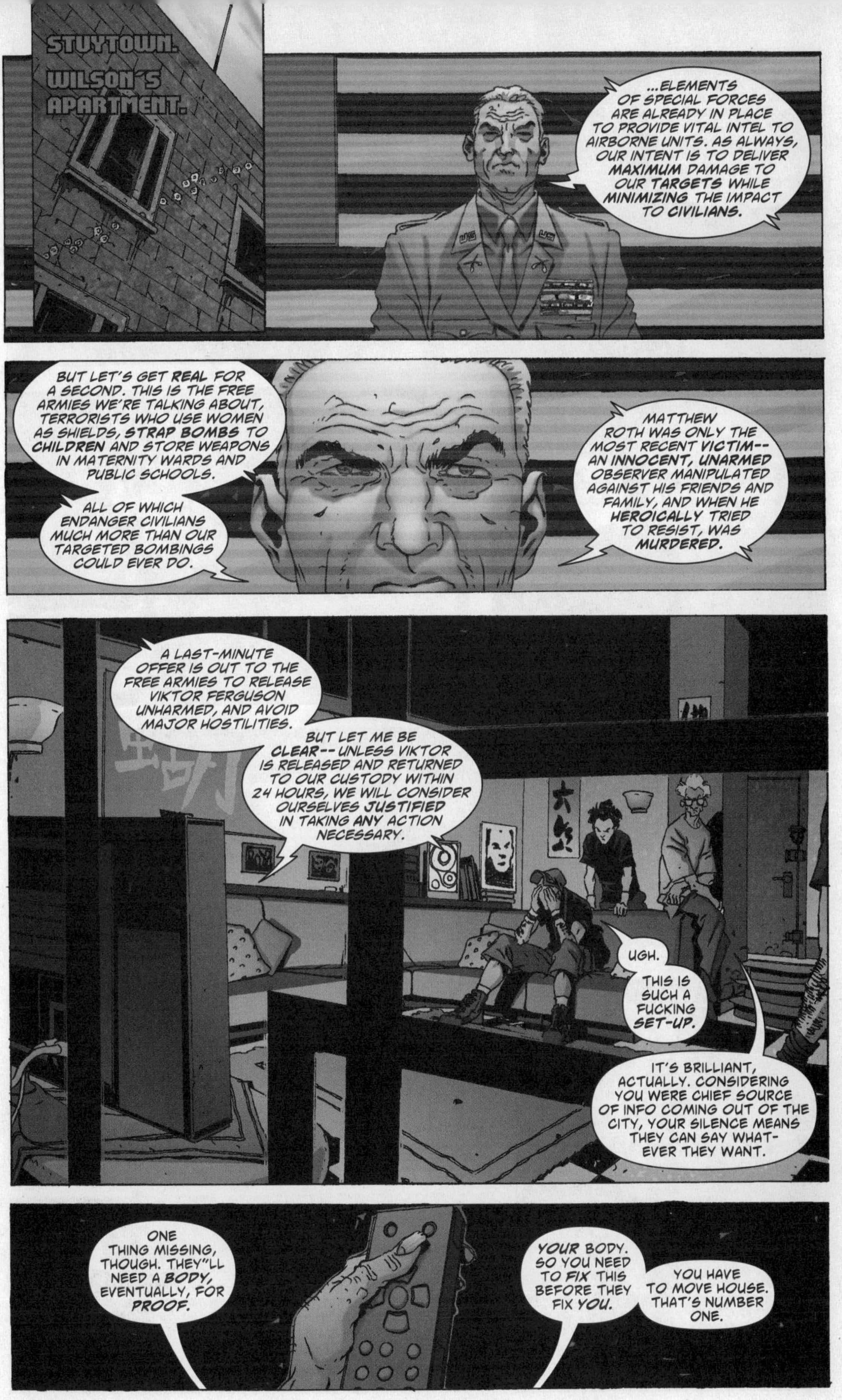
STUYTOWN.
WILSON'S APARTMENT.
...ELEMENTS OF SPECIAL FORCES ARE ALREADY IN PLACE TO PROVIDE VITAL INTEL TO AIRBORNE UNITS. AS ALWAYS, OUR INTENT IS TO DELIVER MAXIMUM DAMAGE TO OUR TARGETS WHILE MINIMIZING THE IMPACT TO CIVILIANS.
BUT LET'S GET REAL FOR A SECOND. THIS IS THE FREE ARMIES WE'RE TALKING ABOUT, TERRORISTS WHO USE WOMEN AS SHIELDS, STRAP BOMBS TO CHILDREN AND STORE WEAPONS IN MATERNITY WARDS AND PUBLIC SCHOOLS.
ALL OF WHICH ENDANGER CIVILIANS MUCH MORE THAN OUR TARGETED BOMBINGS COULD EVER DO.
MATTHEW ROTH WAS ONLY THE MOST RECENT VICTIM-- AN INNOCENT, UNARMED OBSERVER MANIPULATED AGAINST HIS FRIENDS AND FAMILY, AND WHEN HE HEROICALLY TRIED TO RESIST, WAS MURDERED.
A LAST-MINUTE OFFER IS OUT TO THE FREE ARMIES TO RELEASE VIKTOR FERGUSON UNHARMED, AND AVOID MAJOR HOSTILITIES.
BUT LET ME BE CLEAR-- UNLESS VIKTOR IS RELEASED AND RETURNED TO OUR CUSTODY WITHIN 24 HOURS, WE WILL CONSIDER OURSELVES JUSTIFIED IN TAKING ANY ACTION NECESSARY.
UGH.
THIS IS SUCH A FUCKING SET-UP.
IT'S BRILLIANT, ACTUALLY. CONSIDERING YOU WERE CHIEF SOURCE OF INFO COMING OUT OF THE CITY, YOUR SILENCE MEANS THEY CAN SAY WHAT-EVER THEY WANT.
ONE THING MISSING, THOUGH. THEY'LL NEED A BODY, EVENTUALLY, FOR PROOF.
YOUR BODY. SO YOU NEED TO FIX THIS BEFORE THEY FIX YOU.
YOU HAVE TO MOVE HOUSE. THAT'S NUMBER ONE.

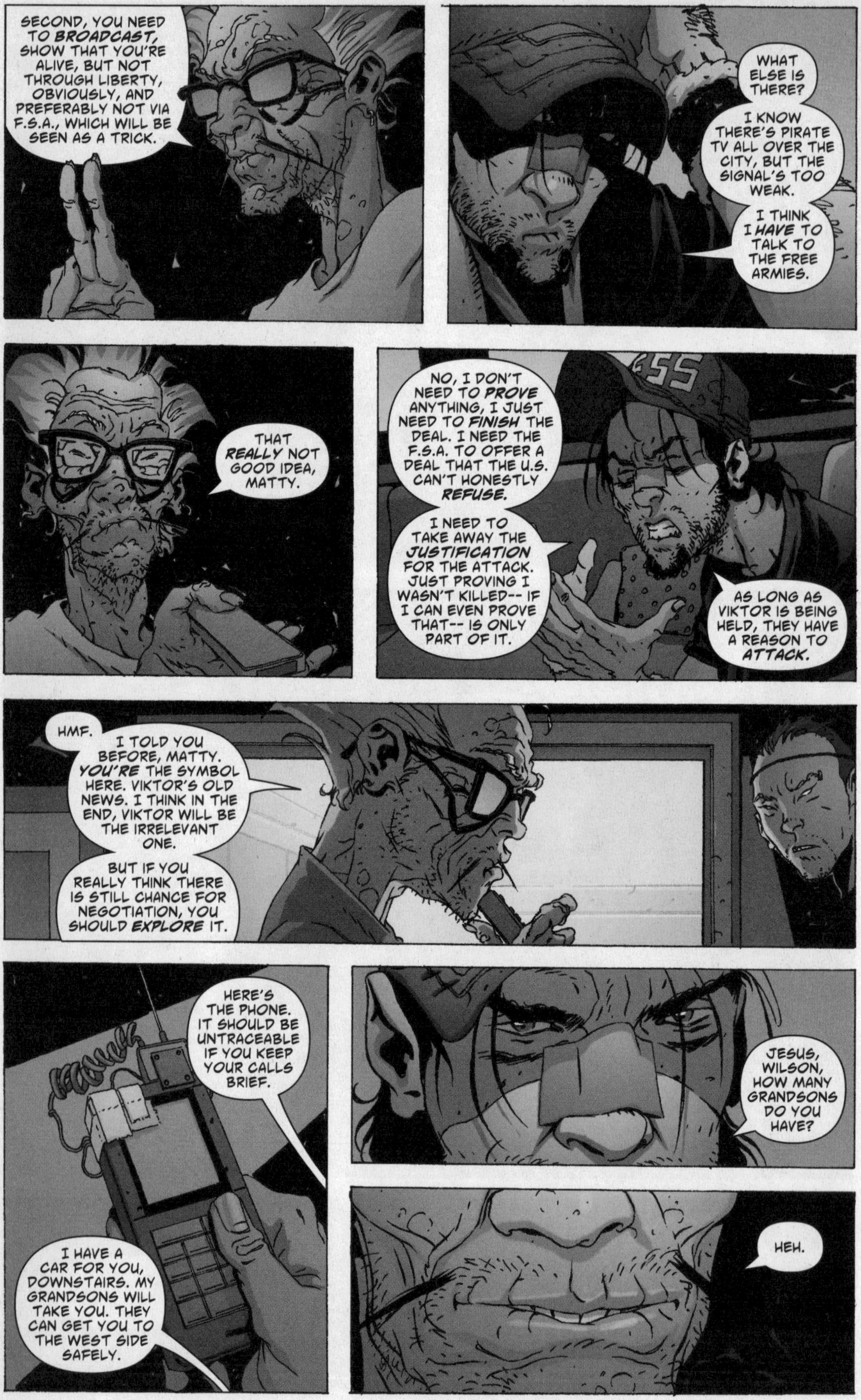
SECOND, YOU NEED TO BROADCAST, SHOW THAT YOU'RE ALIVE, BUT NOT THROUGH LIBERTY, OBVIOUSLY, AND PREFERABLY NOT VIA F.S.A., WHICH WILL BE SEEN AS A TRICK.
WHAT ELSE IS THERE?
I KNOW THERE'S PIRATE TV ALL OVER THE CITY, BUT THE SIGNAL'S TOO WEAK.
I THINK I HAVE TO TALK TO THE FREE ARMIES.
THAT REALLY NOT GOOD IDEA, MATTY.
NO, I DON'T NEED TO PROVE ANYTHING, I JUST NEED TO FINISH THE DEAL. I NEED THE F.S.A. TO OFFER A DEAL THAT THE U.S. CAN'T HONESTLY REFUSE.
I NEED TO TAKE AWAY THE JUSTIFICATION FOR THE ATTACK. JUST PROVING I WASN'T KILLED-- IF I CAN EVEN PROVE THAT-- IS ONLY PART OF IT.
AS LONG AS VIKTOR IS BEING HELD, THEY HAVE A REASON TO ATTACK.
HMF.
I TOLD YOU BEFORE, MATTY. YOU'RE THE SYMBOL HERE. VIKTOR'S OLD NEWS. I THINK IN THE END, VIKTOR WILL BE THE IRRELEVANT ONE.
BUT IF YOU REALLY THINK THERE IS STILL CHANCE FOR NEGOTIATION, YOU SHOULD EXPLORE IT.
HERE'S THE PHONE. IT SHOULD BE UNTRACEABLE IF YOU KEEP YOUR CALLS BRIEF.
I HAVE A CAR FOR YOU, DOWNSTAIRS. MY GRANDSONS WILL TAKE YOU. THEY CAN GET YOU TO THE WEST SIDE SAFELY.
JESUS, WILSON, HOW MANY GRANDSONS DO YOU HAVE?
HEH.

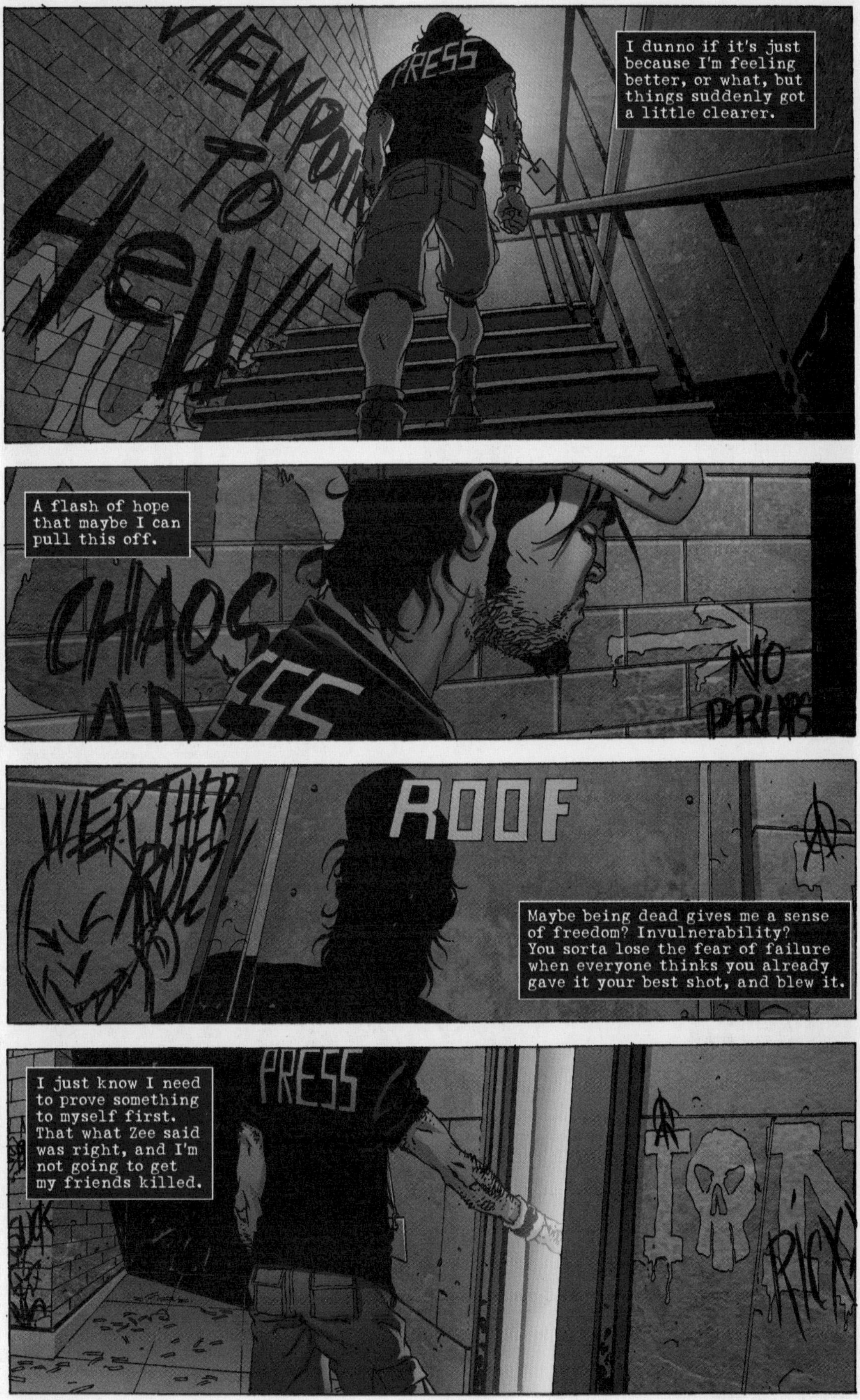
PRESS
TO
I dunno if it's just because I'm feeling better, or what, but things suddenly got a little clearer.
A flash of hope that maybe I can pull this off.
CHAOS
NO
ROOF
Maybe being dead gives me a sense of freedom? Invulnerability? You sorta lose the fear of failure when everyone thinks you already gave it your best shot, and blew it.
PRESS
I just know I need to prove something to myself first. That what Zee said was right, and I'm not going to get my friends killed.

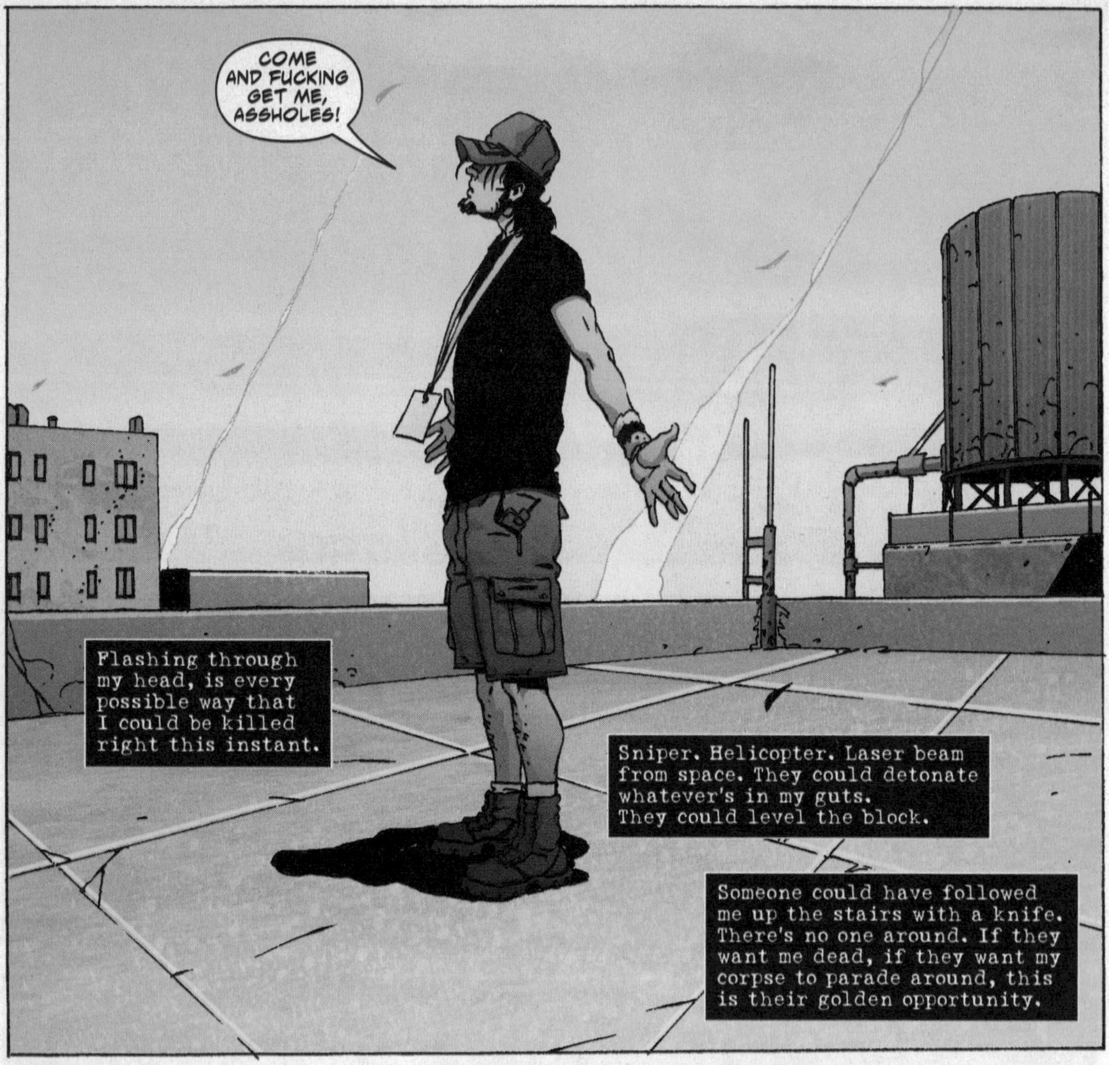
COME AND FUCKING GET ME, ASSHOLES!
Flashing through my head, is every possible way that I could be killed right this instant.
Sniper. Helicopter. Laser beam from space. They could detonate whatever's in my guts. They could level the block.
Someone could have followed me up the stairs with a knife. There's no one around. If they want me dead, if they want my corpse to parade around, this is their golden opportunity.

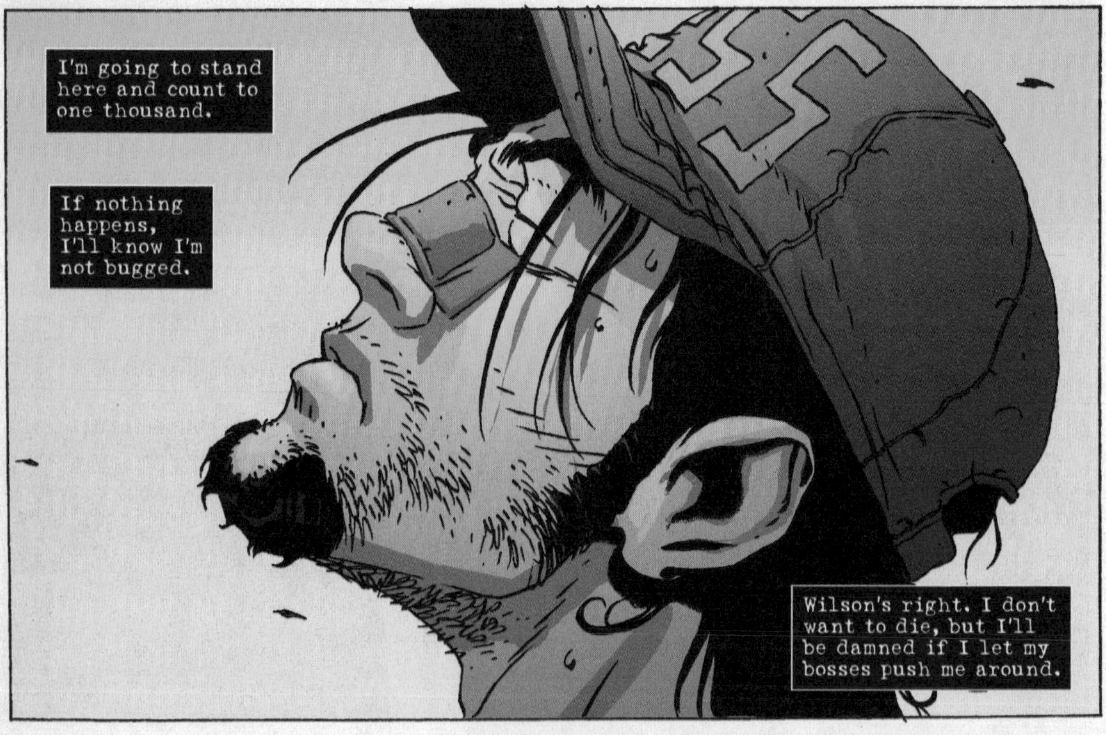
I'm going to stand here and count to one thousand.
If nothing happens, I'll know I'm not bugged.
Wilson's right. I don't want to die, but I'll be damned if I let my bosses push me around.

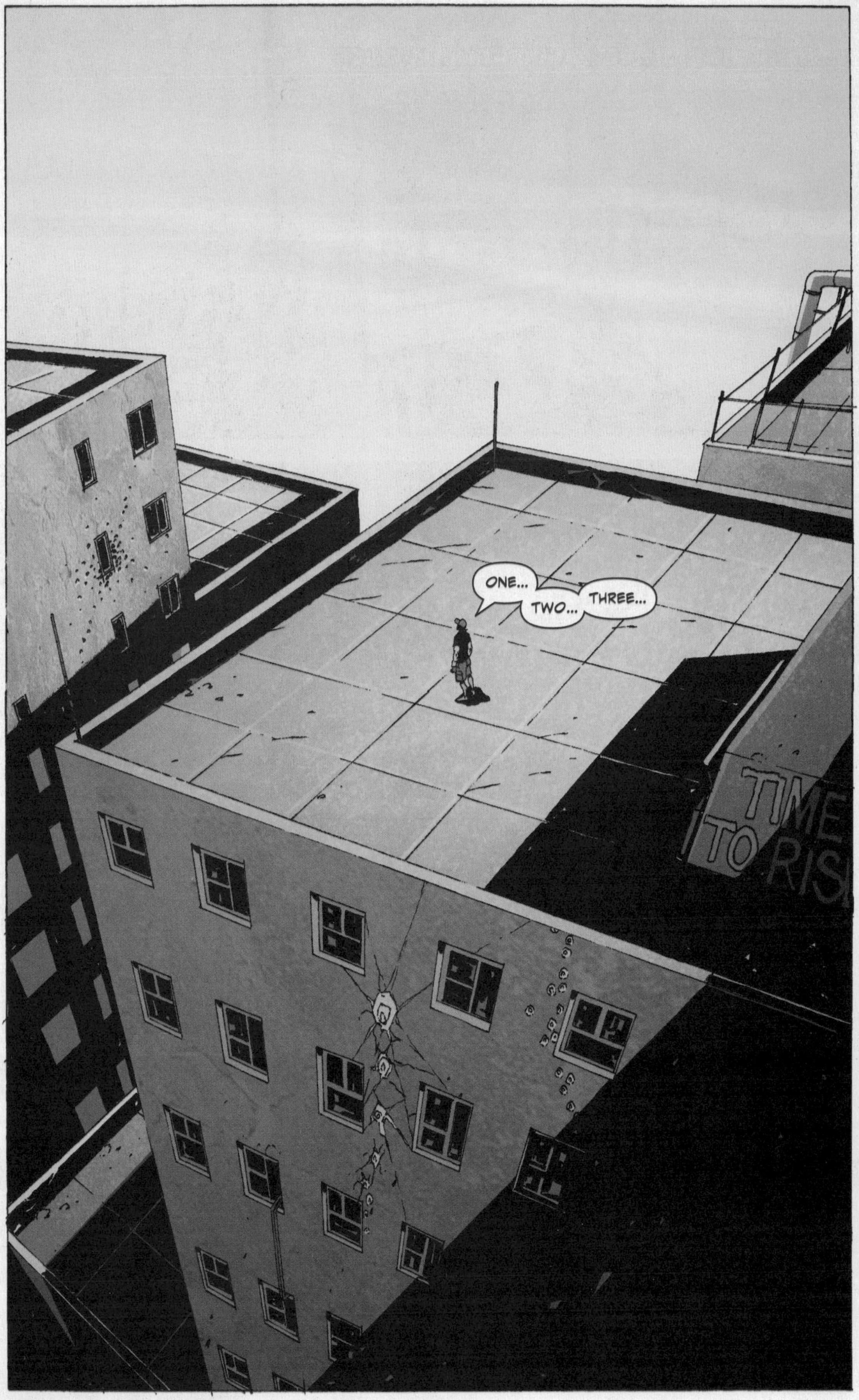
ONE...
TWO...
THREE...
TIME
TO RIS

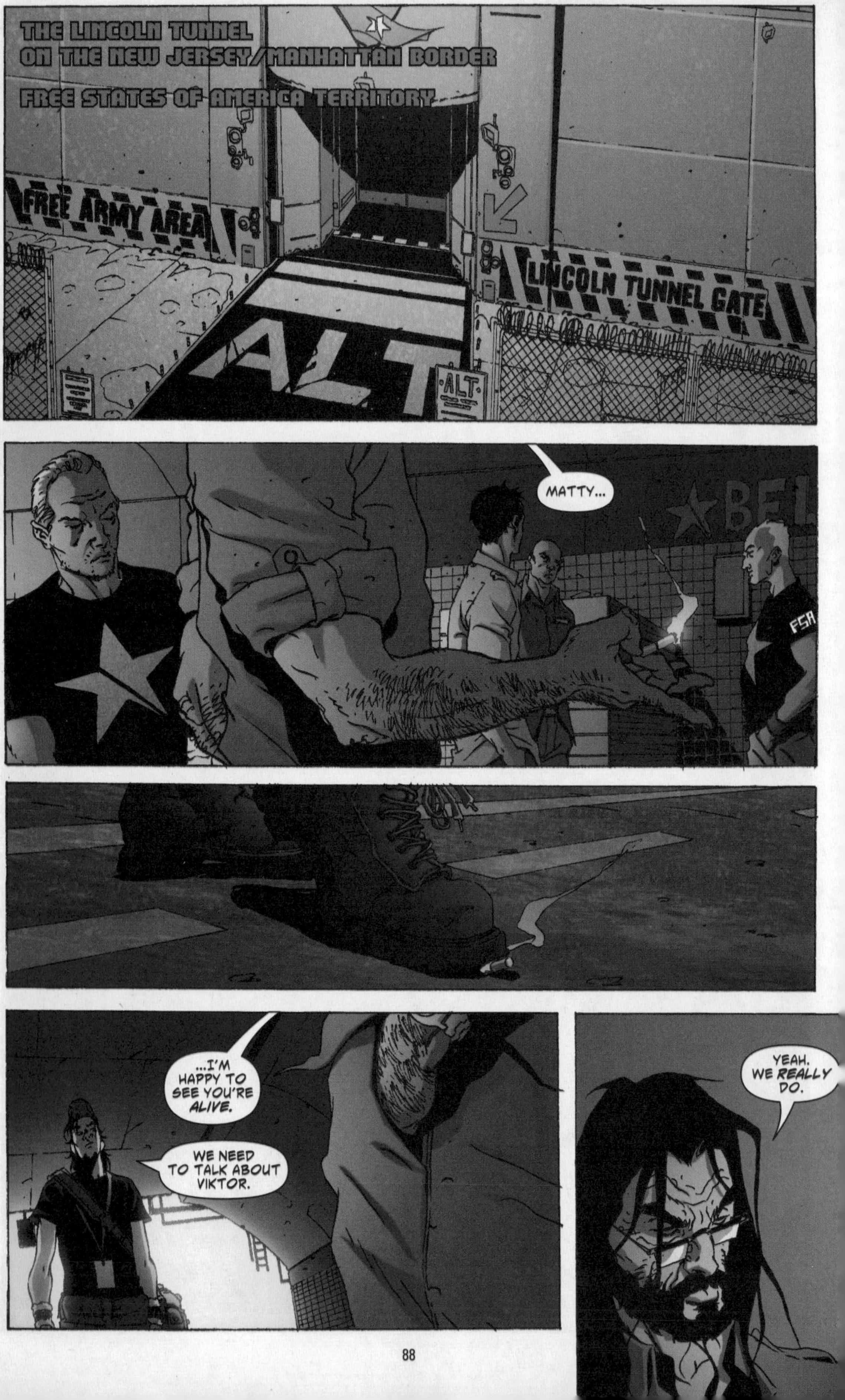
THE LINCOLN TUNNEL
ON THE NEW JERSEY/MANHATTAN BORDER
FREE STATES OF AMERICA TERRITORY
FREE ARMY AREA
LINCOLN TUNNEL GATE
ALT
ALT
MATTY...
FSA
...I'M HAPPY TO SEE YOU'RE *ALIVE.*
WE NEED TO TALK ABOUT VIKTOR.
YEAH. WE *REALLY* DO.

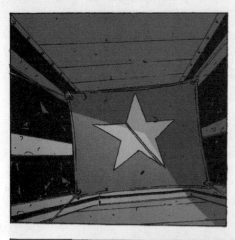

I DON'T GET IT. HOW THE *FUCK* DO YOU LOSE A GUY YOU HAVE LOCKED UP IN THE BACK OF A TRUCK?

WE HAVE A *TRAITOR,* IT SEEMS.

WE KNOW HE'S BEEN MISSING FOR APPROXIMATELY THIRTY MINUTES, WHICH MEANS HE COULD ALREADY BE ACROSS THE EAST RIVER.

BUT RIGHT NOW I'M LESS CONCERNED WITH THE LOSS OF OUR BARGAINING CHIP AND MORE CONCERNED WITH GETTING *HIT.*

ESPECIALLY NOW IF IT'S FOR *NO* REASON.

SO WHAT THE *FUCK* DO WE DO? I NEED TO PROVE VIKTOR'S ALIVE AND PROVE *I'M* ALIVE. I JUST DON'T KNOW HOW...

HOLD ON.

BEEP BEEP BEEP

LOAD UP! WE HAVE A SIGHTING ON HOUSTON AND VARICK! TWO VEHICLES, LET'S GO!

YOU *UP* FOR IT?

HELL YEAH.

PRESS

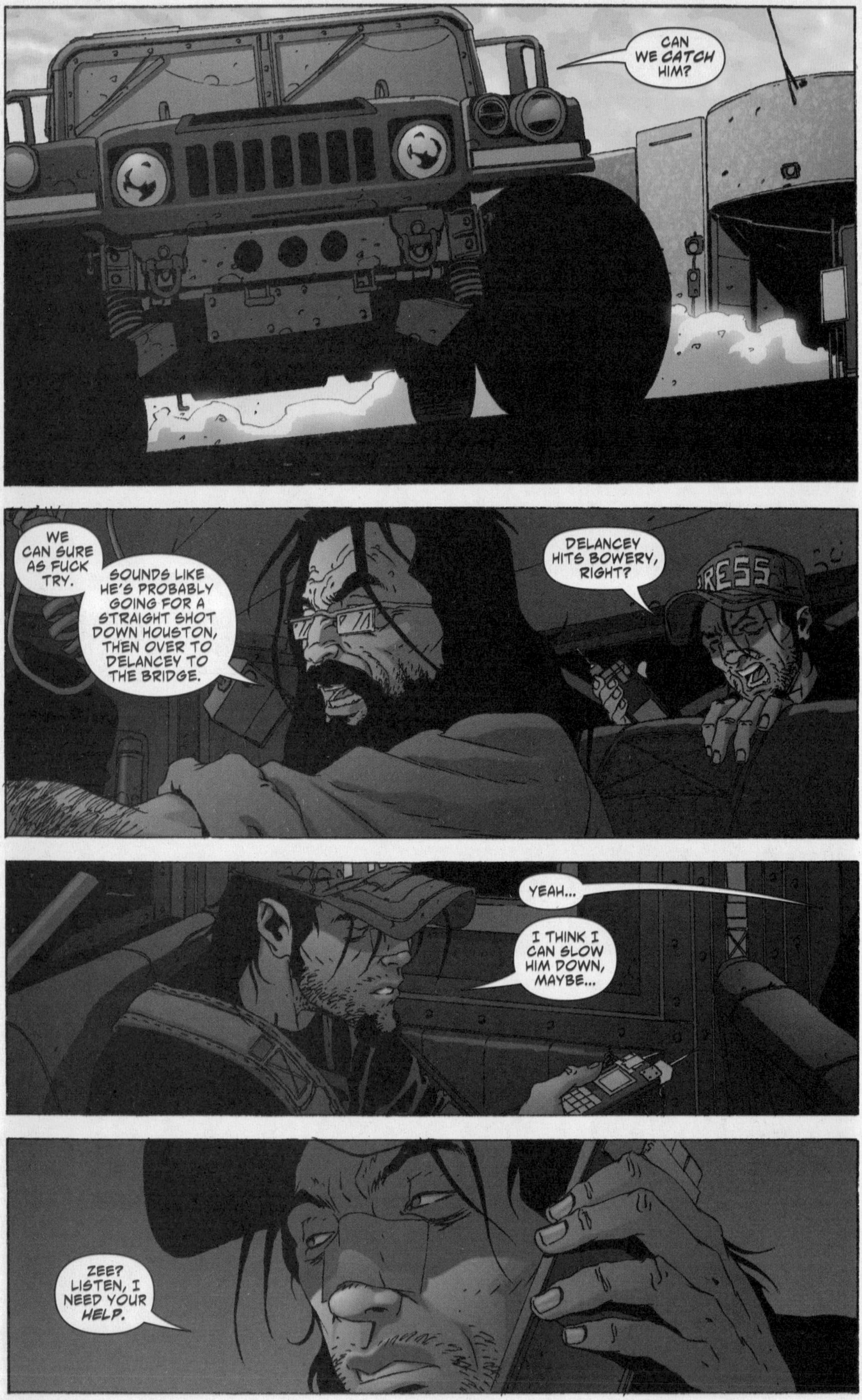
CAN WE CATCH HIM?
WE CAN SURE AS FUCK TRY.
SOUNDS LIKE HE'S PROBABLY GOING FOR A STRAIGHT SHOT DOWN HOUSTON, THEN OVER TO DELANCEY TO THE BRIDGE.
DELANCEY HITS BOWERY, RIGHT?
PRESS
YEAH...
I THINK I CAN SLOW HIM DOWN, MAYBE...
ZEE? LISTEN, I NEED YOUR HELP.

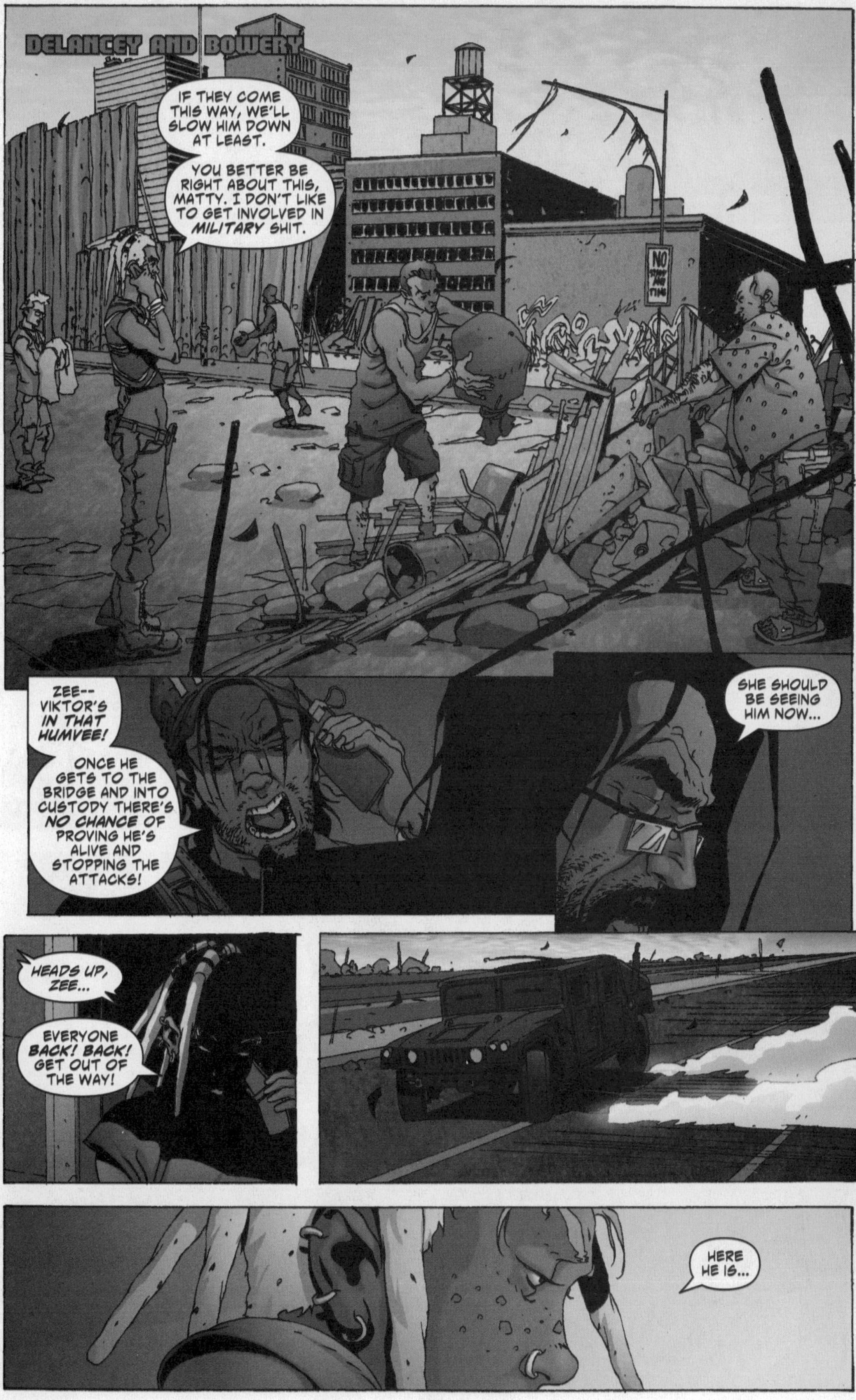
DELANCEY AND BOWERY
IF THEY COME THIS WAY, WE'LL SLOW HIM DOWN AT LEAST.
YOU BETTER BE RIGHT ABOUT THIS, MATTY. I DON'T LIKE TO GET INVOLVED IN MILITARY SHIT.
ZEE-- VIKTOR'S IN THAT HUMVEE!
ONCE HE GETS TO THE BRIDGE AND INTO CUSTODY THERE'S NO CHANCE OF PROVING HE'S ALIVE AND STOPPING THE ATTACKS!
SHE SHOULD BE SEEING HIM NOW...
HEADS UP, ZEE...
EVERYONE BACK! BACK! GET OUT OF THE WAY!
HERE HE IS...

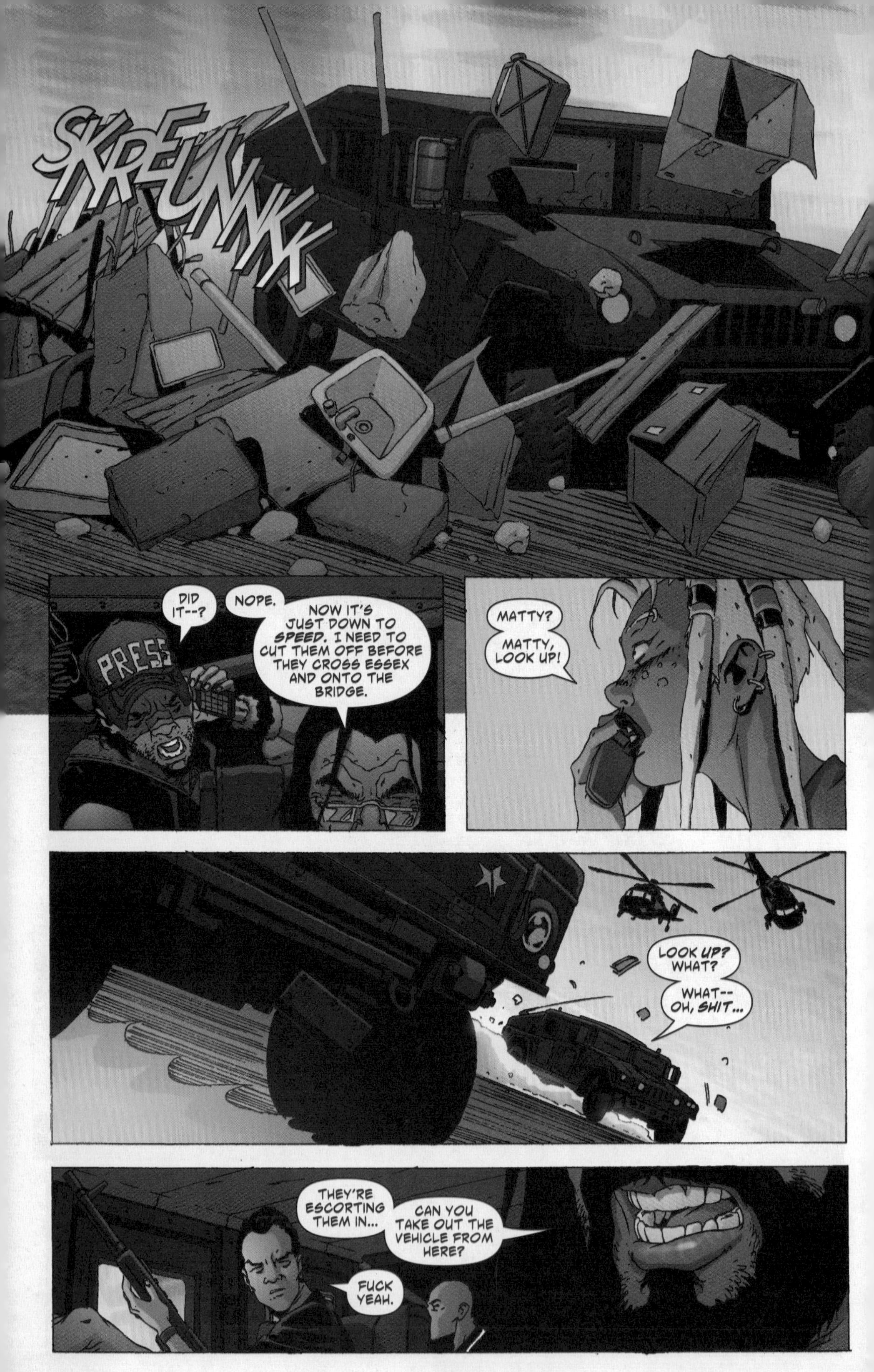
SKREUNNKK
DID IT--?
NOPE.
NOW IT'S JUST DOWN TO SPEED. I NEED TO CUT THEM OFF BEFORE THEY CROSS ESSEX AND ONTO THE BRIDGE.
MATTY?
MATTY, LOOK UP!
LOOK UP? WHAT?
WHAT-- OH, SHIT...
THEY'RE ESCORTING THEM IN...
CAN YOU TAKE OUT THE VEHICLE FROM HERE?
FUCK YEAH.

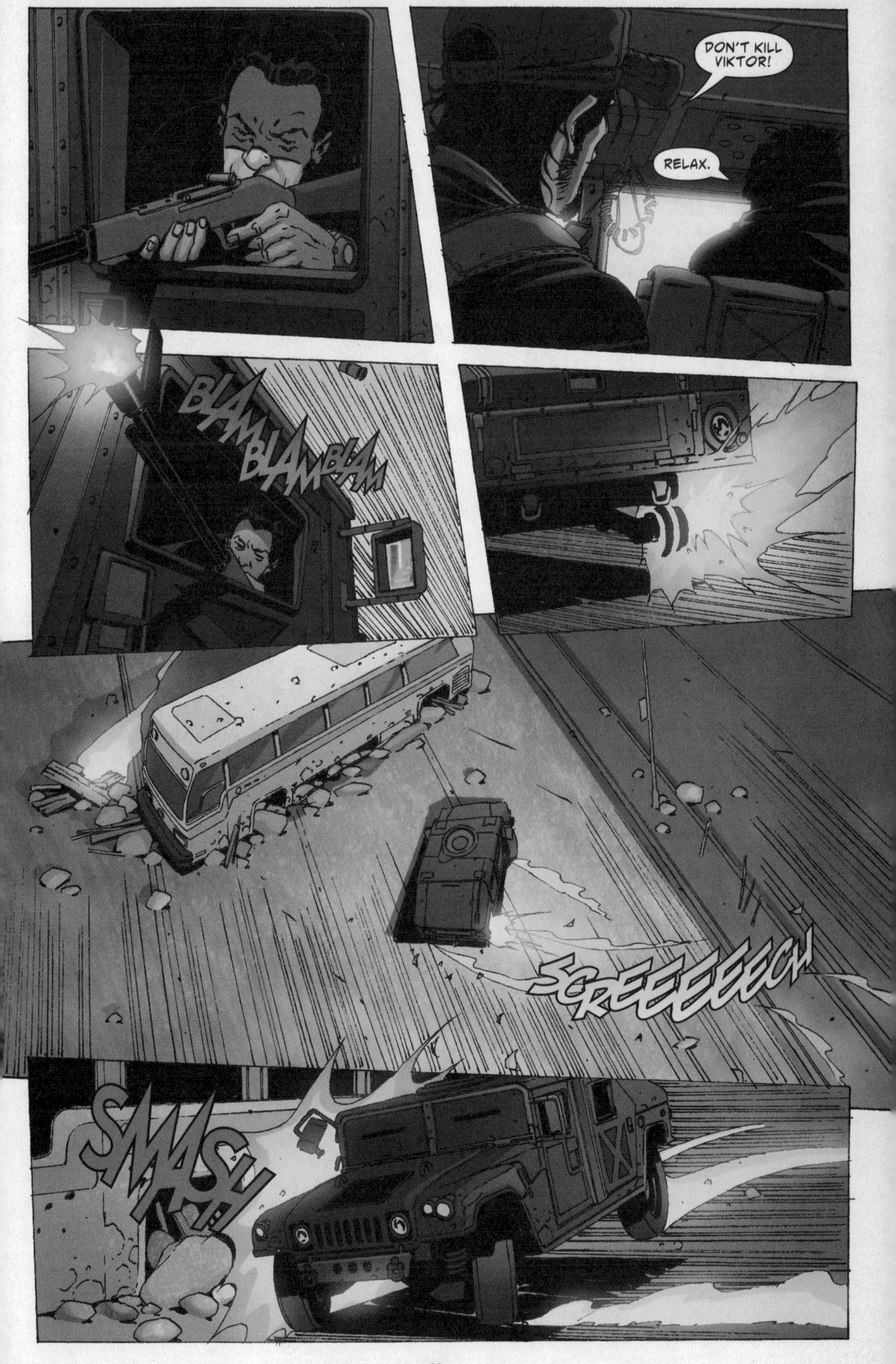
DON'T KILL VIKTOR!
RELAX.
BLAM BLAM BLAM BLAM
SCREEEEEECH
SMASH

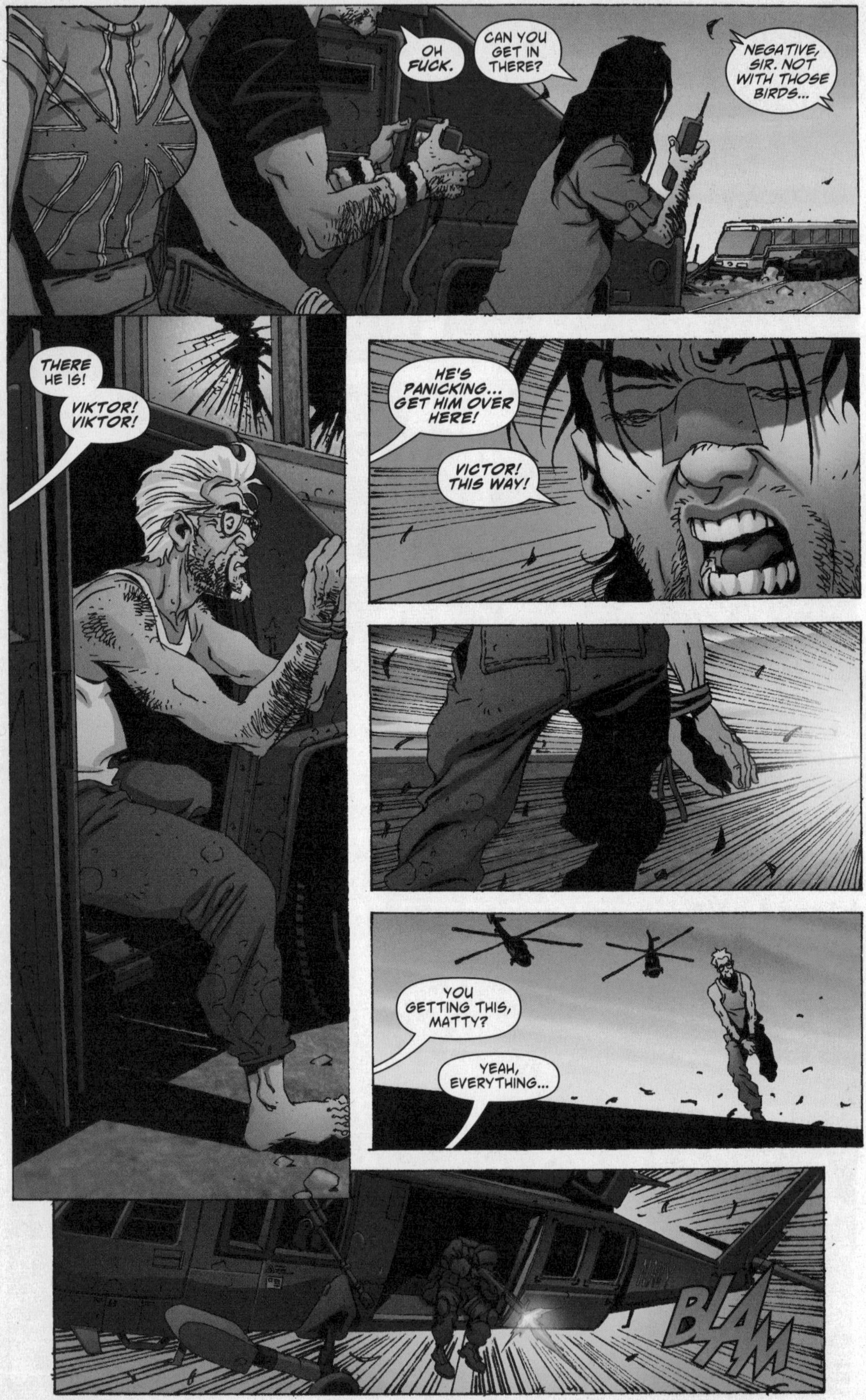
OH FUCK.
CAN YOU GET IN THERE?
NEGATIVE, SIR. NOT WITH THOSE BIRDS...
THERE HE IS!
VIKTOR! VIKTOR!
HE'S PANICKING... GET HIM OVER HERE!
VICTOR! THIS WAY!
YOU GETTING THIS, MATTY?
YEAH, EVERYTHING...
BLAM

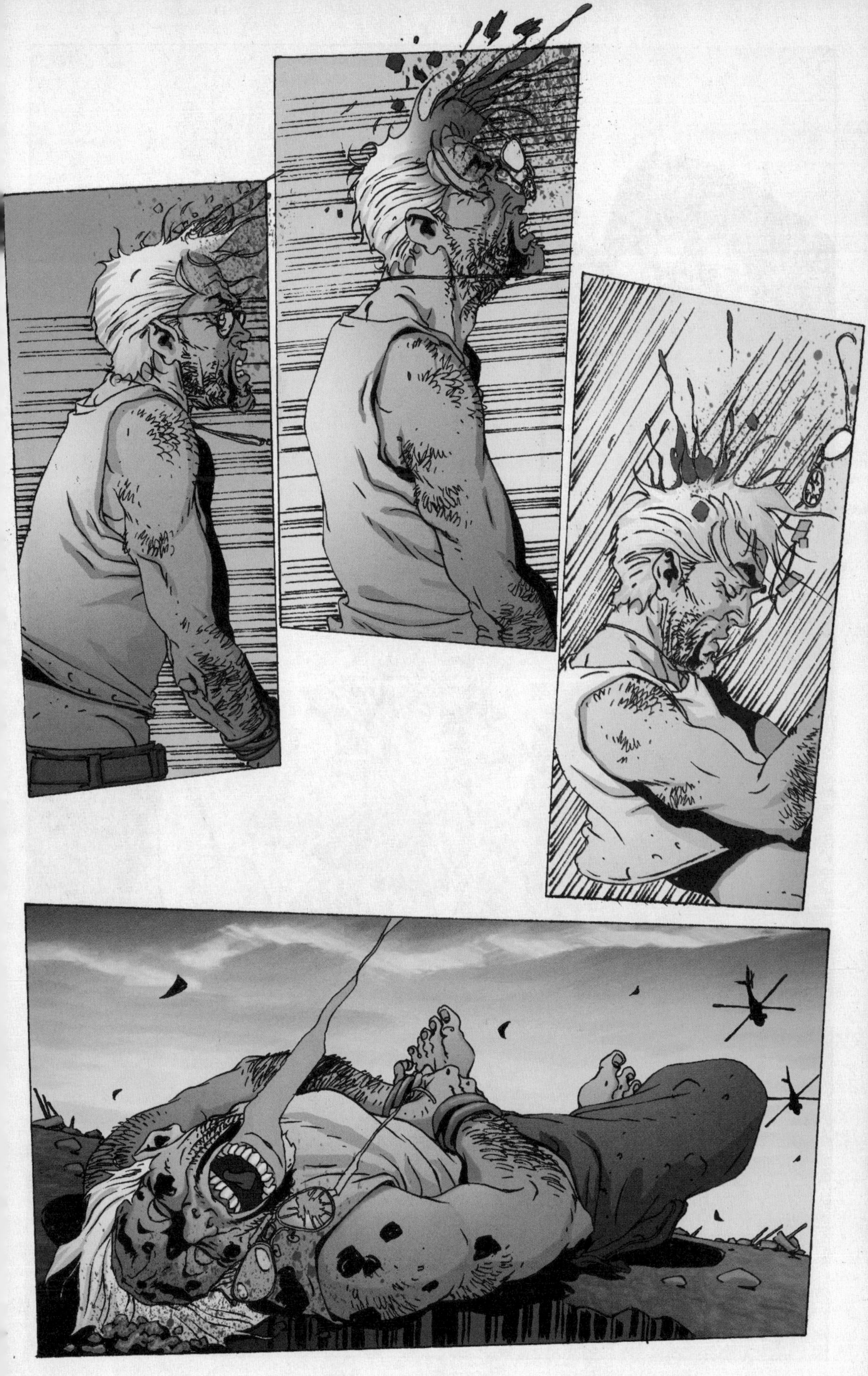

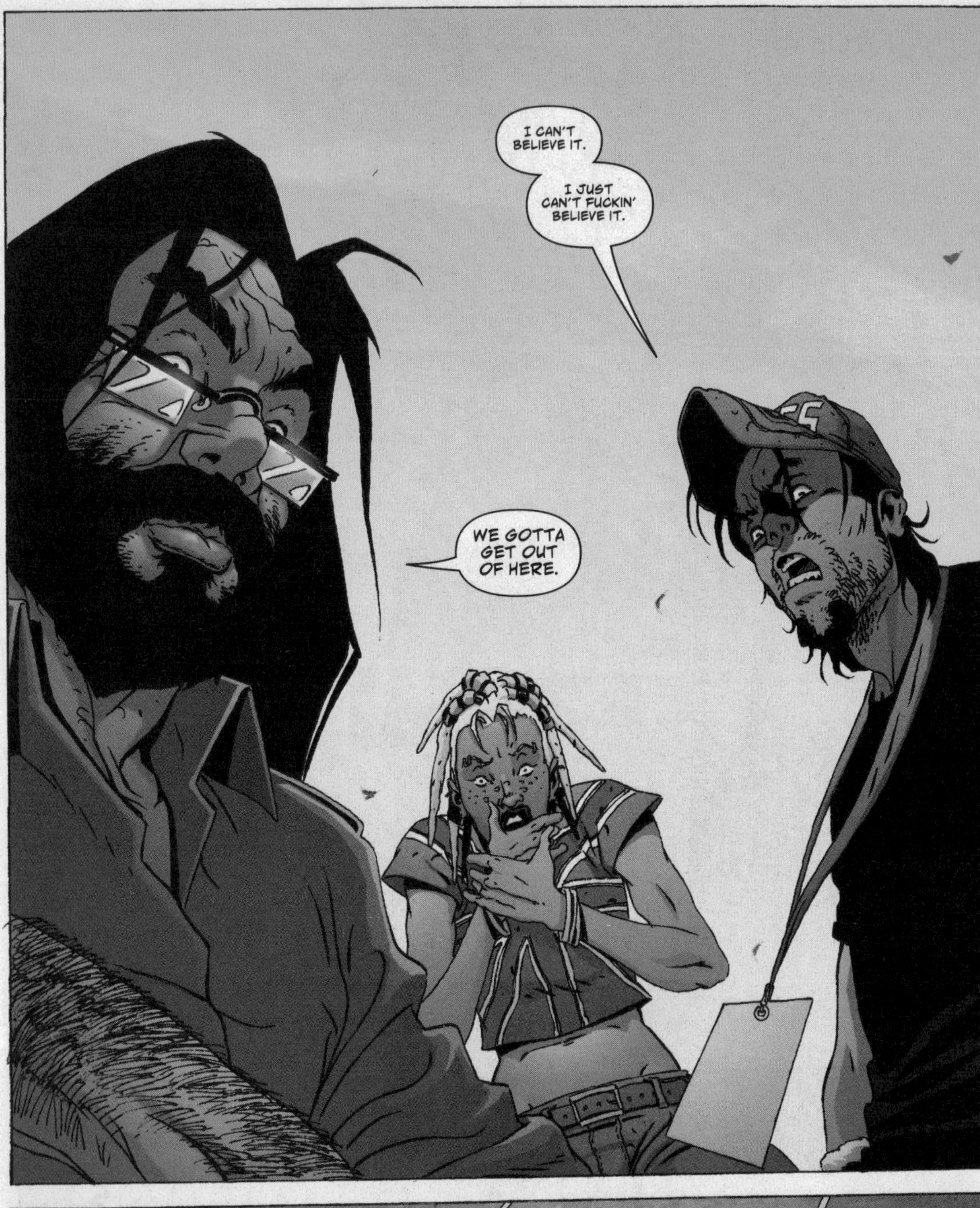
I CAN'T BELIEVE IT.
I JUST CAN'T FUCKIN' BELIEVE IT.
WE GOTTA GET OUT OF HERE.

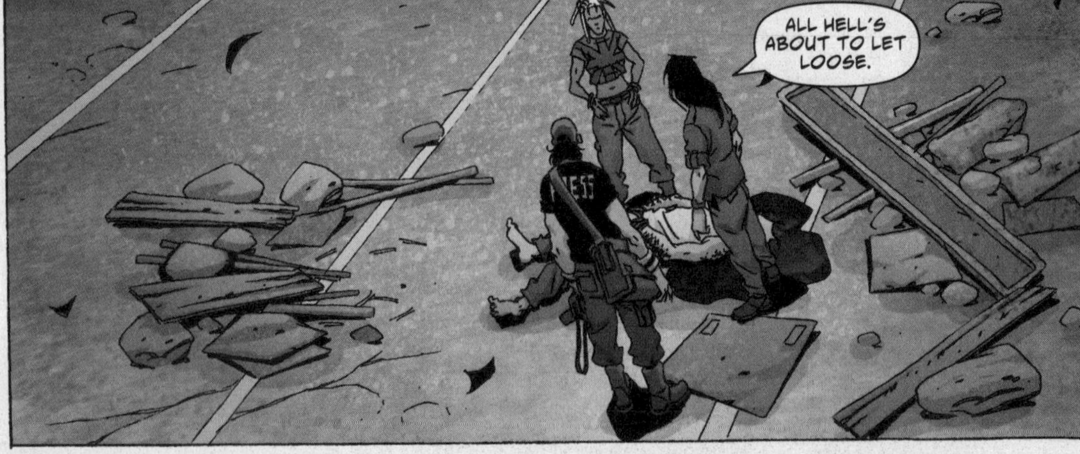
ALL HELL'S ABOUT TO LET LOOSE.

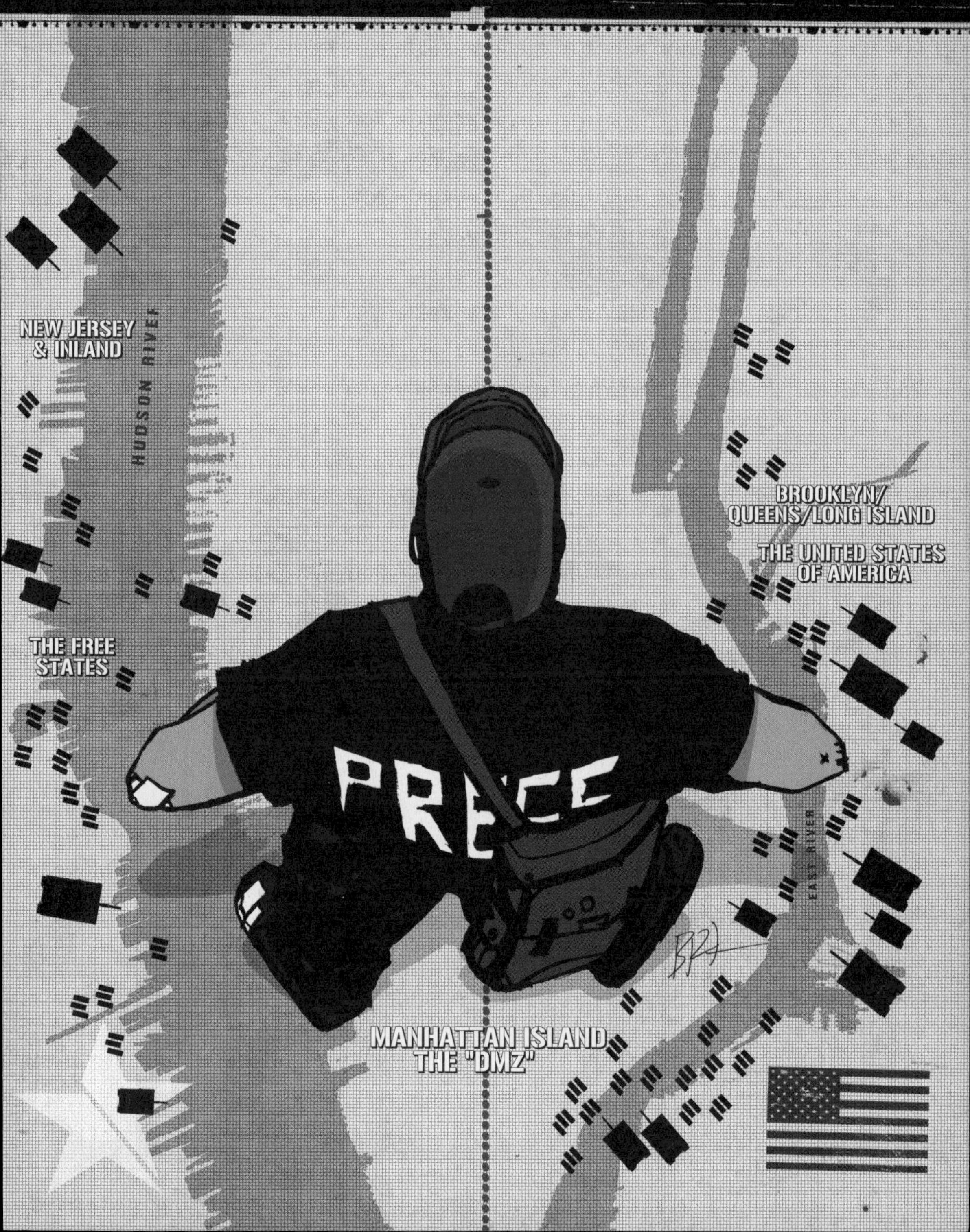
NEW JERSEY
& INLAND
HUDSON RIVER
THE FREE
STATES
PRESS
BROOKLYN/
QUEENS/LONG ISLAND
THE UNITED STATES
OF AMERICA
EAST RIVER
MANHATTAN ISLAND
THE "DMZ"

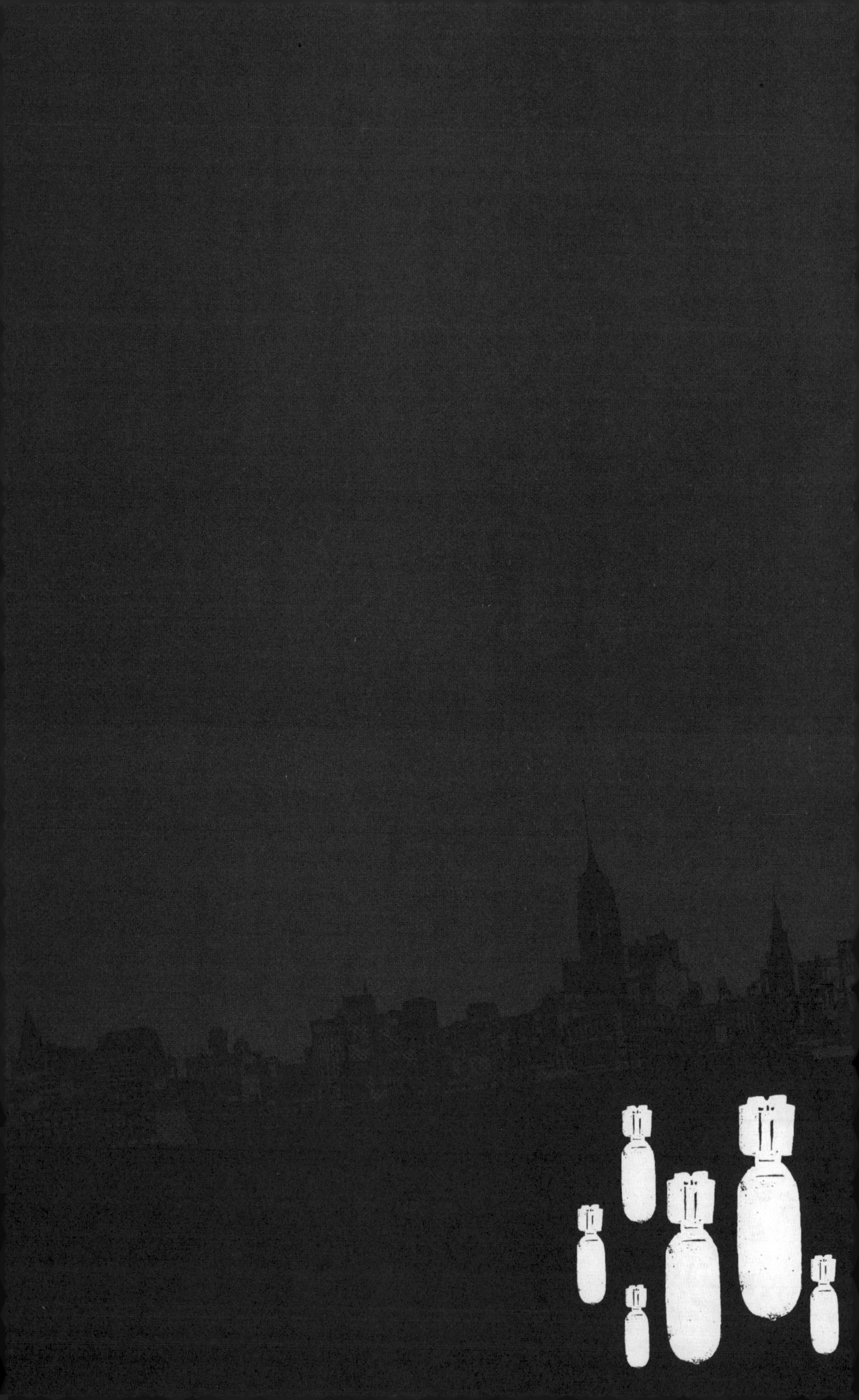

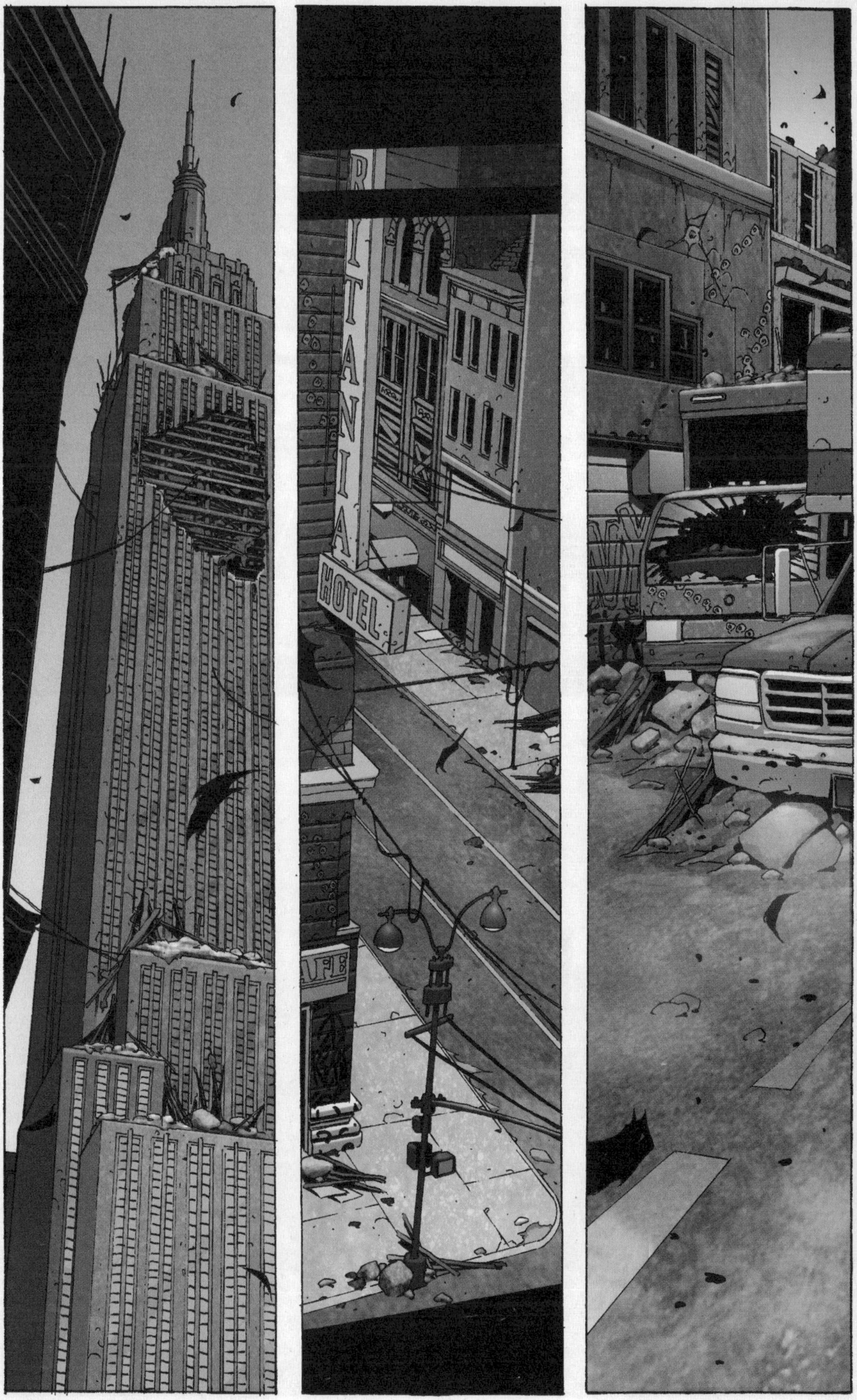

HOTEL
CAFE

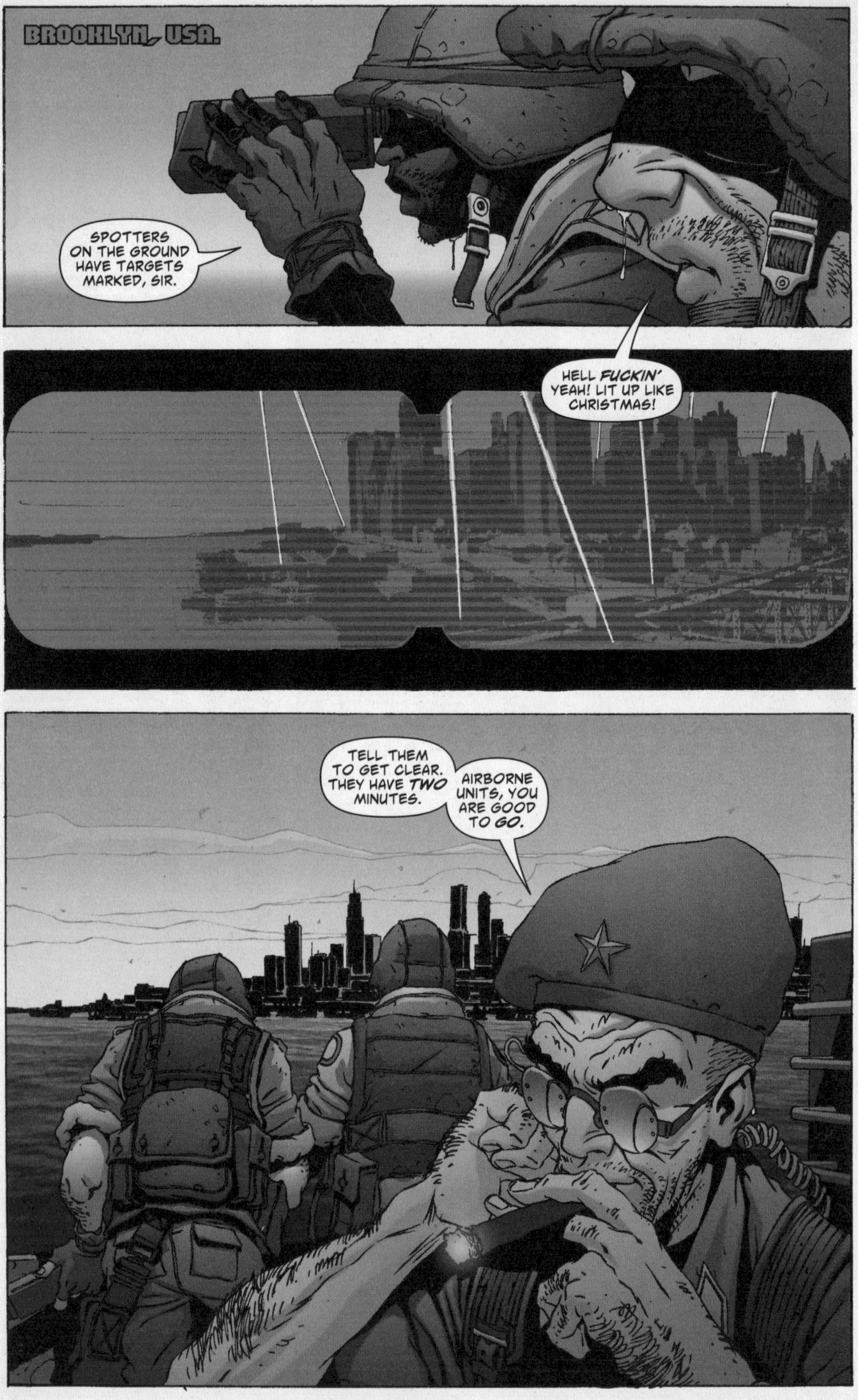
BROOKLYN, USA.
SPOTTERS ON THE GROUND HAVE TARGETS MARKED, SIR.
HELL FUCKIN' YEAH! LIT UP LIKE CHRISTMAS!
TELL THEM TO GET CLEAR. THEY HAVE TWO MINUTES.
AIRBORNE UNITS, YOU ARE GOOD TO GO.

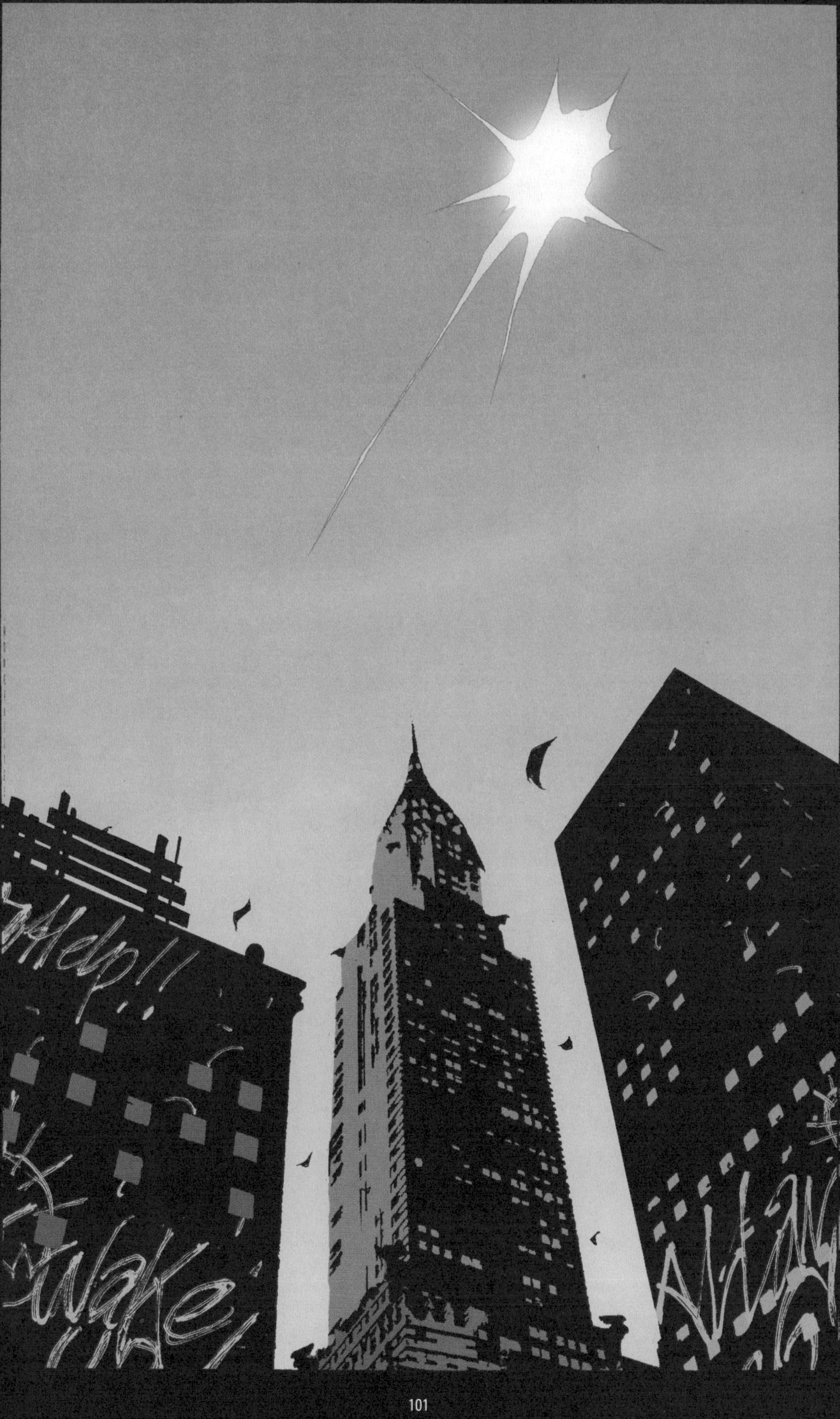
Help!!
Wake

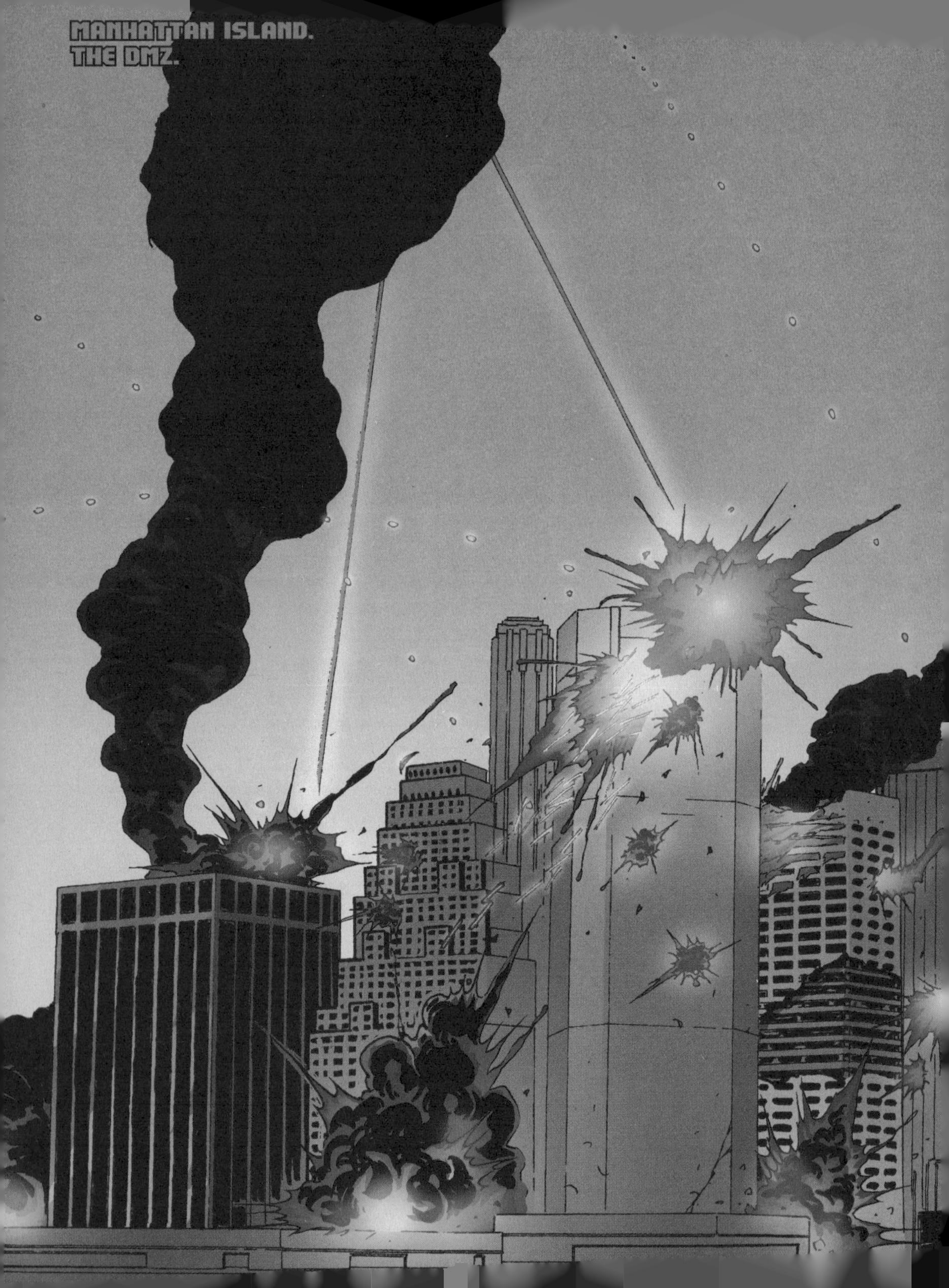
MANHATTAN ISLAND.
THE DMZ.

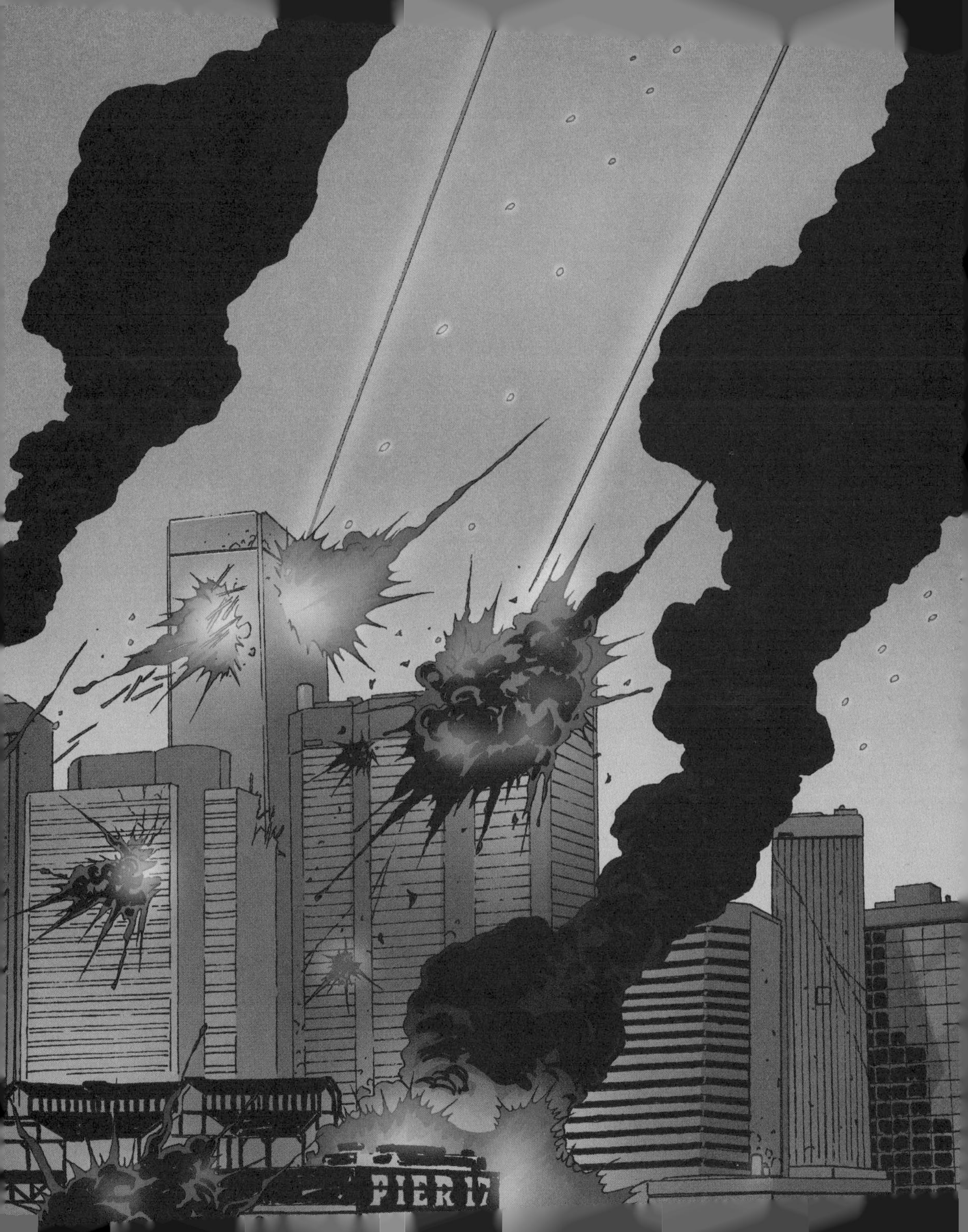
PIER 17

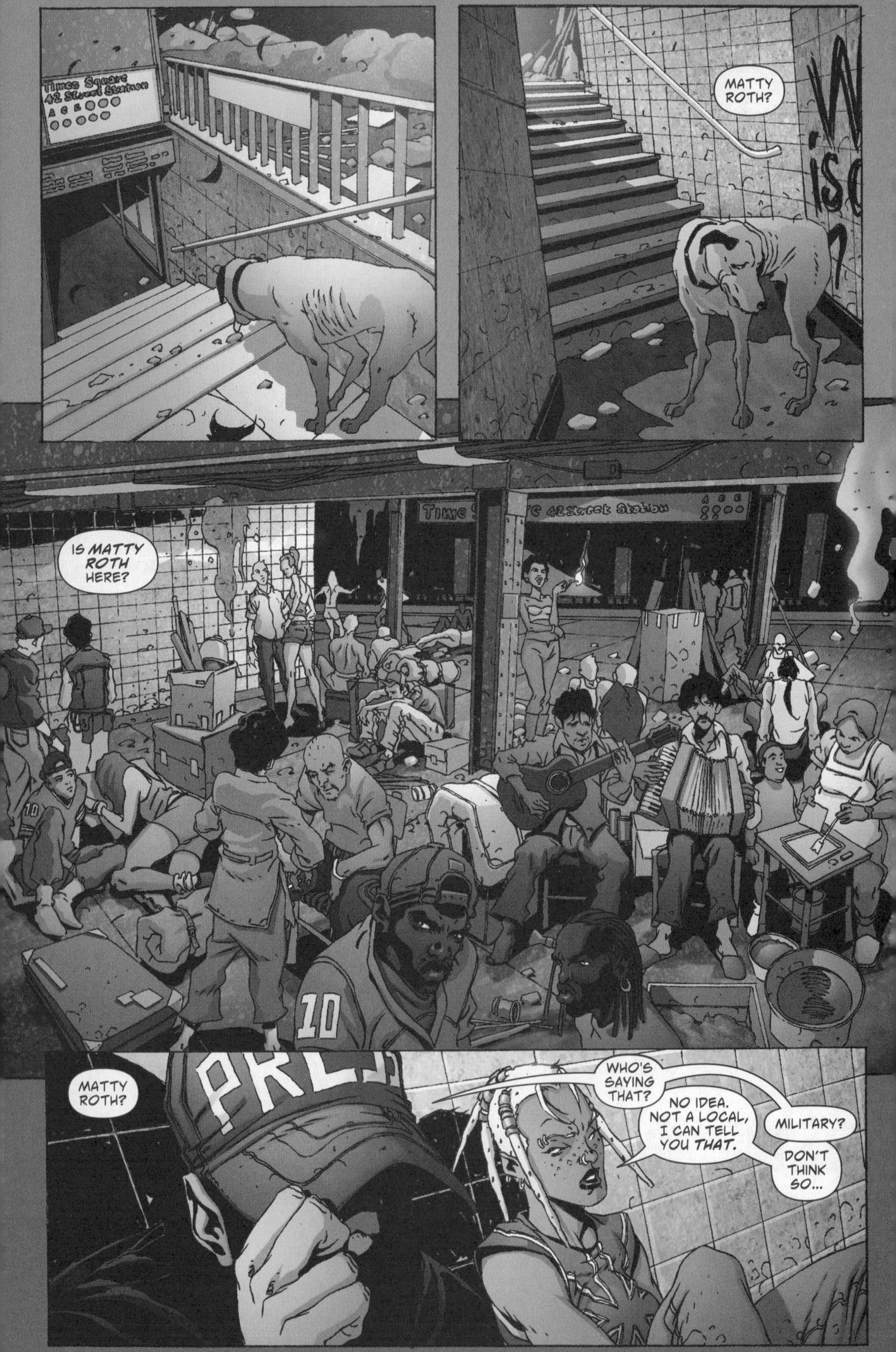
Times Square
42 Street Station
MATTY ROTH?
IS MATTY ROTH HERE?
MATTY ROTH?
WHO'S SAYING THAT?
NO IDEA. NOT A LOCAL, I CAN TELL YOU THAT.
MILITARY?
DON'T THINK SO...

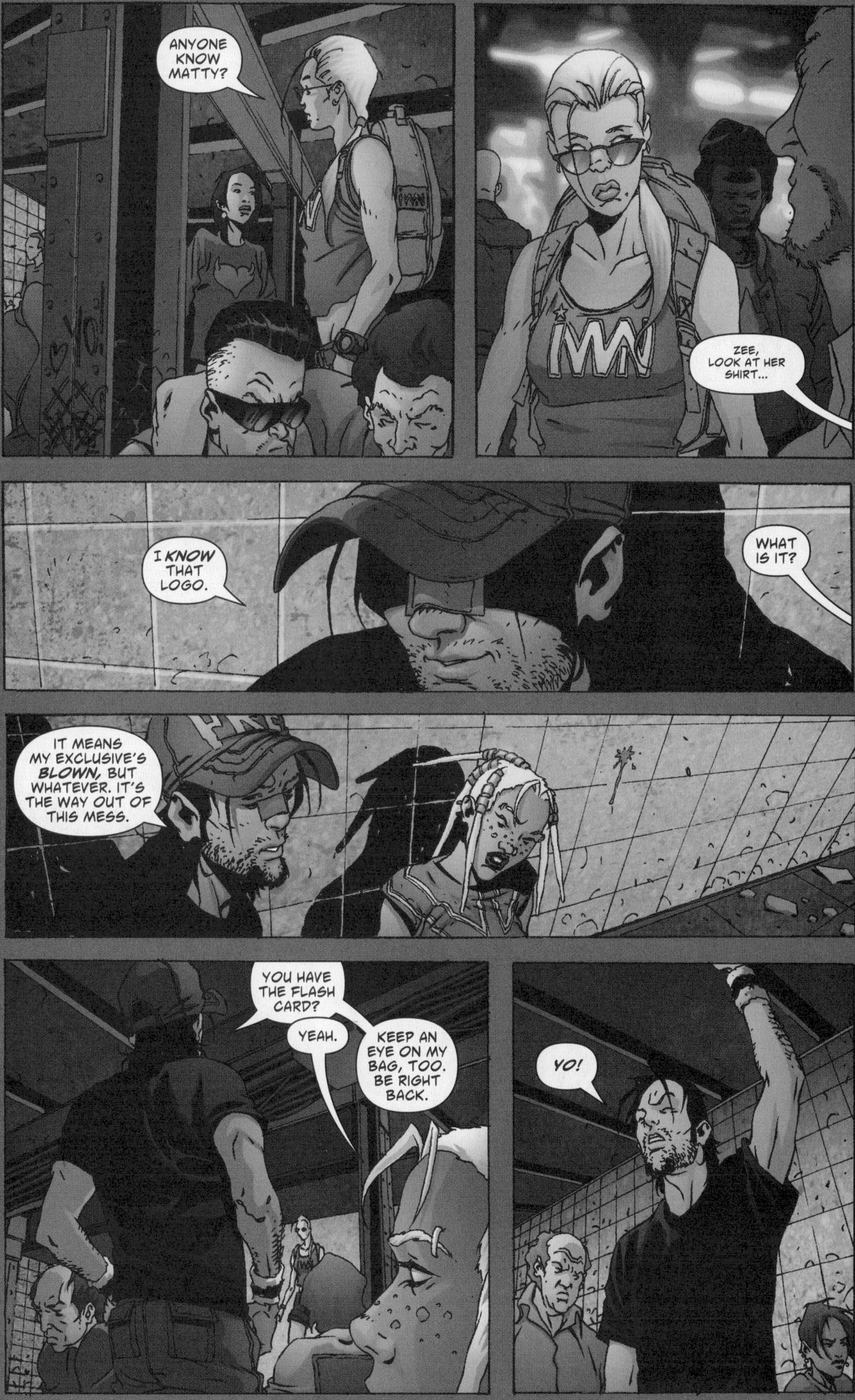
ANYONE KNOW MATTY?
ZEE, LOOK AT HER SHIRT...
I KNOW THAT LOGO.
WHAT IS IT?
IT MEANS MY EXCLUSIVE'S BLOWN, BUT WHATEVER. IT'S THE WAY OUT OF THIS MESS.
YOU HAVE THE FLASH CARD?
YEAH.
KEEP AN EYE ON MY BAG, TOO. BE RIGHT BACK.
YO!

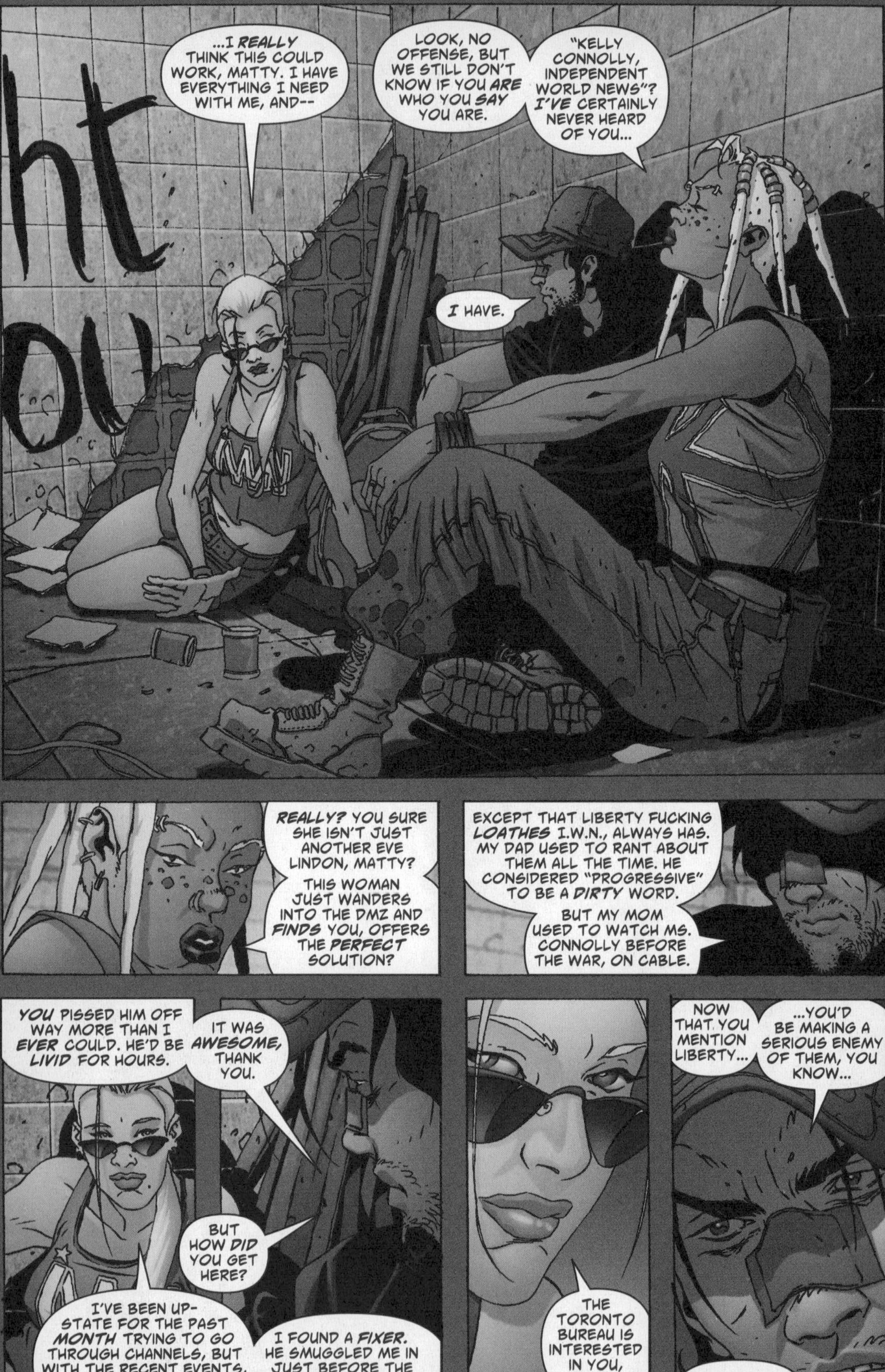
...I REALLY THINK THIS COULD WORK, MATTY. I HAVE EVERYTHING I NEED WITH ME, AND--
LOOK, NO OFFENSE, BUT WE STILL DON'T KNOW IF YOU ARE WHO YOU SAY YOU ARE.
"KELLY CONNOLLY, INDEPENDENT WORLD NEWS"? I'VE CERTAINLY NEVER HEARD OF YOU...
I HAVE.
REALLY? YOU SURE SHE ISN'T JUST ANOTHER EVE LINDON, MATTY?
THIS WOMAN JUST WANDERS INTO THE DMZ AND FINDS YOU, OFFERS THE PERFECT SOLUTION?
EXCEPT THAT LIBERTY FUCKING LOATHES I.W.N., ALWAYS HAS. MY DAD USED TO RANT ABOUT THEM ALL THE TIME. HE CONSIDERED "PROGRESSIVE" TO BE A DIRTY WORD.
BUT MY MOM USED TO WATCH MS. CONNOLLY BEFORE THE WAR, ON CABLE.
YOU PISSED HIM OFF WAY MORE THAN I EVER COULD. HE'D BE LIVID FOR HOURS.
IT WAS AWESOME, THANK YOU.
BUT HOW DID YOU GET HERE?
I'VE BEEN UP-STATE FOR THE PAST MONTH TRYING TO GO THROUGH CHANNELS, BUT WITH THE RECENT EVENTS, THEY WEREN'T LETTING PRESS ANYWHERE NEAR THE CITY.
I FOUND A FIXER. HE SMUGGLED ME IN JUST BEFORE THE ATTACK. I HAD A GOOD IDEA WHERE IN THE CITY TO LOOK, BASED ON YOUR PAST REPORTS.
THE TORONTO BUREAU IS INTERESTED IN YOU, MATTY.
LIBERTY CLEARLY HAS NO USE FOR YOU ANYMORE.
NOW THAT YOU MENTION LIBERTY...
...YOU'D BE MAKING A SERIOUS ENEMY OF THEM, YOU KNOW...
...CONSIDERING WHAT I'M CARRYING RIGHT NOW.

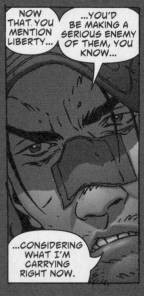

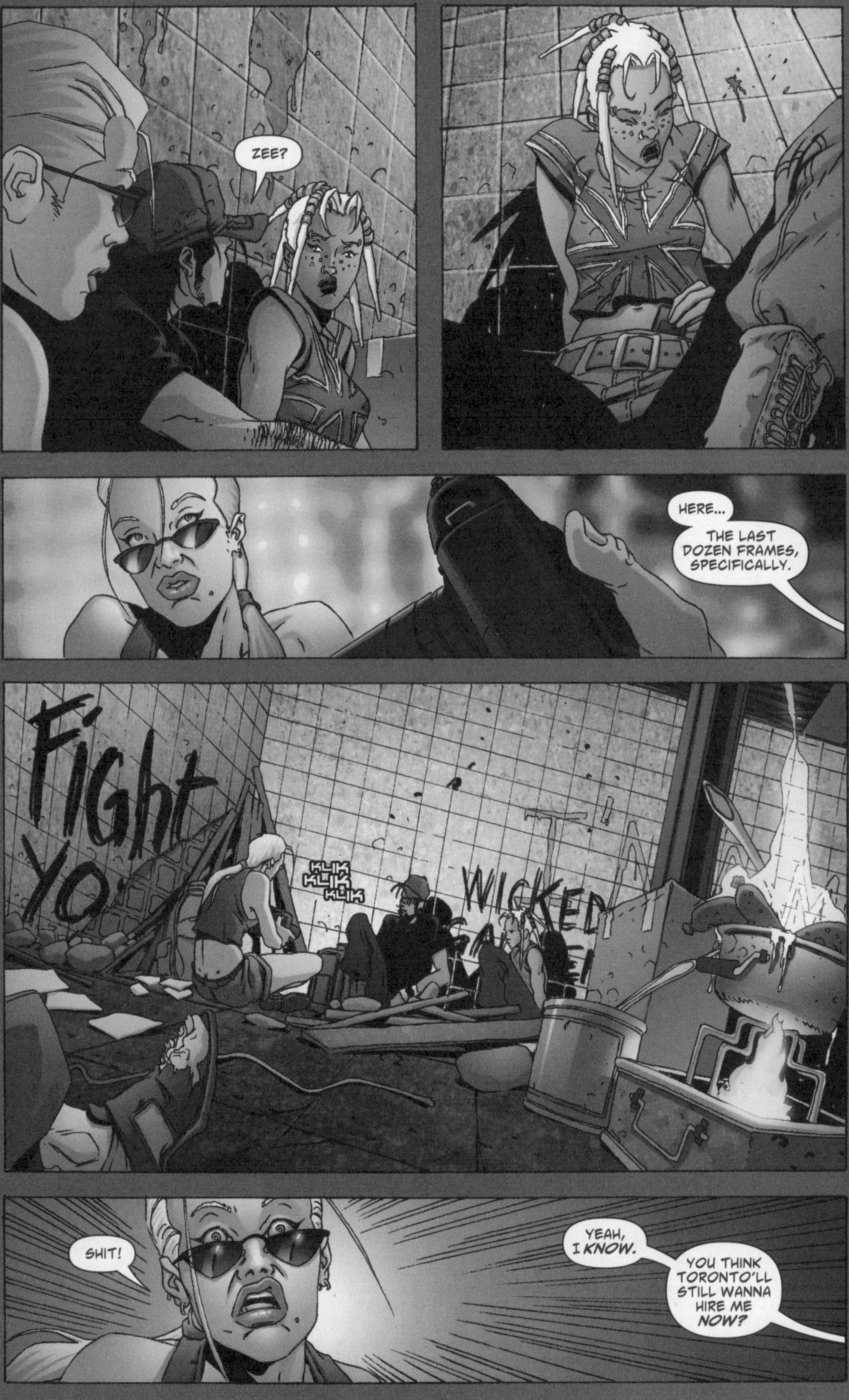
ZEE?
HERE...
THE LAST DOZEN FRAMES, SPECIFICALLY.
FIGHT YO
KLIK KLIK KLIK
WICKED
SHIT!
YEAH, I KNOW.
YOU THINK TORONTO'LL STILL WANNA HIRE ME NOW?

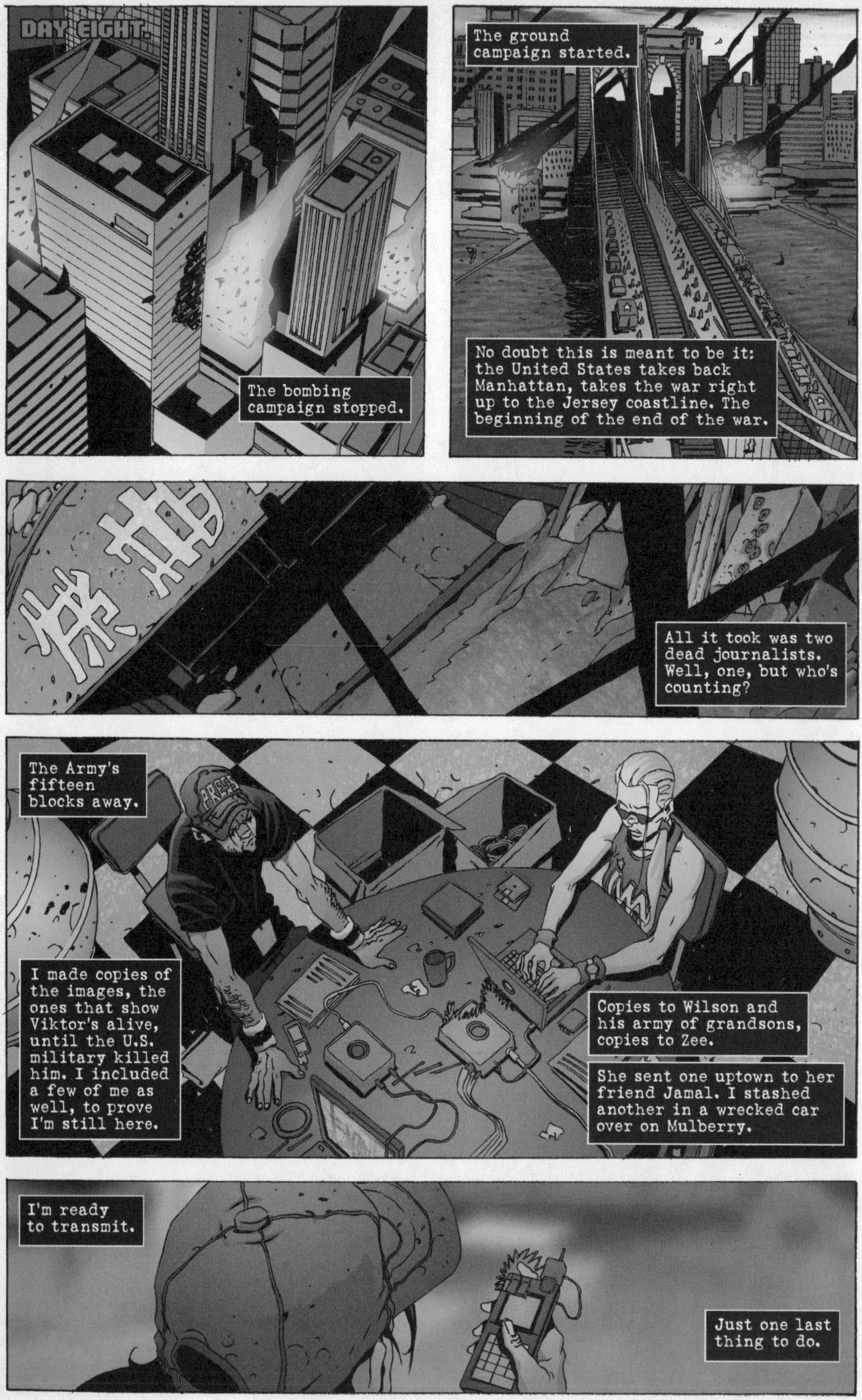
DAY EIGHT.
The bombing campaign stopped.
The ground campaign started.
No doubt this is meant to be it: the United States takes back Manhattan, takes the war right up to the Jersey coastline. The beginning of the end of the war.
All it took was two dead journalists. Well, one, but who's counting?
The Army's fifteen blocks away.
I made copies of the images, the ones that show Viktor's alive, until the U.S. military killed him. I included a few of me as well, to prove I'm still here.
Copies to Wilson and his army of grandsons, copies to Zee.
She sent one uptown to her friend Jamal. I stashed another in a wrecked car over on Mulberry.
I'm ready to transmit.
Just one last thing to do.

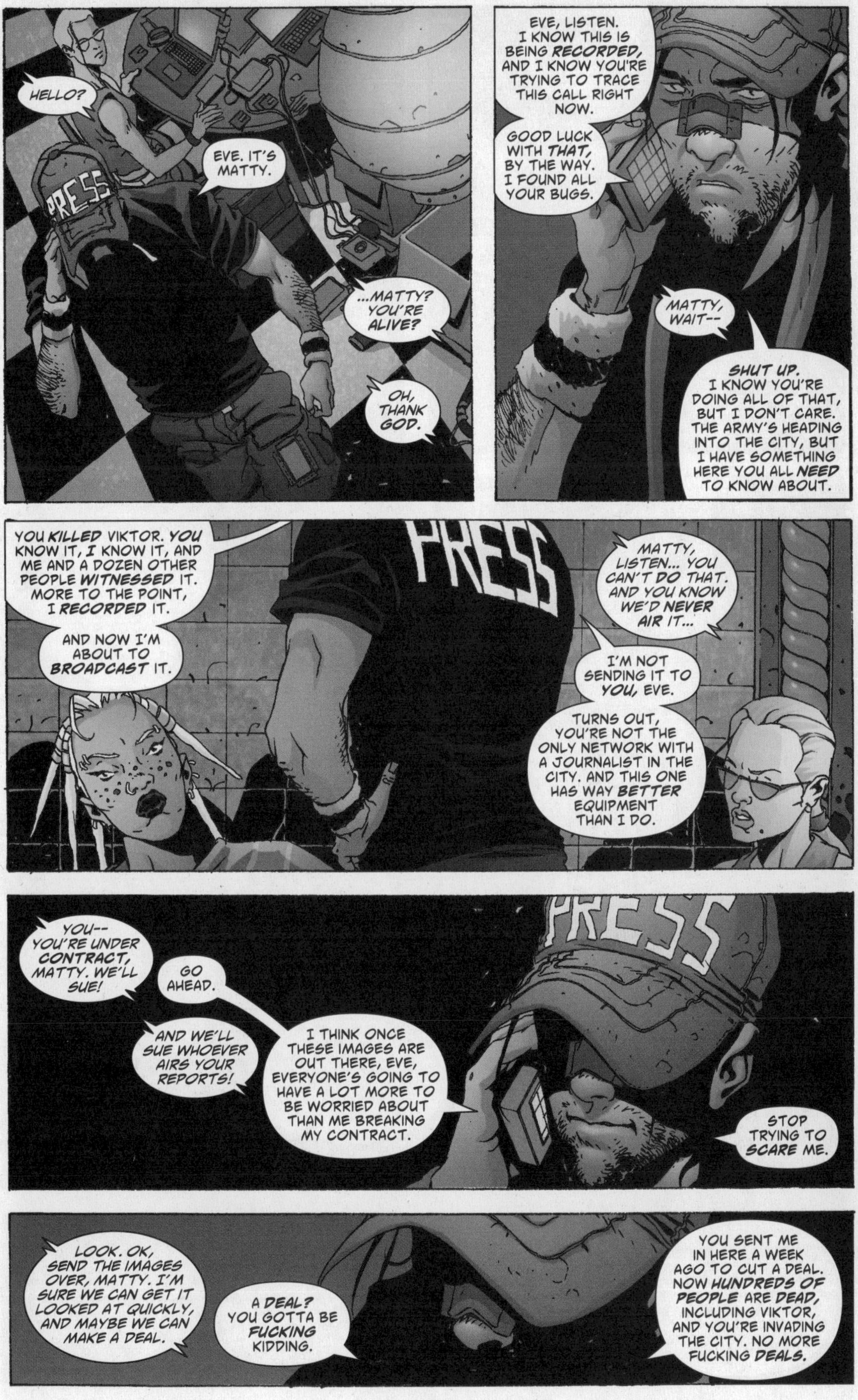
HELLO?
EVE. IT'S MATTY.
...MATTY? YOU'RE ALIVE?
OH, THANK GOD.
EVE, LISTEN. I KNOW THIS IS BEING RECORDED, AND I KNOW YOU'RE TRYING TO TRACE THIS CALL RIGHT NOW.
GOOD LUCK WITH THAT, BY THE WAY. I FOUND ALL YOUR BUGS.
MATTY, WAIT--
SHUT UP. I KNOW YOU'RE DOING ALL OF THAT, BUT I DON'T CARE. THE ARMY'S HEADING INTO THE CITY, BUT I HAVE SOMETHING HERE YOU ALL NEED TO KNOW ABOUT.
YOU KILLED VIKTOR. YOU KNOW IT, I KNOW IT, AND ME AND A DOZEN OTHER PEOPLE WITNESSED IT. MORE TO THE POINT, I RECORDED IT.
AND NOW I'M ABOUT TO BROADCAST IT.
MATTY, LISTEN... YOU CAN'T DO THAT. AND YOU KNOW WE'D NEVER AIR IT...
I'M NOT SENDING IT TO YOU, EVE.
TURNS OUT, YOU'RE NOT THE ONLY NETWORK WITH A JOURNALIST IN THE CITY. AND THIS ONE HAS WAY BETTER EQUIPMENT THAN I DO.
YOU-- YOU'RE UNDER CONTRACT, MATTY. WE'LL SUE!
GO AHEAD.
AND WE'LL SUE WHOEVER AIRS YOUR REPORTS!
I THINK ONCE THESE IMAGES ARE OUT THERE, EVE, EVERYONE'S GOING TO HAVE A LOT MORE TO BE WORRIED ABOUT THAN ME BREAKING MY CONTRACT.
STOP TRYING TO SCARE ME.
LOOK. OK, SEND THE IMAGES OVER, MATTY. I'M SURE WE CAN GET IT LOOKED AT QUICKLY, AND MAYBE WE CAN MAKE A DEAL.
A DEAL? YOU GOTTA BE FUCKING KIDDING.
YOU SENT ME IN HERE A WEEK AGO TO CUT A DEAL. NOW HUNDREDS OF PEOPLE ARE DEAD, INCLUDING VIKTOR, AND YOU'RE INVADING THE CITY. NO MORE FUCKING DEALS.

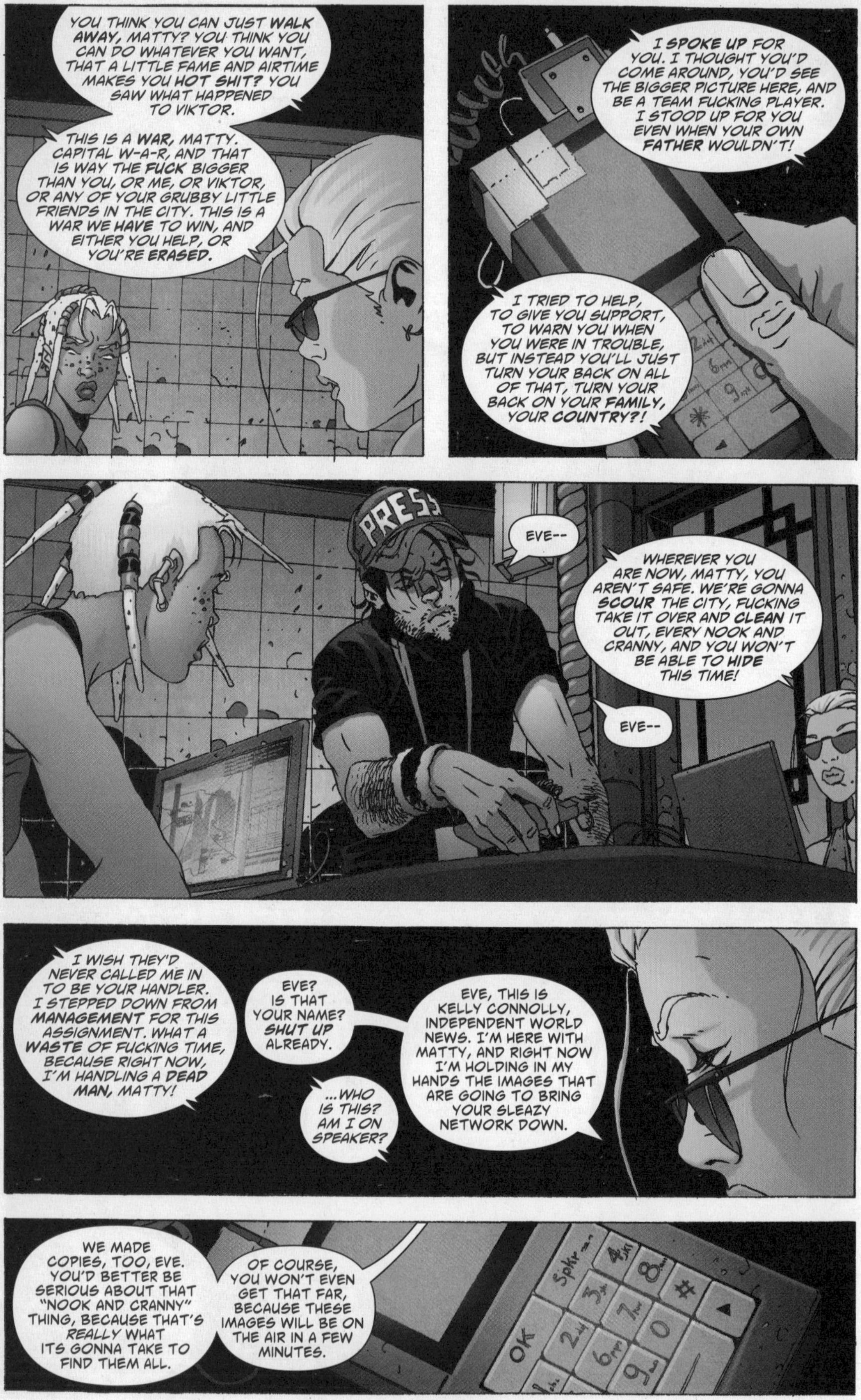
YOU THINK YOU CAN JUST WALK AWAY, MATTY? YOU THINK YOU CAN DO WHATEVER YOU WANT, THAT A LITTLE FAME AND AIRTIME MAKES YOU HOT SHIT? YOU SAW WHAT HAPPENED TO VIKTOR.
THIS IS A WAR, MATTY. CAPITAL W-A-R, AND THAT IS WAY THE FUCK BIGGER THAN YOU, OR ME, OR VIKTOR, OR ANY OF YOUR GRUBBY LITTLE FRIENDS IN THE CITY. THIS IS A WAR WE HAVE TO WIN, AND EITHER YOU HELP, OR YOU'RE ERASED.
I SPOKE UP FOR YOU. I THOUGHT YOU'D COME AROUND, YOU'D SEE THE BIGGER PICTURE HERE, AND BE A TEAM FUCKING PLAYER. I STOOD UP FOR YOU EVEN WHEN YOUR OWN FATHER WOULDN'T!
I TRIED TO HELP, TO GIVE YOU SUPPORT, TO WARN YOU WHEN YOU WERE IN TROUBLE, BUT INSTEAD YOU'LL JUST TURN YOUR BACK ON ALL OF THAT, TURN YOUR BACK ON YOUR FAMILY, YOUR COUNTRY?!
PRESS
EVE--
WHEREVER YOU ARE NOW, MATTY, YOU AREN'T SAFE. WE'RE GONNA SCOUR THE CITY, FUCKING TAKE IT OVER AND CLEAN IT OUT, EVERY NOOK AND CRANNY, AND YOU WON'T BE ABLE TO HIDE THIS TIME!
EVE--
I WISH THEY'D NEVER CALLED ME IN TO BE YOUR HANDLER. I STEPPED DOWN FROM MANAGEMENT FOR THIS ASSIGNMENT. WHAT A WASTE OF FUCKING TIME, BECAUSE RIGHT NOW, I'M HANDLING A DEAD MAN, MATTY!
EVE? IS THAT YOUR NAME? SHUT UP ALREADY.
EVE, THIS IS KELLY CONNOLLY, INDEPENDENT WORLD NEWS. I'M HERE WITH MATTY, AND RIGHT NOW I'M HOLDING IN MY HANDS THE IMAGES THAT ARE GOING TO BRING YOUR SLEAZY NETWORK DOWN.
...WHO IS THIS? AM I ON SPEAKER?
WE MADE COPIES, TOO, EVE. YOU'D BETTER BE SERIOUS ABOUT THAT "NOOK AND CRANNY" THING, BECAUSE THAT'S REALLY WHAT ITS GONNA TAKE TO FIND THEM ALL.
OF COURSE, YOU WON'T EVEN GET THAT FAR, BECAUSE THESE IMAGES WILL BE ON THE AIR IN A FEW MINUTES.

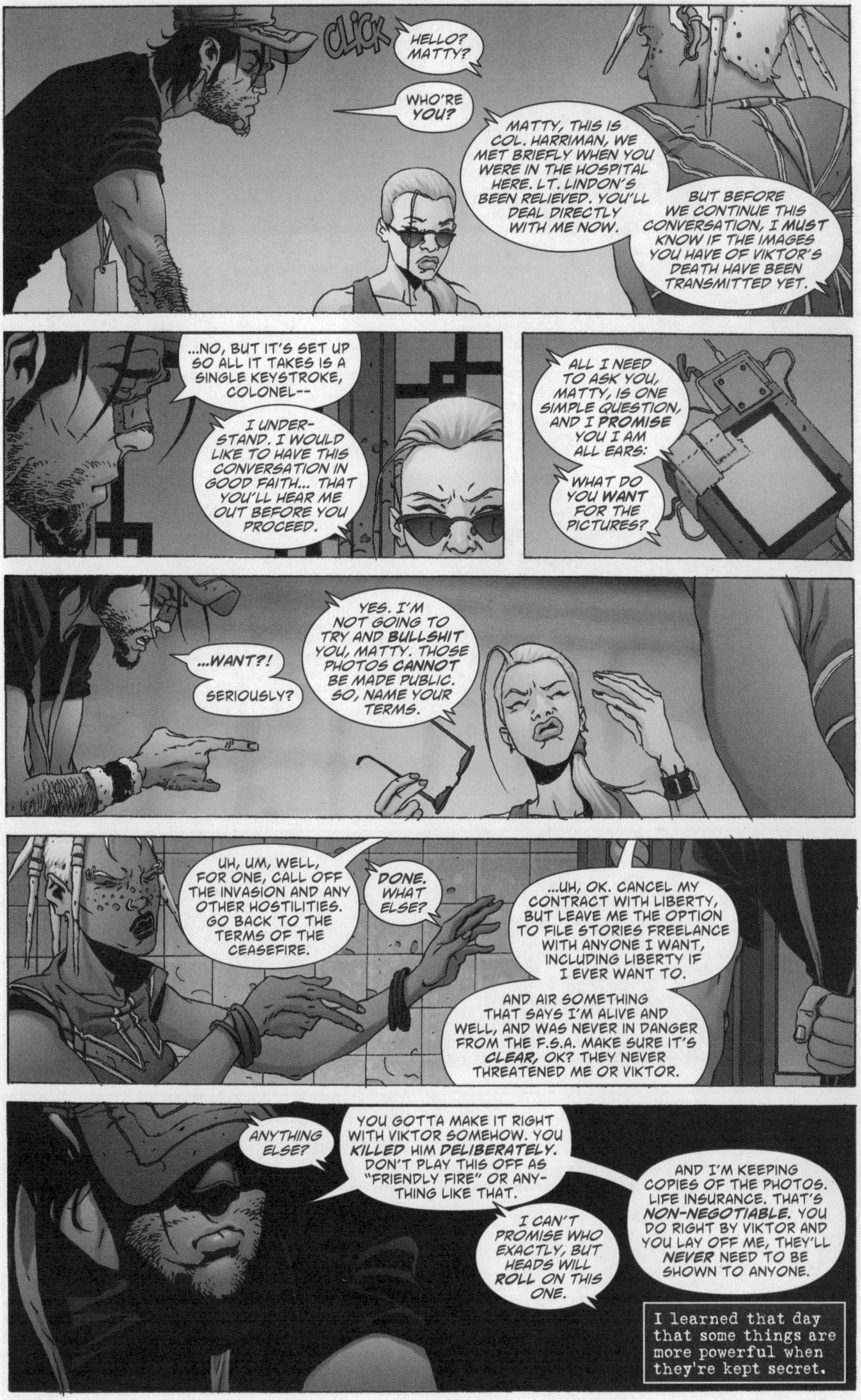

CLICK
HELLO? MATTY?
WHO'RE YOU?
MATTY, THIS IS COL. HARRIMAN, WE MET BRIEFLY WHEN YOU WERE IN THE HOSPITAL HERE. LT. LINDON'S BEEN RELIEVED. YOU'LL DEAL DIRECTLY WITH ME NOW.
BUT BEFORE WE CONTINUE THIS CONVERSATION, I MUST KNOW IF THE IMAGES YOU HAVE OF VIKTOR'S DEATH HAVE BEEN TRANSMITTED YET.
...NO, BUT IT'S SET UP SO ALL IT TAKES IS A SINGLE KEYSTROKE, COLONEL--
I UNDERSTAND. I WOULD LIKE TO HAVE THIS CONVERSATION IN GOOD FAITH... THAT YOU'LL HEAR ME OUT BEFORE YOU PROCEED.
ALL I NEED TO ASK YOU, MATTY, IS ONE SIMPLE QUESTION, AND I PROMISE YOU I AM ALL EARS:
WHAT DO YOU WANT FOR THE PICTURES?
...WANT?!
SERIOUSLY?
YES. I'M NOT GOING TO TRY AND BULLSHIT YOU, MATTY. THOSE PHOTOS CANNOT BE MADE PUBLIC. SO, NAME YOUR TERMS.
UH, UM, WELL, FOR ONE, CALL OFF THE INVASION AND ANY OTHER HOSTILITIES. GO BACK TO THE TERMS OF THE CEASEFIRE.
DONE. WHAT ELSE?
...UH, OK. CANCEL MY CONTRACT WITH LIBERTY, BUT LEAVE ME THE OPTION TO FILE STORIES FREELANCE WITH ANYONE I WANT, INCLUDING LIBERTY IF I EVER WANT TO.
AND AIR SOMETHING THAT SAYS I'M ALIVE AND WELL, AND WAS NEVER IN DANGER FROM THE F.S.A. MAKE SURE IT'S CLEAR, OK? THEY NEVER THREATENED ME OR VIKTOR.
ANYTHING ELSE?
YOU GOTTA MAKE IT RIGHT WITH VIKTOR SOMEHOW. YOU KILLED HIM DELIBERATELY. DON'T PLAY THIS OFF AS "FRIENDLY FIRE" OR ANYTHING LIKE THAT.
I CAN'T PROMISE WHO EXACTLY, BUT HEADS WILL ROLL ON THIS ONE.
AND I'M KEEPING COPIES OF THE PHOTOS. LIFE INSURANCE. THAT'S NON-NEGOTIABLE. YOU DO RIGHT BY VIKTOR AND YOU LAY OFF ME, THEY'LL NEVER NEED TO BE SHOWN TO ANYONE.
I learned that day that some things are more powerful when they're kept secret.

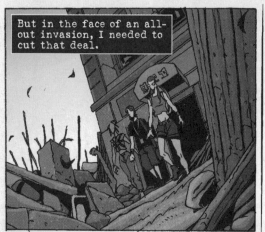

But in the face of an all-out invasion, I needed to cut that deal.

Zee said something to me once that sticks with me.

This is all because of me.

Just my presence in the DMZ is volatile and affects my friends as much as it affects me. I have a responsibility.

To my friends, and to everyone else.

I've been in the city almost a year...

...and now I finally feel like I'm part of it.

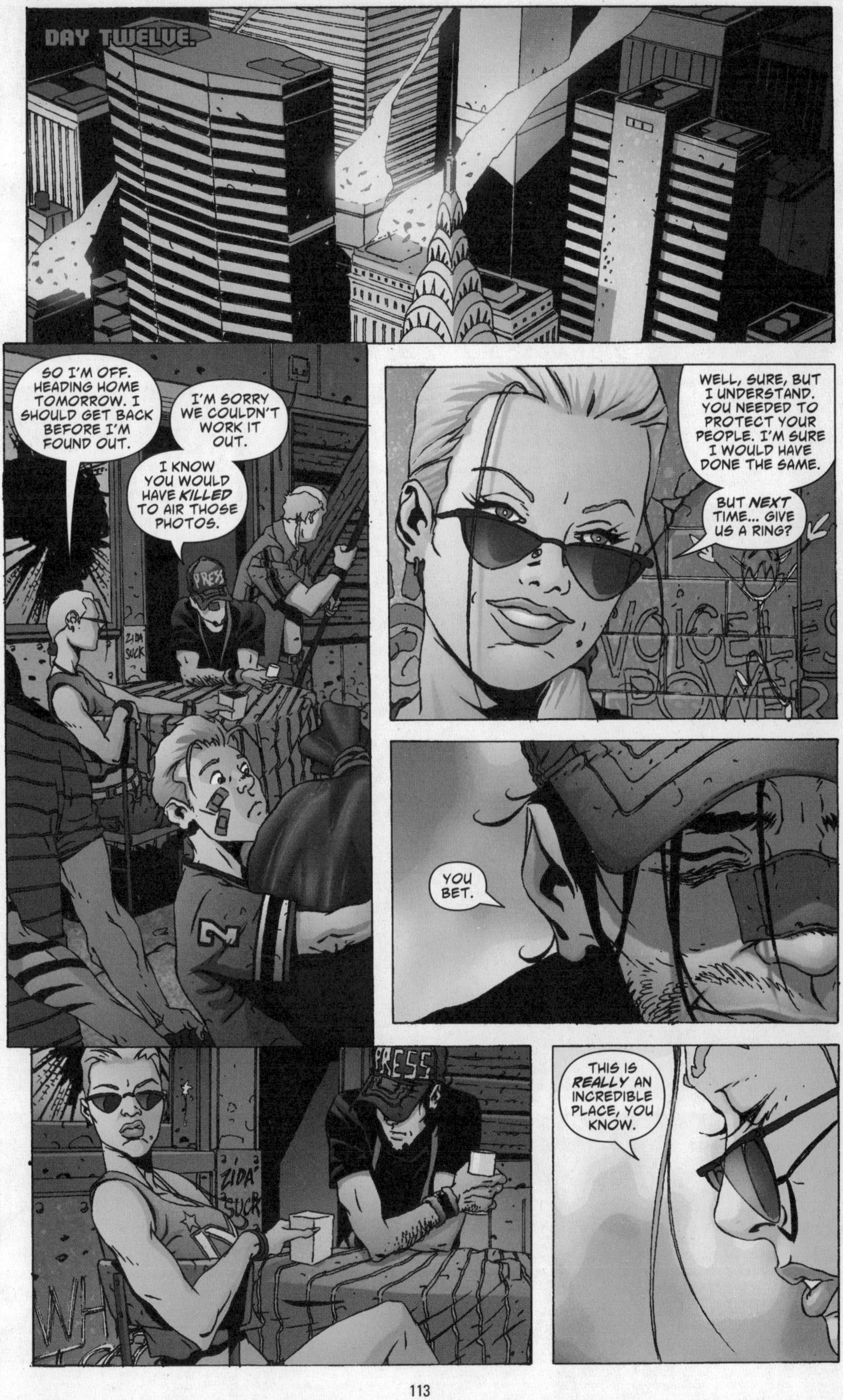
DAY TWELVE.
SO I'M OFF. HEADING HOME TOMORROW. I SHOULD GET BACK BEFORE I'M FOUND OUT.
I'M SORRY WE COULDN'T WORK IT OUT.
I KNOW YOU WOULD HAVE *KILLED* TO AIR THOSE PHOTOS.
PRESS
ZIDA SUCK
WELL, SURE, BUT I UNDERSTAND. YOU NEEDED TO PROTECT YOUR PEOPLE. I'M SURE I WOULD HAVE DONE THE SAME.
BUT *NEXT* TIME... GIVE US A RING?
VOICELESS POWER
YOU BET.
PRESS
ZIDA SUCK
THIS IS *REALLY* AN INCREDIBLE PLACE, YOU KNOW.

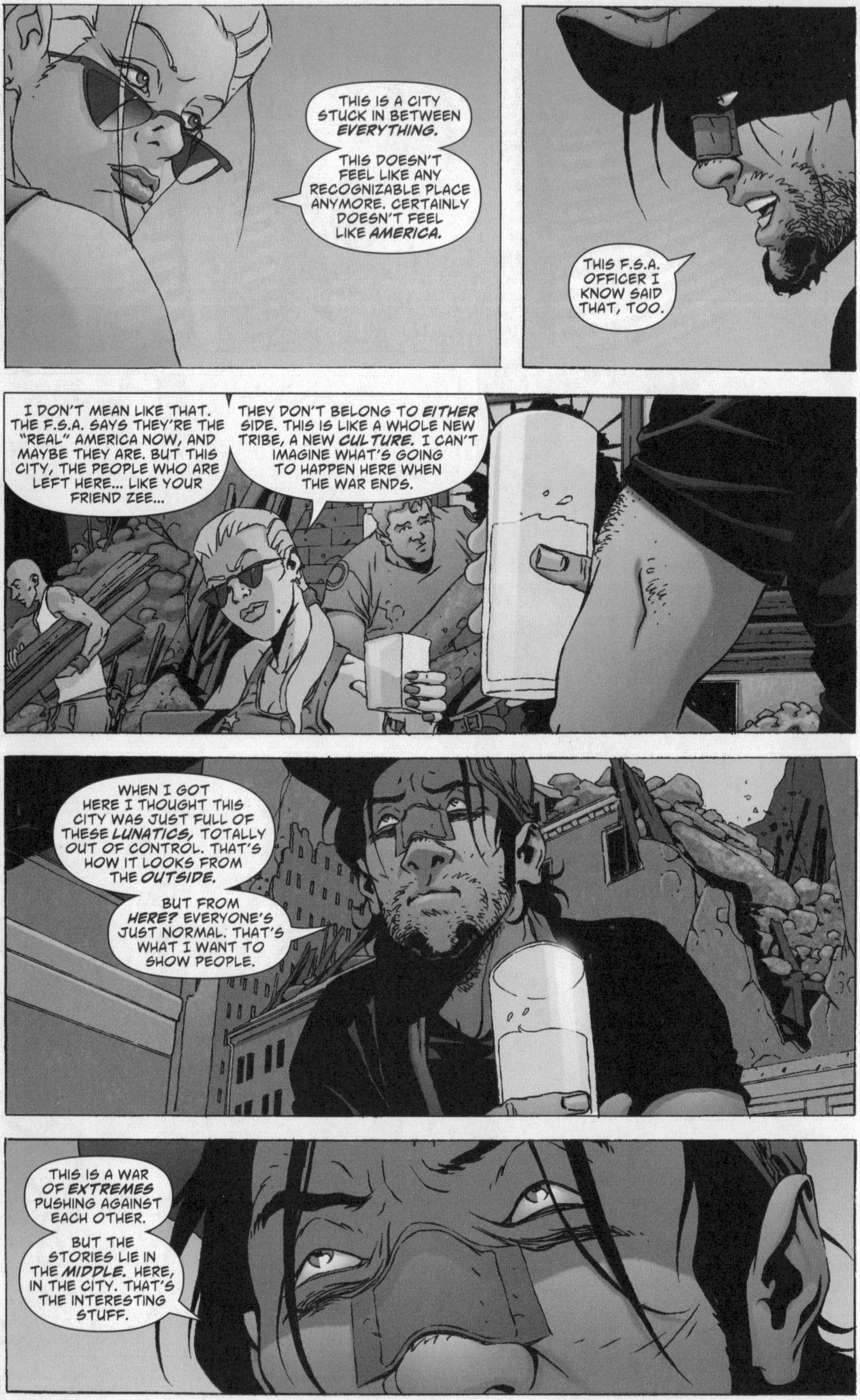
THIS IS A CITY STUCK IN BETWEEN *EVERYTHING.*
THIS DOESN'T FEEL LIKE ANY RECOGNIZABLE PLACE ANYMORE. CERTAINLY DOESN'T FEEL LIKE *AMERICA.*
THIS F.S.A. OFFICER I KNOW SAID THAT, TOO.
I DON'T MEAN LIKE THAT. THE F.S.A. SAYS THEY'RE THE "REAL" AMERICA NOW, AND MAYBE THEY ARE. BUT THIS CITY, THE PEOPLE WHO ARE LEFT HERE... LIKE YOUR FRIEND ZEE...
THEY DON'T BELONG TO *EITHER* SIDE. THIS IS LIKE A WHOLE NEW TRIBE, A NEW *CULTURE.* I CAN'T IMAGINE WHAT'S GOING TO HAPPEN HERE WHEN THE WAR ENDS.
WHEN I GOT HERE I THOUGHT THIS CITY WAS JUST FULL OF THESE *LUNATICS,* TOTALLY OUT OF CONTROL. THAT'S HOW IT LOOKS FROM THE *OUTSIDE.*
BUT FROM *HERE?* EVERYONE'S JUST NORMAL. THAT'S WHAT I WANT TO SHOW PEOPLE.
THIS IS A WAR OF *EXTREMES* PUSHING AGAINST EACH OTHER.
BUT THE STORIES LIE IN THE *MIDDLE.* HERE, IN THE CITY. THAT'S THE INTERESTING STUFF.

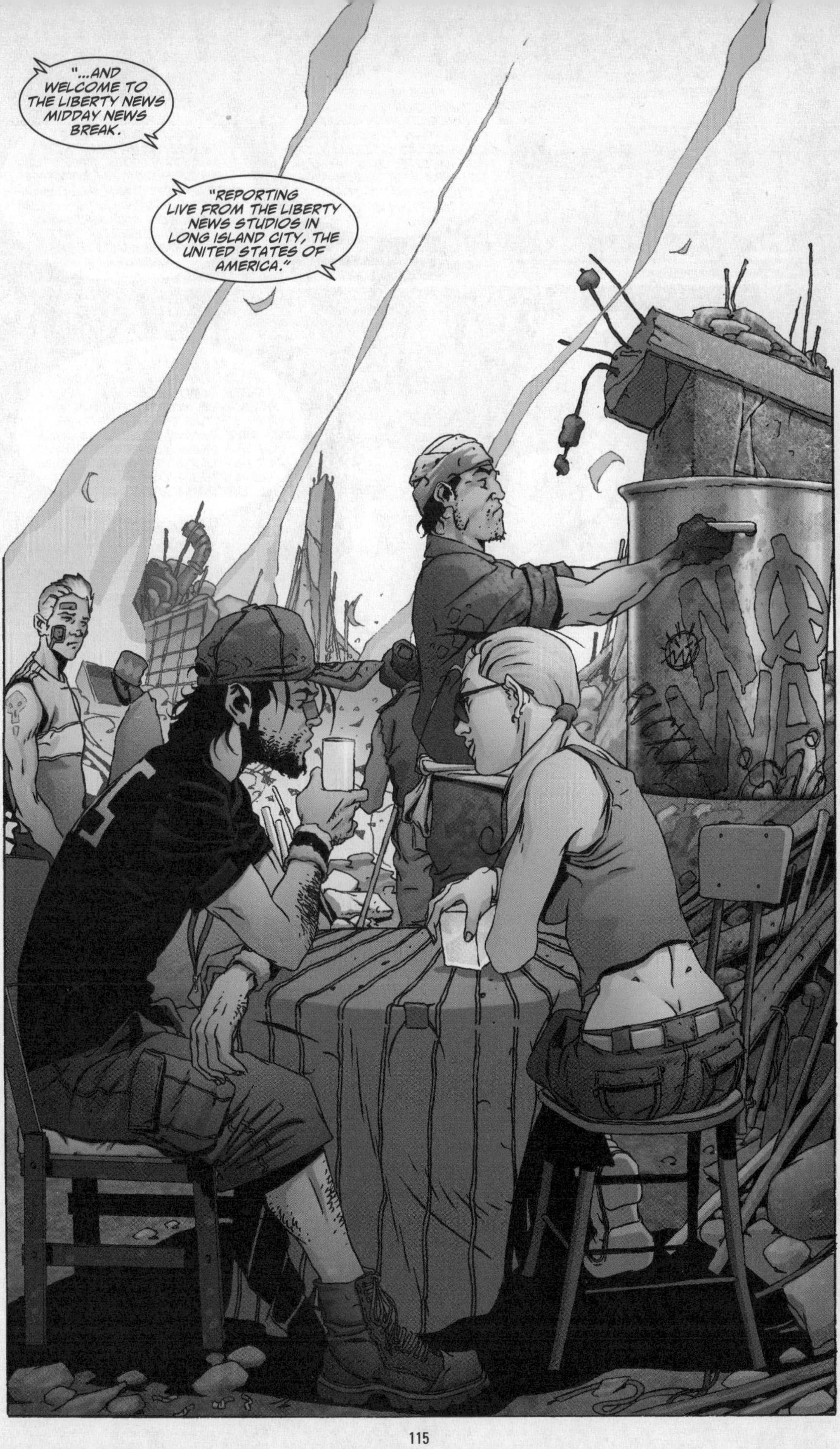
"...AND WELCOME TO THE LIBERTY NEWS MIDDAY NEWS BREAK.
"REPORTING LIVE FROM THE LIBERTY NEWS STUDIOS IN LONG ISLAND CITY, THE UNITED STATES OF AMERICA."

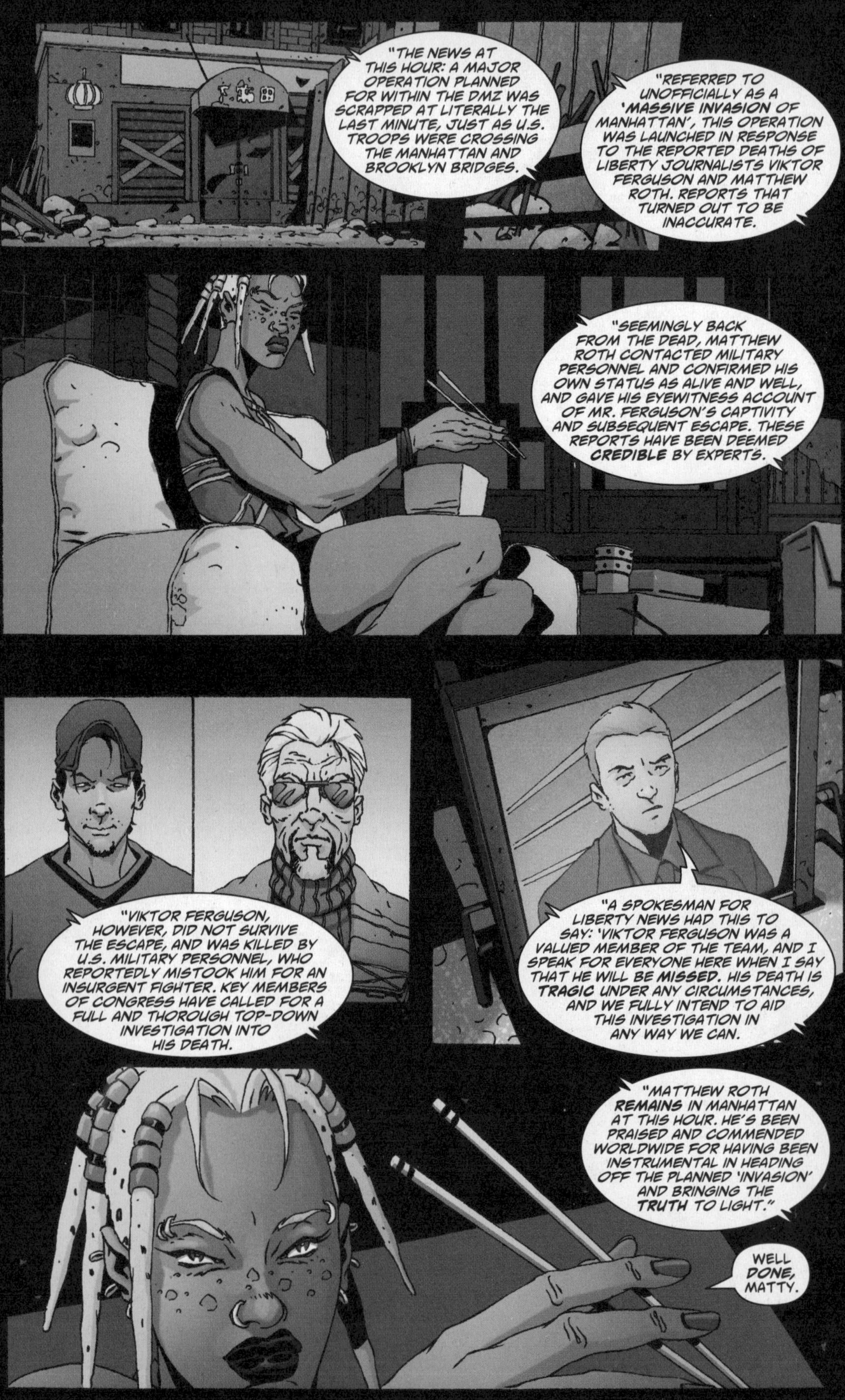
"THE NEWS AT THIS HOUR: A MAJOR OPERATION PLANNED FOR WITHIN THE DMZ WAS SCRAPPED AT LITERALLY THE LAST MINUTE, JUST AS U.S. TROOPS WERE CROSSING THE MANHATTAN AND BROOKLYN BRIDGES.
"REFERRED TO UNOFFICIALLY AS A 'MASSIVE INVASION OF MANHATTAN', THIS OPERATION WAS LAUNCHED IN RESPONSE TO THE REPORTED DEATHS OF LIBERTY JOURNALISTS VIKTOR FERGUSON AND MATTHEW ROTH. REPORTS THAT TURNED OUT TO BE INACCURATE.
"SEEMINGLY BACK FROM THE DEAD, MATTHEW ROTH CONTACTED MILITARY PERSONNEL AND CONFIRMED HIS OWN STATUS AS ALIVE AND WELL, AND GAVE HIS EYEWITNESS ACCOUNT OF MR. FERGUSON'S CAPTIVITY AND SUBSEQUENT ESCAPE. THESE REPORTS HAVE BEEN DEEMED CREDIBLE BY EXPERTS.
"VIKTOR FERGUSON, HOWEVER, DID NOT SURVIVE THE ESCAPE, AND WAS KILLED BY U.S. MILITARY PERSONNEL, WHO REPORTEDLY MISTOOK HIM FOR AN INSURGENT FIGHTER. KEY MEMBERS OF CONGRESS HAVE CALLED FOR A FULL AND THOROUGH TOP-DOWN INVESTIGATION INTO HIS DEATH.
"A SPOKESMAN FOR LIBERTY NEWS HAD THIS TO SAY: 'VIKTOR FERGUSON WAS A VALUED MEMBER OF THE TEAM, AND I SPEAK FOR EVERYONE HERE WHEN I SAY THAT HE WILL BE MISSED. HIS DEATH IS TRAGIC UNDER ANY CIRCUMSTANCES, AND WE FULLY INTEND TO AID THIS INVESTIGATION IN ANY WAY WE CAN.
"MATTHEW ROTH REMAINS IN MANHATTAN AT THIS HOUR. HE'S BEEN PRAISED AND COMMENDED WORLDWIDE FOR HAVING BEEN INSTRUMENTAL IN HEADING OFF THE PLANNED 'INVASION' AND BRINGING THE TRUTH TO LIGHT."
WELL DONE, MATTY.

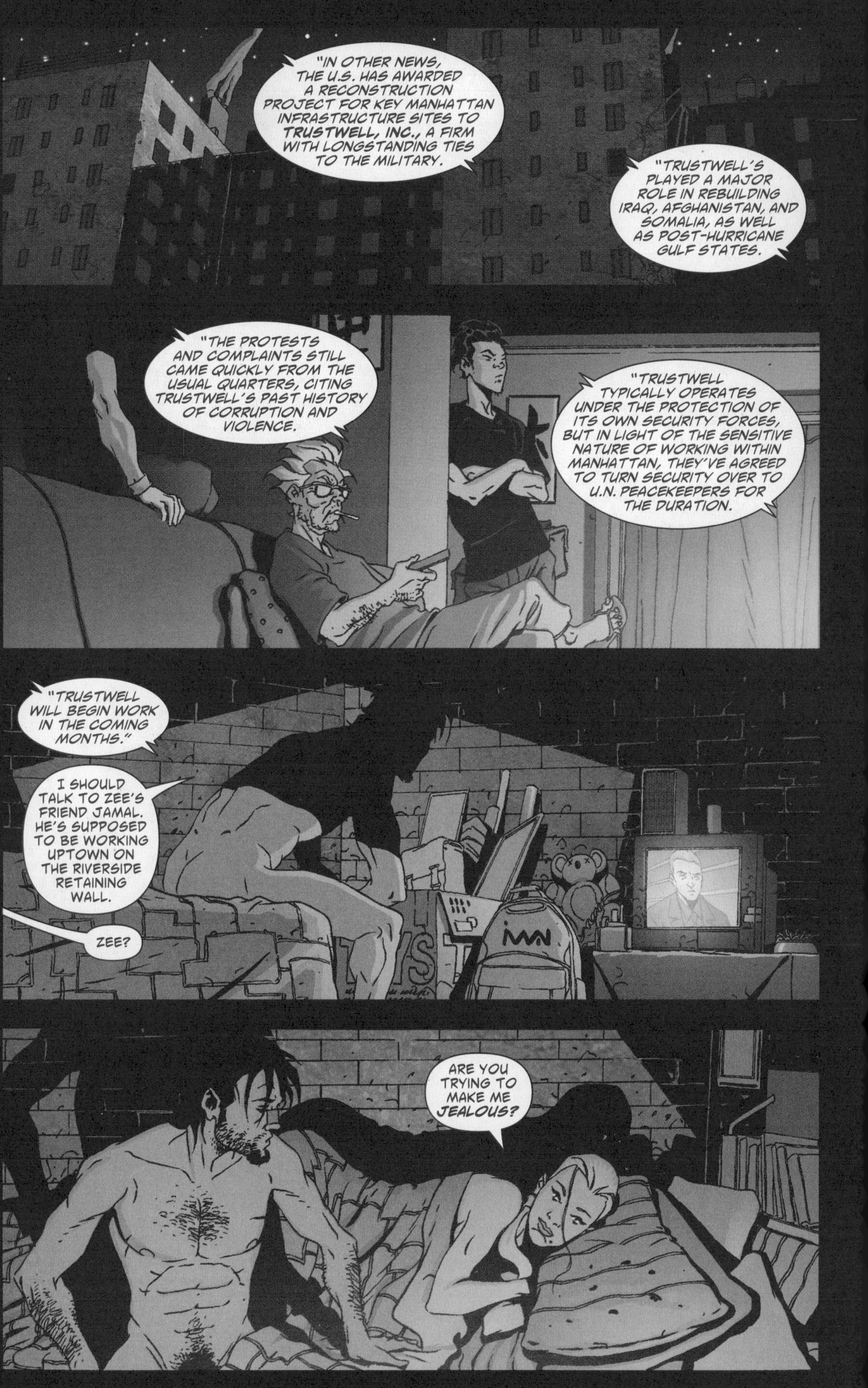
"IN OTHER NEWS, THE U.S. HAS AWARDED A RECONSTRUCTION PROJECT FOR KEY MANHATTAN INFRASTRUCTURE SITES TO TRUSTWELL, INC., A FIRM WITH LONGSTANDING TIES TO THE MILITARY.
"TRUSTWELL'S PLAYED A MAJOR ROLE IN REBUILDING IRAQ, AFGHANISTAN, AND SOMALIA, AS WELL AS POST-HURRICANE GULF STATES.
"THE PROTESTS AND COMPLAINTS STILL CAME QUICKLY FROM THE USUAL QUARTERS, CITING TRUSTWELL'S PAST HISTORY OF CORRUPTION AND VIOLENCE.
"TRUSTWELL TYPICALLY OPERATES UNDER THE PROTECTION OF ITS OWN SECURITY FORCES, BUT IN LIGHT OF THE SENSITIVE NATURE OF WORKING WITHIN MANHATTAN, THEY'VE AGREED TO TURN SECURITY OVER TO U.N. PEACEKEEPERS FOR THE DURATION.
"TRUSTWELL WILL BEGIN WORK IN THE COMING MONTHS."
I SHOULD TALK TO ZEE'S FRIEND JAMAL. HE'S SUPPOSED TO BE WORKING UPTOWN ON THE RIVERSIDE RETAINING WALL.
ZEE?
ARE YOU TRYING TO MAKE ME JEALOUS?

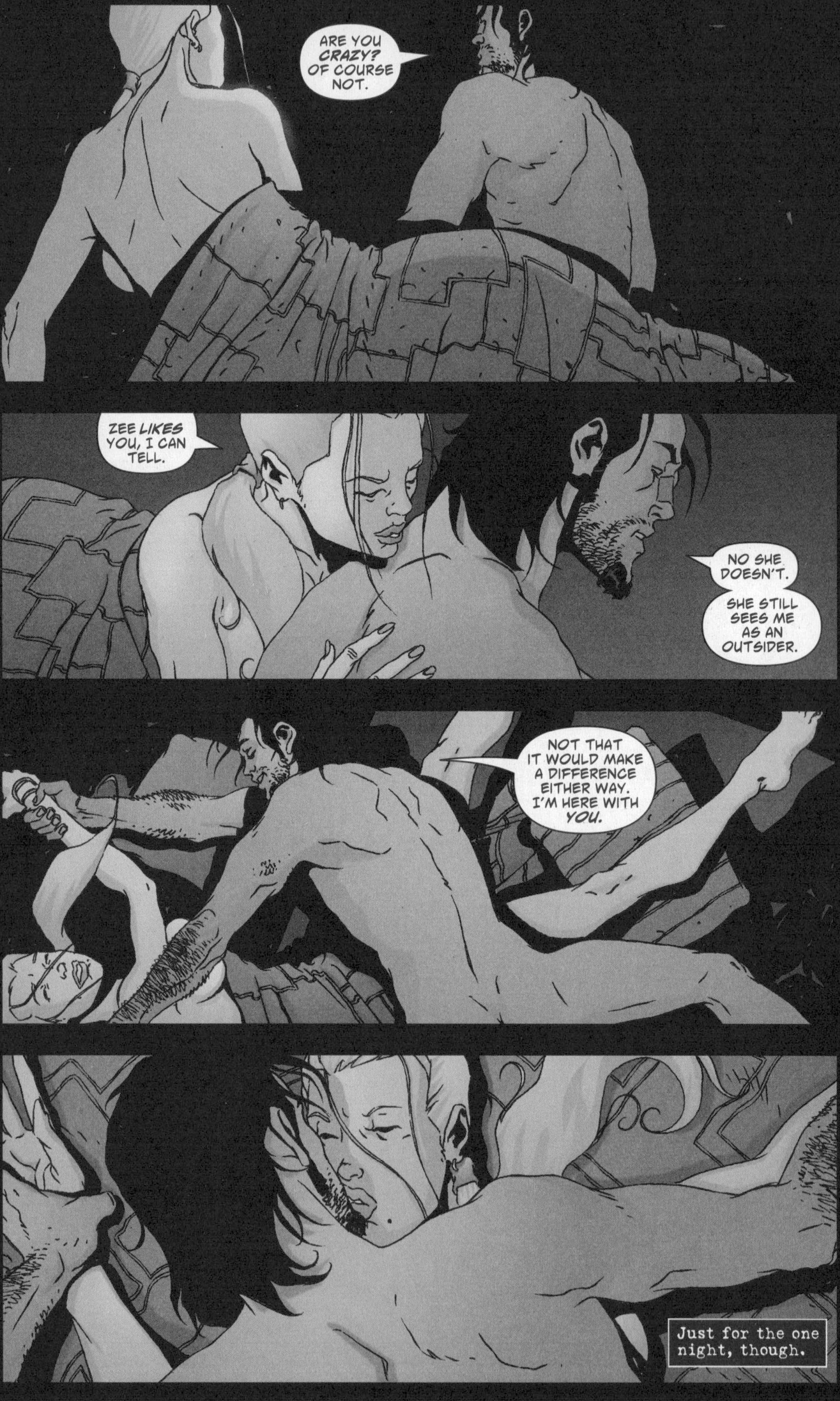
ARE YOU *CRAZY?* OF COURSE NOT.
ZEE *LIKES* YOU, I CAN TELL.
NO SHE DOESN'T.
SHE STILL SEES ME AS AN OUTSIDER.
NOT THAT IT WOULD MAKE A DIFFERENCE EITHER WAY. I'M HERE WITH *YOU.*
Just for the one night, though.

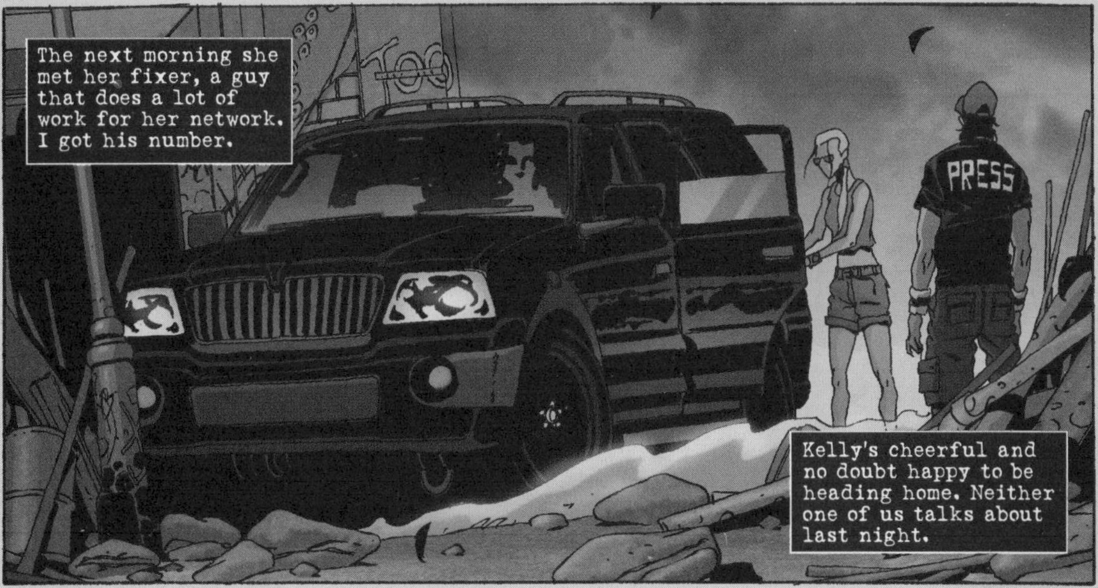
The next morning she met her fixer, a guy that does a lot of work for her network. I got his number.
PRESS
Kelly's cheerful and no doubt happy to be heading home. Neither one of us talks about last night.

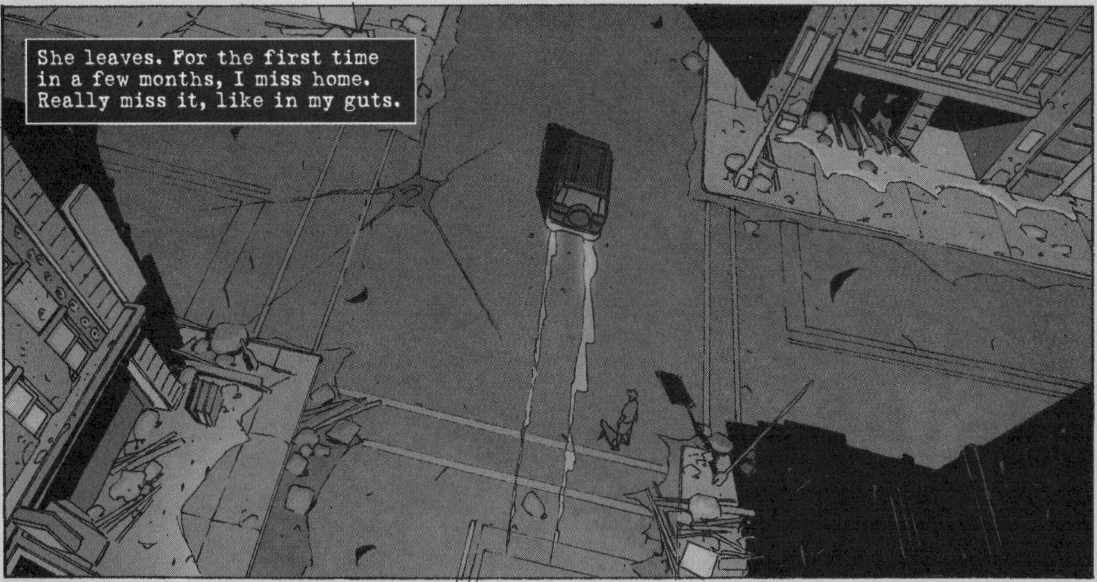
She leaves. For the first time in a few months, I miss home. Really miss it, like in my guts.

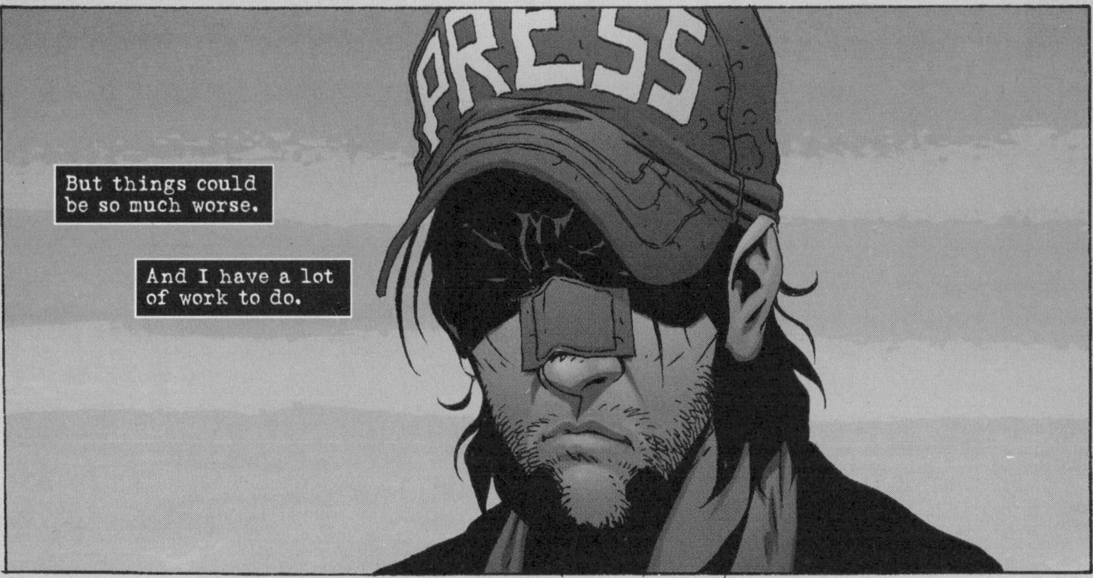
PRESS
But things could be so much worse.
And I have a lot of work to do.

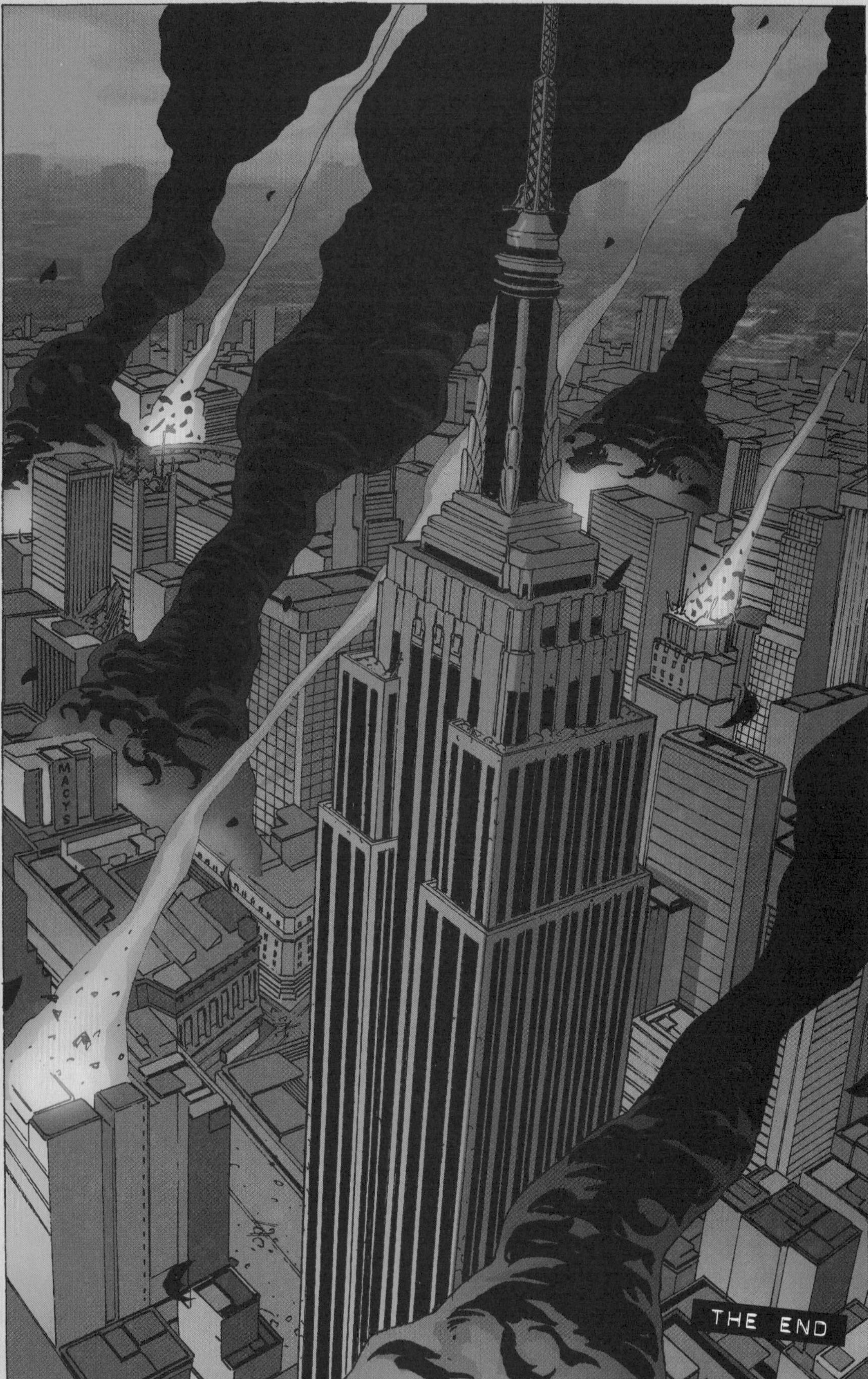
MACYS
THE END

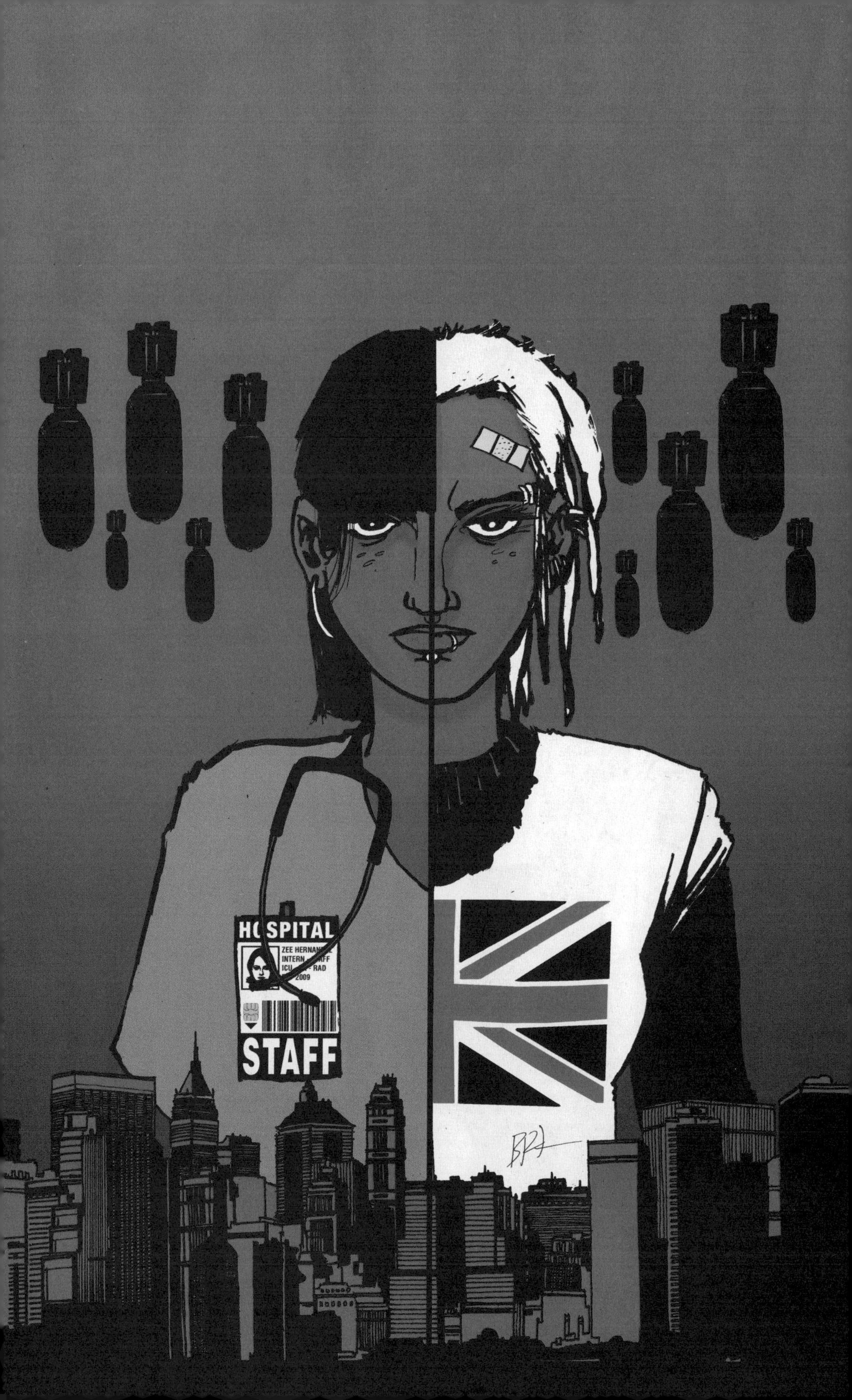
HOSPITAL
STAFF

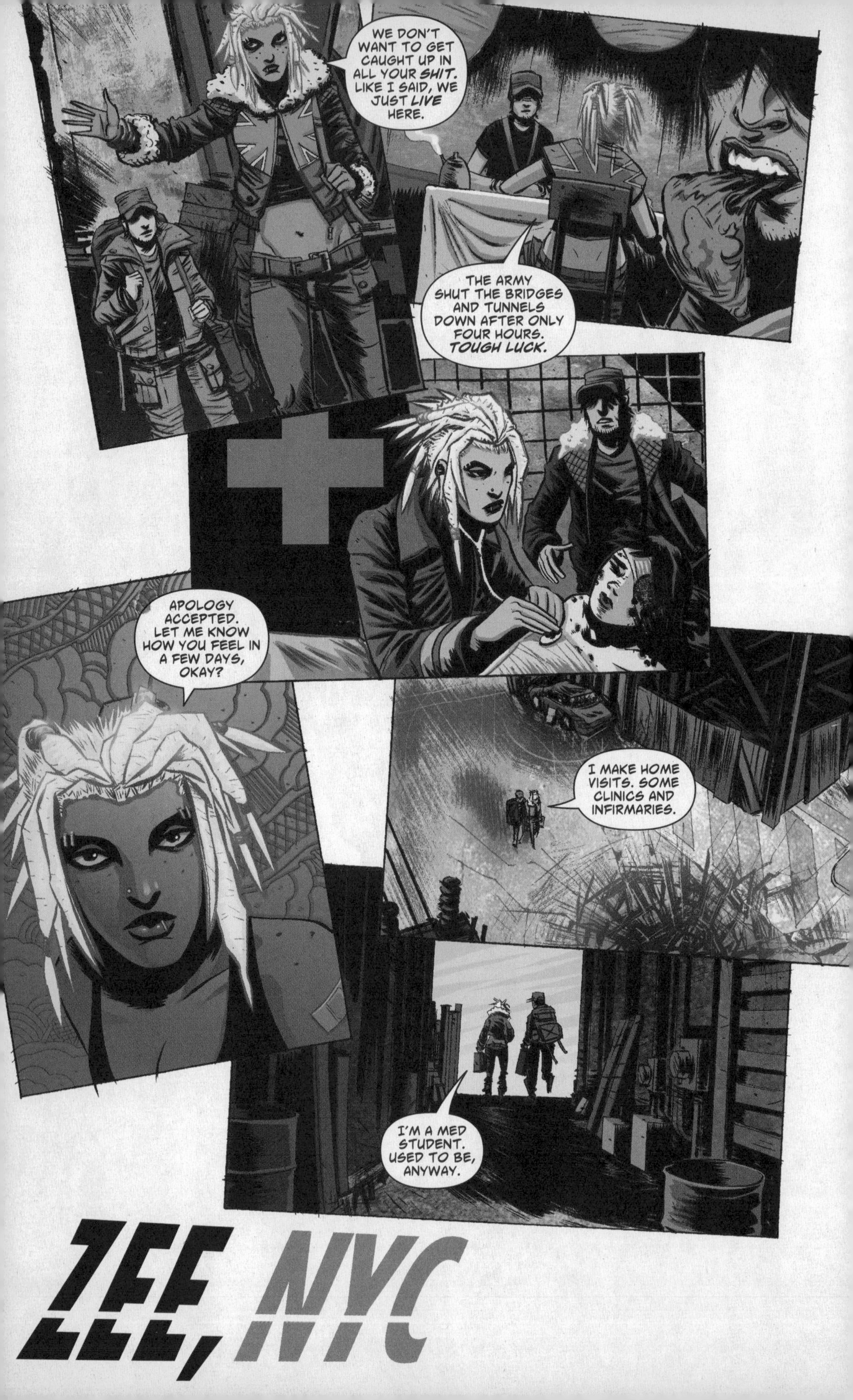
WE DON'T WANT TO GET CAUGHT UP IN ALL YOUR SHIT. LIKE I SAID, WE JUST LIVE HERE.
THE ARMY SHUT THE BRIDGES AND TUNNELS DOWN AFTER ONLY FOUR HOURS. TOUGH LUCK.
APOLOGY ACCEPTED. LET ME KNOW HOW YOU FEEL IN A FEW DAYS, OKAY?
I MAKE HOME VISITS. SOME CLINICS AND INFIRMARIES.
I'M A MED STUDENT. USED TO BE, ANYWAY.
ZEE, NYC

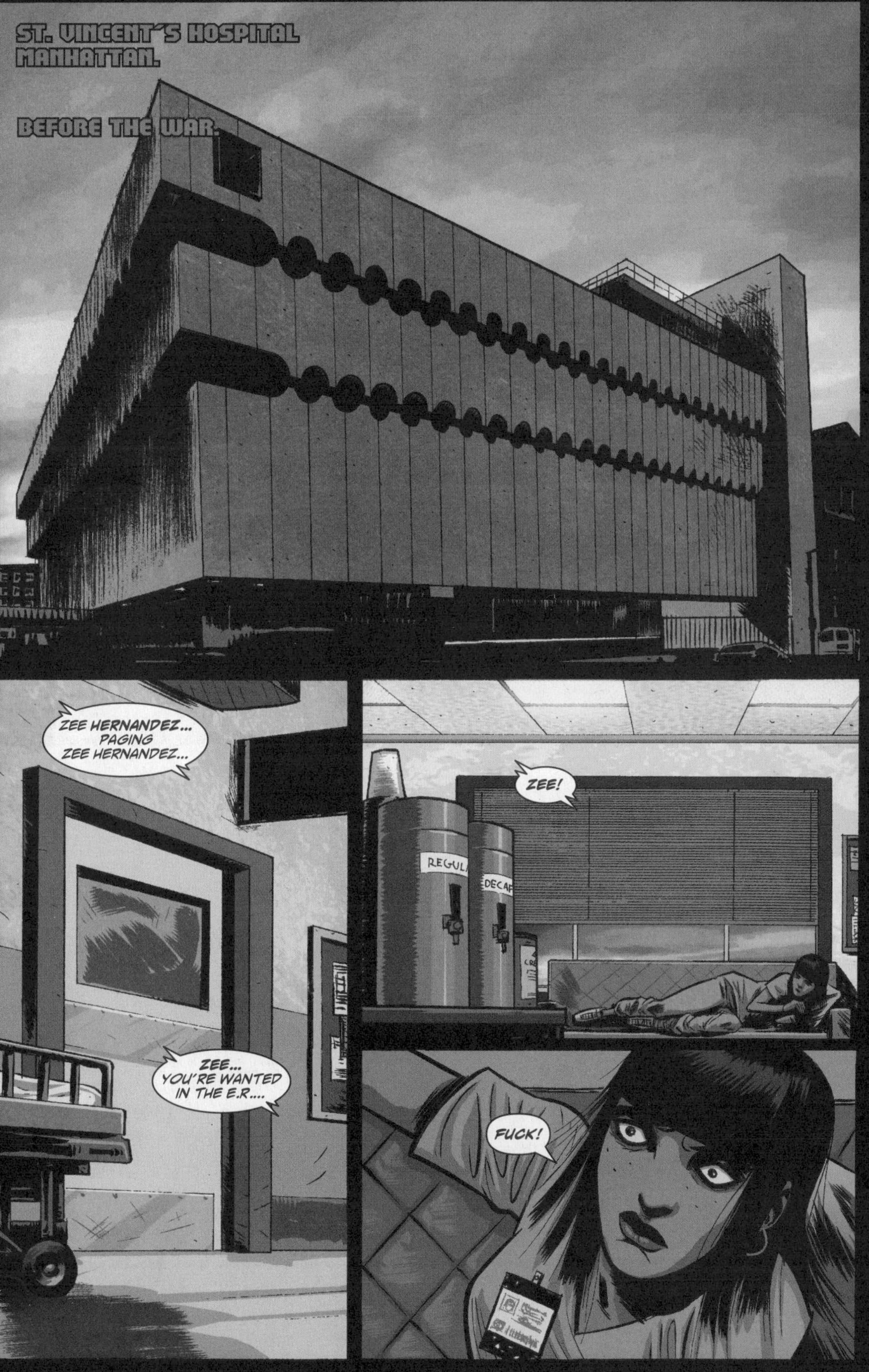
ST. VINCENT'S HOSPITAL
MANHATTAN.
BEFORE THE WAR.
ZEE HERNANDEZ... PAGING ZEE HERNANDEZ...
ZEE... YOU'RE WANTED IN THE E.R....
ZEE!
REGUL
DECAF
FUCK!

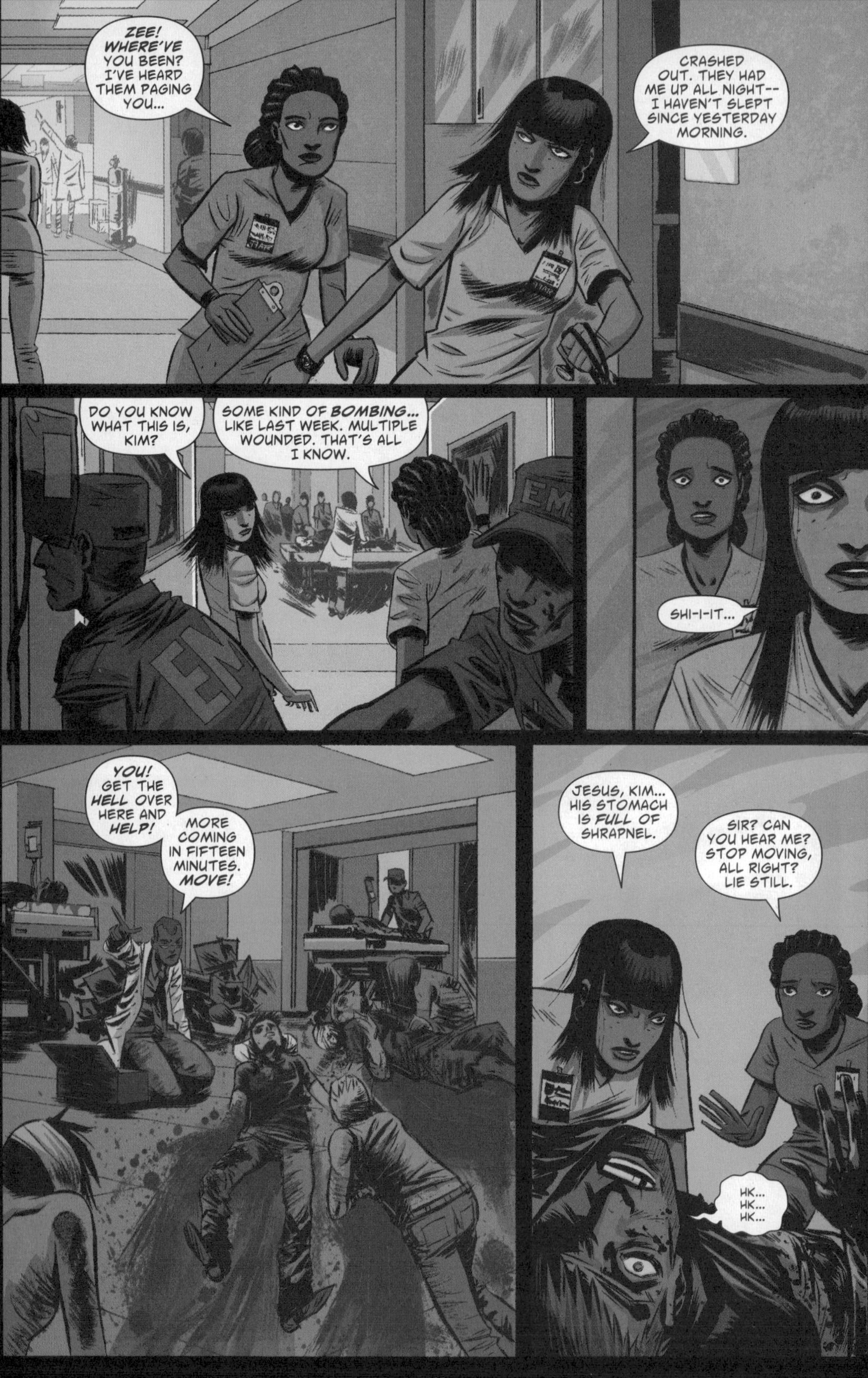
ZEE! WHERE'VE YOU BEEN? I'VE HEARD THEM PAGING YOU...
CRASHED OUT. THEY HAD ME UP ALL NIGHT-- I HAVEN'T SLEPT SINCE YESTERDAY MORNING.
DO YOU KNOW WHAT THIS IS, KIM?
SOME KIND OF BOMBING... LIKE LAST WEEK. MULTIPLE WOUNDED. THAT'S ALL I KNOW.
SHI-I-IT...
YOU! GET THE HELL OVER HERE AND HELP!
MORE COMING IN FIFTEEN MINUTES. MOVE!
JESUS, KIM... HIS STOMACH IS FULL OF SHRAPNEL.
SIR? CAN YOU HEAR ME? STOP MOVING, ALL RIGHT? LIE STILL.
HK... HK... HK...

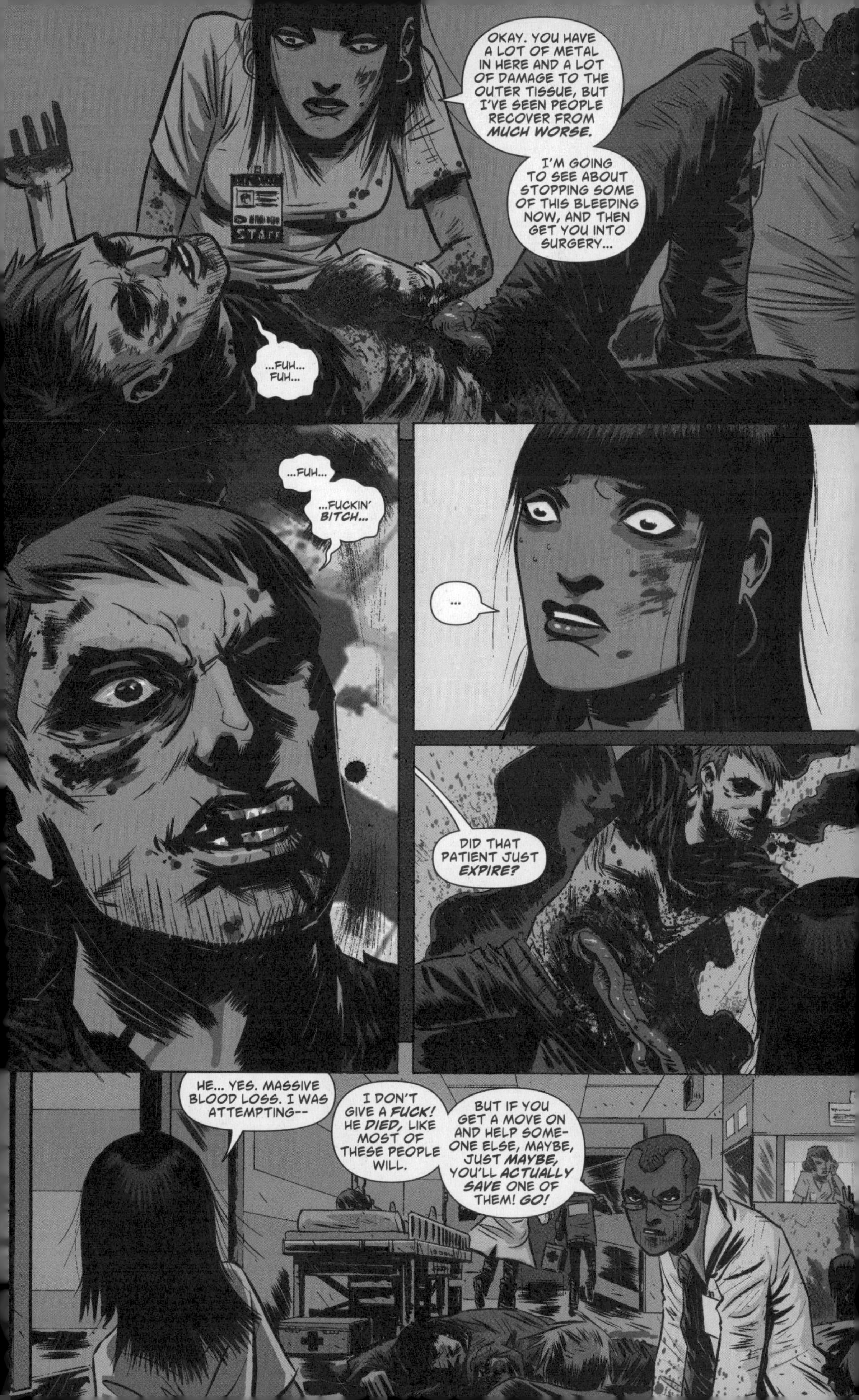
OKAY. YOU HAVE A LOT OF METAL IN HERE AND A LOT OF DAMAGE TO THE OUTER TISSUE, BUT I'VE SEEN PEOPLE RECOVER FROM MUCH WORSE.
I'M GOING TO SEE ABOUT STOPPING SOME OF THIS BLEEDING NOW, AND THEN GET YOU INTO SURGERY...
STAFF
...FUH... FUH...
...FUH...
...FUCKIN' BITCH...
...
DID THAT PATIENT JUST EXPIRE?
HE... YES. MASSIVE BLOOD LOSS. I WAS ATTEMPTING--
I DON'T GIVE A FUCK! HE DIED, LIKE MOST OF THESE PEOPLE WILL.
BUT IF YOU GET A MOVE ON AND HELP SOME-ONE ELSE, MAYBE, JUST MAYBE, YOU'LL ACTUALLY SAVE ONE OF THEM! GO!

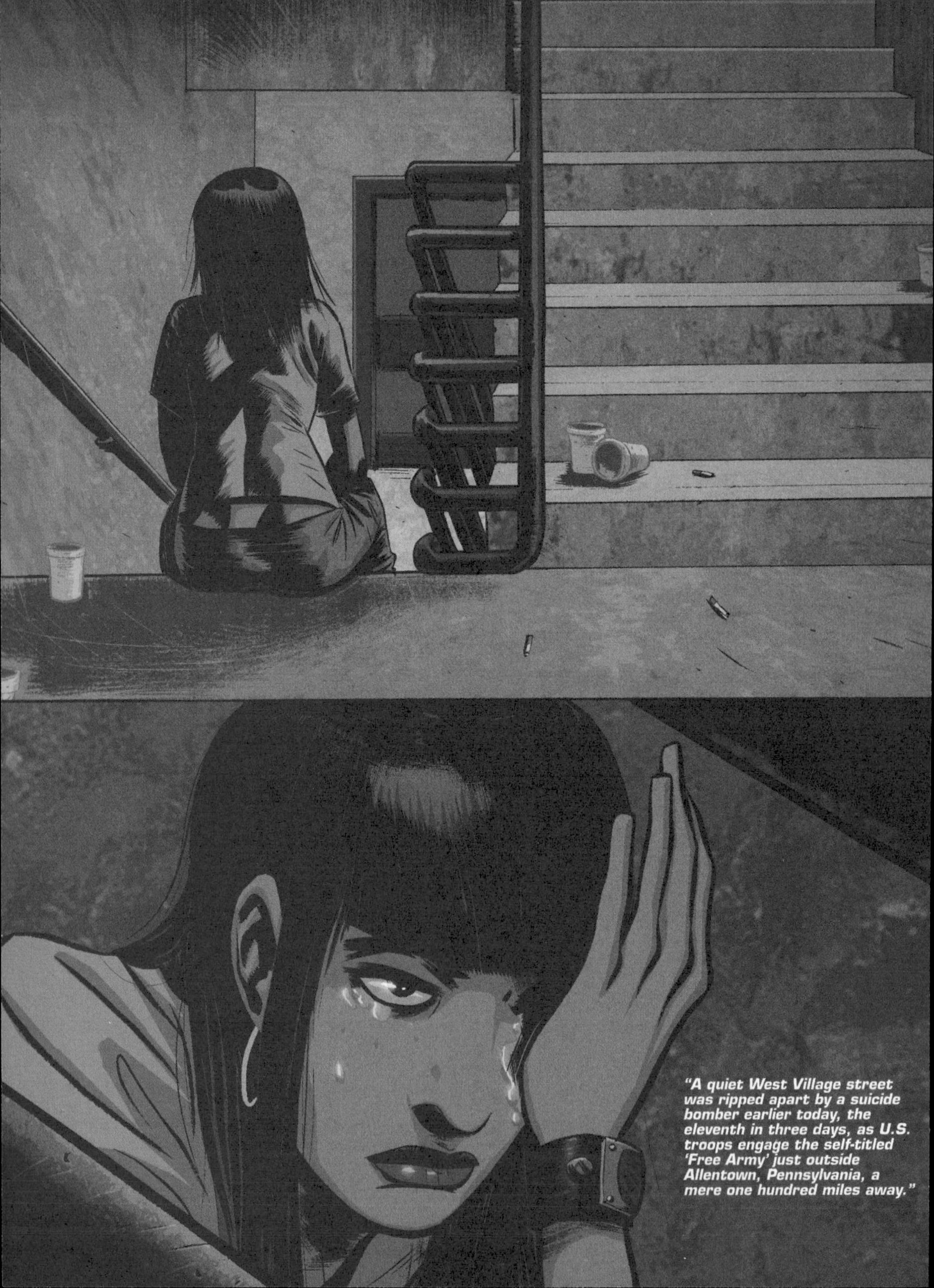
"A quiet West Village street was ripped apart by a suicide bomber earlier today, the eleventh in three days, as U.S. troops engage the self-titled 'Free Army' just outside Allentown, Pennsylvania, a mere one hundred miles away."

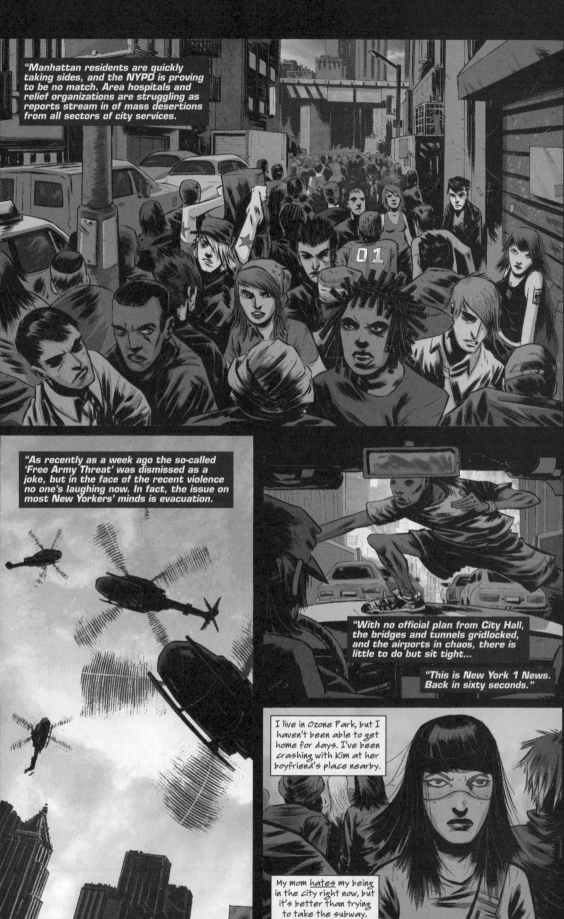

"Manhattan residents are quickly taking sides, and the NYPD is proving to be no match. Area hospitals and relief organizations are struggling as reports stream in of mass desertions from all sectors of city services.

"As recently as a week ago the so-called 'Free Army Threat' was dismissed as a joke, but in the face of the recent violence no one's laughing now. In fact, the issue on most New Yorkers' minds is evacuation.

"With no official plan from City Hall, the bridges and tunnels gridlocked, and the airports in chaos, there is little to do but sit tight...

"This is New York 1 News. Back in sixty seconds."

I live in Ozone Park, but I haven't been able to get home for days. I've been crashing with Kim at her boyfriend's place nearby.

My mom hates my being in the city right now, but it's better than trying to take the subway.

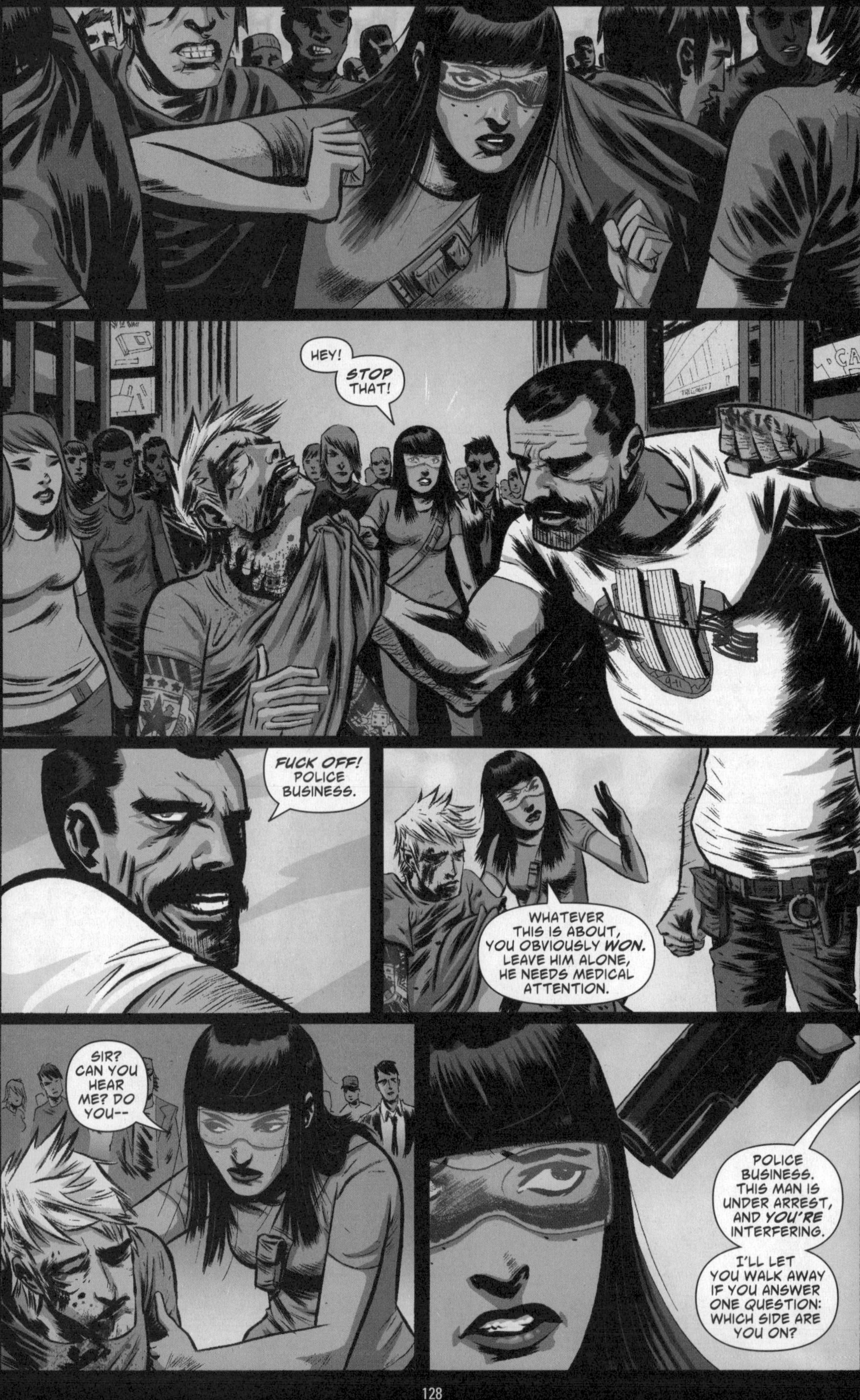
HEY! STOP THAT!
FUCK OFF! POLICE BUSINESS.
WHATEVER THIS IS ABOUT, YOU OBVIOUSLY WON. LEAVE HIM ALONE, HE NEEDS MEDICAL ATTENTION.
SIR? CAN YOU HEAR ME? DO YOU--
POLICE BUSINESS. THIS MAN IS UNDER ARREST, AND YOU'RE INTERFERING.
I'LL LET YOU WALK AWAY IF YOU ANSWER ONE QUESTION: WHICH SIDE ARE YOU ON?

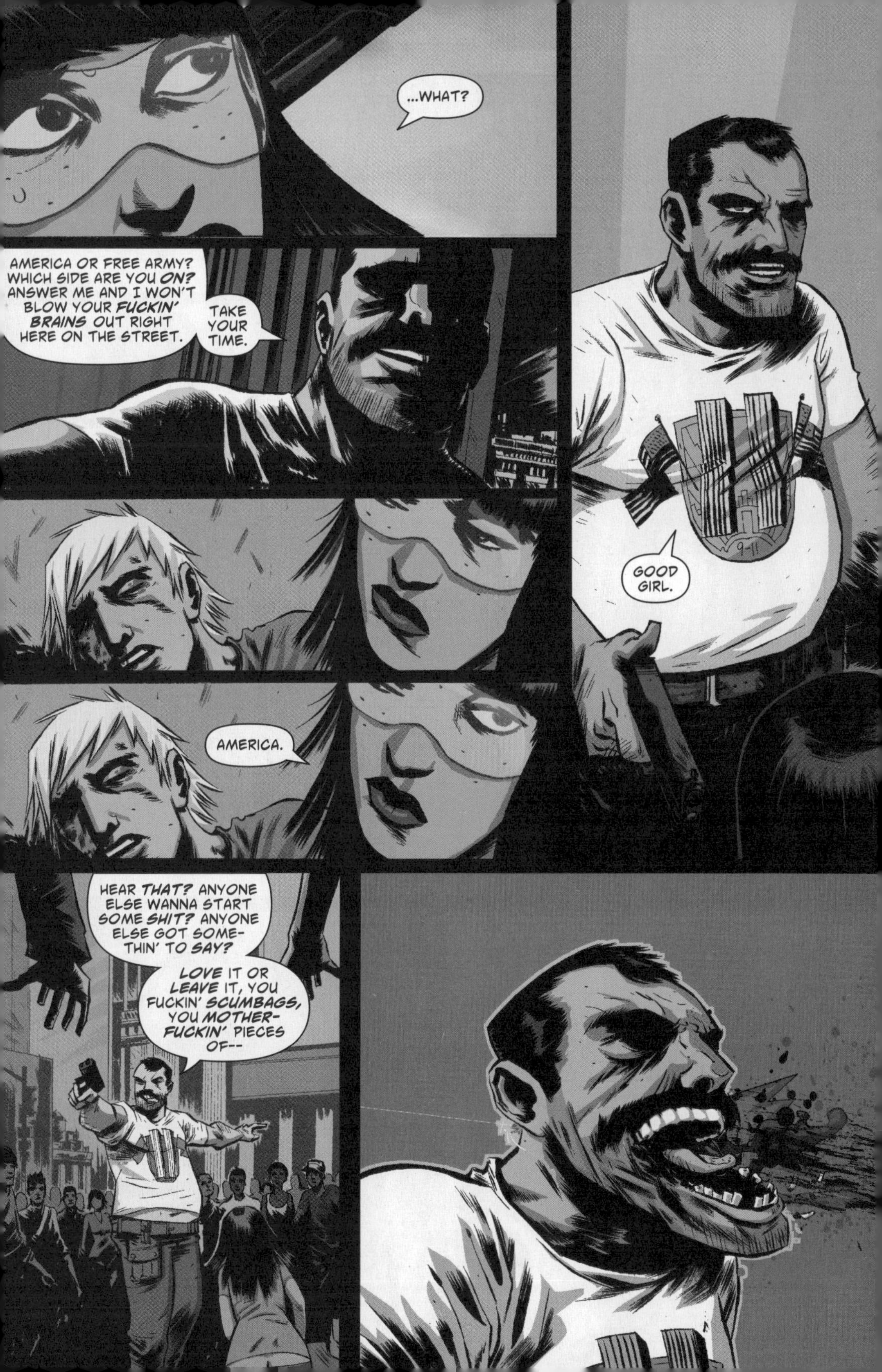
...WHAT?
AMERICA OR FREE ARMY? WHICH SIDE ARE YOU ON? ANSWER ME AND I WON'T BLOW YOUR FUCKIN' BRAINS OUT RIGHT HERE ON THE STREET.
TAKE YOUR TIME.
AMERICA.
GOOD GIRL.
HEAR THAT? ANYONE ELSE WANNA START SOME SHIT? ANYONE ELSE GOT SOME-THIN' TO SAY?
LOVE IT OR LEAVE IT, YOU FUCKIN' SCUMBAGS, YOU MOTHER-FUCKIN' PIECES OF--
9-11

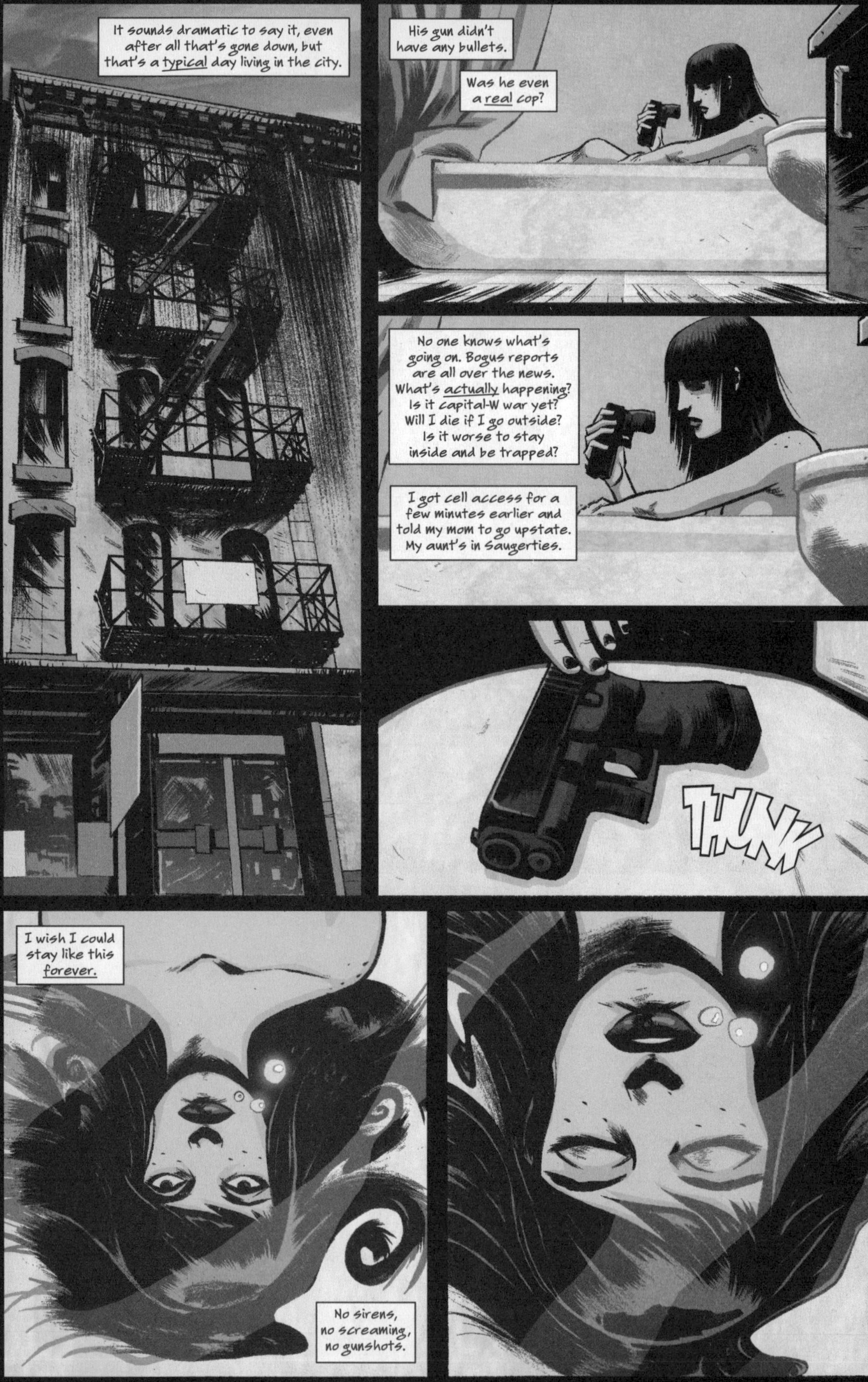
It sounds dramatic to say it, even after all that's gone down, but that's a typical day living in the city.
His gun didn't have any bullets.
Was he even a real cop?
No one knows what's going on. Bogus reports are all over the news. What's actually happening? Is it capital-W war yet? Will I die if I go outside? Is it worse to stay inside and be trapped?
I got cell access for a few minutes earlier and told my mom to go upstate. My aunt's in Saugerties.
THUNK
I wish I could stay like this forever.
No sirens, no screaming, no gunshots.

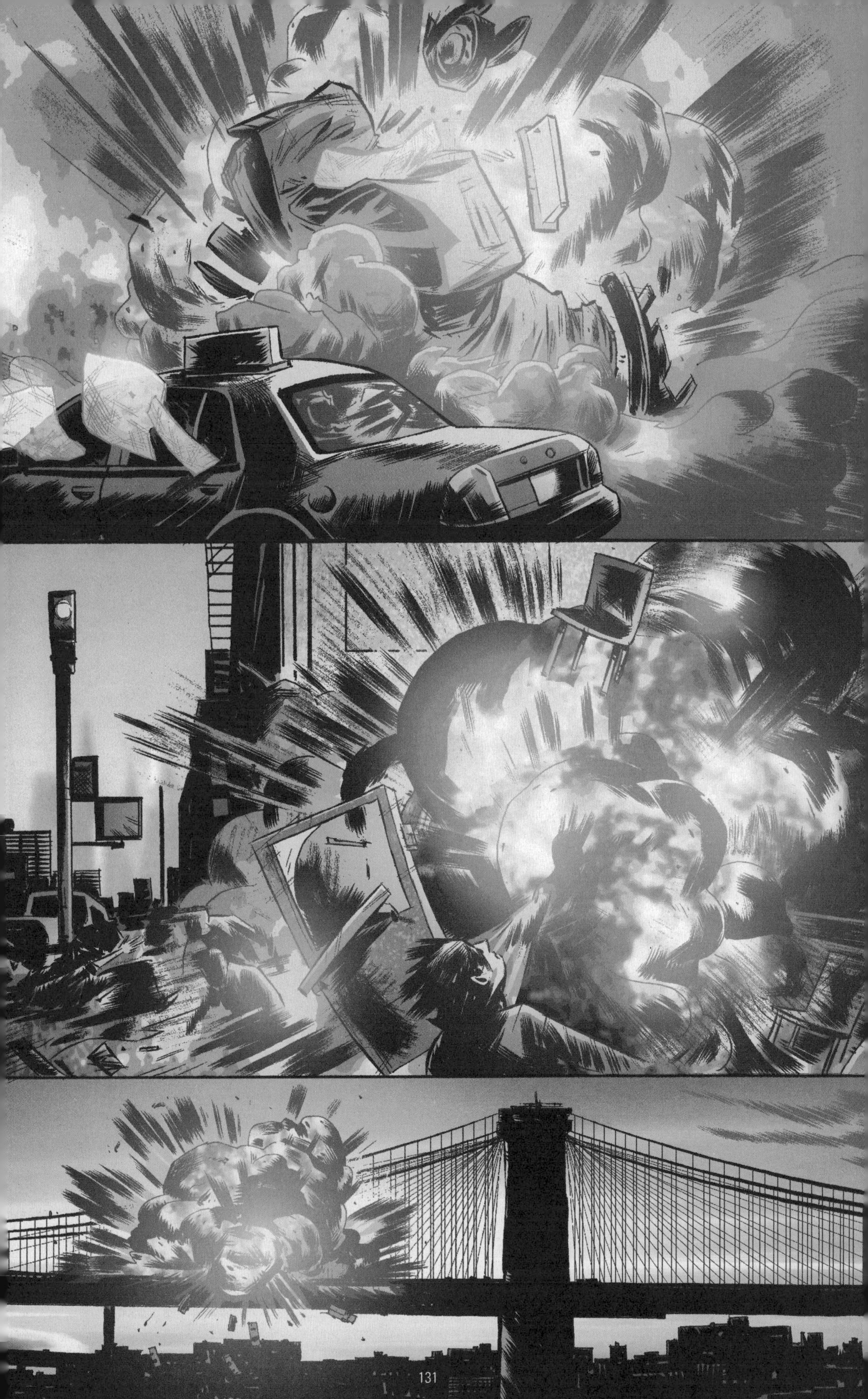

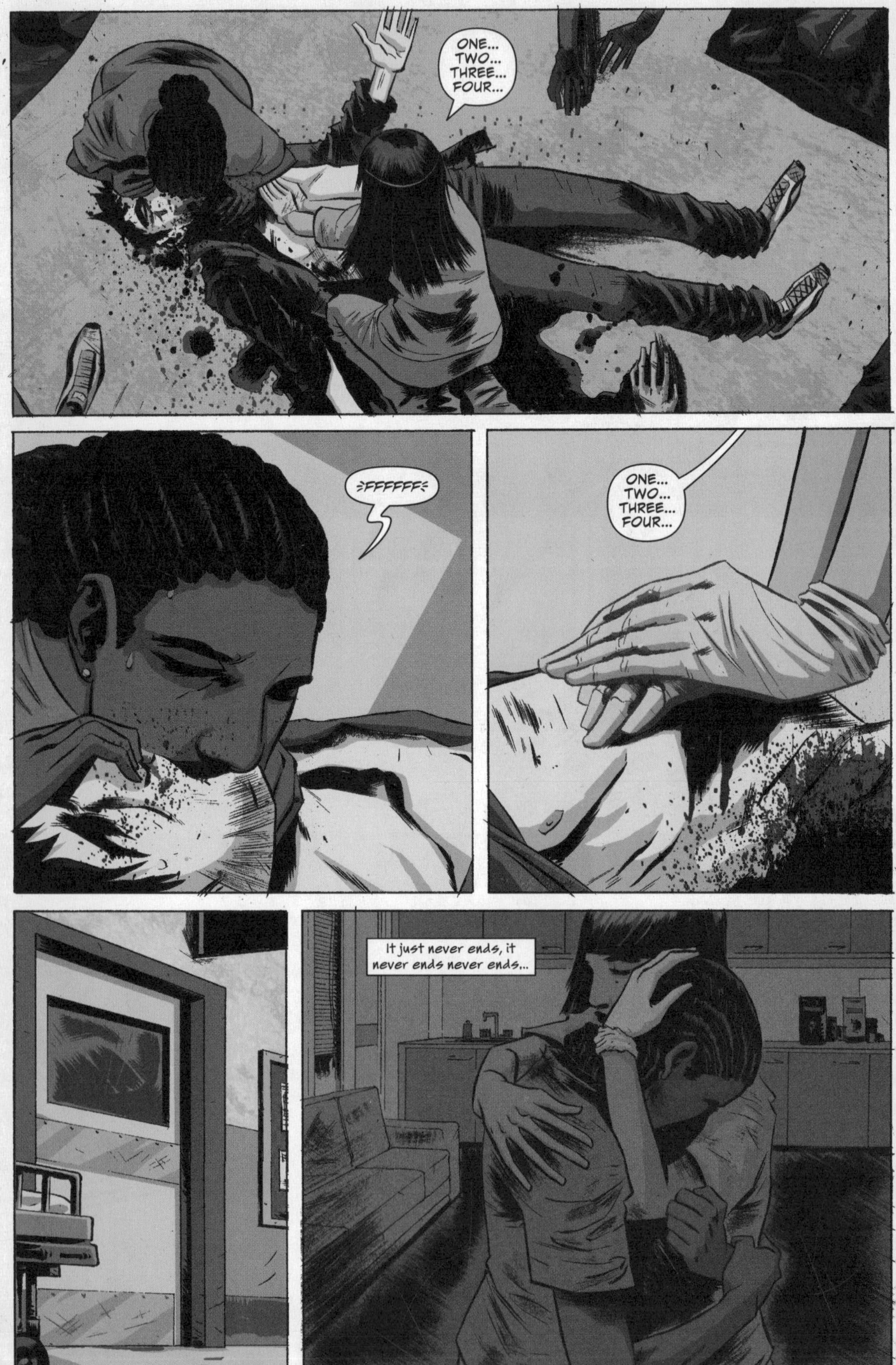
ONE... TWO... THREE... FOUR...
≠FFFFFF≠
ONE... TWO... THREE... FOUR...
It just never ends, it never ends never ends...

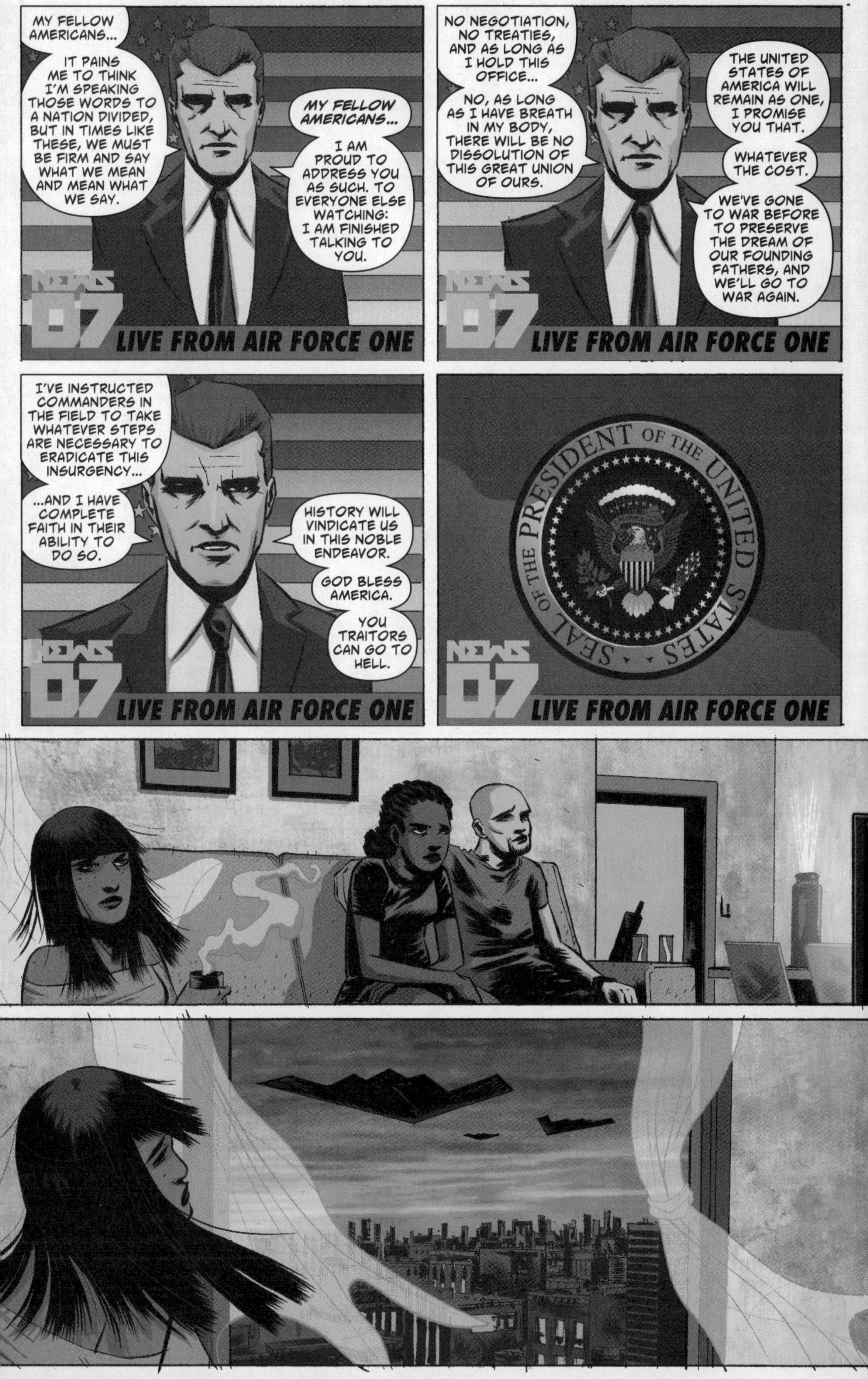
MY FELLOW AMERICANS...
IT PAINS ME TO THINK I'M SPEAKING THOSE WORDS TO A NATION DIVIDED, BUT IN TIMES LIKE THESE, WE MUST BE FIRM AND SAY WHAT WE MEAN AND MEAN WHAT WE SAY.
MY FELLOW AMERICANS...
I AM PROUD TO ADDRESS YOU AS SUCH. TO EVERYONE ELSE WATCHING: I AM FINISHED TALKING TO YOU.
NEWS 07
LIVE FROM AIR FORCE ONE
NO NEGOTIATION, NO TREATIES, AND AS LONG AS I HOLD THIS OFFICE...
NO, AS LONG AS I HAVE BREATH IN MY BODY, THERE WILL BE NO DISSOLUTION OF THIS GREAT UNION OF OURS.
THE UNITED STATES OF AMERICA WILL REMAIN AS ONE, I PROMISE YOU THAT.
WHATEVER THE COST.
WE'VE GONE TO WAR BEFORE TO PRESERVE THE DREAM OF OUR FOUNDING FATHERS, AND WE'LL GO TO WAR AGAIN.
NEWS 07
LIVE FROM AIR FORCE ONE
I'VE INSTRUCTED COMMANDERS IN THE FIELD TO TAKE WHATEVER STEPS ARE NECESSARY TO ERADICATE THIS INSURGENCY...
...AND I HAVE COMPLETE FAITH IN THEIR ABILITY TO DO SO.
HISTORY WILL VINDICATE US IN THIS NOBLE ENDEAVOR.
GOD BLESS AMERICA.
YOU TRAITORS CAN GO TO HELL.
NEWS 07
LIVE FROM AIR FORCE ONE
SEAL OF THE PRESIDENT OF THE UNITED STATES
NEWS 07
LIVE FROM AIR FORCE ONE

STAFF	STATUS
Dr. Dennis	missing.
Dr. Wood	reassigned.
Dr. Zagami	reassigned.
Dr. Brandon	evacuated.
Dr. Macdonald	missing.
Dr. Spears	missing.
Dr. Filardi	critically injured.
Dr. Seijas	evacuated.
Dr. Shannon	missing.
Dr. Hopkins	evacuated.

manhattan is fucked!!

ATTENTION

IMMEDIATE RELOCATION

REPORT TO THE FOLLOWING LOCATIONS FOR FRONTLINE ~~REASSIGNMENT.~~ *DRAFTING <3*

IF EVACUATING WITH FAMILY YOU MUST CONTACT YOUR DEPT. SUPERVISORS OR RISK TERMINATION.

ATT

DO NOT TA
SUPPLIES
AUTHORIZ

I DON'T GET IT. NO ONE IS STAYING HERE... WE'RE ALL BEING MOVED SOMEWHERE ELSE?

WHO'S GOING TO STAY HERE TO TREAT THE WOUNDED?

NO ONE. THEY'RE EVACUATING THE HOSPITAL ENTIRELY. ORDERS FROM THE TOP BRASS. THEY CAN'T ENSURE OUR SAFETY IF WE STAY, AND ANYWAY, THEY'RE GONNA EVACUATE THE ISLAND, RIGHT?

WE'LL DO MORE GOOD AT THESE MILITARY HOSPITALS THEY'RE SENDING US TO.

THEY CAN'T ALL BE EVACUATED IN TIME!

THEY'LL BE STUCK HERE!

BUT THERE'S JUST NO WAY EVERYONE IS GONNA BE ABLE TO LEAVE. THINK ABOUT IT, MAN... HOW MANY MILLION PEOPLE LIVE HERE? IT'S *OBVIOUS* SOME ARE GOING TO BE LEFT BEHIND.

WHAT ABOUT THEM?

THEM? WHAT, THE *TERRORISTS*? YOU WANNA HELP *THEM*? *FUCK* THEM!

WHAT? WHAT "TERRORISTS"? I'M TALKING ABOUT *PEOPLE!* CIVILIANS!

Twenty minutes later I left my badge on my supervisor's desk and walked out.

134

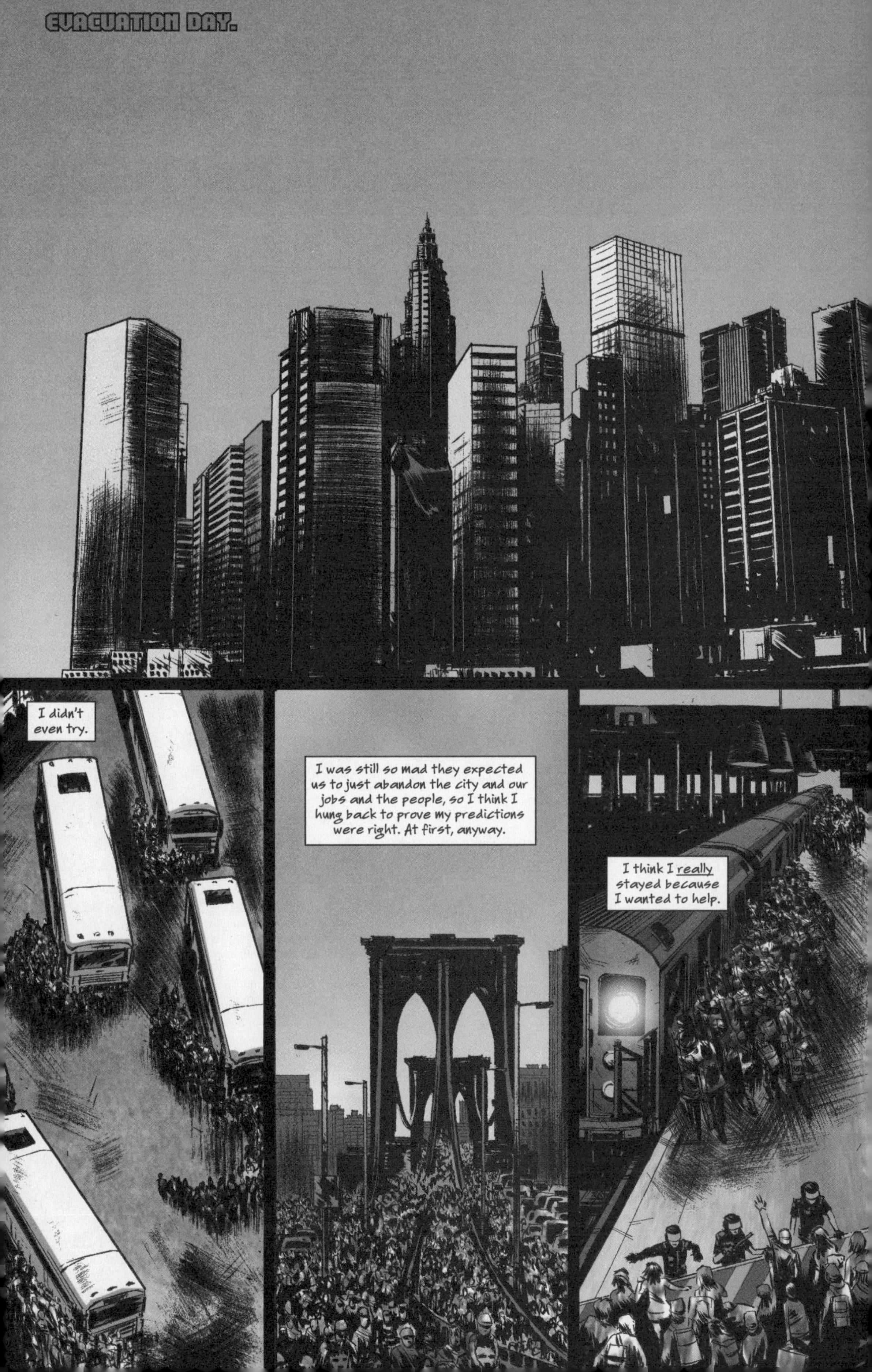
EVACUATION DAY.
I didn't even try.
I was still so mad they expected us to just abandon the city and our jobs and the people, so I think I hung back to prove my predictions were right. At first, anyway.
I think I really stayed because I wanted to help.

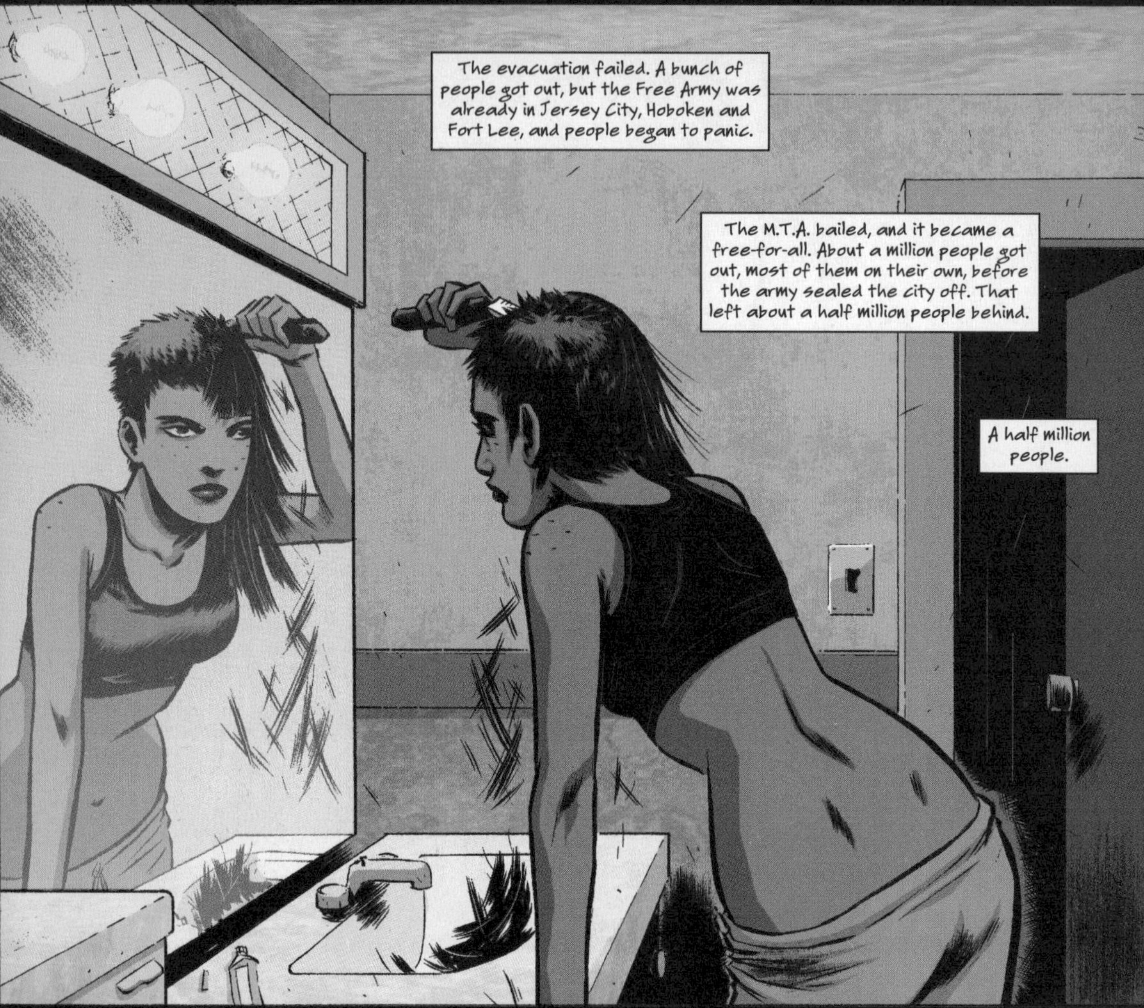
The evacuation failed. A bunch of people got out, but the Free Army was already in Jersey City, Hoboken and Fort Lee, and people began to panic.
The M.T.A. bailed, and it became a free-for-all. About a million people got out, most of them on their own, before the army sealed the city off. That left about a half million people behind.
A half million people.

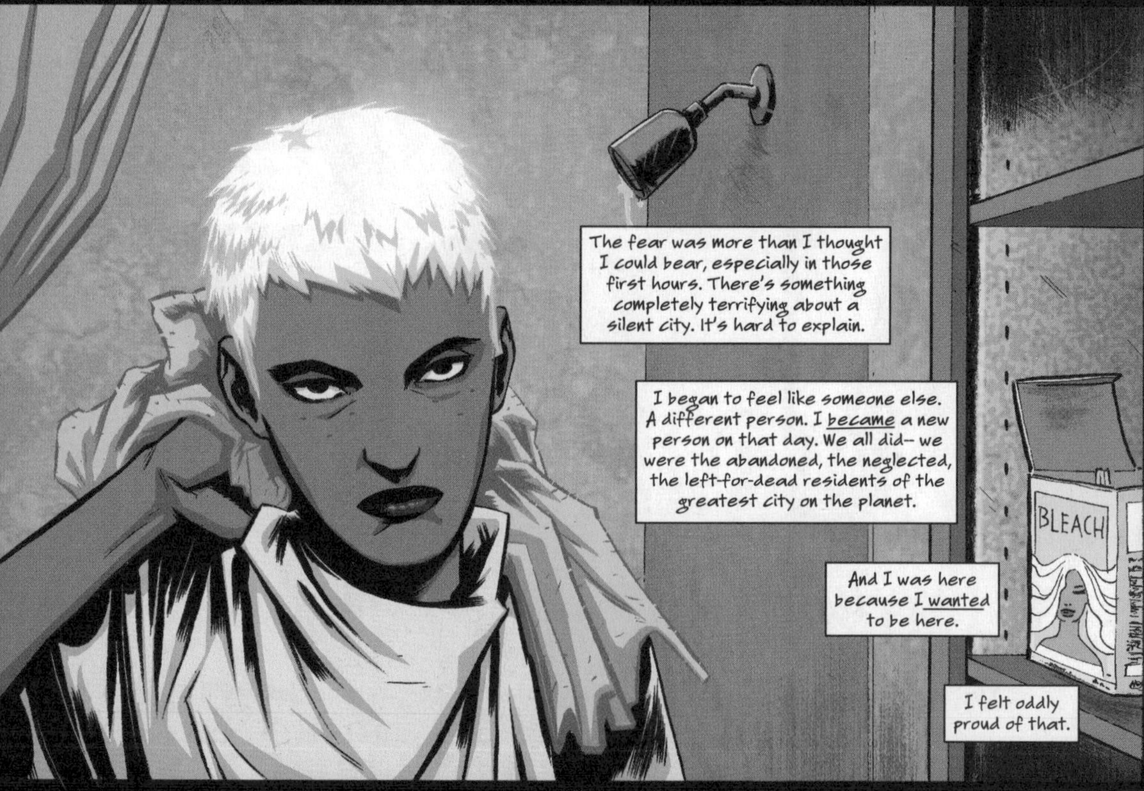
The fear was more than I thought I could bear, especially in those first hours. There's something completely terrifying about a silent city. It's hard to explain.
I began to feel like someone else. A different person. I became a new person on that day. We all did-- we were the abandoned, the neglected, the left-for-dead residents of the greatest city on the planet.
BLEACH
And I was here because I wanted to be here.
I felt oddly proud of that.

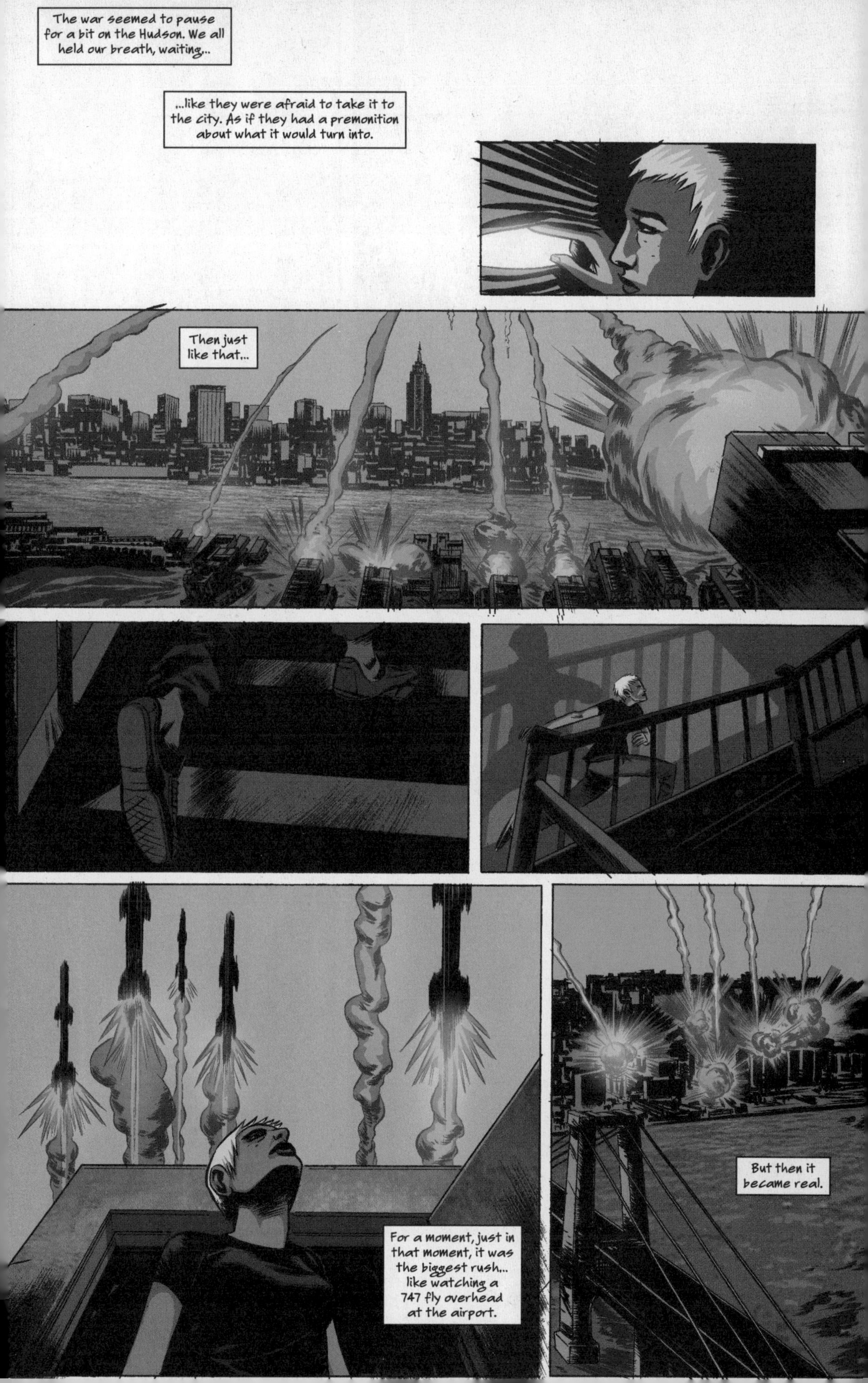
The war seemed to pause for a bit on the Hudson. We all held our breath, waiting...
...like they were afraid to take it to the city. As if they had a premonition about what it would turn into.
Then just like that...
For a moment, just in that moment, it was the biggest rush... like watching a 747 fly overhead at the airport.
But then it became real.

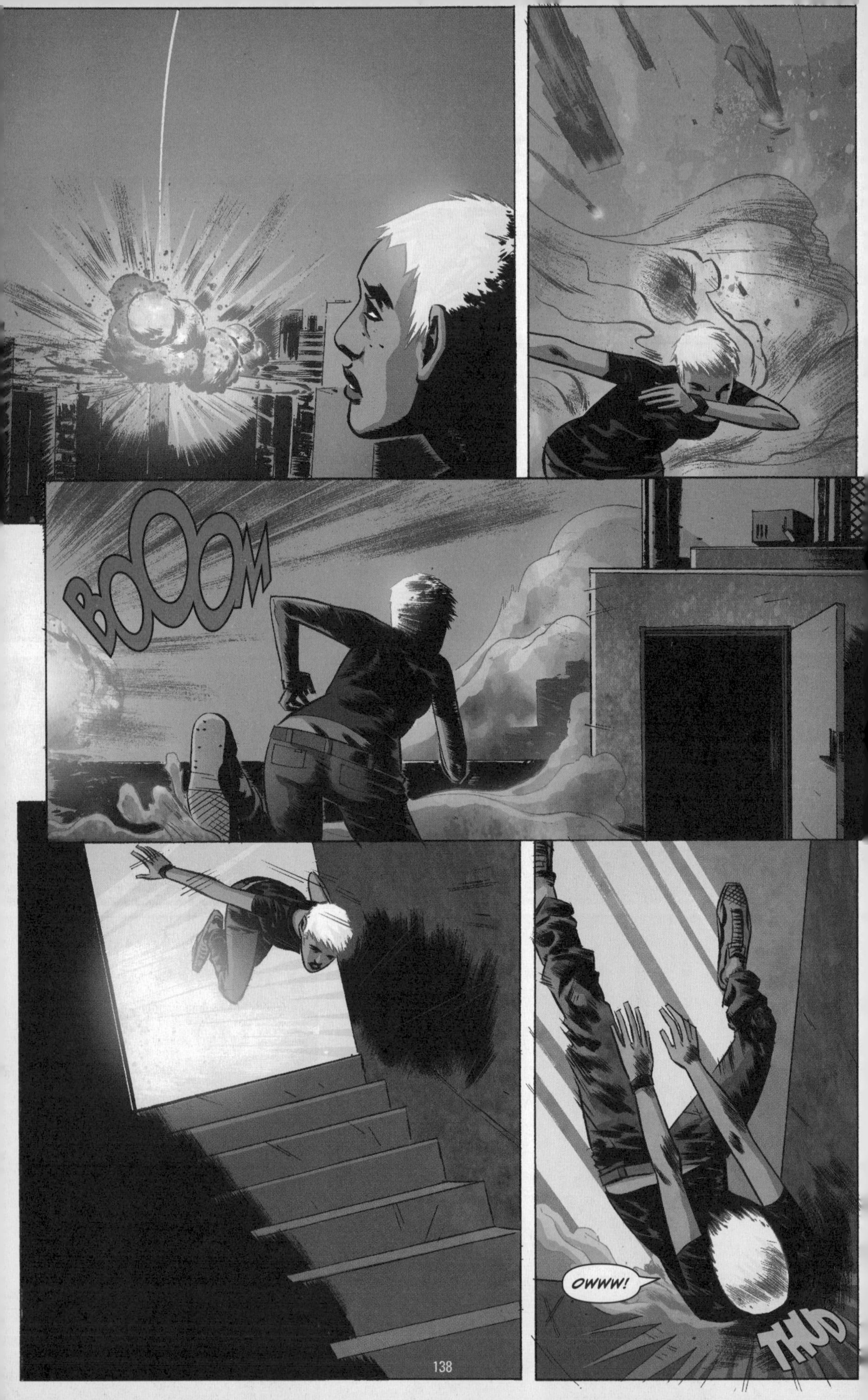
BOOOM
OWWW!
THUD

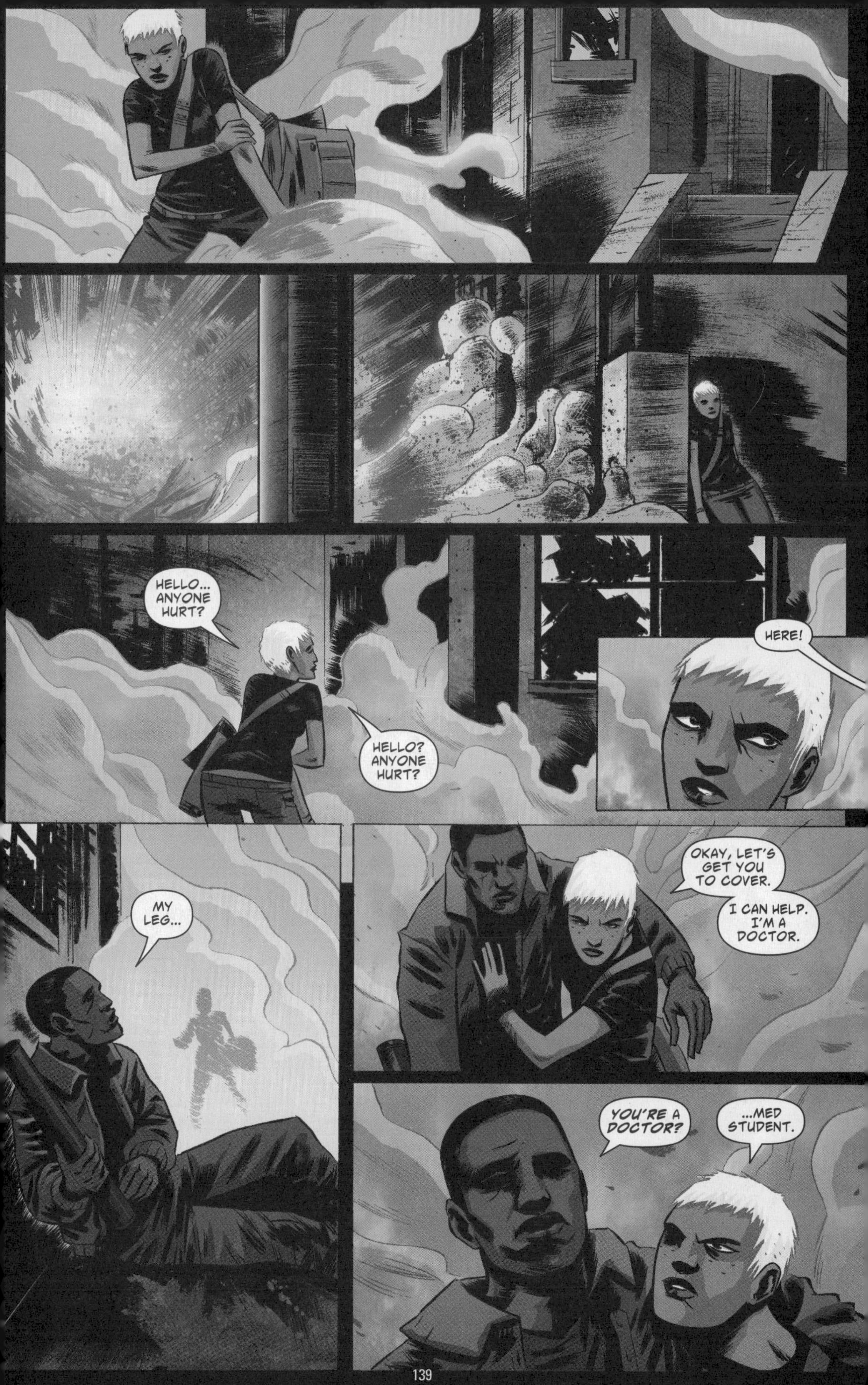
HELLO... ANYONE HURT?
HELLO? ANYONE HURT?
HERE!
MY LEG...
OKAY, LET'S GET YOU TO COVER.
I CAN HELP. I'M A DOCTOR.
YOU'RE A DOCTOR?
...MED STUDENT.

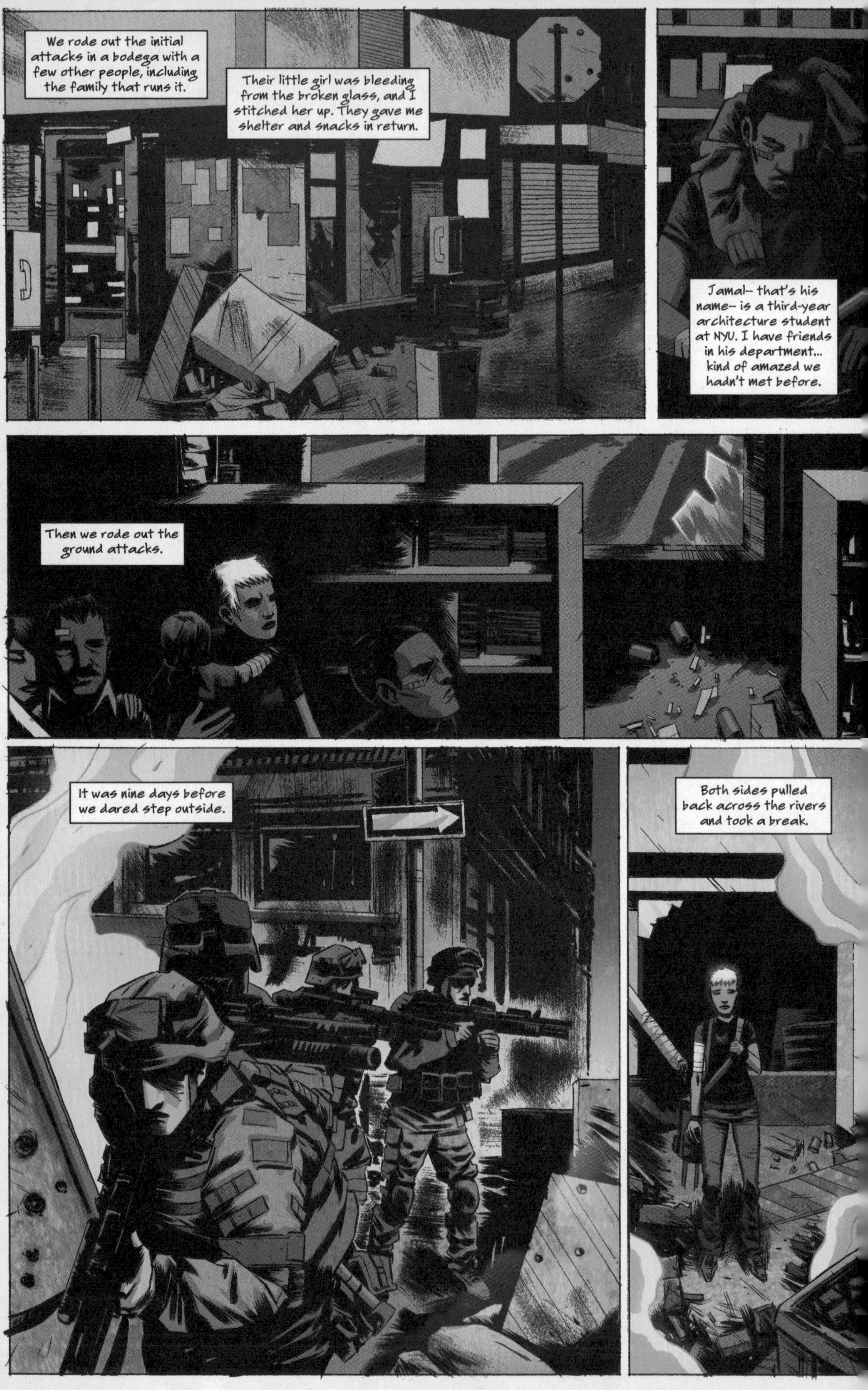
We rode out the initial attacks in a bodega with a few other people, including the family that runs it.
Their little girl was bleeding from the broken glass, and I stitched her up. They gave me shelter and snacks in return.
Jamal– that's his name– is a third-year architecture student at NYU. I have friends in his department... kind of amazed we hadn't met before.
Then we rode out the ground attacks.
It was nine days before we dared step outside.
Both sides pulled back across the rivers and took a break.

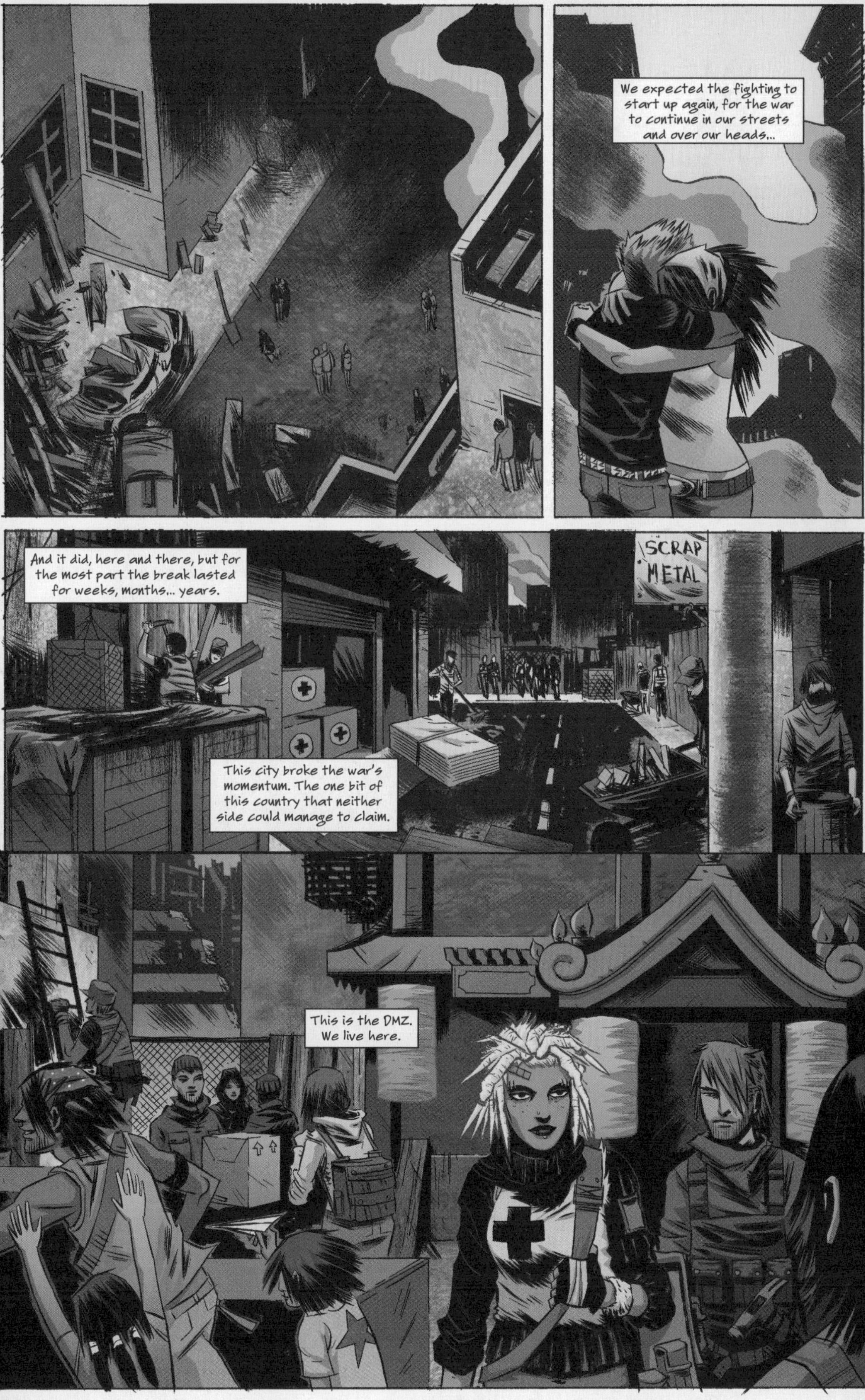
We expected the fighting to start up again, for the war to continue in our streets and over our heads...
And it did, here and there, but for the most part the break lasted for weeks, months... years.
SCRAP METAL
This city broke the war's momentum. The one bit of this country that neither side could manage to claim.
This is the DMZ. We live here.

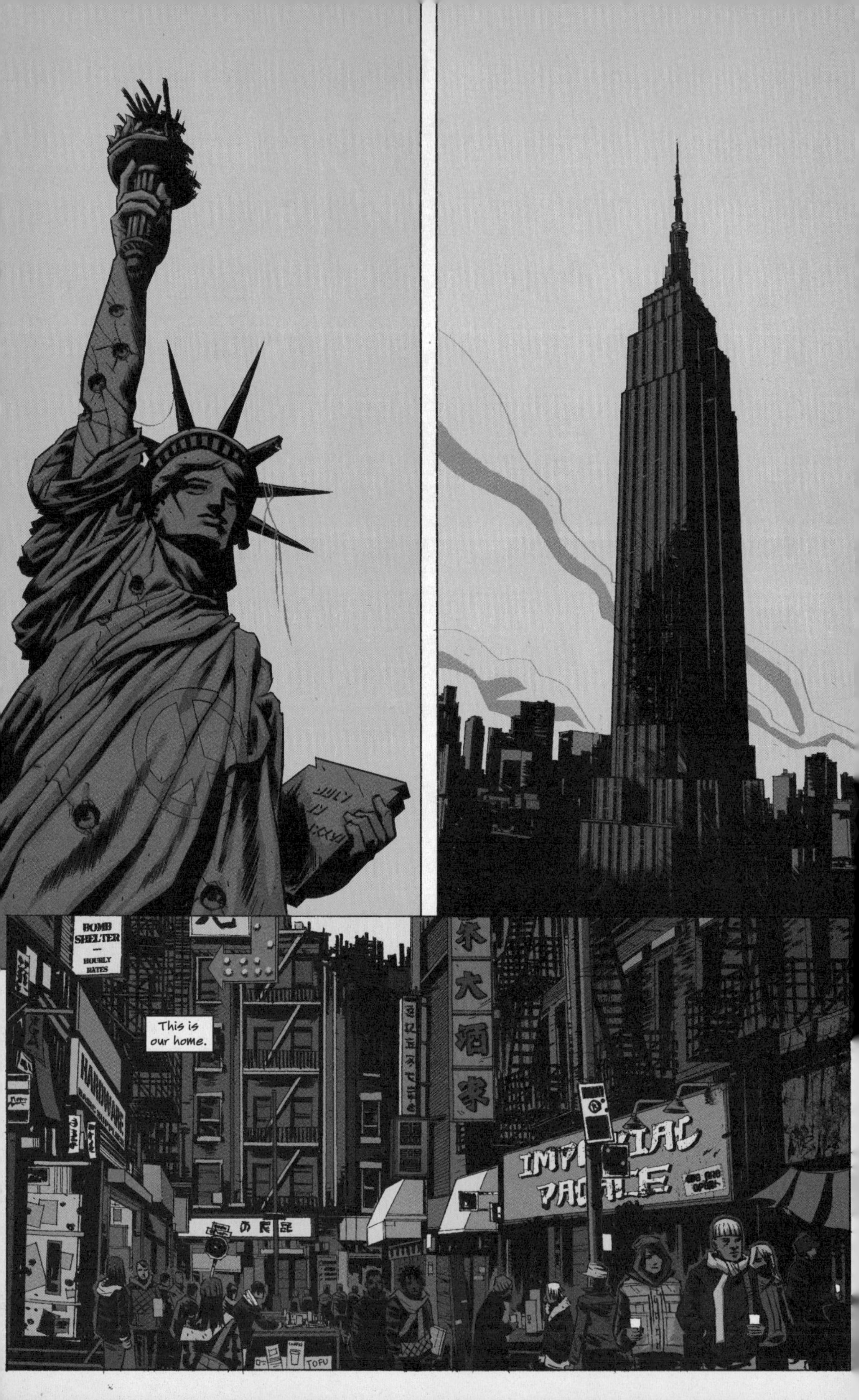
BOMB SHELTER
HOURLY RATES
This is our home.
TOFU

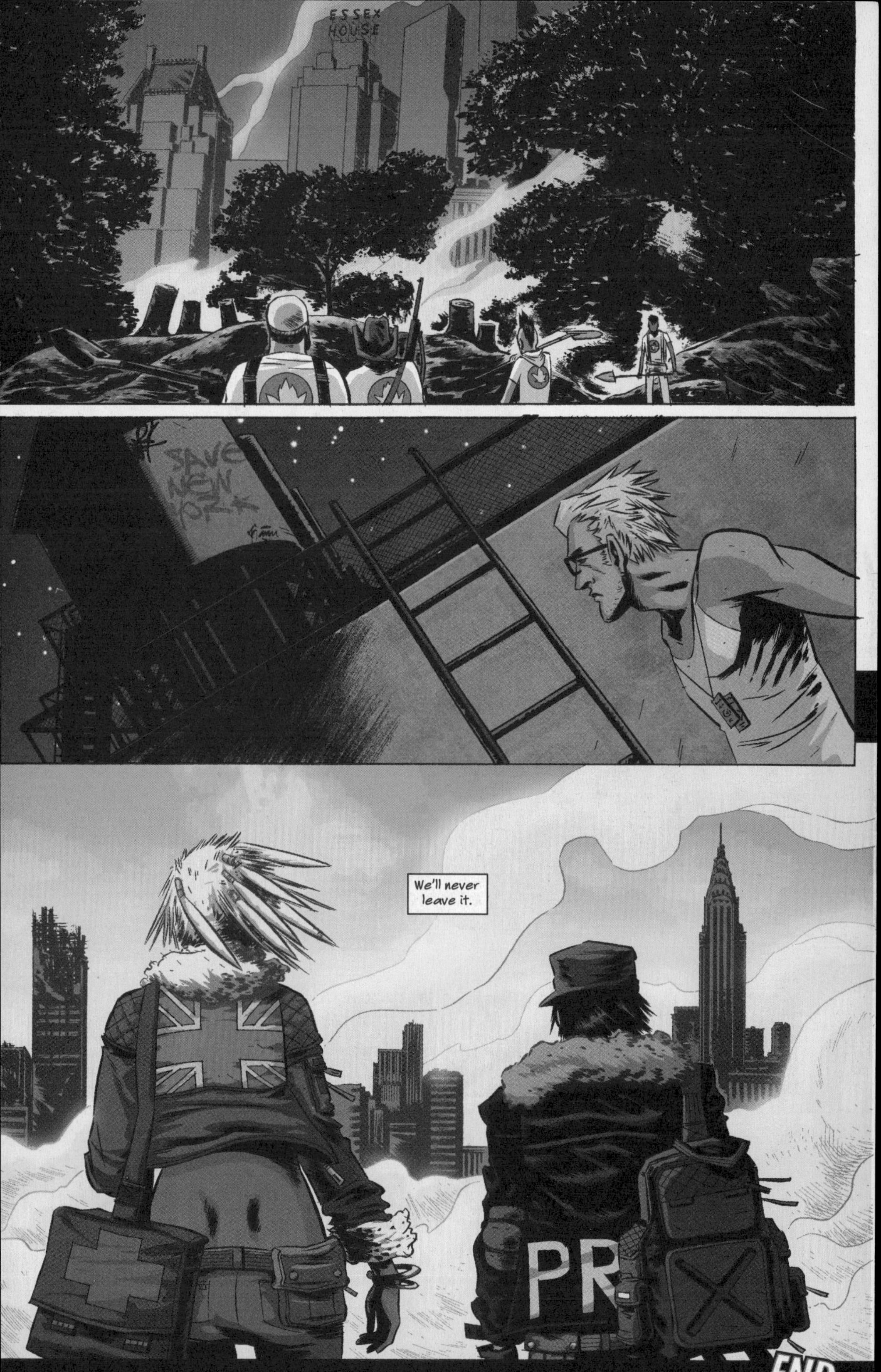
ESSEX HOUSE
SAVE NEW YORK
We'll never leave it.
PR
END

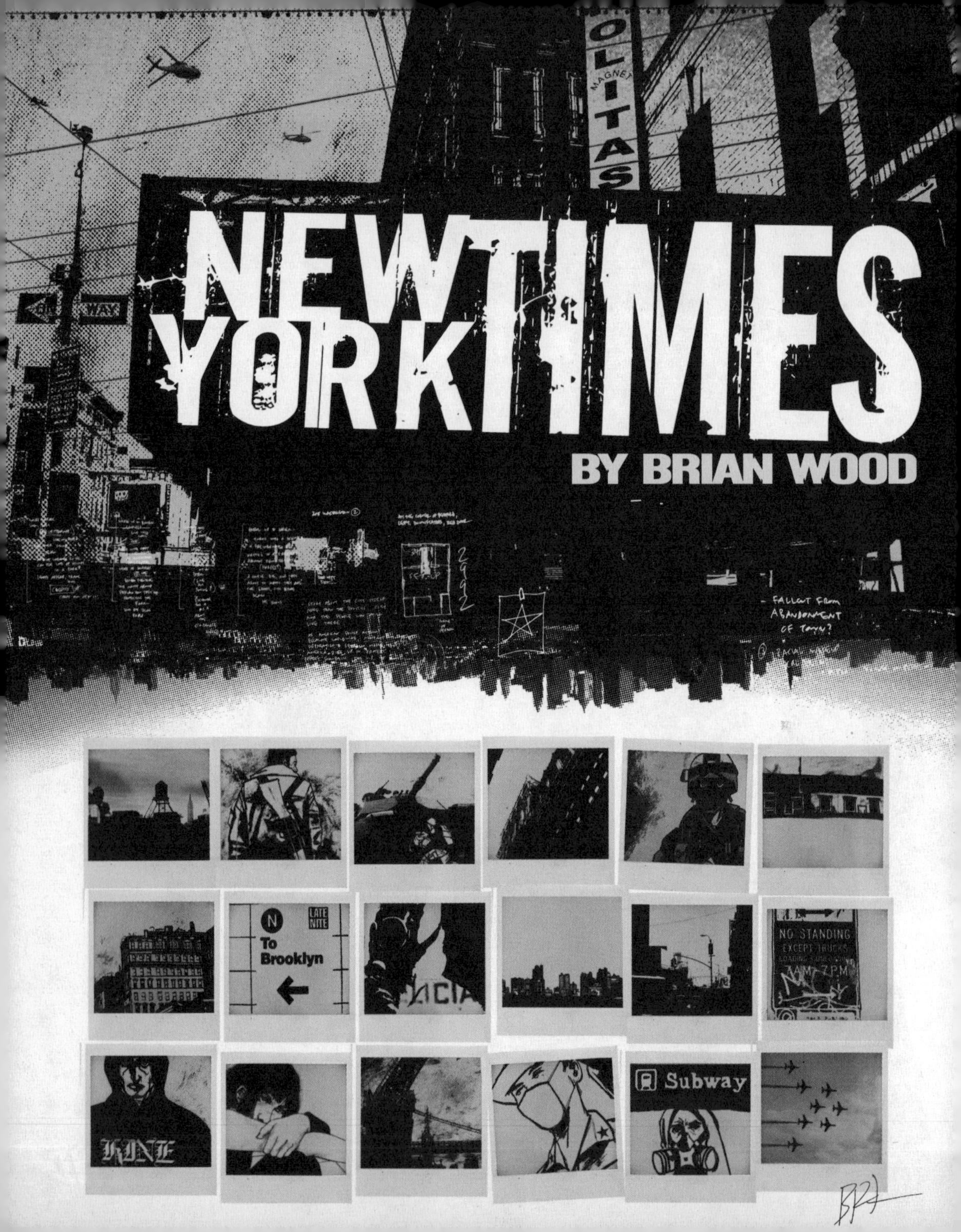
NEW YORK TIMES
BY BRIAN WOOD
OLITAS
WAY
- FALLOUT FROM ABANDONMENT OF TOWN?
N
LATE NITE
To Brooklyn
NO STANDING
EXCEPT TRUCKS
Subway
KINE

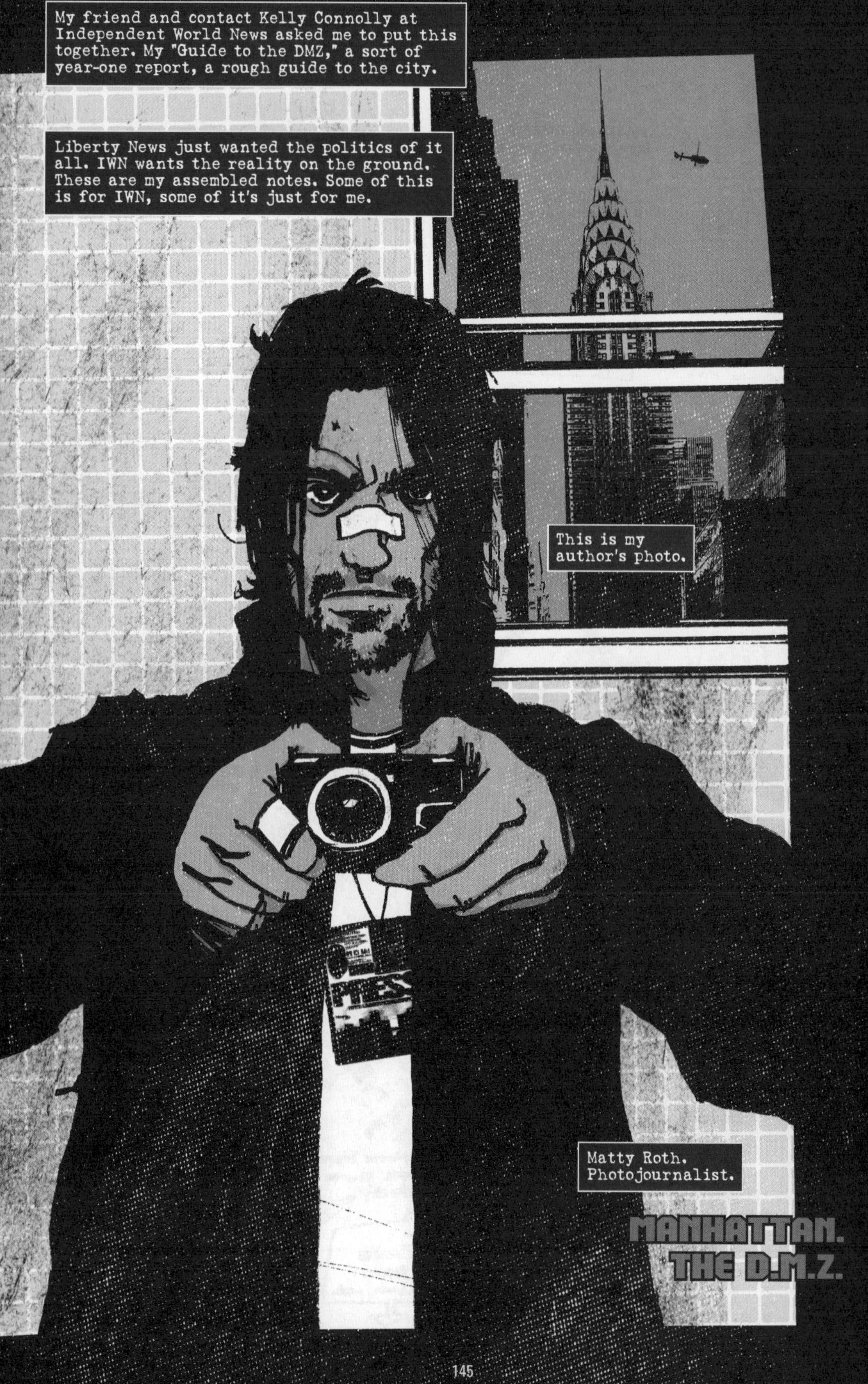
My friend and contact Kelly Connolly at Independent World News asked me to put this together. My "Guide to the DMZ," a sort of year-one report, a rough guide to the city.
Liberty News just wanted the politics of it all. IWN wants the reality on the ground. These are my assembled notes. Some of this is for IWN, some of it's just for me.
This is my author's photo.
Matty Roth. Photojournalist.
MANHATTAN. THE D.M.Z.

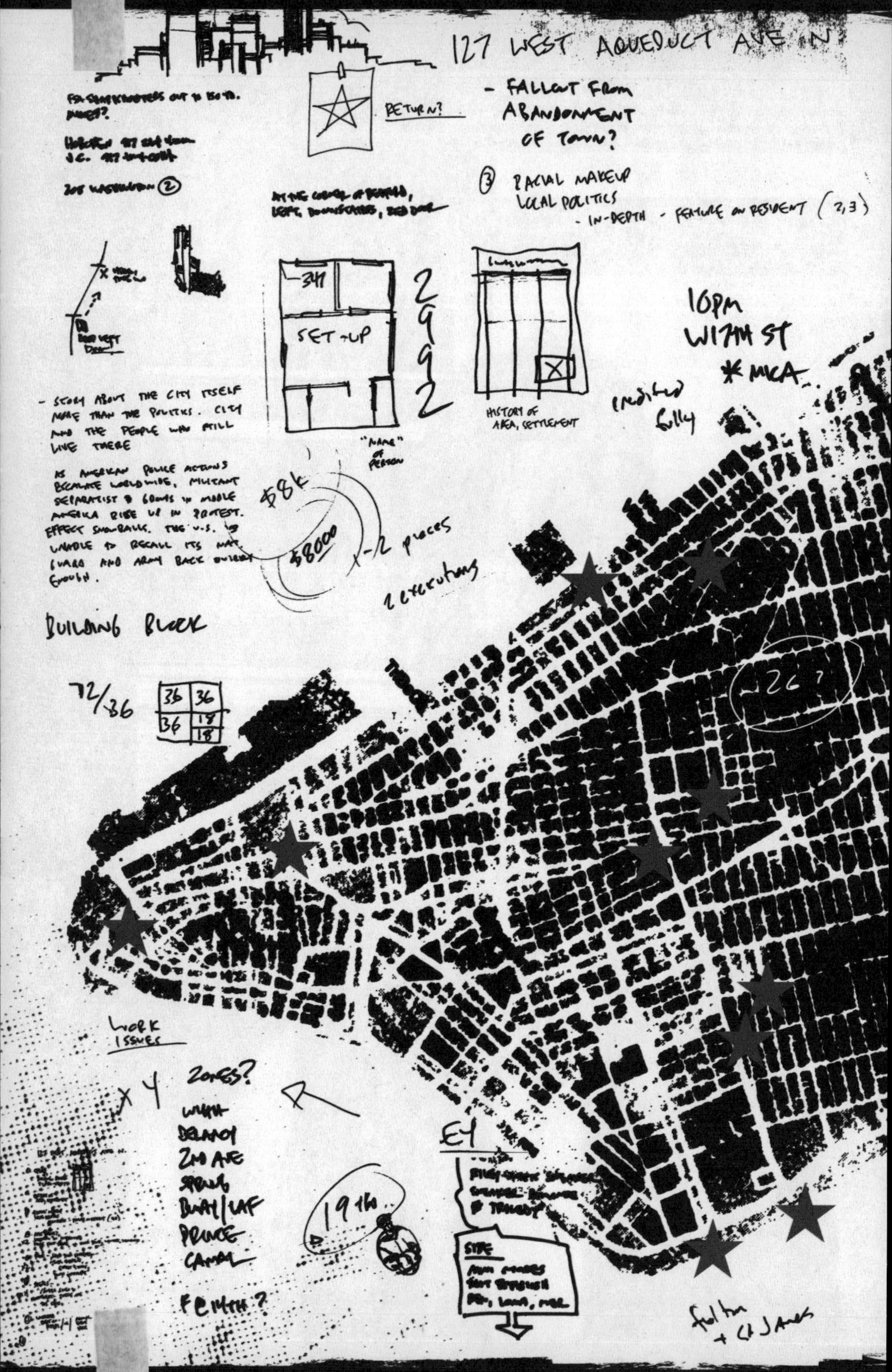
127 WEST AQUEDUCT AVE N
RETURN?
- FALLOUT FROM ABANDONMENT OF TOWN?
③ RACIAL MAKEUP
LOCAL POLITICS
- IN-DEPTH - FEATURE ON RESIDENT (2,3)
341
SET-UP
2992
"NAME" OF PERSON
HISTORY OF AREA, SETTLEMENT
10PM
W17TH ST
* MICA
- STORY ABOUT THE CITY ITSELF MORE THAN THE POLITICS. CITY AND THE PEOPLE WHO STILL LIVE THERE
AS AMERICAN POLICE ACTIONS ESCALATE WORLDWIDE, MILITANT SEPARATIST & GROUPS IN MIDDLE AMERICA RISE UP IN PROTEST. EFFECT SNOWBALLS. THE U.S. IS UNABLE TO RECALL ITS NAT. GUARD AND ARMY BACK QUICKLY ENOUGH.
$8K
$8000
x-2 pieces
2 executions
BUILDING BLOCK
72/36
36 36
36 18
18
~26?
WORK ISSUES
x 4 ZONES?
DELANCY
2ND AVE
SPRING
PRINCE
CANAL
19th
FEMTH?

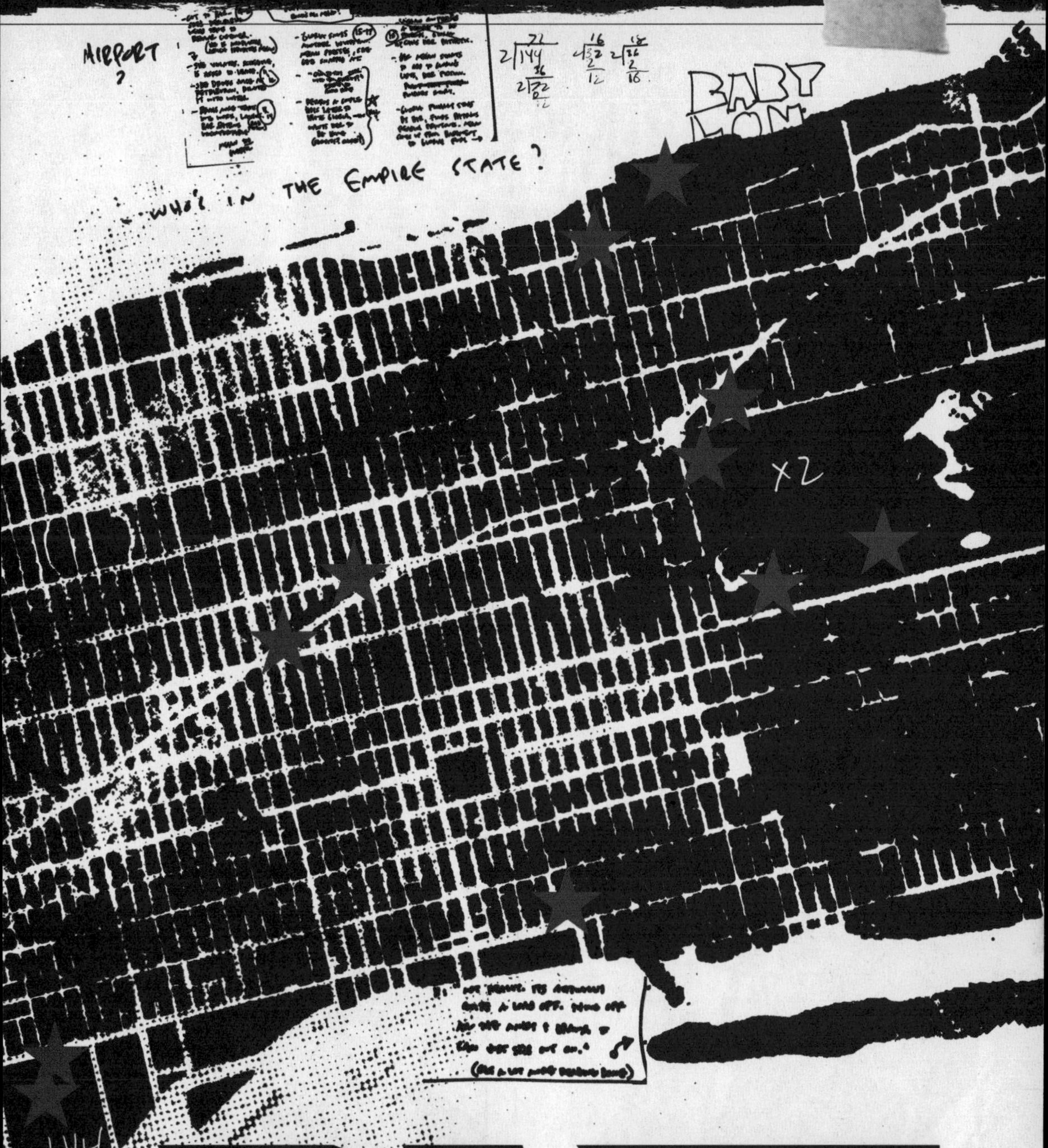
AIRPORT ?
BABY MOM
WHO'S IN THE EMPIRE STATE?
X2
144

DMZ

NEW YORK TIMES

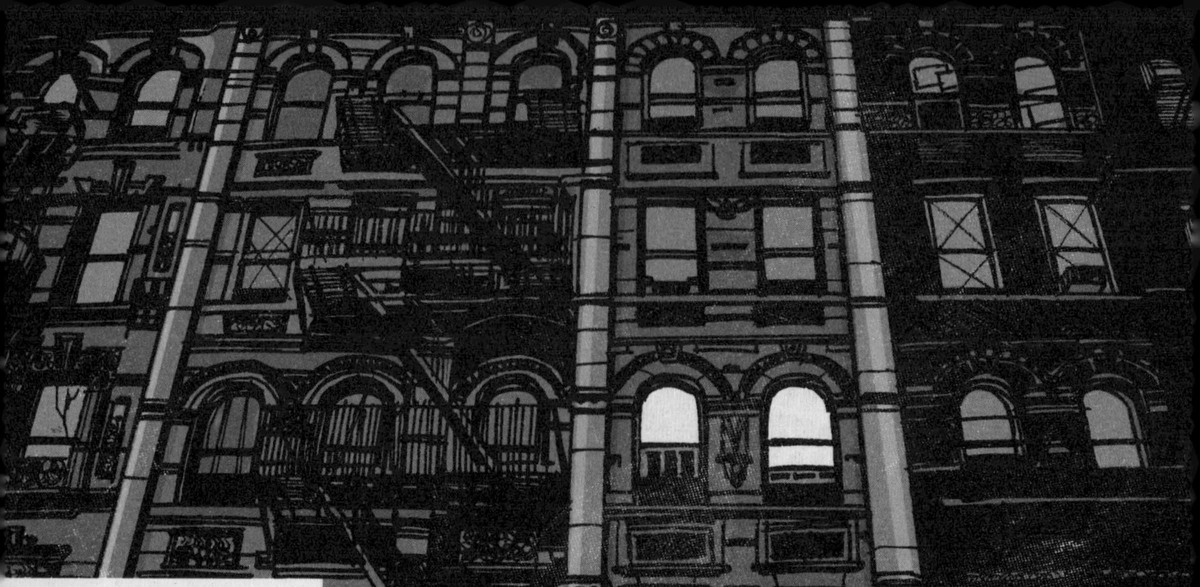

NEIGHBORHOODS

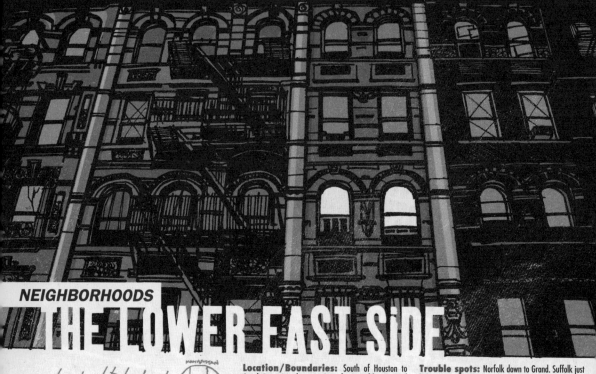

THE LOWER EAST SiDE

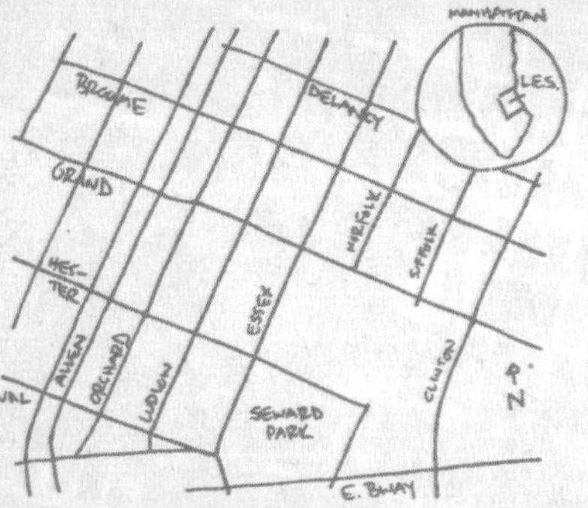
MANHATTAN
L.E.S.
BROOME
DELANCEY
GRAND
HES-TER
NORFOLK
SUFFOLK
ESSEX
ALLEN
ORCHARD
LUDLOW
CLINTON
CANAL
SEWARD PARK
E. B'WAY
N

Location/Boundaries: South of Houston to Canal, Bowery to the river. Sort of a mix of hipsters and the immigrant working class, based on existing signage and the people who hang around. Ruined museum on Orchard protected by extremist local types suggests tenement culture in the past, and the recreated old-style immigrant tenement building they've preserved becomes an ironic statement... I can think of several families now who wish they had it that good.

Zee lives near here. Neighborhood milita is a circus... by my count, close to twenty groups have carved up this area, some only occupying a block or two. Bizarre, Trotsky-esque lunatics have the lockdown on Zee's block. They're the assholes who took out the helicopter I came in on, and they won't talk to me. Zee says to leave them alone. They don't talk to anyone.

Trouble spots: Norfolk down to Grand. Suffolk just below Houston. Hester any time of day or night. Militias keep Seward Park stable, but all I ever see going on there are Chinese doing tai-chi in the morning. Grand belongs to Wilson's Grandsons. The playgrounds that run along Allen St. are fucking deathzones.

U.S. Military's got good line-of-sight on a lot of this neighborhood, and the proximity to the bridges can be tricky. I've documented seventeen cases of random killings from U.S. sniper fire... bored river guards? People learn to keep a building between them and the water. Leaves streets like Houston and Delancey and Canal pretty empty.

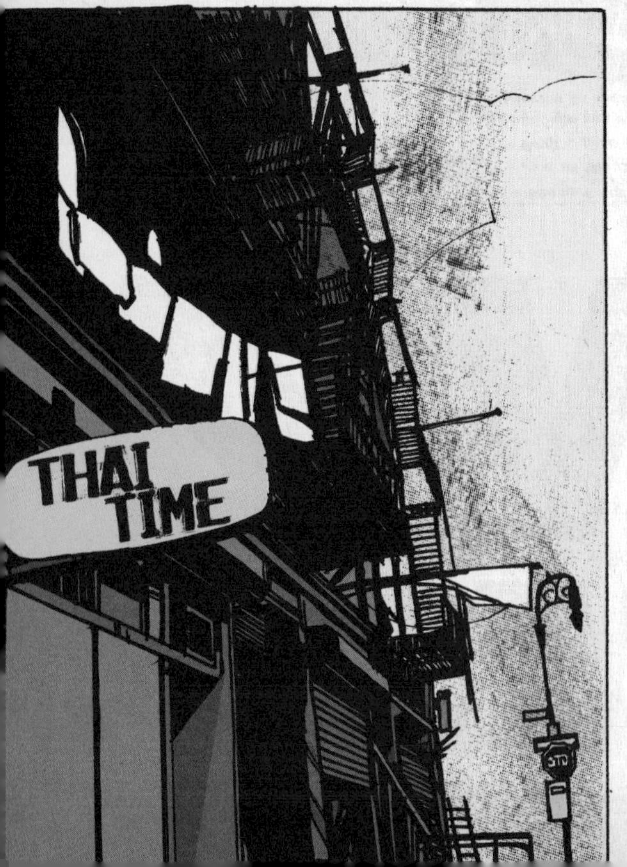
THAI TIME

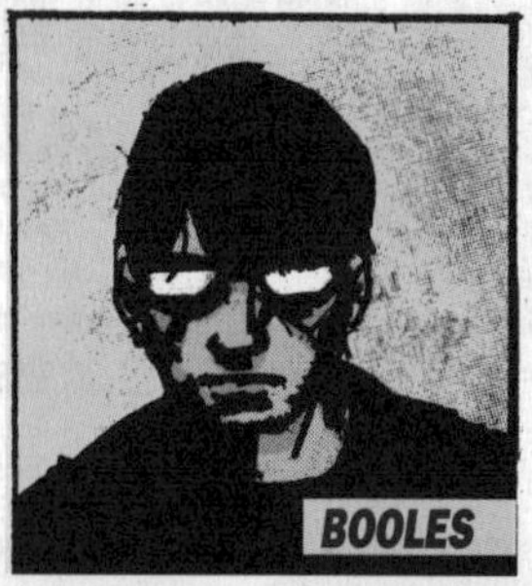

BOOLES

(Ageless, raceless hipster somehow claiming an entire building on lower Eldridge. Filthy black denim everything, looks like he might have been a roadie for The Ramones. Everyone leaves him alone, except me, it seems. –Matty)

Name: Booles ***Age:*** Pre-War

X Factor: Live and let live, man.

Personality: What? I don't know.

Days Spent: Walking my block, picking up shit, looking for valuables. Staying out of the way, in bed by 9 p.m. before the nighttime shit starts up.

On the War: Trashed my city, shrunk my world. Now my world's my home, my roof garden, my two hands. Before, I had rent to worry about, ConEd, late fees, asshole bar-hopping pretty boys and smoking bans. So who knows? Could be worse.

Anything Else? Watch what you breathe, man. Air's poisoned.

NOTES

THAI TIME: Where the old Pink Pony was (I'm told). Zee takes me there. They open in the morning. Soy roti made on the premises, back garden devoted to growing fresh produce. Vegan, but cool.

PIANOS: Music venue. Weirdly closed scene – you gotta know people. I get in as "Press" most of the time.

HESTER MILITIA: Unstable crew, but a Colombian cat named Parco gets me through if necessary. Prefer to take the long way around. Parco's shifty, one of those lazy-looking guys who's already worked out a few ways to kill you five mins after meeting you.

SUBWAYS: Not worth it. Army nutbags walk the F tracks from the York stop in DUMBO into the city, start shit for laughs. Plus you never know what third rails are live.

BARS: A lot of booze flows in the L.E.S. How? No one knows, no one cares. Safe spots: Welcome to the Johnsons, Arlene's, Fat Baby, Verlaine.

OVERALL VIBE: Lot of nooks and quiet blocks, militias too distracted to bother civilians most of the time. Apartments are hard to come by – this place is dense with people, but close to the river you can find unclaimed spots if you're desperate and crazy enough. You can find better spots uptown, but this is where civilization's happening, where the culture is.

NEIGHBORHOODS
CENTRAL PARK

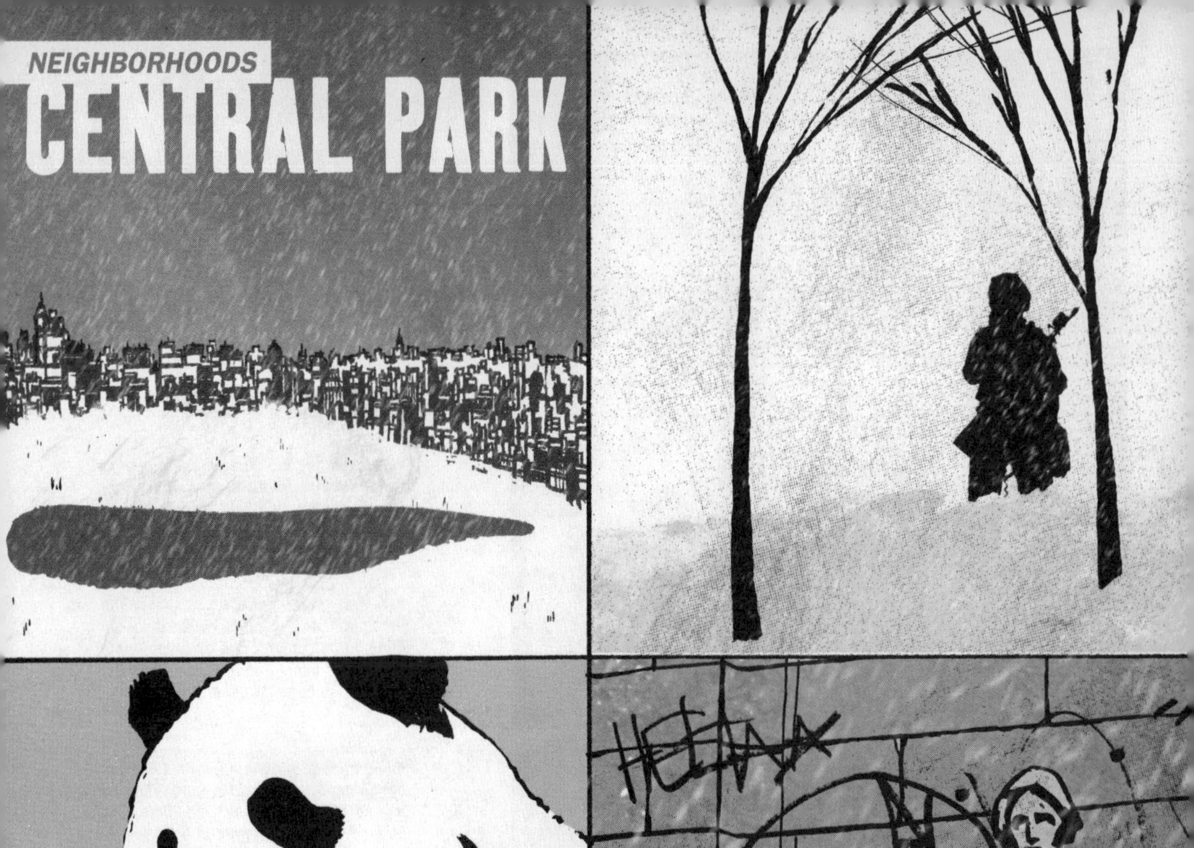

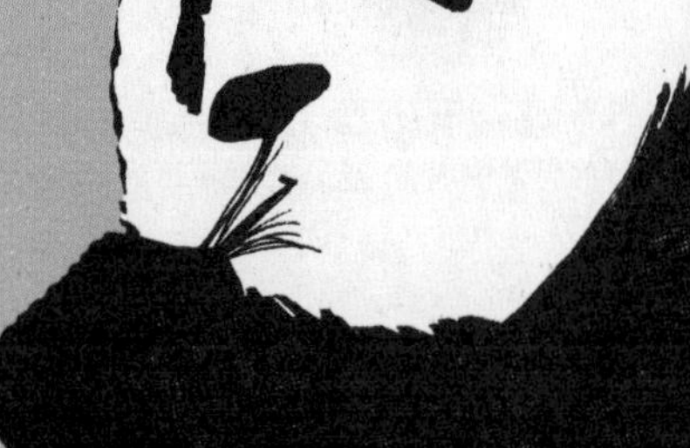
SOAMES

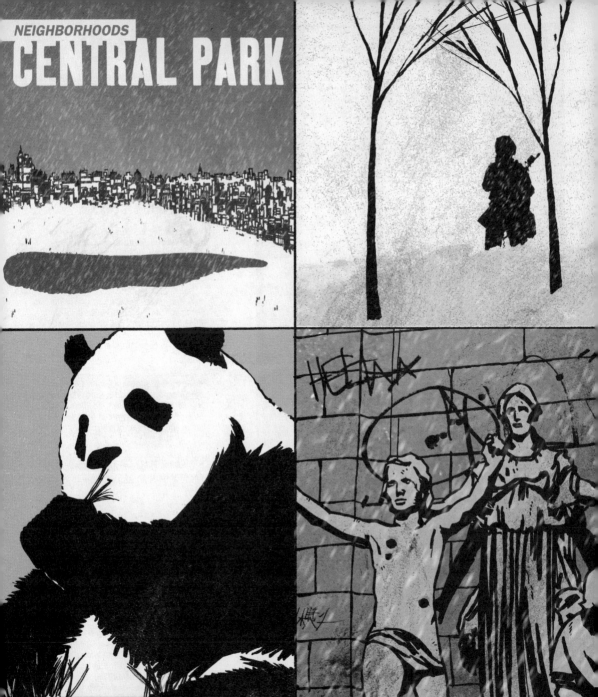

THE GHOSTS

Protectors of the park, the trees, the zoo animals. Model conservationists for all of Uptown. Rogue special forces gone into hiding (probably). I was up there last winter. Liberty wouldn't air the story I did about them, under pressure from the military who wants these guys back. Soames sends guys downtown regardless with care packages from the park – bamboo.

I've heard from people like Wilson that Soames and his crew no doubt came in during the first days of the war – part of that great offensive that ended up killing so many thousands, and he's absolutely got a lot of blood on his hands.

Doesn't matter what kind of saint he is now.

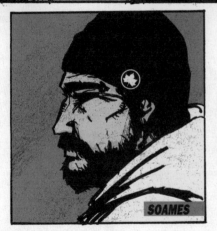

ANATOMY OF A STREET BATTLE

West 14th between 8th and 9th

BACKGROUND

Free States Army (FSA)-backed militants pretty much control that western edge of the city, from about 9th or 10th Ave to the river, with support from snipers and artillery from Jersey. They made some moves a few months ago to extend further, moving closer to 8th Ave. The Union Square West (USW) crew moved to intercept.

- Storefront explosion here. No one knows who caused it or how, but it provided some confusion and smoke cover for the FSA elements to make their way east.

- Vehicles provide additional cover. Some of these aren't wrecks but fresh trucks that the FSA drove in just prior to the explosion. Lends support to the notion that the storefront explosion was all part of a plan.

- Snipers seem to have the block covered to about here. Oddly, they didn't continue to move forward as the ground units did. Once those units got beyond the sphere of protection the snipers afforded, they were in trouble.

- Additional FSA-backed fighters appeared over these rooftops.

- The intersection. Torched buses block the way, and the fighting gets bogged down. Random street crazies engage the FSA fighters here and slow them up enough for the USW fighters to reach 8th Ave. Corners and intersections are the worst possible place to linger in the DMZ, anywhere... too many angles, too many crazies, too much strategic value.

- USW fighters start to appear in larger numbers. FSA snipers still not moving forward. The FSA fighters control the intersection, thanks to the buses, but have zero flank support and cannot continue eastward. USW has probably sent men the long way around, back to 7th Ave and west on 13th and 15th to come around on the sides, but they never show up in time.

- A second storefront explosion here. The USW fighters scatter, probably thinking the blast came from above, even drone aircraft. More likely a bullet clipped a gasline, or a boobytrap was triggered.

- USW moves back to this point. FSA stays put in the buses. Some shots fired from north and south along the avenue, but nothing coordinated. FSA retreats after dark, probably laying traps. In the morning locals rope off the buses and post warnings for the block. No one moves in to occupy.

EAST>>

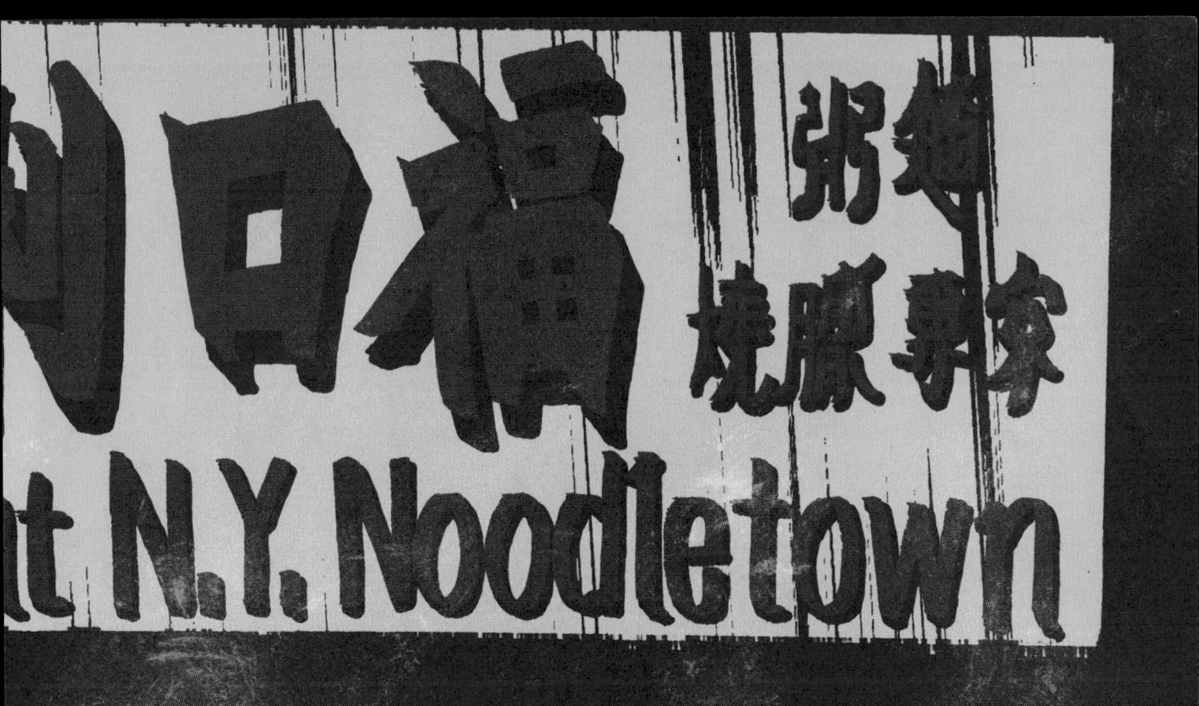

N.Y. Noodletown

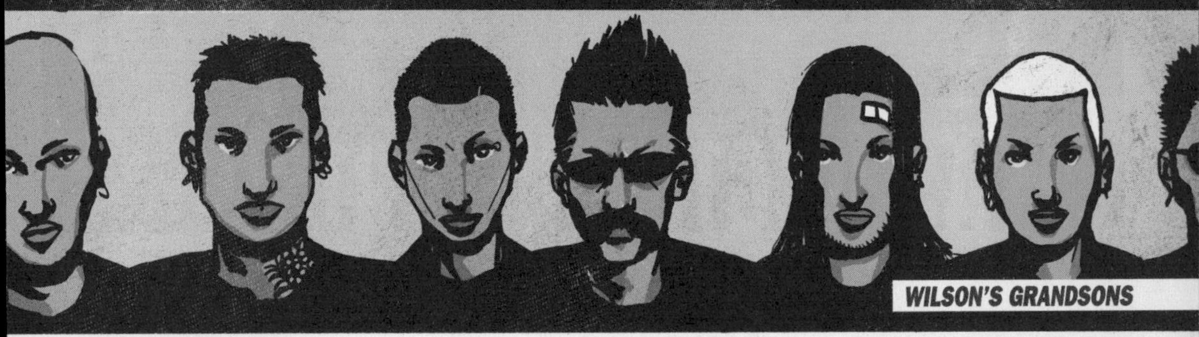

WILSON'S GRANDSONS

NEIGHBORHOODS

CHINATOWN

ASIANS – Probably the largest ethnic group ignored during the evacuations. Now they completely occupy their neighborhood and pretty much shut the doors behind them. Tourists (assuming there would be some) can no longer score Prada knockoffs on Canal, yuppies can't get bubble tea, hipsters can't find bootlegs of HK flicks, and I can't get noodles from N.Y. Noodle Town whenever I want.

The U.S. military's reach extends into parts of Chinatown ust like it does the Lower East Side, but for some reason it's less of a danger down here. Canal is still left pretty vacant, but the entrance to the Manhattan Bridge is *right there,* and the Bowery is a busy street. The U.S. leaves Chinatown alone.

I'd ask Wilson why, but I'm a little afraid of what the answer might be.

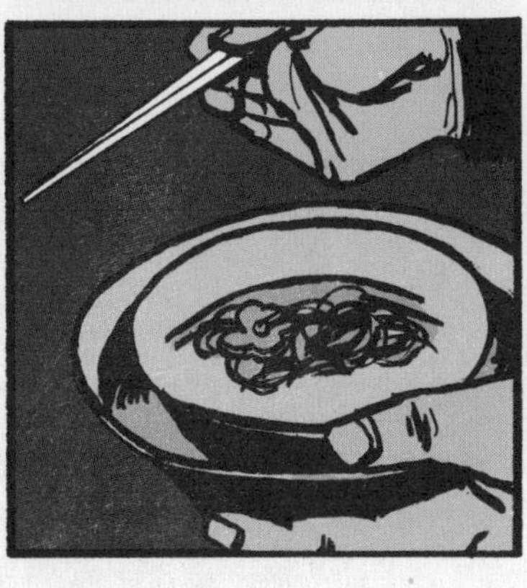

NOTES

Wilson threw some kind of old-style wedding party for one of his granddaughters (don't ask), and I was invited. Total token white guy, but with camera. Here I am, well-known photojournalist working for two networks, and I'm reduced to being Wilson's wedding photographer.

CONSUMED WHILE ON THE JOB:

Roast Pork and Noodle Soup
Ha Moon Mai Fun
Salt Fish and Chicken Rice
Chinese Vegetables with Oyster Sauce
A dozen Heineken

A Grandson brought me home. I was lit. Felt good – first time in a year I could let my guard down and know people were looking out for me.

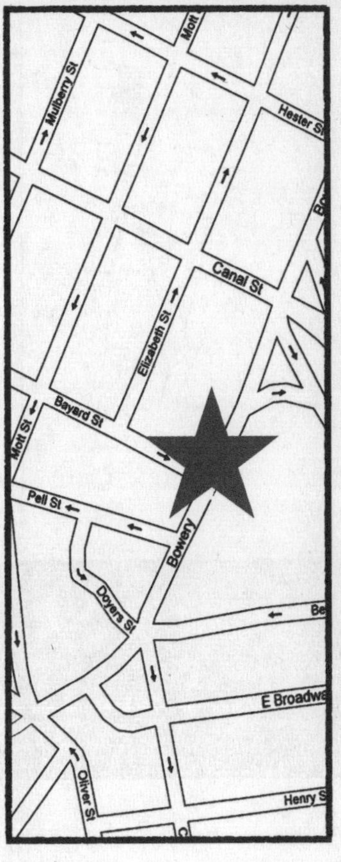

Mott
Mulberry St
Hester St
Canal St
Elizabeth St
Bayard St
Mott St
Pell St
Bowery
Doyers St
Oliver St

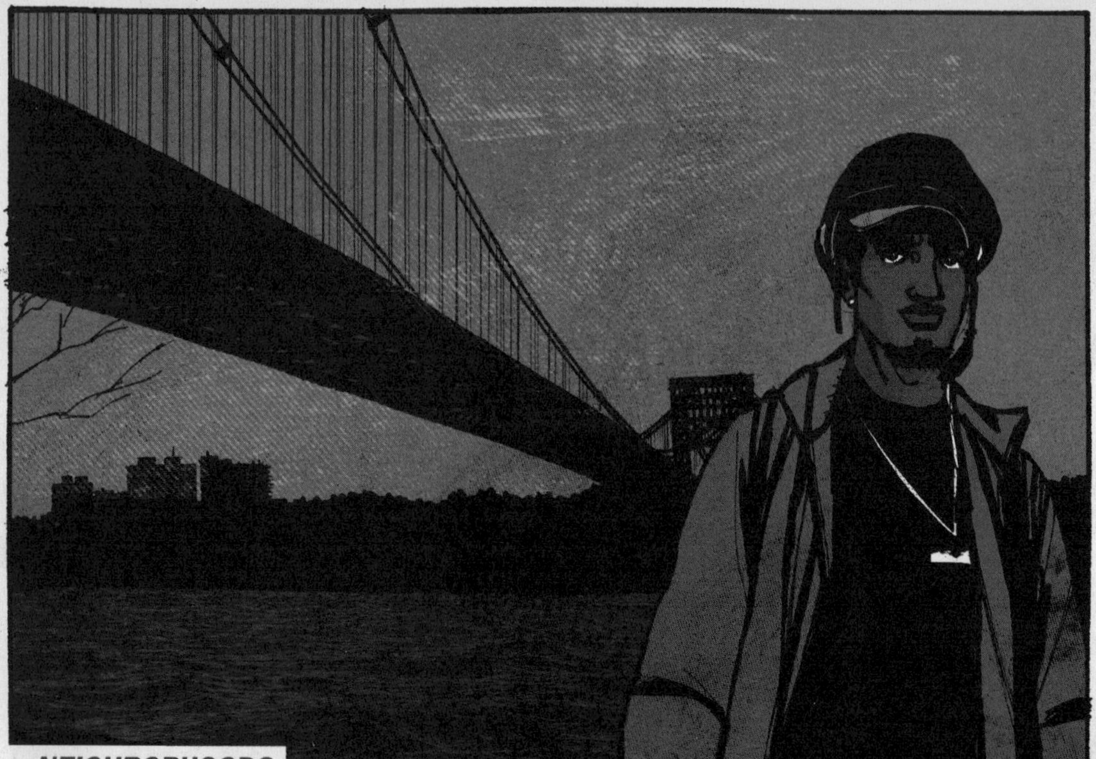

NEIGHBORHOODS

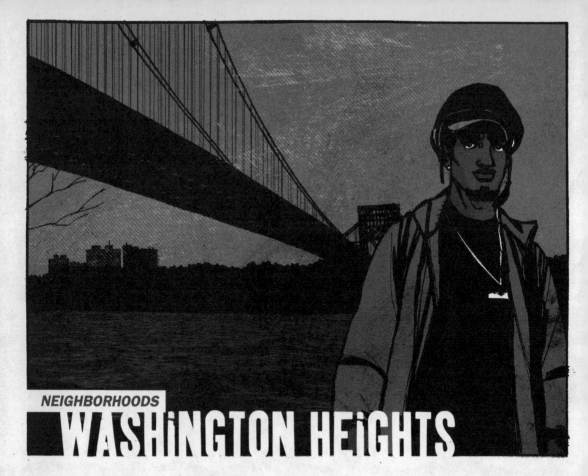

WASHINGTON HEIGHTS

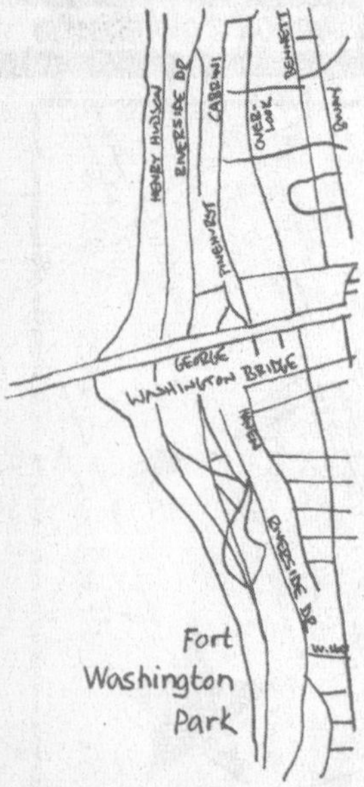
HENRY HUDSON
RIVERSIDE DR
CABRINI
OVERLOOK
BENNETT
GEORGE
WASHINGTON BRIDGE
RIVERSIDE DR
Fort
Washington
Park

Massive residential neighborhood uptown, north of Harlem. Strange to see hundreds, if not thousands, of beautiful pre-war buildings sitting vacant. Faces peer at you from windows here and there, but most people who stayed behind moved downtown. I don't blame them, it's spooky as hell up here. And I think there is something inside us, on an instinctual, animal level, to seek the protection of groups. The people are all downtown, as is most of the food and power and culture.

Uptown is the realm of animals, shut-ins, looters, and mass graves.

Zee's friend Jamal, along with his crew of engineers and architects, have been working on the retaining walls that run along the Henry Hudson. They're crumbling, and it's not really the sort of problem that can be ignored if anyone is ever going to want to live along Riverside Drive ever again. They're fixing them for free, but rumor has it this is one of the sites that Trustwell is being paid to take care of when they move in next month.

JAMAL

Name: Jamal Greene

Age: 23

X Factor: Skill and pride in my work.

Where's Home? Born and raised on Bennett Ave and 186th.

Days Spent: I live in a tent in Riverside Park, but it's nicer than it sounds. Some of the buildings along Riverside still have working plumbing, pulling water from the roof towers, so I can shower and flush a toilet.

On the War: Am I an asshole for seeing a bright side? I'm a 23-yo ex-student with no degree, and here I am working on these walls. This is the sort of work I dreamed about when I was young: designing and building something that'll make a real difference to my city. I wouldn't be doing this right now if the war hadn't happened, I bet.

Anything Else? Take good care of each other. We're family.

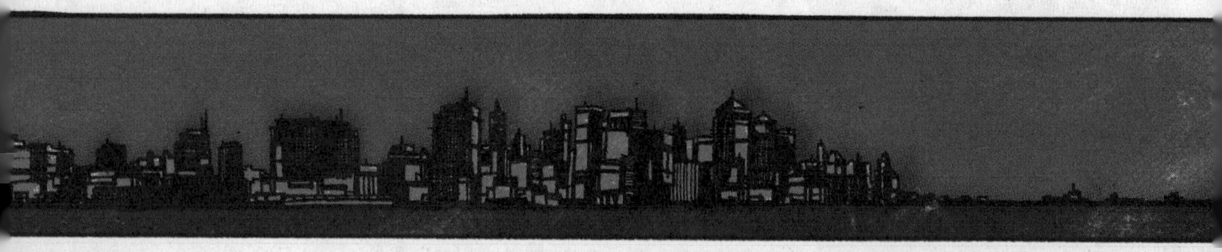

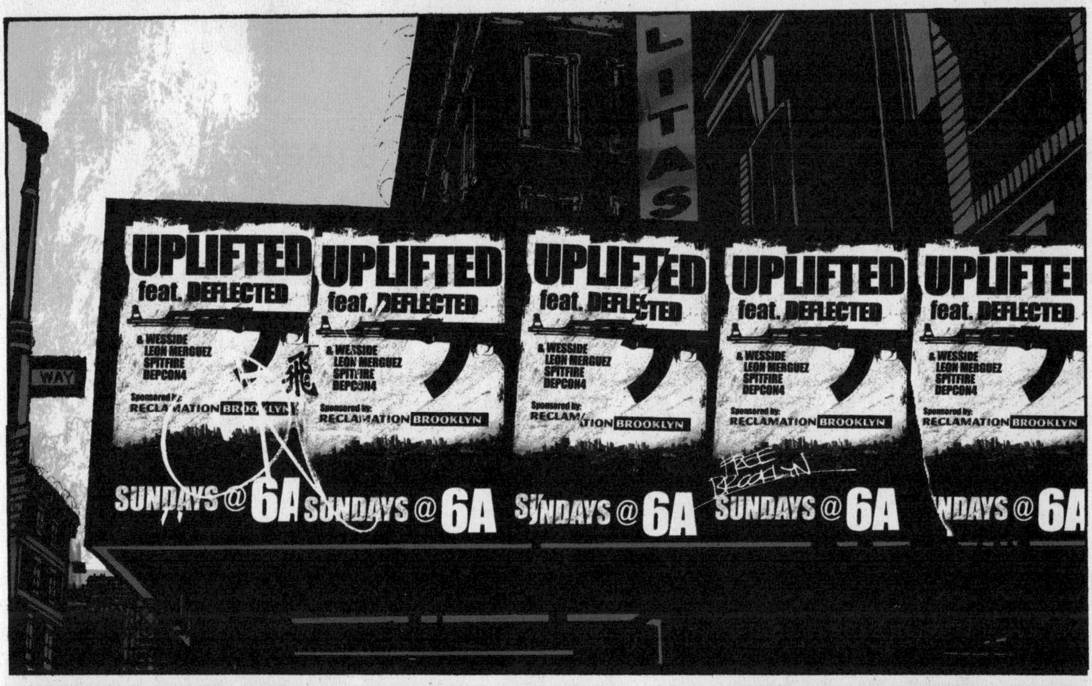
LITAS
WAY
UPLIFTED
feat. DEFLECTED
& WESSIDE
LEON MERGUEZ
SPITFIRE
DEPCON4
Sponsored by:
RECLAMATION BROOKLYN
SUNDAYS @ 6A
FREE BROOKLYN

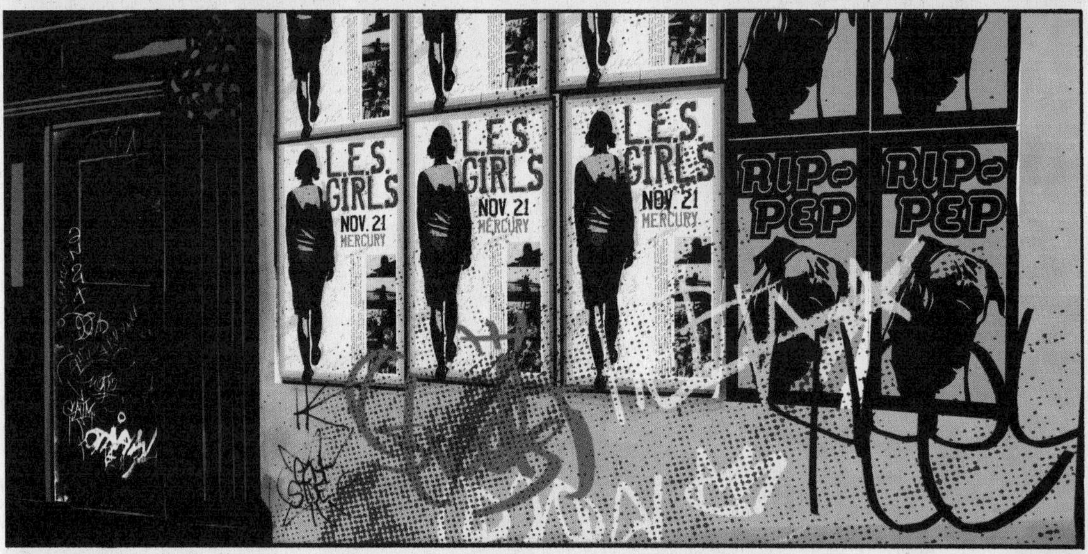
L.E.S. GIRLS
NOV. 21
MERCURY
RIP-PEP

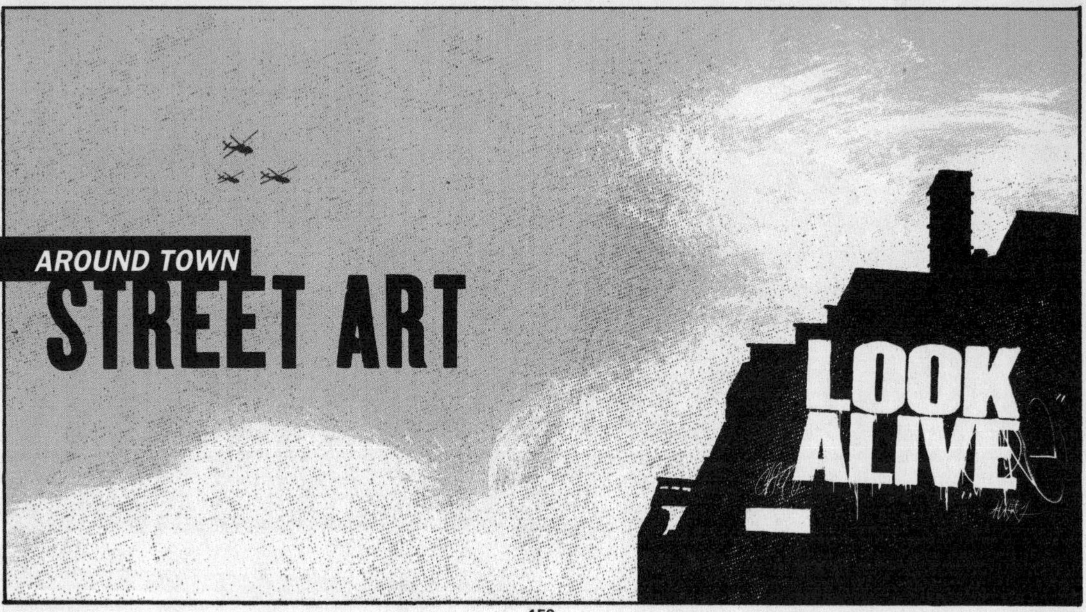
AROUND TOWN
STREET ART
LOOK ALIVE

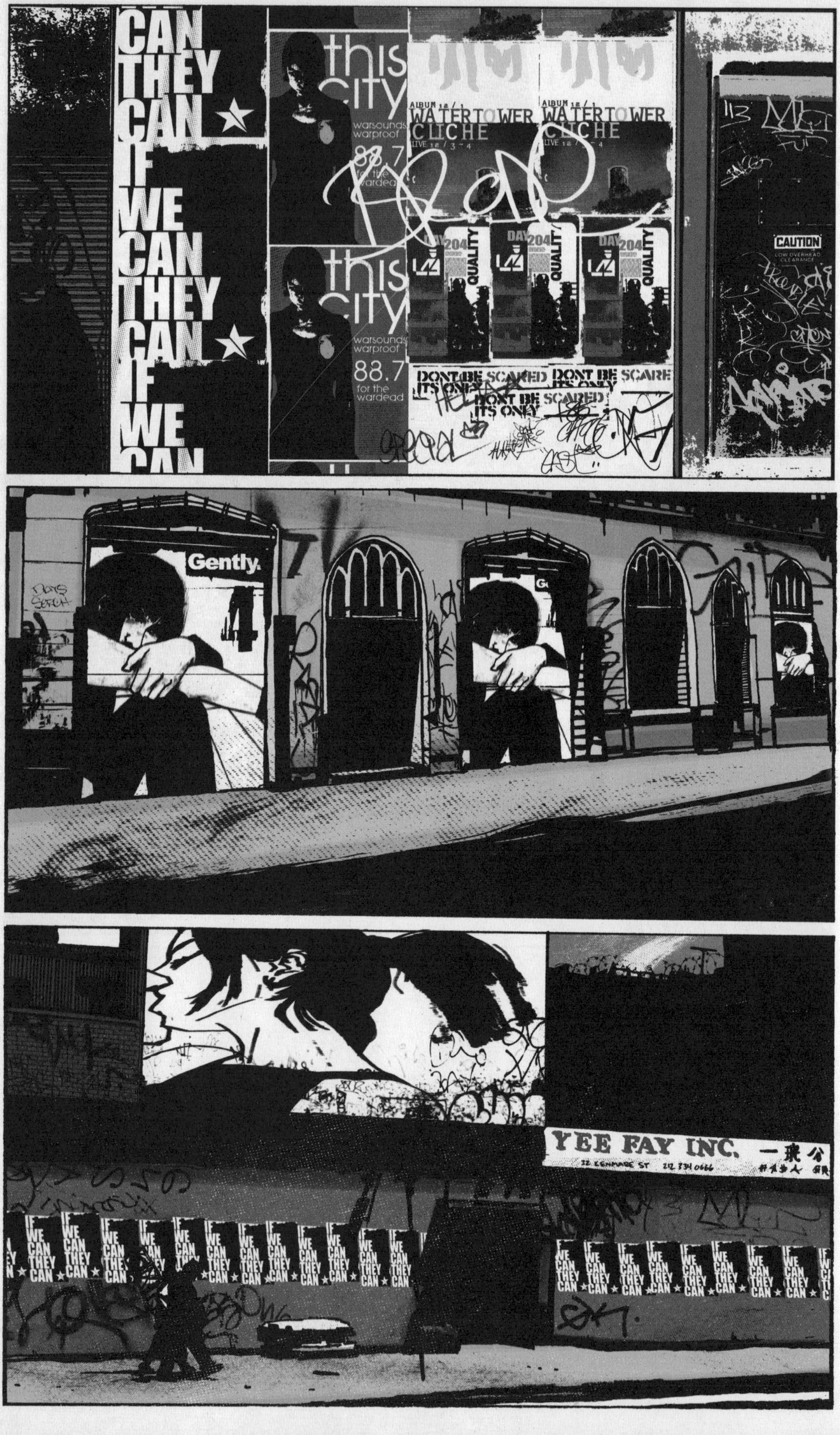
CAN THEY CAN IF WE CAN THEY CAN IF WE
this city
warsounds warproof
88.7
for the wardead
this city
warsounds warproof
88.7
for the wardead
ALBUM 12 / 1
WATERTOWER CLICHE
LIVE 12 / 3 - 4
ALBUM 12 / 1
WATERTOWER CLICHE
DAY 204
QUALITY
DONT BE SCARED ITS ONLY
DONT BE SCARE
DONT BE SCARED ITS ONLY
CAUTION
LOW OVERHEAD CLEARANCE
Gently.
4
YEE FAY INC.
22 KENMARE ST 212 334 0666
IF WE CAN THEY CAN

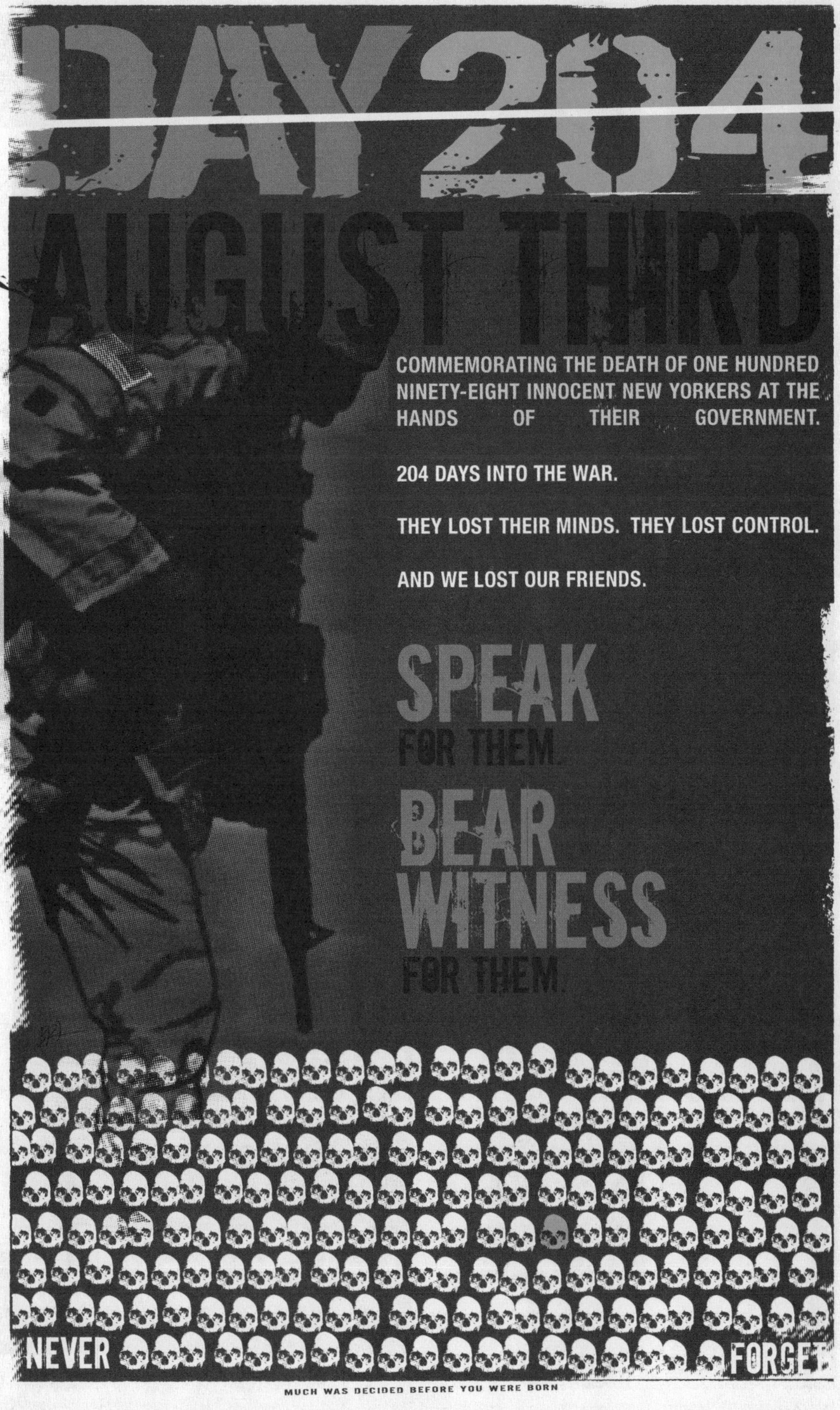
DAY 204
AUGUST THIRD
COMMEMORATING THE DEATH OF ONE HUNDRED NINETY-EIGHT INNOCENT NEW YORKERS AT THE HANDS OF THEIR GOVERNMENT.
204 DAYS INTO THE WAR.
THEY LOST THEIR MINDS. THEY LOST CONTROL.
AND WE LOST OUR FRIENDS.
SPEAK
FOR THEM.
BEAR WITNESS
FOR THEM.
NEVER
FORGET

MUCH WAS DECIDED BEFORE YOU WERE BORN

Name: Delo

Age: 27

Where's Home?
Washington Square Park

On the War: "You do what it takes to get by, whatever the situation. War, no war, not much seemed to change for me day-to-day."

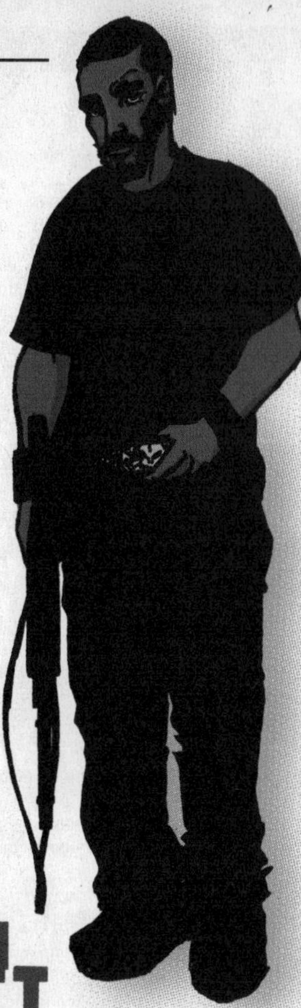

Name: Rosa **Age:** 39 **Occupation:** Artist

How Do You Deal? "You can't be a recluse. You can't stay inside and hide from the war. It's been so many years now and you learn what to wear, where to walk, who to trust. I love my life. In many ways I feel freer than I did before the war."

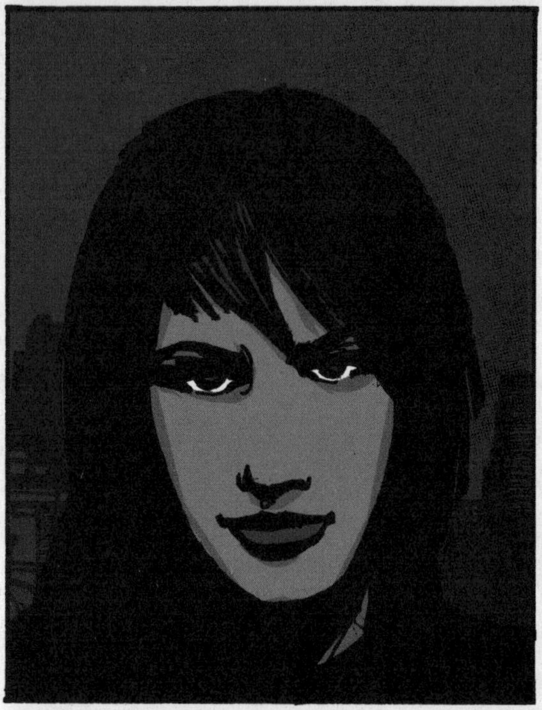

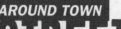

AROUND TOWN

STREET CULTURE

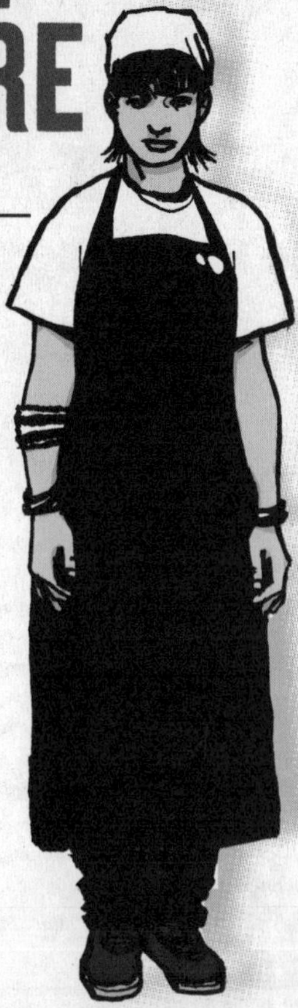

Name: Annie

Age: 32

What Do You Do?
"Vegetarian chef for my own restaurant, Risen. We built a small greenhouse in the back and can grow everything we need year-round."

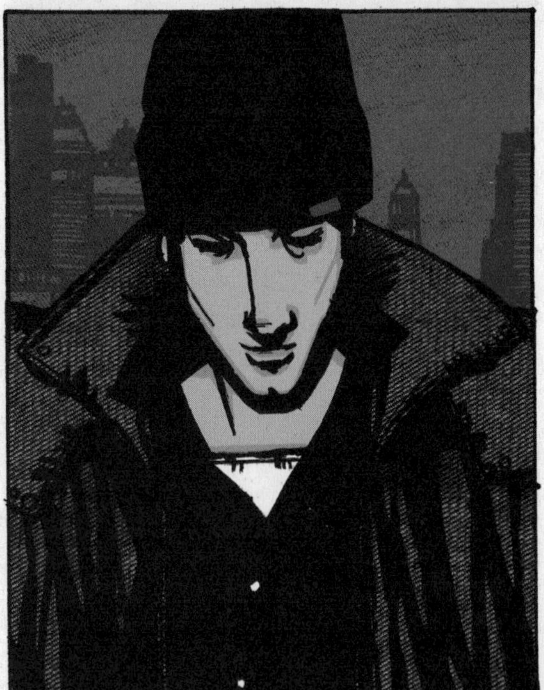

Name: Random Fire **Age:** 19 **Occupation:** DJ

On the War: "Everything's underground now, music, fashion, culture. Block by block, everyone does their thing. We're all fueled by innovation and style, not money, so it's pure, it's all pure now."

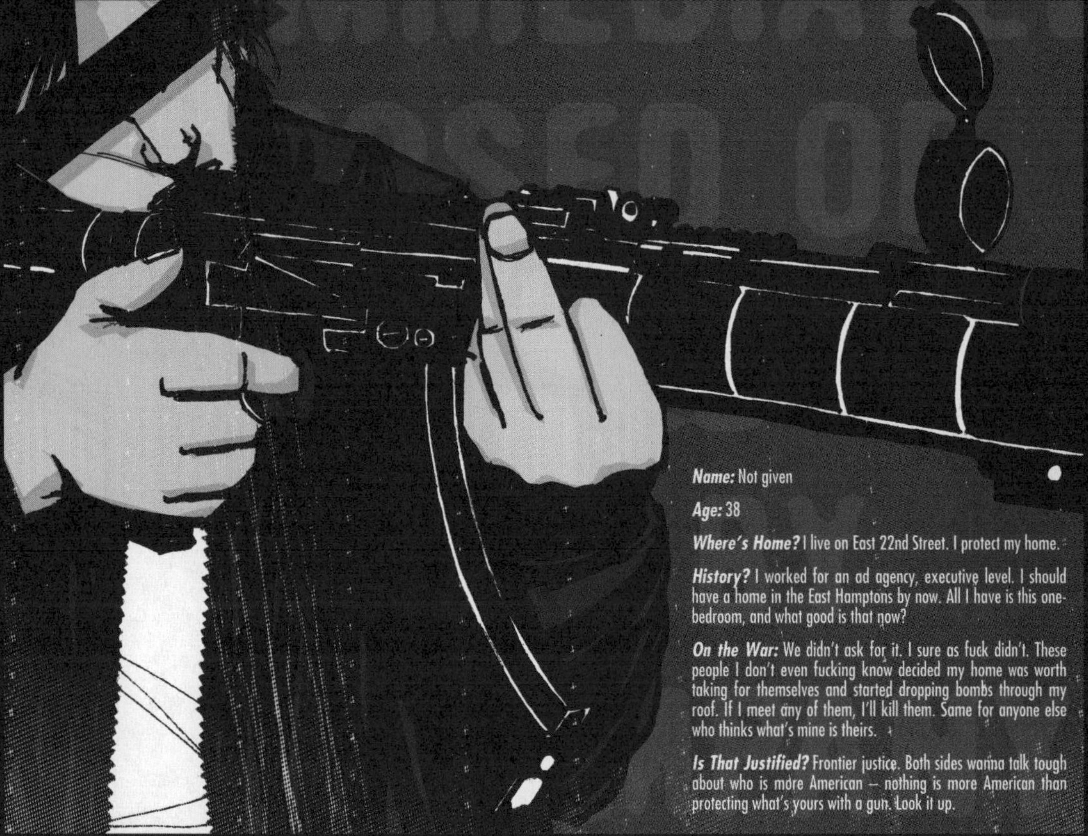

Name: Not given

Age: 38

Where's Home? I live on East 22nd Street. I protect my home.

History? I worked for an ad agency, executive level. I should have a home in the East Hamptons by now. All I have is this one-bedroom, and what good is that now?

On the War: We didn't ask for it. I sure as fuck didn't. These people I don't even fucking know decided my home was worth taking for themselves and started dropping bombs through my roof. If I meet any of them, I'll kill them. Same for anyone else who thinks what's mine is theirs.

Is That Justified? Frontier justice. Both sides wanna talk tough about who is more American – nothing is more American than protecting what's yours with a gun. Look it up.

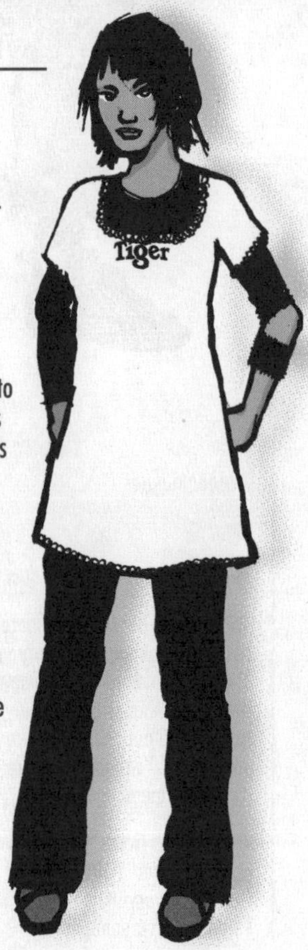

Tiger

Name: Jenny

Age: 20

Where's Home? East 9th St.

What Do You Do? I sell vintage clothes from a storefront near me.

Vintage Clothes? Clothes don't have to be that old now to be vintage. My boyfriend finds entire wardrobes in apartments in the Upper East Side, just sitting there in these huge walk-ins. I have an entire rack of Gucci.

On the War: I'm from Parsippany, here as a student. I don't know where my family is, but my boyfriend and I take care of each other.

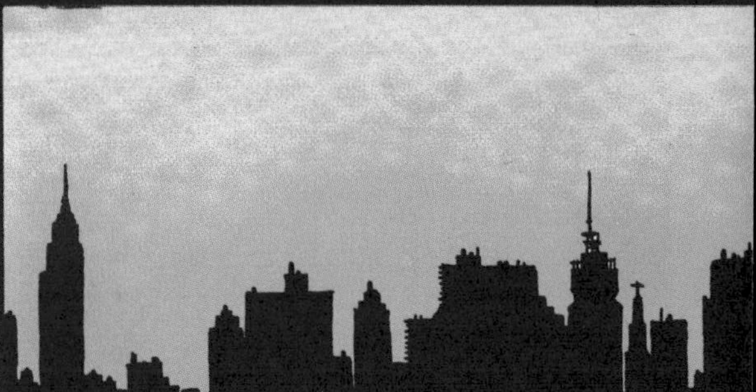

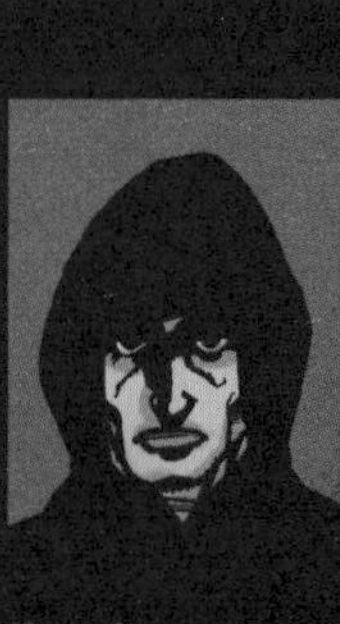

Name: César

Age: 29

"I grew up in Bay Ridge. My fucking bad luck to be in the city when the bombing started. Haven't been able to get home since."

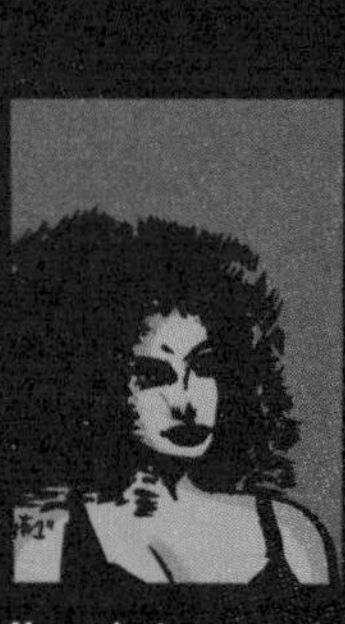

Name: Angie

Age: 25

"I'm not political, but this war is all about politics. I don't know what to say, except that if everyone was just cool with each other..."

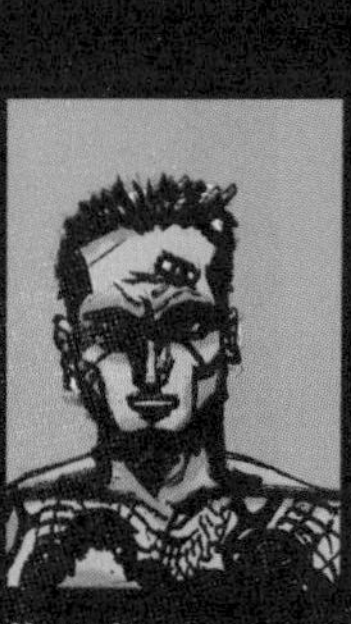

Name: Jin

Age: 24

"Life is better, definitely. Everything is easier to do and to get. I love the war."

Name: Sue **Age:** 11 **Affiliation:** Thompkins Square Militia

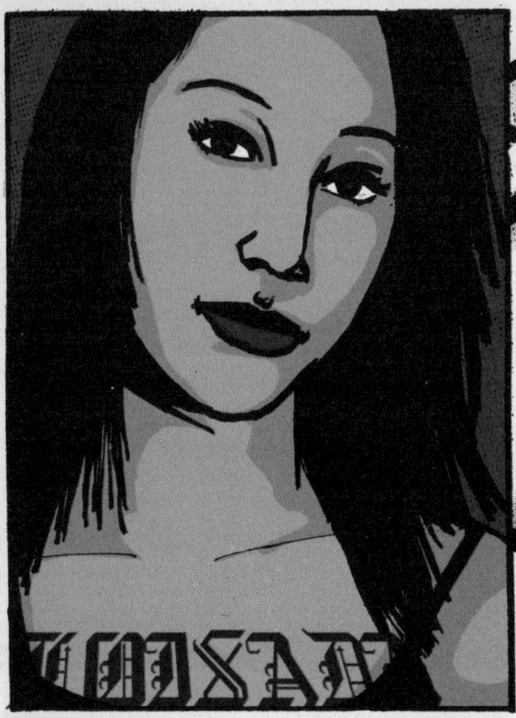

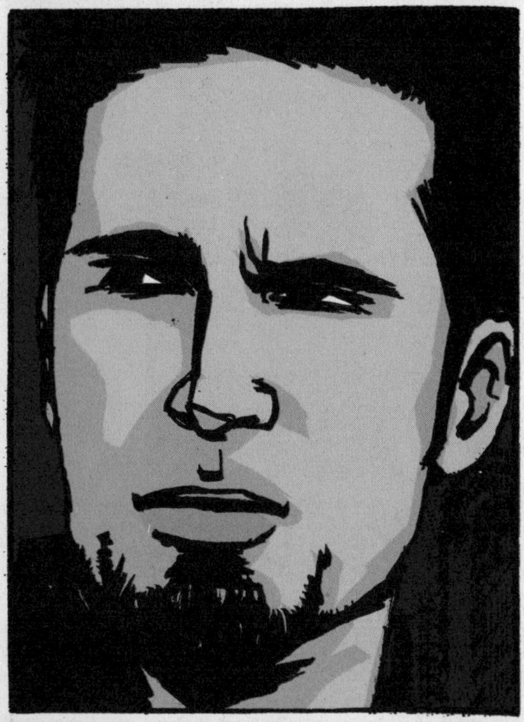

Name: Mike **Age:** 36 **Affiliation:** The Nation of Fearghus

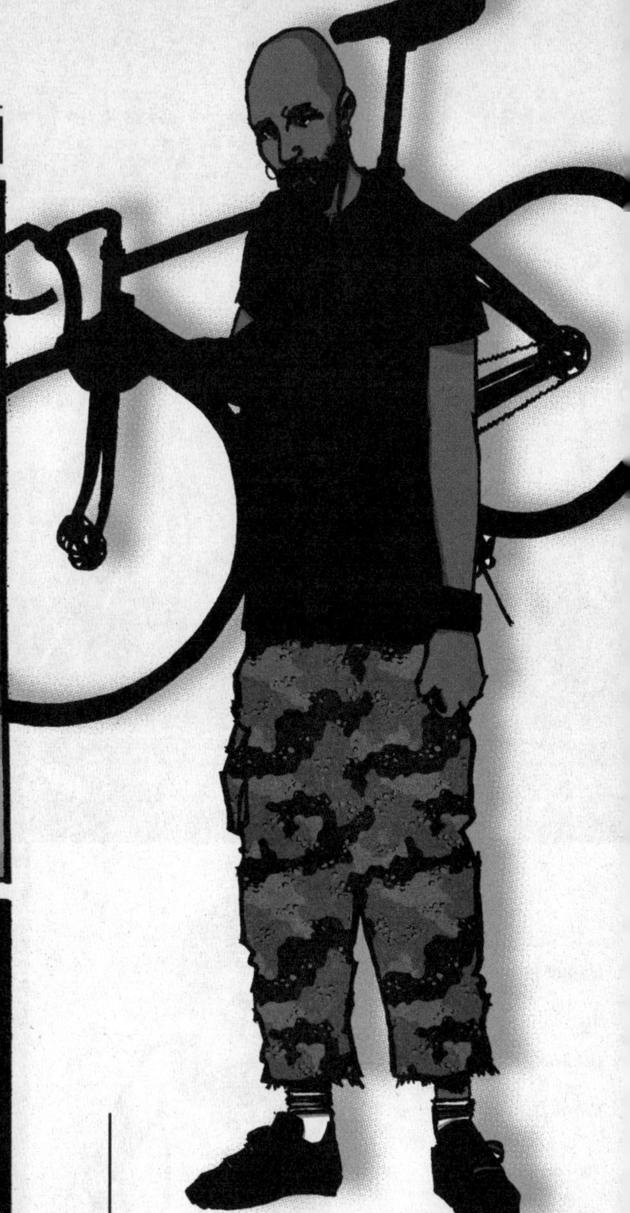

Name: Magnus

Age: 42

Where's Home? Varick, just below Houston

What Do You Do? Freelance bike messenger. I've been a messenger for twenty years. I predate this war. I've always ridden a bike. They can crater the streets, they can embargo the oil, they can ban traffic, but nothing will ever beat the bike for efficiency and practicality. I can go anywhere in this city. No one shoots the messenger!

Affiliation: None. Myself. I'll deliver for anyone who pays. I've seen every corner of this city, and as far as I can tell, everyone's fucking bonkers. So who cares? I work for everyone.

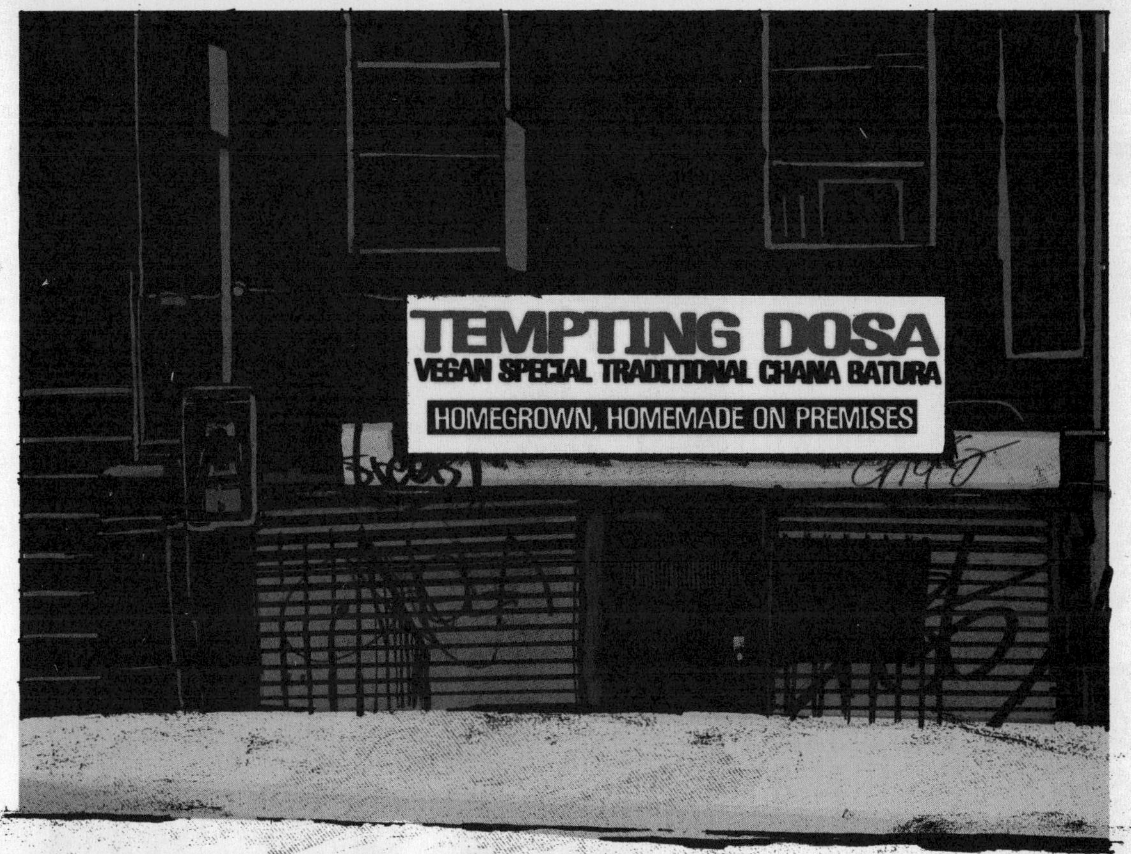
TEMPTING DOSA
VEGAN SPECIAL TRADITIONAL CHANA BATURA
HOMEGROWN, HOMEMADE ON PREMISES

DiNiNG OUT

I ate here once with Zee – her culinary instincts have never let me down – and what the hell do I know about vegan food or dosas? Nothing, and I was ready to revolt when this thing came out as big as a football. Huge goddamn dosas! is what I was told. Amen.

Like a lot of places around here, they grow their own food out back, in the basements (sprouts grow well in the dark, who knew?) and on the roofs. And also like many places, you don't need any money. They'll accept any sort of beneficial trade. I used to pay in cash when Liberty was funding me, but now I pay with all sorts of crap: working lightbulbs, extension cords I find, broken furniture they can mend, other food, beer stolen from Wilson, bamboo... or a press review or even some manual labor in the gardens. Money's not super-valuable to the average person here. It's about the day-to-day, living off the grid, getting by and being happy. The people who try and hoard money and stash goods are the ones living only for the day when the war ends, but who knows when that'll happen? In the meantime they're the miserable ones.

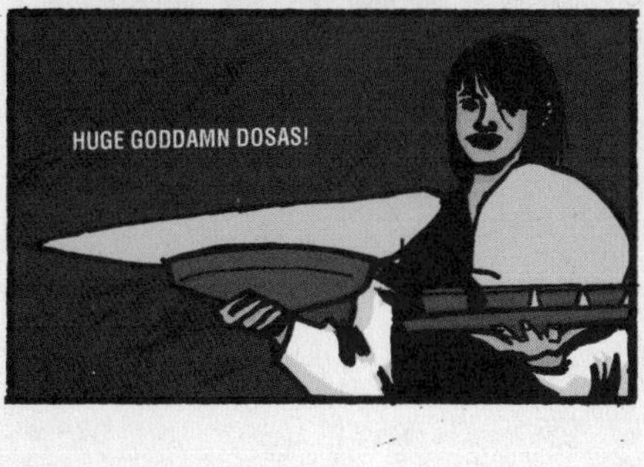
HUGE GODDAMN DOSAS!

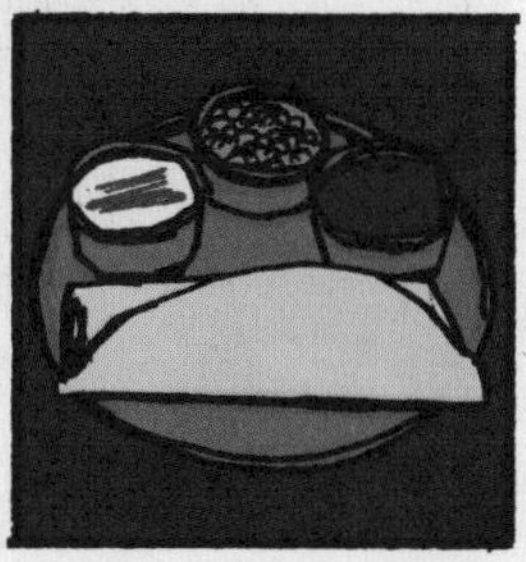

Tempting Dosa... I eat here a few days a week. They make a real effort, and it shows. It's on Grand Street, technically part of Wilson's territory, but they make an exception and let anyone come eat. They get respect for the food and their cool attitude, and it pays off. It's a safe block.

I usually order dosa and cold tea, but I'd recommend the Medu Wada, the rice and lentil pancakes, and in the winter either of the soups.

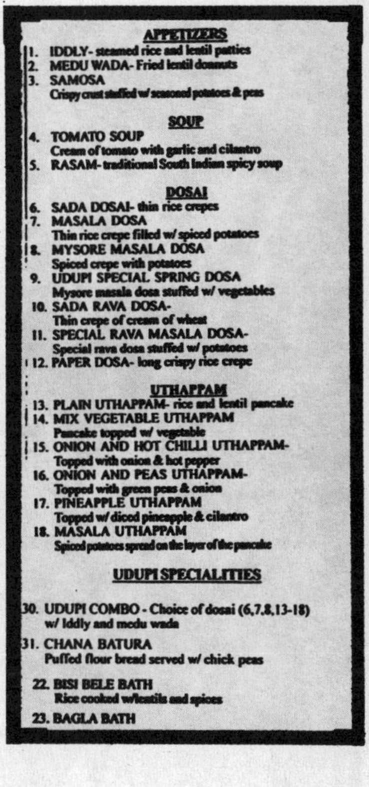

APPETIZERS

1. IDDLY- steamed rice and lentil patties
2. MEDU WADA- Fried lentil donnuts
3. SAMOSA
Crispy crust stuffed w/ seasoned potatoes & peas

SOUP

4. TOMATO SOUP
Cream of tomato with garlic and cilantro
5. RASAM- traditional South Indian spicy soup

DOSAI

6. SADA DOSAI- thin rice crepes
7. MASALA DOSA
Thin rice crepe filled w/ spiced potatoes
8. MYSORE MASALA DOSA
Spiced crepe with potatoes
9. UDUPI SPECIAL SPRING DOSA
Mysore masala dosa stuffed w/ vegetables
10. SADA RAVA DOSA-
Thin crepe of cream of wheat
11. SPECIAL RAVA MASALA DOSA-
Special rava dosa stuffed w/ potatoes
12. PAPER DOSA- long crispy rice crepe

UTHAPPAM

13. PLAIN UTHAPPAM- rice and lentil pancake
14. MIX VEGETABLE UTHAPPAM
Pancake topped w/ vegetable
15. ONION AND HOT CHILLI UTHAPPAM-
Topped with onion & hot pepper
16. ONION AND PEAS UTHAPPAM-
Topped with green peas & onion
17. PINEAPPLE UTHAPPAM
Topped w/ diced pineapple & cilantro
18. MASALA UTHAPPAM
Spiced potatoes spread on the layer of the pancake

UDUPI SPECIALITIES

30. UDUPI COMBO - Choice of dosai (6,7,8,13-18)
w/ Iddly and medu wada
31. CHANA BATURA
Puffed flour bread served w/ chick peas
22. BISI BELE BATH
Rice cooked w/lentils and spices
23. BAGLA BATH

ARTS
MUSIC

One of the biggest surprises I got when I came here was that the arts scene is fucking booming. I guess it's always booming here, but I dunno... I didn't think people would be in the mood because of the war. That sounds stupid, but that's how I thought back then.

VENUES

These are the places you can hear music most nights. It's informal — you show up and see who's playing each night. No such thing as a schedule.

DELANCY'S KITCHEN: Delancey is an iffy street in terms of security, and that fucking subway entrance is right in front. Never queue up in front of this place if you can help it. If snipers don't take shots at you from the bridge, the subway lunatics will. But this is one of the best places to see bands, so if you can get in safely, do it.

N.S.F.W.'s: Still around. There is a sense of pride about this place, and pride always leads to violence. The Nation of Fearghus used to control it, but they got ousted by some unknown set, so avoid N.S.F.W.'s until that settles down.

ANNIE'S BODEGA: I love Annie's. Great place.

STEREO LOUNGE: Same security risk as Delancy's. Worth it most nights.

TRAILERPARK: Avoid. Too close to the river.

INTERCONTINENTAL: Right in the middle of one of the busiest areas of the city, especially at night. Makes me a little nervous because of the proximity to Little Tokyo and the Polish sector, and this place has a weird vibe, this smelly black box of a club with horrible bands.

Simon Strong's not a real rock star, but he plays one in the DMZ. Weekly fixture at Trailerpark. Not recommended.

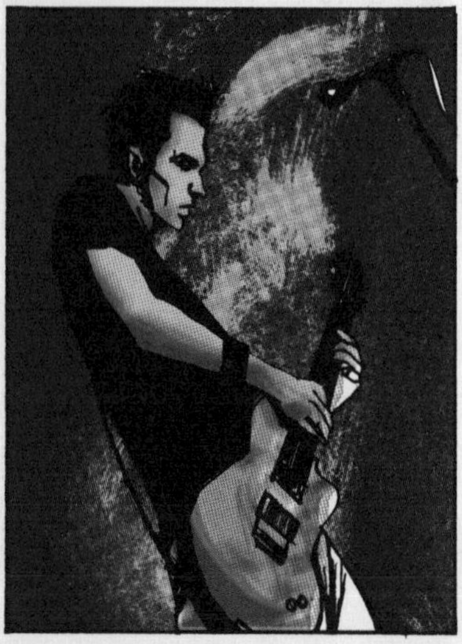

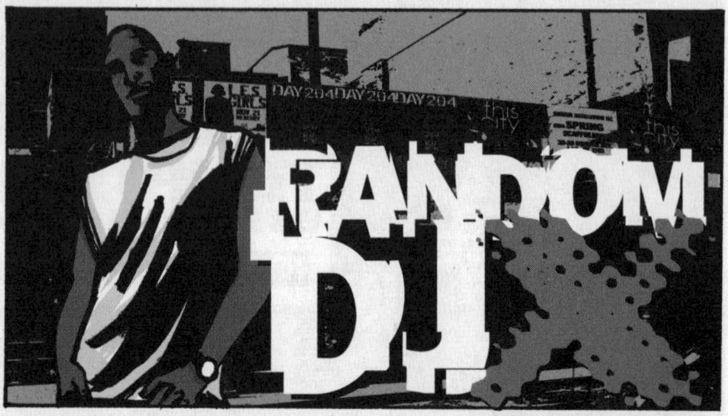
RANDOM DJ

RANDOM DJ X: Frequent fixture at Gulag. Kind of a Spooky/Shadow kind of sound by way of Hank Shocklee. Records a lot of street noise. Quiet, ambient stuff, lays it over this blistering shit that sounds like War. People like it. Random makes war sound cool.

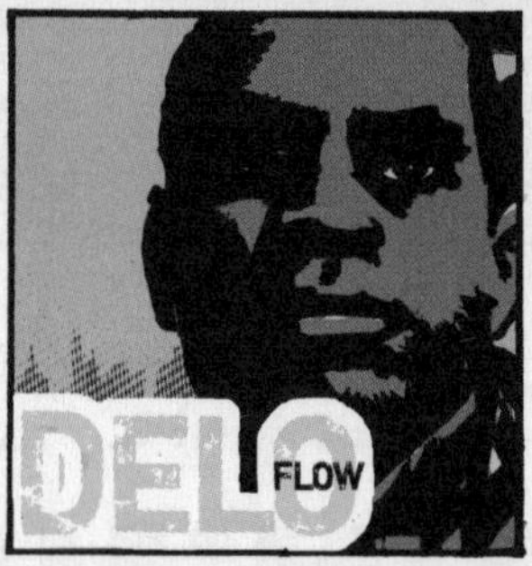
DELO
FLOW

DELO: One of several people who release CD's on a regular basis, found pretty easily on the street. Sounds like it was made with the built-in mic on his laptop and a midi keyboard, but the lyrics are genuine and his is one of the very few insights anyone here gets on what living above the park is like. Shit, most of us don't even go above 14th St. if we can help it. Again, compelling stuff that people really like.

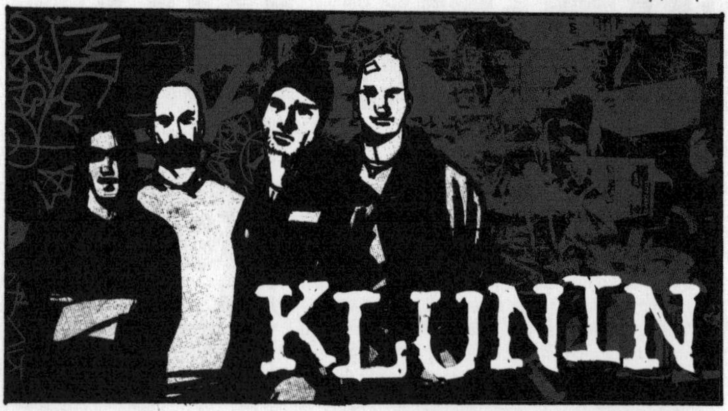
KLUNIN

KLUNIN: I firmly believe these are ex-fratboy NYU students who stayed here because they thought the war would be cool. Terrifying death metal with operatic, Scandinavian overtones. They've been performing with HELENA (pictured right), who really amps the Valkyrie vibe up, up, up. Catch them at Intercontinental, natch.

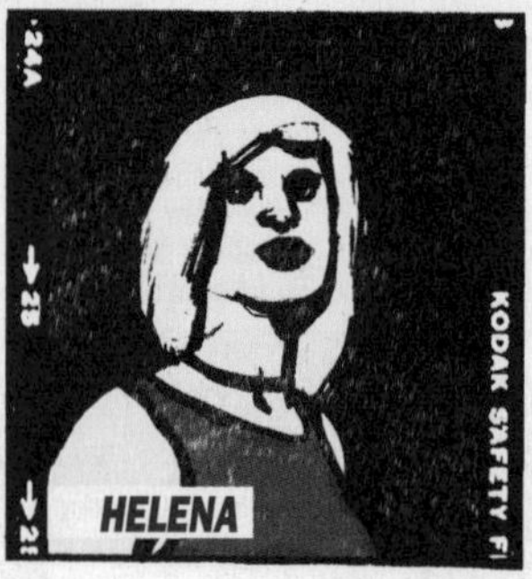
HELENA
KODAK SAFETY

Occasionally real-world bootlegs get smuggled into the city, and based on what I've heard, the music is just as shitty out there as it is in here, but with one exception: There's no money to be made from music in the DMZ, so it feels more genuine on average.

ARTS

BOOKS/ZiNES

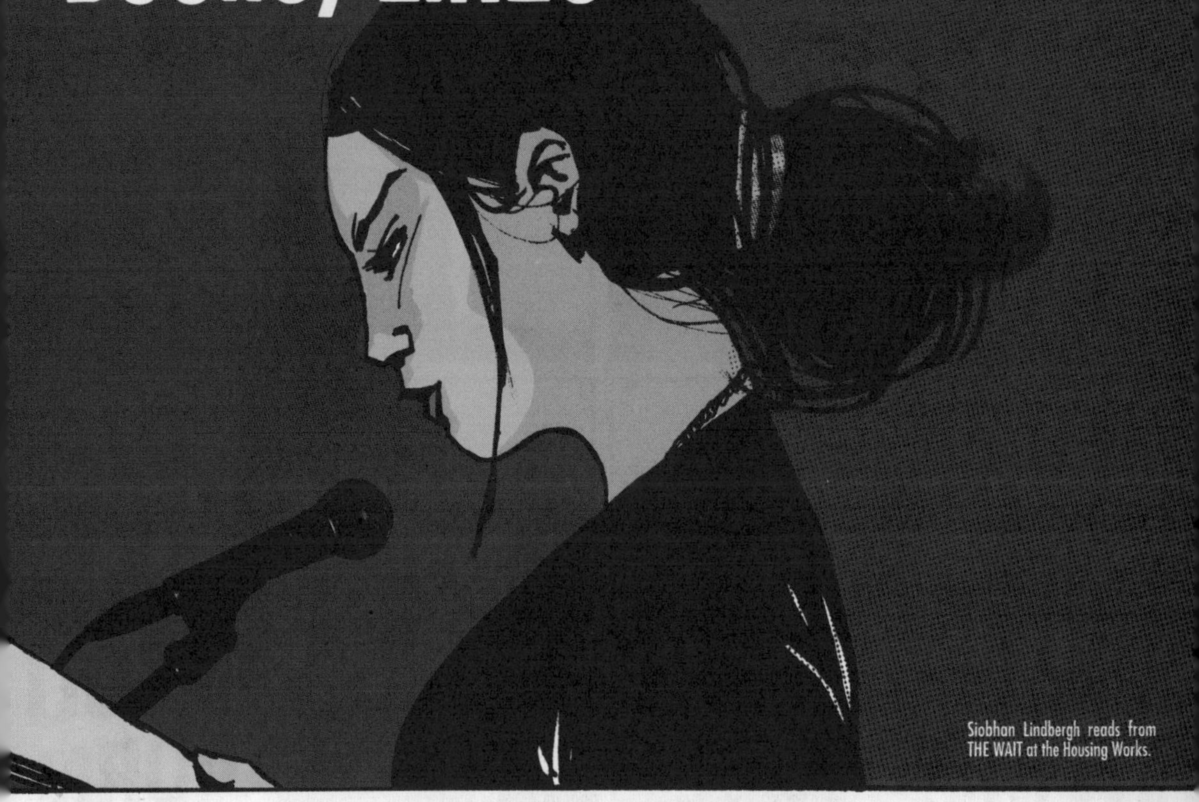

Siobhan Lindbergh reads from THE WAIT at the Housing Works.

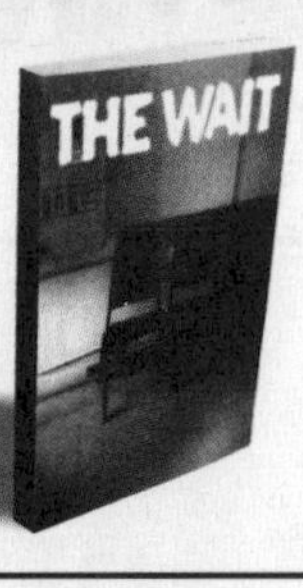
THE WAIT

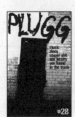

THE WAIT by Siobhan Lindbergh

Ms. Lindbergh calls this book nonfiction, but I have my doubts. While I would never claim that life in the DMZ is easy for anyone, it's hard to imagine anyone having such a miserable time as she claims to have had. From the fantastically depressing to the harrowing and violent, it's truly amazing to think that the five-foot, soft-spoken writer who read with such confidence last week at the Housing Works is the owner of these experiences. But, putting that aside for the moment, the writing is good and could give outsiders an idea of what could potentially happen to people here. Put a copy of THE WAIT into the hands of the U.N. General Assembly and I bet humanitarian aid would triple.

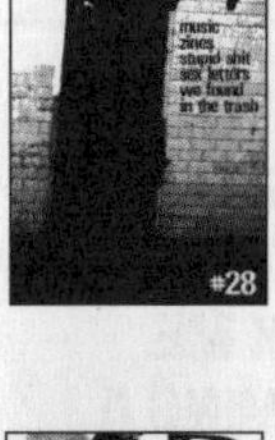
PLUGG
#28

PLUGG #28

If you're worried that you can't read PLUGG #28 until you've read the preceding 27 volumes, don't. PLUGG is a weird assortment of found objects and clippings from newspapers, often with snarky commentary. Good for quite a few laughs. How many more of these will be published? Rumor is the creators of PLUGG occupy an old Kinko's and have quite a stockpile of toner and paper.

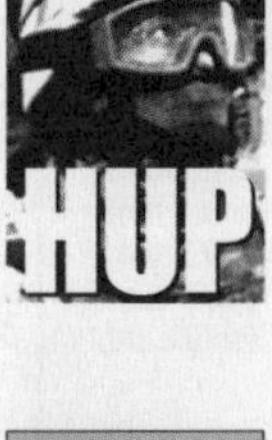
HUP

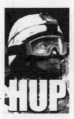

HUP

The creator of HUP, whoever he/she is, must be one of the most-wanted men in the city. A batch of G.I. mail, actual paper letters, was intercepted and reprinted, unedited, to make HUP. Hilarious, embarrassing, depressing, and offensive all at once. A spooky look into the minds of the people pointing weapons at us. Must read.

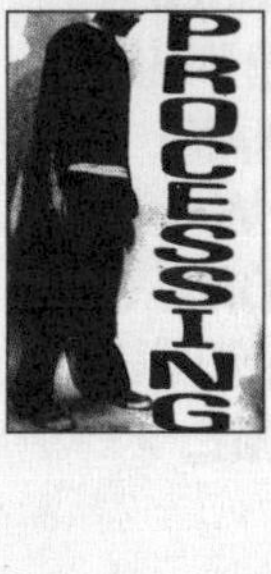
PROCESSING

PROCESSING

Menagerie of short fiction and poetry from a large group of people processing the war, never more than a single page each. Sounds horrible, but is strangely compelling. Open the book up at random and start reading.

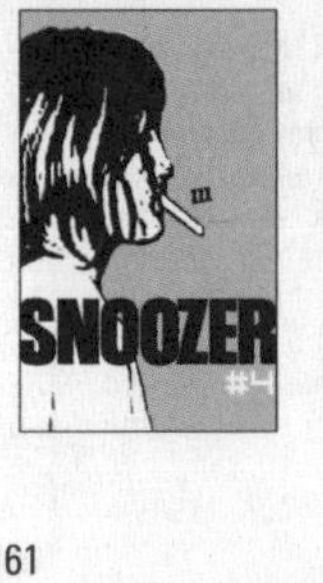
SNOOZER
#4

SNOOZER #4

Snoozer is determined to sleep through the war or die trying. She documents her efforts, mostly through sheer force of will, to sleep as much as humanly possible, and it's fascinating to read. The inner workings of a very clearly mentally ill woman, but she's charming and funny and bitter and extremely likable. I want to meet Snoozer.

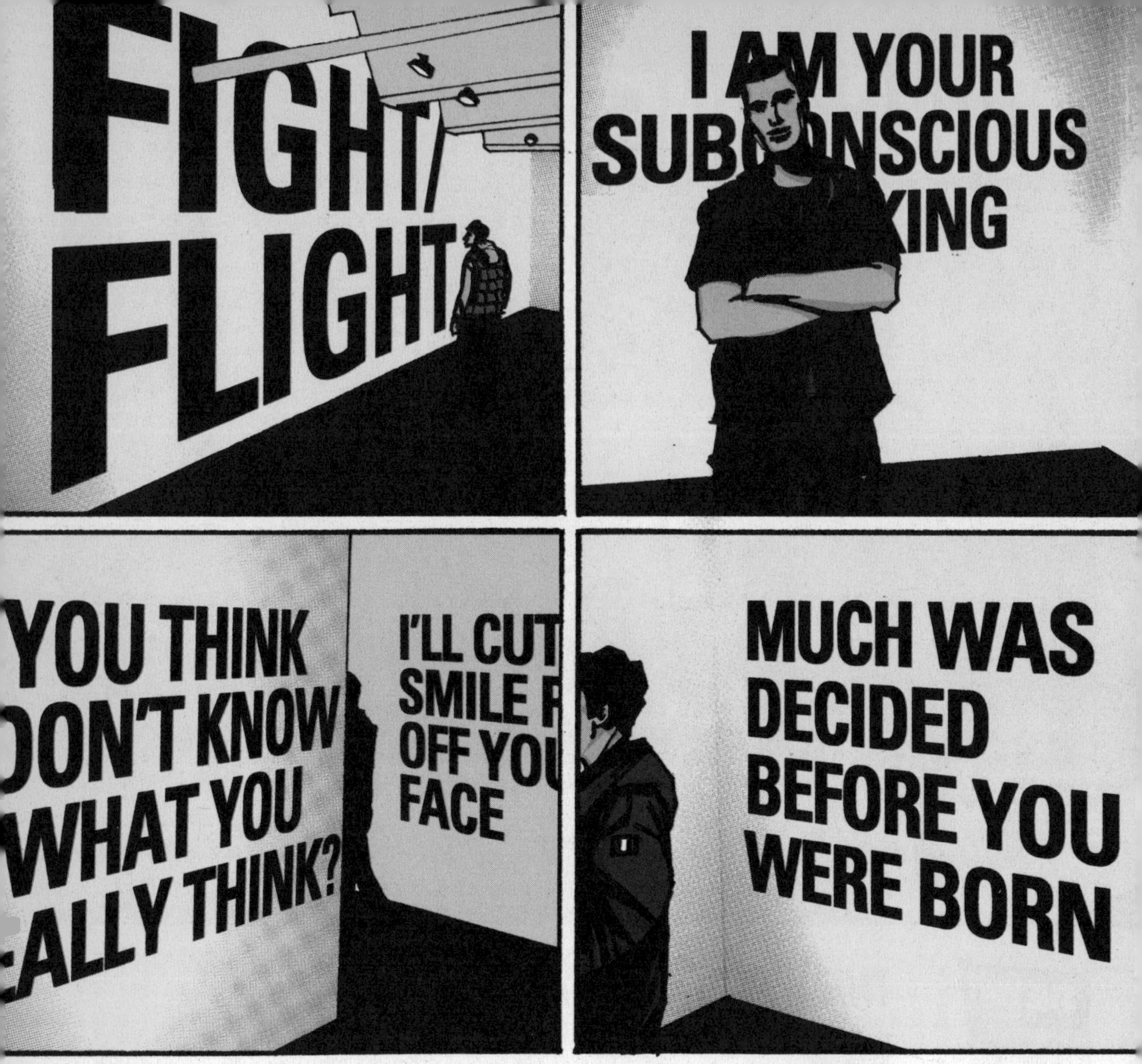
FIGHT/
FLIGHT
I AM YOUR
SUBCONSCIOUS
KING
YOU THINK
ON'T KNOW
WHAT YOU
ALLY THINK?
I'LL CUT
SMILE R
OFF YOU
FACE
MUCH WAS
DECIDED
BEFORE YOU
WERE BORN

ARTS

GALLERIES

Walking firmly in the footsteps of Barbara Kruger, Jenny Holzer, and even de la Vega, the 44-yo artist who goes by the name Decade Later screens slogans on walls and gets away with it in every sense.

The first reaction you get after having the words I AM YOUR SUBCONSCIOUS TALKING is to say "fuck you!" because it's so assumptive and self-righteous. But it makes you want to walk around and see what else he claims you're secretly thinking, if only to say "fuck you!" a few more times. After a few minutes, though, you think he may be right.

I notice people silently mouthing the phrases to themselves as they read them, trying them out, seeing how they feel on their lips. They feel great. In a direct homage to Holzer, Decade tells us I'LL CUT THE SMILE RIGHT OFF YOUR FACE, which is incredibly satisfying to say. BETTER LUCK NEXT TIME (lower right) is a stream-of-consciousness rant of familiar clichés that don't sit well with residents of this city, too used to being manipulated and lied to by slimy politicians. FIGHT OR FLIGHT towers over you, intimidating you as the viewer can't help but mentally recall close calls and dangerous situations.

Decade Later isn't breaking new ground with anything he's doing, but by placing familiar words and phrases and clichés into a new setting, into the DMZ, they take on very specific meanings that we're all already thinking about.

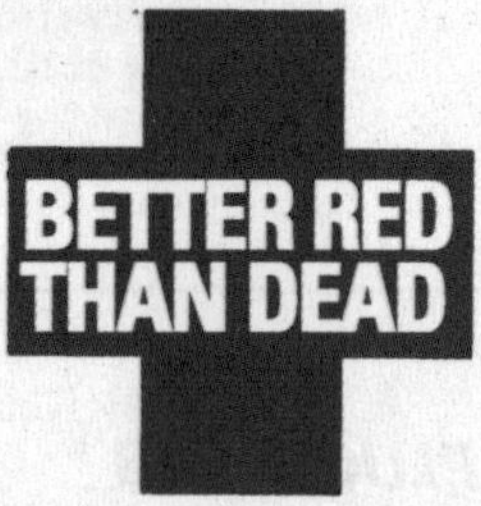
BETTER RED
THAN DEAD

I WASN'T BORN YESTERDAY. THERE'S A SUCKER BORN EVERY MINUTE, BUT THAT'S NOT ME. I DIDN'T JUST FALL OFF THE TURNIP TRUCK. YOU WON'T TRICK ME. FOOL ME NEVER. I SAW THAT COMING A MILE AWAY. DO I LOOK STUPID TO YOU? YOU'RE SO TRANSPARENT YOU MAKE WATER LOOK BAD. YOU NEED TO WAKE UP PRETTY EARLY. NICE TRY. GOOD ONE. YOU THINK YOU'RE PRETTY SLICK. CLOSE BUT NO CIGAR. BETTER LUCK NEXT TIME.

History: This is one of the craziest places in the city. A lot of people won't even talk about it, or they get really mad about it. Even the ones who don't care still don't have a lot to say. It feels like there's so much history, so many promises broken, so many people sick from the air and the dust, so much bullshit connected to it that it's just too much to process. So they pretend it's not here.

Except for the politicians. They talk about it. But they don't have to live with it.

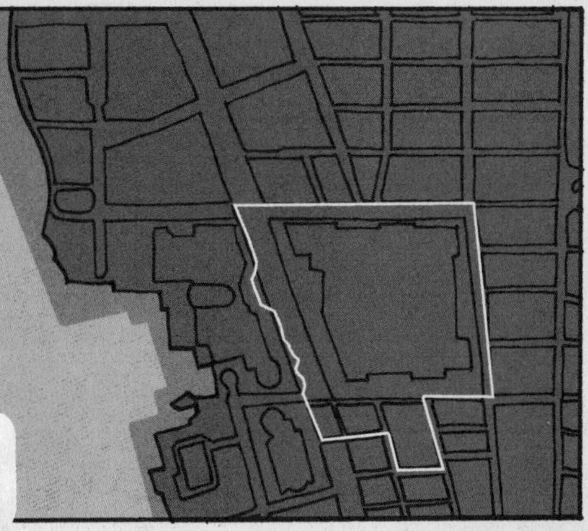

GROUND ZERO

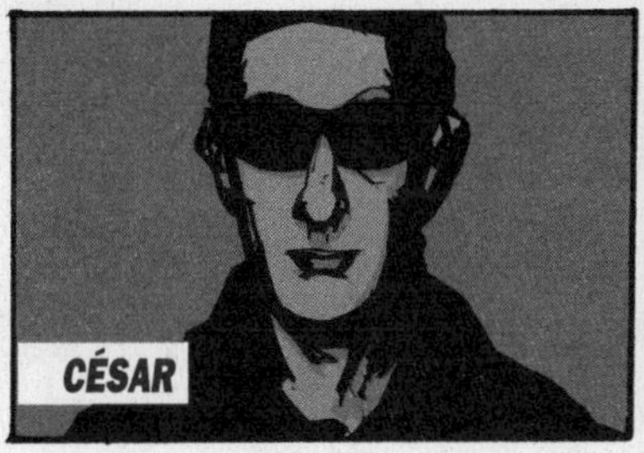
CÉSAR

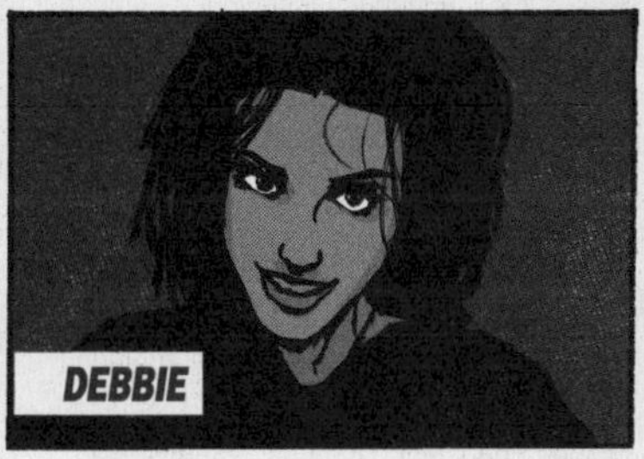
DEBBIE

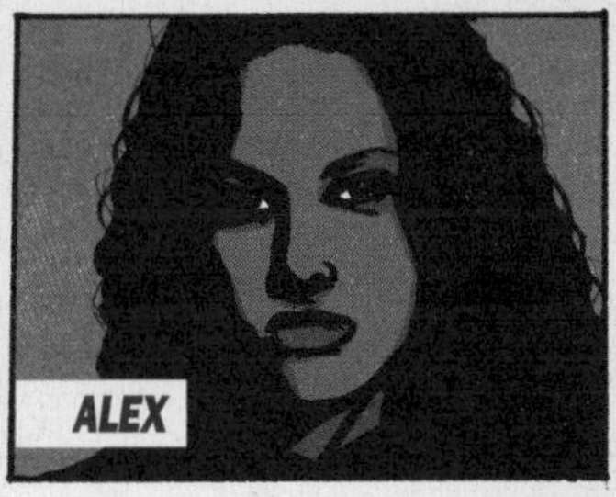
ALEX

Name: César

Age: 31

"People call it sacred. It's just four walls around a vacant lot. The rest of the world got over it – why can't we? I'm sick of having to watch what I say."

Name: Debbie

Age: 23

"I heard that grass and trees are growing in there. I think that's nice. It should just be left alone. All the other open areas in the city are filthy and dangerous. We need clean spaces for later."

Name: Alex

Age: 30

"I lost a cousin on 9/11, and I'm not afraid to talk about it. Where's the memorial? Where's the Freedom Tower? Why can't I go down there? I do and people shoot at me. I was born in this city."

The area around the site is actually controlled by U.S. troops. Feels political to me, like they need to have it in hand so the President can try and whip us up about the horrible tragedy of it all and justify their policies...

But what if it was just a field of grass and wildflowers behind those walls? I guess that wouldn't make people think about getting revenge.

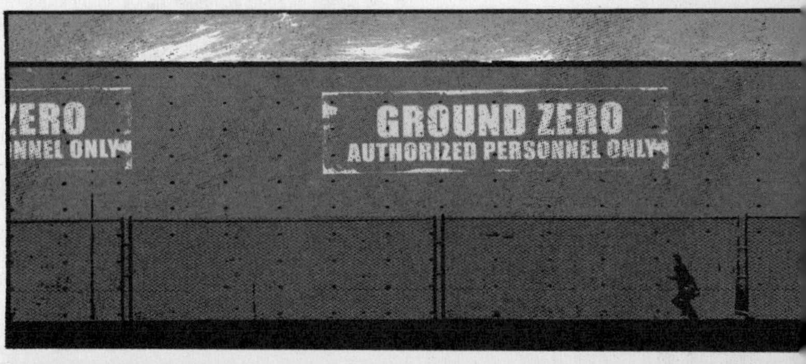
ZERO
NNEL ONLY
GROUND ZERO
AUTHORIZED PERSONNEL ONLY

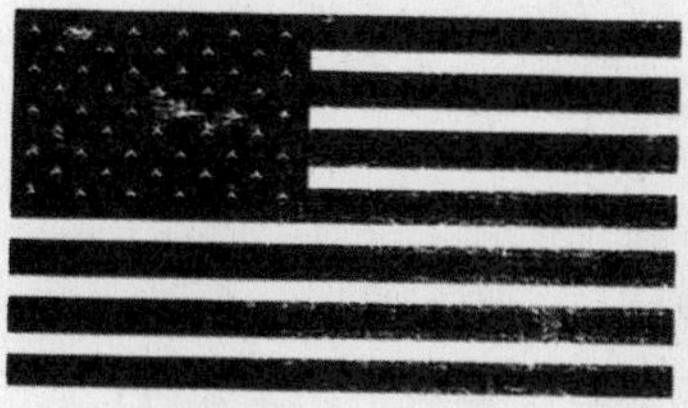

I went up to the observation deck ages ago during a class trip in middle school. I don't miss the towers, though. It's not "sacred ground." For people who actually live here, there's not a block in this city that doesn't have someone's blood staining it, so how can one thing be sacred and not another?

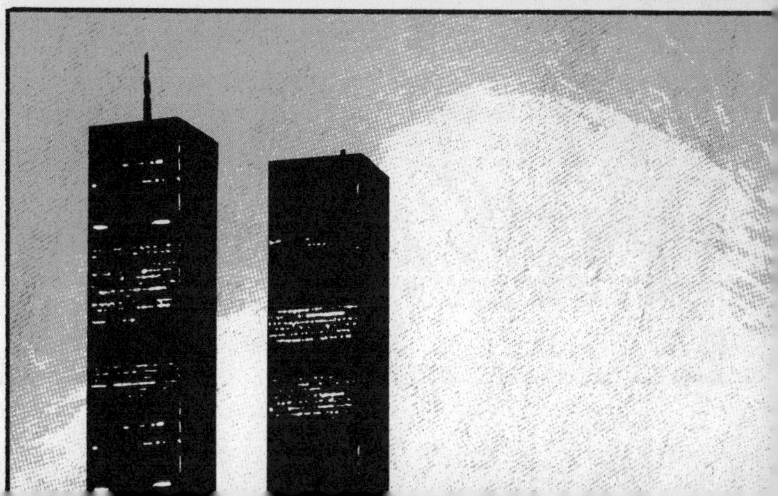

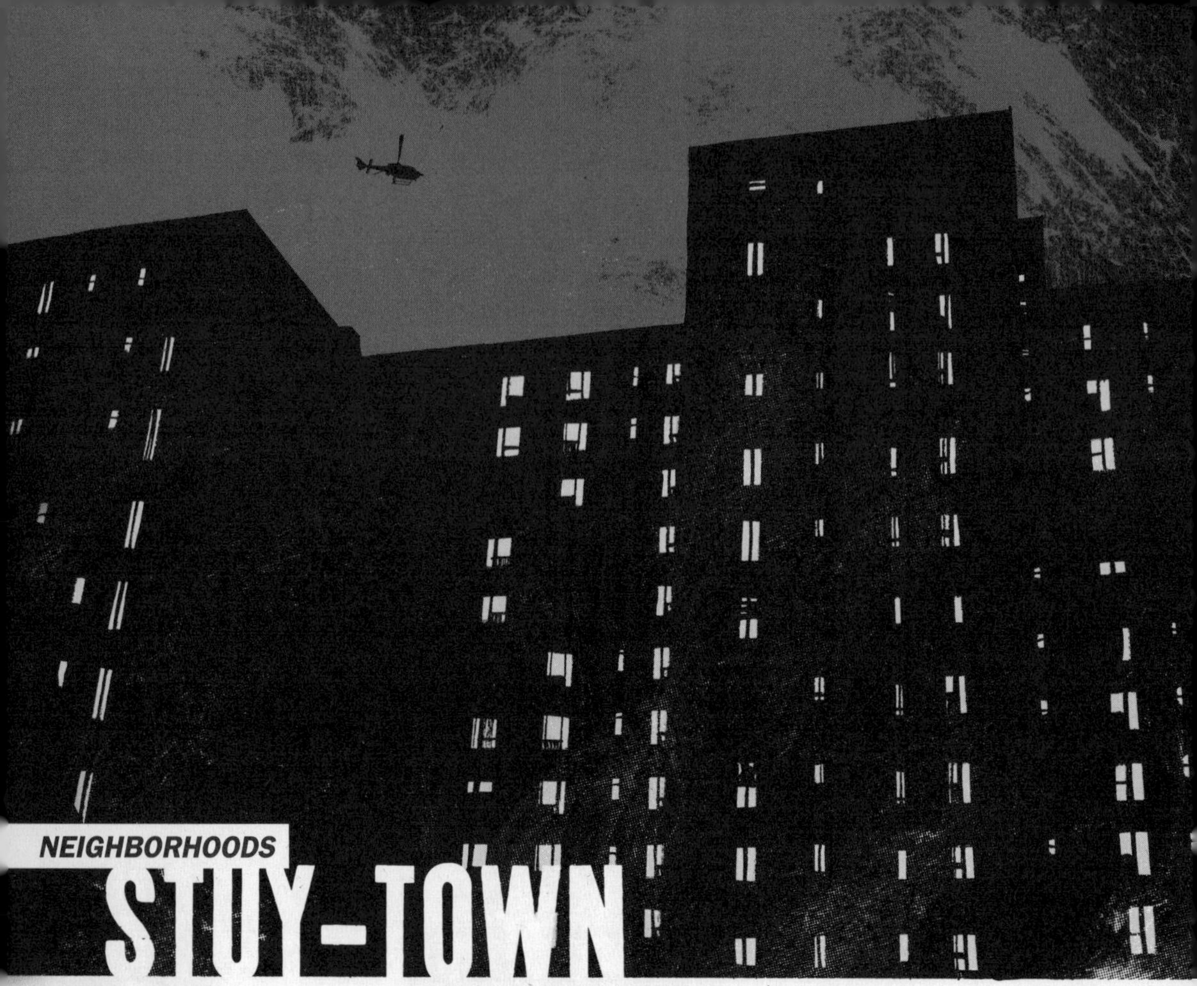

NEIGHBORHOODS

STUY-TOWN

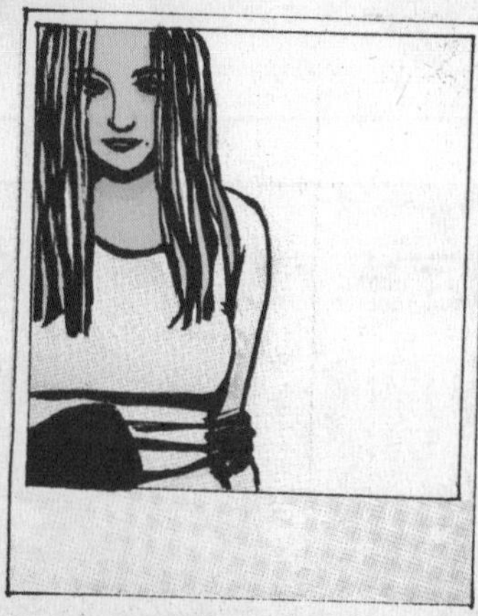

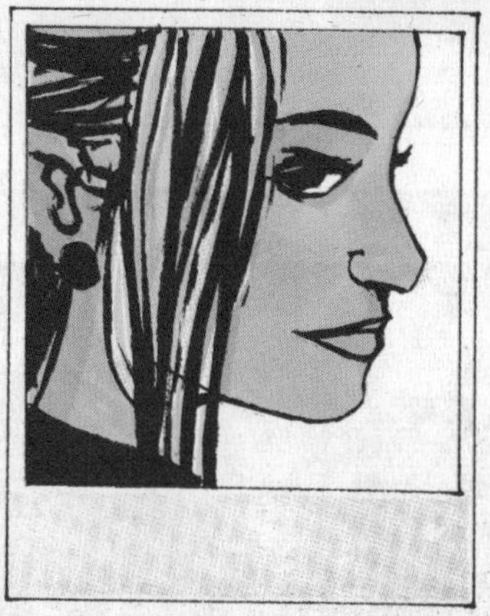

My apartment was given to me by one of The Ghosts, for me to watch over until the war ended and his family came back to claim it. I've taken good care of it, but it's time to move on. In light of recent events, I need to be not so easily found.

Stuy-town is one of the sanest places I've seen here. It's naturally defendable, and lucky for it the people who claim and protect it are decent. We all take care of it, help out with repairs, share food and resources and generally keep an eye out. The towers by Ave C are too exposed to the river for anyone to live in, so they plunder it for parts.

I have an older cousin who lived here years ago while she went to Hunter.

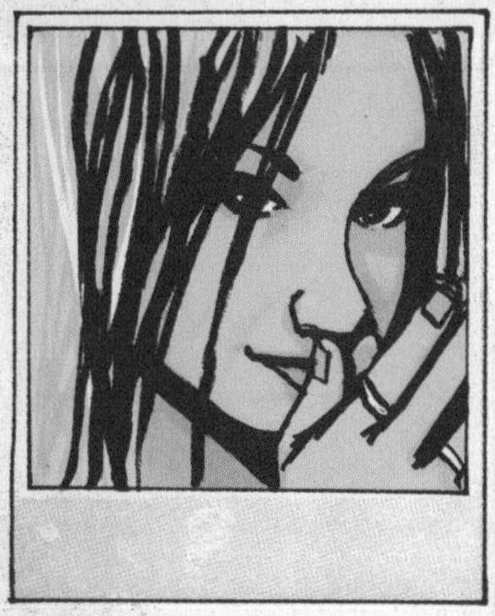

KELLY CONNOLLY

I met Kelly on a filthy, hot subway platform. She'd walked down from Midtown during active hostilities to find me. Suffice it to say neither of us was looking their best, but neither of us seemed to care.

Canadian citizen, reporter for IWN. I used to watch her on cable before I came to the city. Reminds me of home.

She visits me when she can, which isn't often enough.

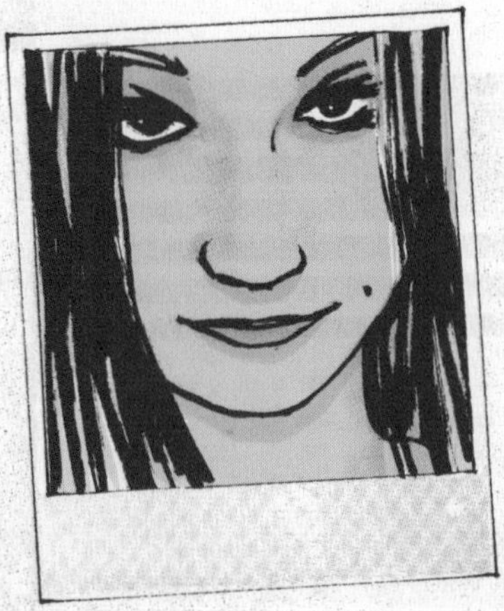

PEOPLE

ZEE

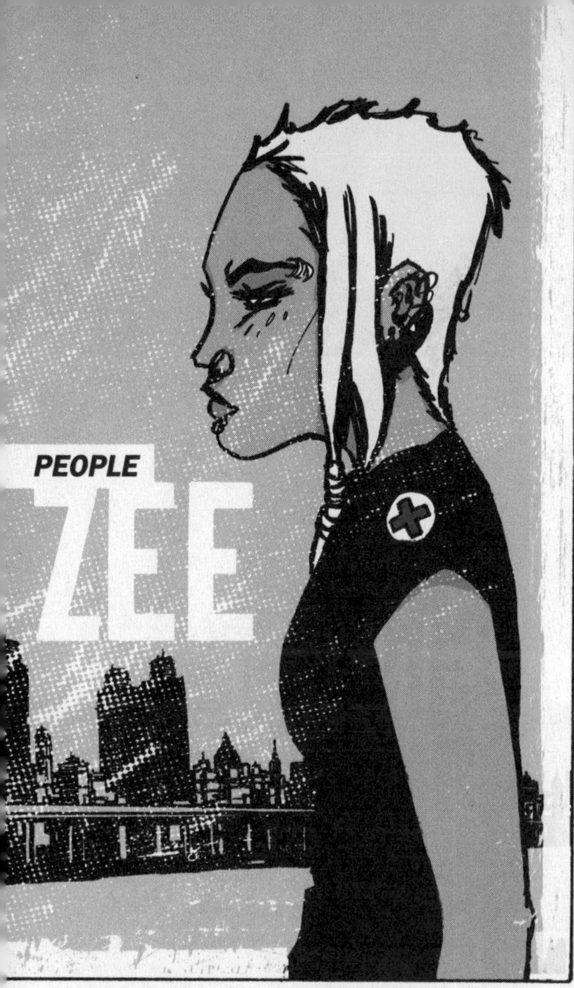

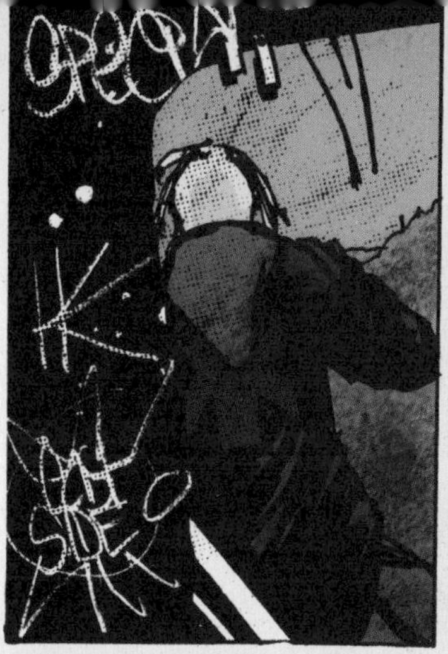

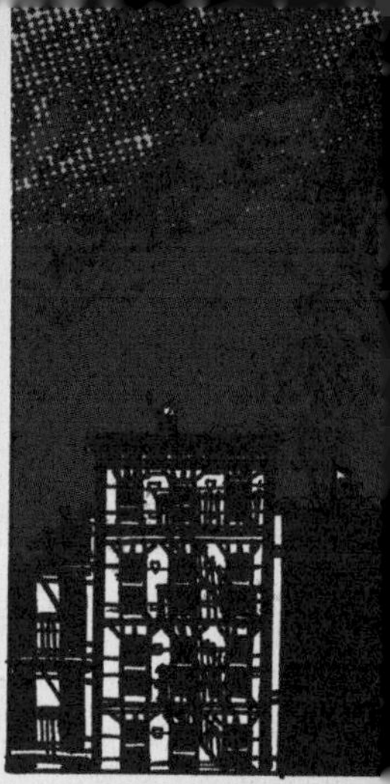

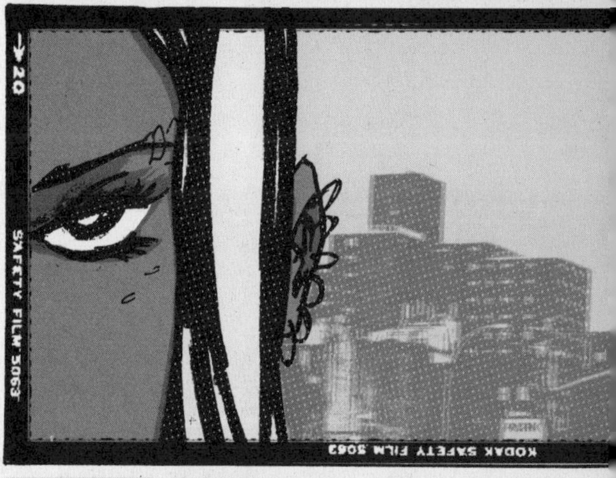
20
SAFETY FILM 5063
KODAK SAFETY FILM 5063

My first night in the city, Zee put a gun in my face. Later she gave me breakfast and a guided tour of her neighborhood. She comes off all snarling and bitter, but I understand where some of that comes from now. She's a protector... she protects her friends, her block, her patients, and her right to be here.

Kelly says Zee likes me. I think Zee tolerates me, at best. She may trust me soon, but it will be a while yet before she *likes* me.

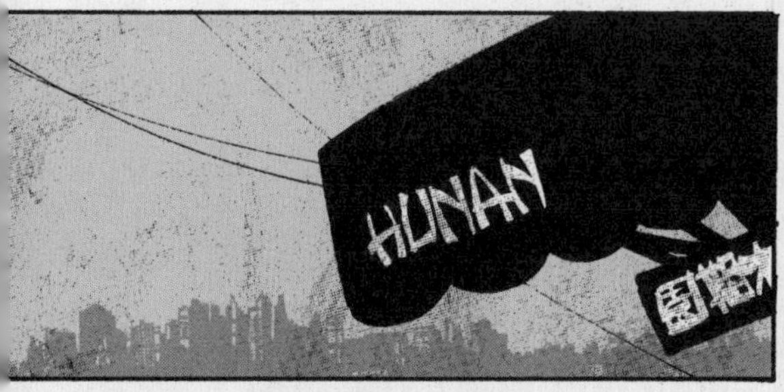
HUNAN

Zee's a hoarder and a thief. She runs a clinic, pretty much all by herself, and every day does rounds around the city. Whenever Red Cross or other relief supplies make it to the city, she's there and does whatever she can to personally receive medical supplies. What she isn't given, she steals. Better to get it directly, she tells me, because by the time it makes its way through the corrupt distribution network, everyone's siphoned off some of it for themselves and she's lucky to end up with a bottle of aspirin and a roll of gauze.

Having said all that, Zee's the most honest person I've met in the city. That gets in the way of her having a lot of friends, but her work is what matters most to her. I can respect that.

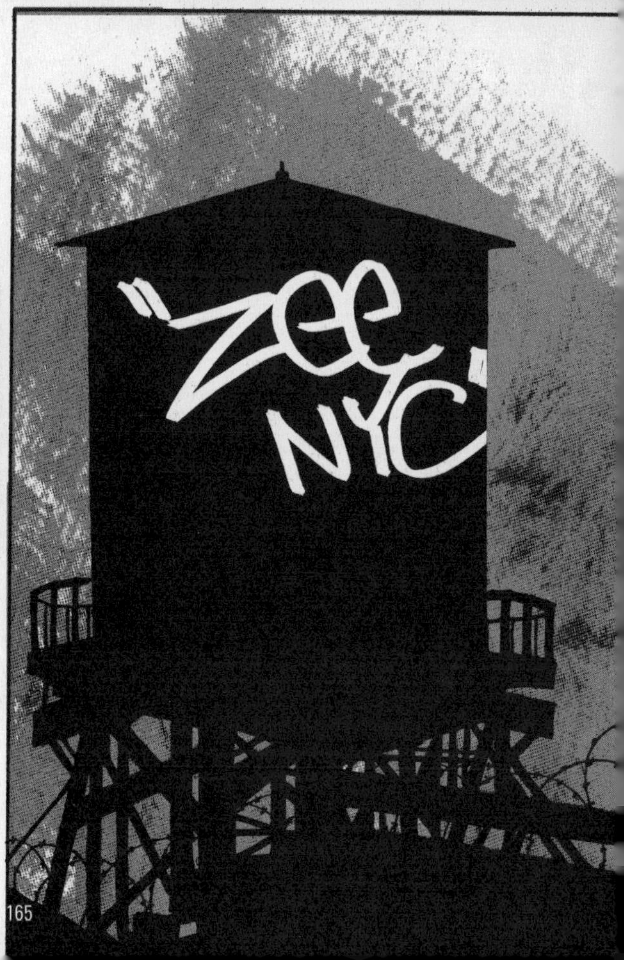
"ZEE NYC"

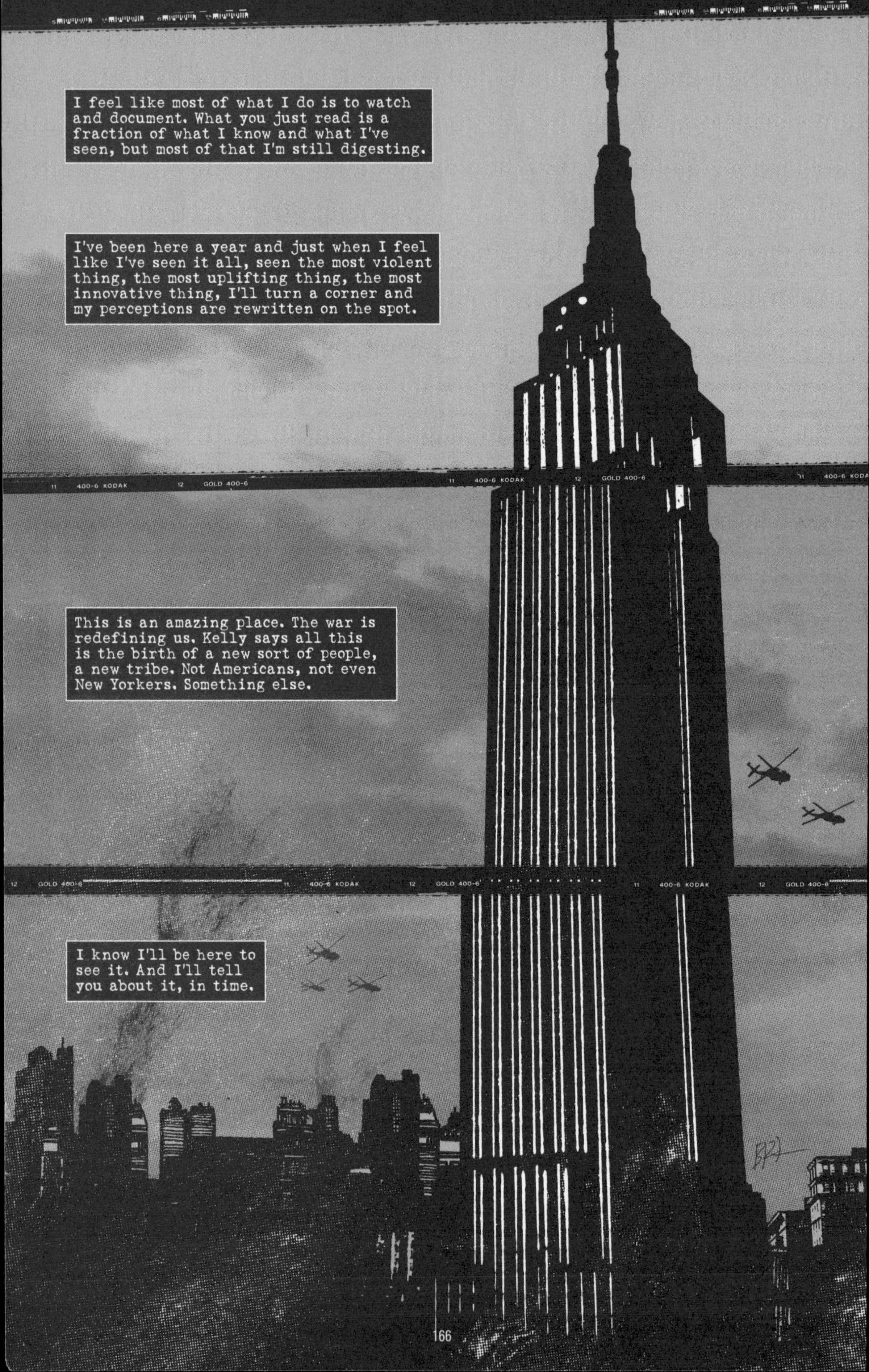
I feel like most of what I do is to watch and document. What you just read is a fraction of what I know and what I've seen, but most of that I'm still digesting.
I've been here a year and just when I feel like I've seen it all, seen the most violent thing, the most uplifting thing, the most innovative thing, I'll turn a corner and my perceptions are rewritten on the spot.
This is an amazing place. The war is redefining us. Kelly says all this is the birth of a new sort of people, a new tribe. Not Americans, not even New Yorkers. Something else.
I know I'll be here to see it. And I'll tell you about it, in time.

ALSO AVAILABLE AT BOOKSTORES

**DMZ: ON THE GROUND
VOL. 1**

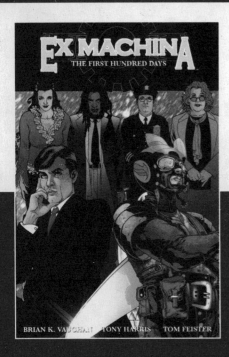